OECD/G20 Base Erosion and Profit Shifting Project

Harmful Tax Practices – 2017 Peer Review Reports on the Exchange of Information on Tax Rulings

INCLUSIVE FRAMEWORK ON BEPS: ACTION 5

OECD
BETTER POLICIES FOR BETTER LIVES

This document, as well as any data and any map included herein, are without prejudice to the status of or sovereignty over any territory, to the delimitation of international frontiers and boundaries and to the name of any territory, city or area.

Please cite this publication as:
OECD (2018), *Harmful Tax Practices – 2017 Peer Review Reports on the Exchange of Information on Tax Rulings: Inclusive Framework on BEPS: Action 5*, OECD/G20 Base Erosion and Profit Shifting Project, OECD Publishing, Paris.
https://doi.org/10.1787/9789264309586-en

ISBN 978-92-64-30957-9 (print)
ISBN 978-92-64-30958-6 (pdf)

Series: OECD/G20 Base Erosion and Profit Shifting Project
ISSN 2313-2604 (print)
ISSN 2313-2612 (online)

The statistical data for Israel are supplied by and under the responsibility of the relevant Israeli authorities. The use of such data by the OECD is without prejudice to the status of the Golan Heights, East Jerusalem and Israeli settlements in the West Bank under the terms of international law.

Photo credits: © ninog-Fotolia.com.

Corrigenda to OECD publications may be found on line at: *www.oecd.org/publishing/corrigenda*.

Foreword

The integration of national economies and markets has increased substantially in recent years, putting a strain on the international tax rules, which were designed more than a century ago. Weaknesses in the current rules create opportunities for base erosion and profit shifting (BEPS), requiring bold moves by policy makers to restore confidence in the system and ensure that profits are taxed where economic activities take place and value is created.

Following the release of the report Addressing Base Erosion and Profit Shifting in February 2013, OECD and G20 countries adopted a 15-point Action Plan to address BEPS in September 2013. The Action Plan identified 15 actions along three key pillars: introducing coherence in the domestic rules that affect cross-border activities, reinforcing substance requirements in the existing international standards, and improving transparency as well as certainty.

After two years of work, measures in response to the 15 actions were delivered to G20 Leaders in Antalya in November 2015. All the different outputs, including those delivered in an interim form in 2014, were consolidated into a comprehensive package. The BEPS package of measures represents the first substantial renovation of the international tax rules in almost a century. Once the new measures become applicable, it is expected that profits will be reported where the economic activities that generate them are carried out and where value is created. BEPS planning strategies that rely on outdated rules or on poorly co-ordinated domestic measures will be rendered ineffective.

Implementation is now the focus of this work. The BEPS package is designed to be implemented via changes in domestic law and practices, and in tax treaties. With the negotiation of a multilateral instrument (MLI) having been finalised in 2016 to facilitate the implementation of the treaty related BEPS measures, over 80 jurisdictions are covered by the MLI. The entry into force of the MLI on 1 July 2018 paves the way for swift implementation of the treaty related measures. OECD and G20 countries also agreed to continue to work together to ensure a consistent and co-ordinated implementation of the BEPS recommendations and to make the project more inclusive. Globalisation requires that global solutions and a global dialogue be established which go beyond OECD and G20 countries.

A better understanding of how the BEPS recommendations are implemented in practice could reduce misunderstandings and disputes between governments. Greater focus on implementation and tax administration should therefore be mutually beneficial to governments and business. Proposed improvements to data and analysis will help support ongoing evaluation of the quantitative impact of BEPS, as well as evaluating the impact of the countermeasures developed under the BEPS Project.

As a result, the OECD established the Inclusive Framework on BEPS, bringing all interested and committed countries and jurisdictions on an equal footing in the Committee on Fiscal Affairs and all its subsidiary bodies. The Inclusive Framework, which already has more than 120 members, is monitoring and peer reviewing the implementation of the minimum standards as well as completing the work on standard setting to address BEPS issues. In addition to BEPS members, other international organisations and regional tax bodies are involved in the work of the Inclusive Framework, which also consults business and the civil society on its different work streams.

This report was approved by the Inclusive Framework on BEPS on 13 November 2018 and prepared for publication by the OECD Secretariat.

Table of contents

Abbreviations and acronyms

AAR	Authority for Advance Rulings
AFIP	Federal Administration of Public Revenues (Argentina)
AGT	Administração Geral Tributária (Angola)
APA	Advance pricing arrangement
APMA	Advance Pricing and Mutual Agreement
AR	Advance tax ruling
ATA	Andorran Tax Administration
ATR	Advance tax ruling
ATO	Australian Taxation Office
AXIS	Automatic Exchange and Analysis of Foreign Financial Information System
BEPS	Base Erosion and Profit Shifting
BIR	Bureau of Internal Revenue (Philippines)
BRA	Barbados Revenue Authority
CASD	Competent Authority Services Division
CBDT	Central Board of Direct Tax (India)
CD	Central Directory
CE-in-C	Chief Executive in Council of Hong Kong
CRA	Canada Revenue Agency
CTS	Common Transmission System
DEI	Development and Expansion Incentive
DGI	Dirección General de Ingresos (Panamanian Tax Administration)
DIAN	National Tax and Customs Administration (Colombia)
DSTA	Department of Special Tax Audits
DTA	Double Taxation Agreement
EC	European Commission
ECIL	Encouragement of Capital Investments Law
EOI	Exchange of Information

ETCB	Estonian Tax and Customs Board
EU	European Union
FA	Fiscal Authority
FHTP	Forum on Harmful Tax Practices
FCTO	Federal Central Tax Office
FTS	Federal Tax Service of Russia
HMRC	Her Majesty's Revenue and Customs
IAPR	Independent Authority for Public Revenues (Greece Tax Administration)
INER	Strategy and Risk Unit (*Intendencia Nacional de Estrategias y Riesgos)*
INJT	Central Legal Area (*Intendencia Nacional Jurídica Tributaria)*
IP	Intellectual Property
IPCN	Central Office of Large National Taxpayers (*Intendencia de Principales Contribuyentes Nacionales)*
IRAS	Inland Revenue Authority of Singapore
IBRN	Inland Revenue Board Malaysia
IRD	Inland Revenue Department of Hong Kong/ Directorate of Internal Revenue (Icelandic Tax Administration)/ Inland Revenue Department (New Zealand)
ITAD	International Affairs Division (Philippines)
ITB	International Tax Branch (Singapore)
ITO	Income Tax Office
ITS	International Taxation Section (Mauritius)
ITRD	Income Tax Rulings Directorate
JTO	Jersey Taxes Office
LIAATM	Law on International Administrative Assistance in Tax Matters
LTD	Large Taxpayers Department (Mauritius)
LoA	Letter of awards
MHQ	Multinational Companies Headquarters
MNE	Multinational Enterprise
MoF	Ministry of Finance
MRA	Mauritius Revenue Authority
MSC	Multimedia Super Corridor
MSTD	Medium and Small Taxpayers Department (Mauritius)
NRA	National Revenue Administration (Poland)
NTA	National Tax Agency (Japan)

NTCA	National Tax and Customs Administration
NTS	National Tax Service (Korea)
PE	Permanent Establishment
PBR	Private Bindings Rulings
R&D	Research and Development
RFN	*Receita Federal do Brazil* (Brazilian Tax Administration)
SAARC	South Asian Association for Regional Cooperation
SARS	South African Revenue Service
SAT	State Administration of Taxation (Chinese Tax Administration)
SEOI	Spontaneous Exchange of Information
SEM	Sedes de Empresas Multinacionales (Multinational Companies Headquarters)
SII	Servicio de Impuestos Internos (Chilean Tax Administration)
SPOC	Single Point of Contact
SRC	Seychelles Revenue Commission
SRS	State Revenue Service (Latvia)
STI	State Tax Inspectorate (Lithuania)
SUNAT	Superintendencia Nacional de Aduanas y de Administración Tributaria (Peru)
STA	Swedish Tax Agency
TAAA	Tax Administrative Assistance Act
TAAO	Tax Administrative Assistance Ordinance
TRNC	Turkish Republic of Northern Cyprus
ToR	Terms of reference
XML	Extensible Mark-Up Language

Executive summary

Context for the exchange of information on tax rulings (the "transparency framework")

1. The BEPS Action 5 minimum standard on the compulsory spontaneous exchange of information on tax rulings (the "transparency framework") provides tax administrations with timely information on rulings that have been granted to a foreign related party of their resident taxpayer or a permanent establishment, which can be used in conducting risk assessments and which, in the absence of exchange, could give rise to BEPS concerns.

2. The transparency framework requires spontaneous exchange of information on five categories of taxpayer-specific rulings: (i) rulings related to certain preferential regimes, (ii) unilateral advance pricing arrangements (APAs) or other cross-border unilateral rulings in respect of transfer pricing, (iii) rulings providing for a downward adjustment of taxable profits, (iv) permanent establishment (PE) rulings; and (v) related party conduit rulings.[1] The requirement to exchange information on the rulings in the above categories includes certain past rulings as well as future rulings, pursuant to pre-defined periods which are outlined in each jurisdiction's report. The exchanges occur pursuant to international exchange of information agreements, which ensure taxpayer confidentiality.

3. The inclusion of the above categories of rulings in the scope of the transparency framework is not intended to suggest that the issuance of such rulings constitutes a preferential regime or a harmful tax practice. In practice, tax rulings can be an effective way to provide certainty to taxpayers and reduce the risk of disputes. Rather, the need for transparency on rulings is that a tax administration's lack of knowledge or information on the tax treatment of a taxpayer in another jurisdiction can impact the transactions or arrangements undertaken with a related taxpayer resident in their own jurisdiction and thus lead to BEPS concerns. The availability of timely and targeted information about such rulings, as agreed in the template in Annex C of the Action 5 Report, *Countering Harmful Tax Practices More Effectively, Taking Into Account Transparency and Substance* (OECD, 2015), will be beneficial in enabling tax authorities to quickly identify risk areas.

Scope of this review

4. This is the second annual peer review of the transparency framework. It covers 92 jurisdictions. This includes all OECD and G20 countries and the countries that were in the OECD accession process throughout the BEPS project (which were reviewed in the first annual peer review published in 2017) and also Inclusive Framework members that joined prior to 1 September 2017 and Jurisdictions of Relevance identified by the Inclusive Framework prior to 1 September 2017. Five of these jurisdictions have not been assessed under the transparency framework, namely Bermuda, the British Virgin Islands, the Cayman Islands, Sint Maarten and the Turks and Caicos Islands. Sint Maarten was affected by a natural disaster during the year in review, and therefore it was considered

appropriate that the peer review of the jurisdiction be deferred to the next annual review. Bermuda, the British Virgin Islands, the Cayman Islands and the Turks and Caicos Islands are jurisdictions which do not impose any corporate income tax, and cannot legally issue rulings within scope of the transparency framework and nor should Inclusive Framework members exchange information on rulings with them. Therefore, these jurisdictions are considered to be outside the scope of the transparency framework.

5. The reviews on the implementation of the transparency framework contained in this annual report cover the calendar year 2017. Jurisdictions may have made improvements during the calendar year 2018 which have not been reflected in this report. These may be assessed in the subsequent peer review. The reviews have been prepared using information from each reviewed jurisdiction, input from peers who received exchanges of information under the transparency framework, and input from the delegates of the Forum on Harmful Tax Practices (FHTP).

Key findings

6. Key findings from this first peer review include:

- As at 31 December 2017, almost 16 000 tax rulings in the scope of the transparency framework had been issued by the jurisdictions being reviewed;
- Almost 21 000 exchanges of information took place by 31 December 2017, with almost 14 000 exchanges undertaken during 2017 and over 6 000 exchanges during 2016;
- All jurisdictions already have, or have undertaken steps to implement, the necessary legal framework for spontaneous exchange of information on rulings for the year in review;
- 60 recommendations for improvement have been made for the year in review;
- Of the 49 recommendations for improvement made to the 44 jurisdictions in the previous year peer review, 29 recommendations have been actioned and removed during the year in review;
- In a number of cases, the peer review process has assisted jurisdictions in identifying areas where improvement is required, and jurisdictions have been able to take swift action to implement changes. These changes will be reviewed in the subsequent peer review.

A summary of the recommendations made can be found in the following pages.

Next steps

7. The peer review is an annual process that has taken place in 2017 and 2018, with another two reviews to take place in 2019 and 2020. The next annual peer review will continue to track the progress of jurisdictions and the actions taken to respond to recommendations, and an update on statistics on the exchanges of information. The next annual peer review in 2019 will also include jurisdictions which joined the Inclusive Framework, and jurisdictions of relevance identified by the Inclusive Framework, since 1 September 2017, as well as members of the Inclusive Framework on BEPS that are developing countries and which requested an additional year to implement the transparency framework.

Summary of recommendations made

Aspect of the implementation of the transparency framework that should be improved	Recommendation for improvement
Andorra	
Andorra experienced difficulties in identifying all potential exchange jurisdictions for past rulings (ToR I.4.2.2).	Andorra is recommended to continue to apply the "best efforts approach" to identify potential exchange jurisdictions for all past rulings.
Andorra experienced difficulties in identifying all potential exchange jurisdictions for future rulings (ToR I.4.2.1).	Andorra is recommended to ensure that all potential exchange jurisdictions are identified swiftly for all future rulings.
Andorra did not undertake spontaneous exchange of information on tax rulings within scope of the transparency framework during the year in review (ToR II.5).	Andorra is recommended to continue its efforts to complete the templates for all relevant rulings and to ensure that the exchanges of information on rulings occur as soon as possible.
Angola	
Angola has not yet finalised the steps to have in place its necessary information and gathering process (ToR.I.4).	Angola is recommended to finalise its information gathering process for identifying all past and future rulings and potential exchange jurisdictions, with a review and supervision mechanism, as soon as possible.
Angola has not yet finalised the steps to have effective compulsory spontaneous exchange of information on the tax rulings within the scope of the transparency framework (ToR.I.5).	Angola is recommended to continue to put in place a domestic legal framework allowing spontaneous exchange of information on rulings and to continue its efforts to complete the templates for all relevant rulings and to ensure that the exchanges of information on rulings occur as soon as possible.
Argentina	
Argentina experienced difficulties on the identification of information on future rulings (ToR I.4.1.2).	Argentina is recommended to provide any necessary interpretive guidance and continue its efforts to ensure that there is an effective system for identifying all future rulings in a timely way.
Australia	
	No recommendations are made.
Austria	
Austria encountered delays in the timely exchange of information on past and future rulings. This is a continuing recommendation from the prior year peer review (ToR II.5.6).	Austria is recommended to ensure that all information on past and future rulings is exchanged as soon as possible.
Barbados	
Barbados did not complete the information gathering process during the year in review (ToR I.4).	Barbados is recommended to finalise its information gathering process for identifying all past and future rulings and potential exchange jurisdictions, with a review and supervision mechanism, as soon as possible.
Barbados did not undertake spontaneous exchange of information on tax rulings within scope of the transparency framework during the year in review (ToR II.5).	Barbados is recommended to continue its efforts to complete the templates for all relevant rulings and to ensure that the exchanges of information on rulings occur as soon as possible.
Belgium	
Belgium has not exchanged all information on new taxpayers benefitting from the grandfathered IP regime, and new assets of existing taxpayers benefitting from the grandfathered regime as this information was not able to be collected during the year in review (ToR I.4.1.3).	Belgium is recommended to continue its efforts to identify and exchange information on new entrants to the grandfathered IP regime.
Belize	
	No recommendations are made.
Benin	
	No recommendations are made.
Brazil	
	No recommendations are made.
Brunei Darussalam	
	No recommendations are made.
Bulgaria	
	No recommendations are made.
Burkina Faso	

Aspect of the implementation of the transparency framework that should be improved	Recommendation for improvement
	No recommendations are made.
Cameroon	
It is not known whether Cameroon has an information gathering process in place (ToR.I.4).	Cameroon is recommended to ensure that it has put in place an effective information gathering process to identify all relevant past and future rulings and all potential exchange jurisdictions and to implement a review and supervision mechanism, as soon as possible.
It is not known whether Cameroon has a domestic legal framework allowing spontaneous exchange of information on rulings if needed and has a process in place to ensure the timely exchange of information on rulings in the form required by the transparency framework (ToR.II.5).	Cameroon is recommended to put in place a domestic legal framework allowing spontaneous exchange of information on rulings if needed and to ensure the timely exchange of information on rulings in the form required by the transparency framework.
Canada	
	No recommendations are made.
Chile	
	No recommendations are made.
China (People's Republic of)	
During the year in review, China's Competent Authority collected information on future rulings on an annual basis, which is longer than necessary (ToR II.5.5).	China is recommended to reduce the timelines for providing the information on future rulings to the Competent Authority.
Colombia	
Colombia did not complete exchanges of information on past rulings in accordance with the timelines (ToR II.5.6). This is a continuing recommendation from the prior year peer review.	Colombia is recommended to ensure that all information on past rulings is exchanged as soon as possible.
Congo	
It is not known whether Congo has an information gathering process in place (ToR.I.4).	Congo is recommended to ensure that it has put in place an effective information gathering process to identify all relevant past and future rulings and all potential exchange jurisdictions and to implement a review and supervision mechanism, as soon as possible.
It is not known whether Congo has a domestic legal framework allowing spontaneous exchange of information on rulings if needed and has a process in place to ensure the timely exchange of information on rulings in the form required by the transparency framework (ToR.II.5).	Congo is recommended to put in place a domestic legal framework allowing spontaneous exchange of information on rulings if needed and to ensure the timely exchange of information on rulings in the form required by the transparency framework.
Costa Rica	
For the year in review, Costa Rica did not apply the "best efforts approach" to identify all potential exchange jurisdictions for all past rulings (ToR I.4.2.2).	Costa Rica is recommended to continue to apply the "best efforts approach" to identify potential exchange jurisdictions for all past rulings.
Costa Rica does not yet ensure that information on all potential exchange jurisdictions is always obtained for future rulings (ToR I.4.2.1).	Costa Rica is recommended to continue its efforts to ensure that all potential exchange jurisdictions are identified swiftly for all future rulings.
In the year in review, Costa Rica had not yet finalised the process to complete the templates and submit them to the Competent Authority and had not undertaken any exchanges of information (ToR II.5).	Costa Rica is recommended to continue its efforts to complete the templates for all relevant rulings and to ensure that the exchanges of information on rulings occur as soon as possible.
Côte d'Ivoire	
	No recommendations are made.
Croatia	
	No recommendations are made.
Curaçao	
The information gathering process is still underway in Curaçao with respect to past and future rulings and the classification of these rulings under each category (ToR I.4.1.2).	Curaçao is recommended to continue to finalise its information gathering process identifying all past and future rulings as soon as possible.
Curaçao experienced delays in exchanging information on past and future rulings (ToR II.5.6).	Curaçao is recommended to continue its efforts to ensure all information on past and future rulings is exchanged as soon as possible.
Czech Republic	
The Czech Republic has not completed the exchange of information on past rulings and is experiencing significant delays in the exchange	The Czech Republic is recommended to ensure that all information on past and future rulings is exchanged as soon as possible.

Aspect of the implementation of the transparency framework that should be improved	Recommendation for improvement
of information on future rulings due to the application of the timelines set out in the EU Directive 2011/16/EU, but also exceeding those timelines in complex cases (ToR II.5.6.). This is a continuing recommendation from the prior year peer review.	
Democratic Republic of the Congo	
	No recommendations are made.
Denmark	
	No recommendations are made.
Djibouti	
	No recommendations are made.
Estonia	
	No recommendations are made.
Finland	
	No recommendations are made.
France	
France has experienced delays in exchanging information on future rulings. This is a continuing recommendation from the prior year peer review (ToR II.5.6).	France is recommended to ensure that all information on future rulings is exchanged as soon as possible.
France did not identify or exchange information on new entrants to the IP regime or taxpayers benefitting from the third category of IP asset. This is a continuing recommendation from the prior year peer review (ToR I.4.1.3).	France is recommended to identify and exchange information on all new entrants to the IP regime, and to identify and exchange information on taxpayers benefitting from the third category of IP asset.
Germany	
Germany identified 12 additional past rulings during the year of review and therefore after the timeline of 31 December 2016 due to a misunderstanding of the "still in effect at 1 January 2014" requirement (ToR I.4.1.1).	No recommendation is made because Germany addressed the problem and completed the exchanges of information on all past rulings within the month the rulings were identified and this is not a recurring issue.
Greece	
	No recommendations are made.
Guernsey	
	No recommendations are made.
Haiti	
	No recommendations are made.
Hong Kong (China)	
	No recommendations are made.
Hungary	
Hungary was only able to identify potential exchange jurisdictions for around half of the past rulings issued, even though Hungary may have additional ownership information in its possession or this information is accessible to the tax administration, including through access to company incorporation databases (ToR I.4.2.2).	Hungary is recommended to continue to apply the "best efforts approach" to identify potential exchange jurisdictions for all past rulings.
Hungary was only able to identify potential exchange jurisdictions for around half of the future rulings issued until 31 December 2017, even though Hungary may have additional ownership information in its possession or this information is accessible to the tax administration, including through access to company incorporation databases. It is noted that Hungary has amended its issuing procedure for future rulings as of 1 January 2018 requiring the taxpayers to provide information on relevant exchange jurisdictions (ToR I.4.2.1). This is a continuing recommendation from the prior year peer review.	Hungary is recommended to ensure that all potential exchange jurisdictions are identified swiftly for all future rulings.
Hungary was not able to exchange future and past rulings in the year of review with non EU Member States as it did not have the legal basis to do so. Hungary introduced a new legal basis as of 1 January 2018 and has exchanged information on rulings with all G20 and non-EU Member States. For the exchange of information with EU Member States Hungary did not meet the timelines of the transparency framework (ToR II.5.6). This is a continuing recommendation from the	Hungary is recommended to ensure that all information on future rulings is exchanged as soon as possible.

Aspect of the implementation of the transparency framework that should be improved	Recommendation for improvement
prior year peer review.	
Hungary has not identified and exchanged information on new entrants to the grandfathered IP regime, although information for the 2015 period should be available (ToR I.4.1.3). This is a continuing recommendation from the prior year peer review.	Hungary is recommended to continue its efforts to identify and exchange information on new entrants to the grandfathered IP regime.
Iceland	
	No recommendations are made.
India	
India experienced difficulties to identify immediate parent and ultimate parent companies for past rulings, even though India may have additional ownership information in its possession or this information is accessible to the tax administration, including through access to company incorporation databases and in tax return filings (ToR I.4.2.2). This is a continuing recommendation from the prior year peer review.	India is recommended to continue to apply the "best efforts approach" to identify potential exchange jurisdictions for all past rulings.
India experienced difficulties to identify immediate parent and ultimate parent for future rulings issued between 1 April 2016 until the new issuing procedures take effect. By introducing the new issuing procedures, which requires the taxpayer to provide all necessary information on potential exchange information, India has addressed the issue for future rulings which have been issued after the new issuing procedures come into effect. The issue is therefore limited to future APAs and PE rulings, where taxpayers have applied before the amended application forms were introduced. (ToR I.4.2.1)	India is recommended to ensure that all potential exchange jurisdictions are identified swiftly for all future rulings.
India experienced delays in the exchange of information on past and future APAs. This is a continuing recommendation from the prior year peer review regarding the exchange of APAs. Subsequent to receiving this recommendation in October 2017, India has addressed the delay in the exchange of rulings by amending the issuing procedure for APAs and PE rulings as of 16 June 2017 and 13 July 2018 respectively. (ToR II.5.6)	India is recommended to ensure that all information on past and future APAs is exchanged as soon as possible.
Indonesia	
	No recommendations are made.
Ireland	
	No recommendations are made.
Isle of Man	
	No recommendations are made.
Israel	
Israel experienced delays in the provision of rulings to the Competent Authority during the year in review (ToR II.5.5).	Israel is recommended to reduce the timelines for providing the information on future rulings to the Competent Authority.
Israel encountered delays in the exchange of information for all future rulings issued in 2017 within the scope of the transparency framework issues (ToR II.5.6). This is a continuing recommendation from the prior year peer review.	Israel is recommended to ensure that all information on future rulings is exchanged as soon as possible.
Italy	
Italy amended its procedure to transmit information on future rulings to the Competent Authority on a quarterly basis. However, in practice the information was delayed in its transmission to the Competent Authority, on average within five months and particular delays were encountered with regard to rulings on preferential regimes (ToR II.5.5). This is a continuing recommendation from the prior year peer review. Italy already amended its procedure to address this issue, which will be reviewed in the next peer review report.	Italy is recommended to continue its efforts to reduce the timelines for providing the information on future rulings to the Competent Authority.
Italy has introduced an Inter-Ministerial Decree to identify new entrants of the grandfathered IP regime. However, the Decree only came into force on 6 February 2018 and Italy was not able to identify all relevant information on new entrants to the IP regime that obtained benefits with respect to trademarks during the year of review (ToR I.4.1.3). This is a continuing recommendation from the prior year peer	Italy is recommended to continue its efforts to identify and exchange information on new entrants to the grandfathered IP regime.

Aspect of the implementation of the transparency framework that should be improved	Recommendation for improvement
review.	
Jamaica	
It is not known whether Jamaica has an information gathering process in place (ToR.I.4).	Jamaica is recommended to ensure that it has put in place an effective information gathering process to identify all relevant past and future rulings and all potential exchange jurisdictions and to implement a review and supervision mechanism, as soon as possible.
It is not known whether Jamaica has a domestic legal framework allowing spontaneous exchange of information on rulings and has in place a process for completion of templates and exchange of information on rulings (ToR.II.5).	Jamaica is recommended to put in place a domestic legal framework allowing spontaneous exchange of information on rulings if needed and to ensure the timely exchange of information on rulings in the form required by the transparency framework.
Japan	
	No recommendations are made.
Jersey	
	No recommendations are made.
Jordan	
	No recommendations are made.
Korea	
	No recommendations are made.
Latvia	
The tax administration's internal regulations do not permit spontaneous exchange of information with non-EU countries (ToR II.5.1).	Latvia is recommended to finalise the amendments to the tax administration's internal regulations to permit exchange of information on rulings with non-EU Member States.
Latvia transmits information on future rulings to EU Member States to the Competent Authority at six monthly intervals each year, to align with the EU Directive deadlines, which is longer than necessary (ToR II.5.5).	Latvia is recommended to reduce the timelines for providing the information on future rulings to the Competent Authority.
Liberia	
	No recommendations are made.
Liechtenstein	
	No recommendations are made.
Lithuania	
	No recommendations are made.
Luxembourg	
	No recommendations are made.
Macau (China)	
	No recommendations are made.
Malaysia	
Malaysia did not have a sufficient information gathering process during the year in review (ToR.I.4).	Malaysia is recommended to finalise its information gathering process for identifying all past and future rulings and potential exchange jurisdictions, with a review and supervision mechanism, as soon as possible.
Malaysia did not undertake spontaneous exchange of information on the tax rulings within scope of the transparency framework during the year in review (ToR.II.5).	Malaysia is recommended to continue its efforts to complete the templates for all relevant rulings and to ensure that the exchanges of information on rulings occur as soon as possible.
Malta	
	No recommendations are made.
Mauritius	
	No recommendations are made.
Mexico	
Mexico experienced significant delays in exchanging information on future rulings (ToR II.5.6).	Mexico is recommended to ensure that all information on future rulings is exchanged as soon as possible.
Monaco	
	No recommendations are made.
Montserrat	
	No recommendations are made.

Aspect of the implementation of the transparency framework that should be improved	Recommendation for improvement
The Netherlands	
Although most taxpayers benefitting from the third category of assets in the new IP regime obtain a ruling and are identified and exchanged upon in accordance with the process used for all other rulings, the Netherlands is not yet able to identify taxpayers benefitting from the third category of assets in the IP regime to the extent they do not obtain a ruling (ToR I.4.1.3).	The Netherlands is recommended to continue its efforts to identify and exchange information on taxpayers benefitting from the third category of IP assets as soon as possible.
New Zealand	
	No recommendations are made.
Nigeria	
	No recommendations are made.
Norway	
	No recommendations are made.
Pakistan	
	No recommendations are made.
Panama	
	No recommendations are made.
Papua New Guinea	
	No recommendations are made.
Paraguay	
Paraguay does not yet have in place a process to identify all information on potential exchange jurisdictions (ToR I.4).	Paraguay is recommended to finalise its information gathering process for identifying all past and future rulings and potential exchange jurisdictions, with a review and supervision mechanism, as soon as possible.
Paraguay does not yet have in place a process for completion of templates and exchange of information on rulings (ToR II.5).	Paraguay is recommended to continue to put in place a domestic legal framework allowing spontaneous exchange of information on rulings and to continue its efforts to complete the templates for all relevant rulings and to ensure that the exchanges of information on rulings occur as soon as possible.
Peru	
	No recommendations are made.
Philippines	
The Philippines does not currently collect information on all potential exchange jurisdictions, particularly the ultimate parent company for past rulings (ToR I.4.2.2).	The Philippines is recommended to apply the "best efforts approach" to identify potential exchange jurisdictions for all past rulings.
The Philippines does not currently collect information on all potential exchange jurisdictions, particularly the ultimate parent company for future rulings (ToR I.4.2.1).	The Philippines is recommended to ensure that all potential exchange jurisdictions are identified swiftly for future rulings.
The Philippines does not have a review and supervision mechanism in place to ensure that all relevant information on the identification of rulings and potential exchange jurisdictions is captured adequately (ToR I.4.3).	The Philippines is recommended to have in place a review and supervision mechanism to ensure that all relevant information is captured adequately.
The Philippines does not yet have the necessary legal framework in place for exchanging information on rulings and a process in place to ensure the timely exchange of information on rulings in the form required by the transparency framework (ToR II.5).	The Philippines is recommended to continue to put in place a domestic legal framework allowing spontaneous exchange of information on rulings and to ensure the timely exchange of information on rulings in the form required by the transparency framework.
Poland	
Poland encountered delays in identifying all potential exchange jurisdictions for future rulings other than APAs. This is a continuing recommendation from the prior year peer review (ToR II.4.2.1).	Poland is recommended to ensure that all potential exchange jurisdictions are identified swiftly for future rulings other than APAs.
A number of the exchanges on information on rulings were not sent to all potential exchange jurisdictions (ToR II.5.6).	No recommendation is made because Poland completed the exchanges of information on all past and future rulings by February 2018 and steps have been taken to ensure that this does not recur.

Aspect of the implementation of the transparency framework that should be improved	Recommendation for improvement
Portugal	
Portugal encountered some minor delays in the exchange of information on rulings within scope of the transparency framework. This is a continuing recommendation from the prior year peer review (ToR II.5.6).	Portugal is recommended to ensure that all information on future rulings is exchanged as soon as possible.
Romania	
Romania does not have a review and supervision mechanism in place to ensure that all relevant information on the identification of rulings and potential exchange jurisdictions is captured adequately (ToR I.4.3).	Romania is recommended to have in place a review and supervision mechanism to ensure that all relevant information is captured adequately.
In the year in review, Romania did not have in place a process for completion of templates and exchange of information on rulings (ToR II.5).	Romania is recommended to continue its efforts to complete the templates for all relevant rulings and to ensure that the exchanges of information on rulings occur as soon as possible.
Russian Federation	
	No recommendations are made.
San Marino	
	No recommendations are made.
Saudi Arabia	
	No recommendations are made.
Seychelles	
	No recommendations are made.
Sierra Leone	
	No recommendations are made.
Singapore	
Singapore identified additional 37 past rulings only in 2018 during a review process.	No recommendation is made because Singapore has addressed the issue and it is not expected to recur.
Singapore experienced some delays in exchanging information on past and future rulings.	No recommendation is made because Singapore completed the exchange of all past rulings by May 2018 (except the recently identified LoAs which will be exchanged by August 2018) and this is not a recurring issue. The future rulings were exchanged within a very short period of the deadline and steps have been taken to ensure that this does not recur.
Sint Maarten	
	Review deferred, as the jurisdiction suffered a natural disaster.
Slovak Republic	
	No recommendations are made.
Slovenia	
	No recommendations are made.
South Africa	
	No recommendations are made.
Spain	
Spain has not exchanged information on new assets of existing taxpayers benefitting from the grandfathered regime as this information was not available during the year in review (ToR I.4.1.3).	Spain is recommended to identify and exchange relevant information on new assets of existing taxpayers benefitting from the grandfathered IP regime.
Sri Lanka	
It is not known whether Sri Lanka has an information gathering process in place (ToR I.4).	Sri Lanka is recommended to ensure that it has put in place an effective information gathering process to identify all relevant past and future rulings and all potential exchange jurisdictions and to implement a review and supervision mechanism, as soon as possible.
It is not known whether Sri Lanka has a domestic legal framework allowing spontaneous exchange of information on rulings and has a process in place to ensure the timely exchange of information on rulings in the form required by the transparency framework (ToR II.5).	Sri Lanka is recommended to put in place a domestic legal framework allowing spontaneous exchange of information on rulings if needed and to ensure the timely exchange of information on rulings in the form required by the transparency framework.
Sweden	
Sweden did not identify all past rulings (ToR I.4.1.2).	No recommendation is made because Sweden identified additional past rulings in 2017 which it has exchanged by June 2017 and

Aspect of the implementation of the transparency framework that should be improved	Recommendation for improvement
	Sweden has reviewed its process for identifying past and future rulings to ensure that this is not a recurring issue.
Sweden did not identify all potential exchange jurisdictions for future rulings (ToR I.4.2.1). This is a continuing recommendation from the prior year peer review.	Sweden is recommended to amend its rulings practice to require taxpayers to provide information on all potential exchange jurisdictions for future rulings as soon as possible.
Switzerland	
	No recommendations are made.
Trinidad and Tobago	
	No recommendations are made.
Turkey	
Turkey has not been able to identify and exchange information on new entrants to the grandfathered IP regime (ToR I.4.1.3). This is a continuing recommendation from the prior year peer review.	Turkey is recommended to identify and exchange information on new entrants to the grandfathered IP regime.
United Kingdom	
The United Kingdom experienced some delays exchanging information on future rulings (ToR II.5.6).	No recommendation is made because the United Kingdom completed the exchange of all future rulings in the year of review, implemented new procedures and hired additional staff to prevent further delay, therefore it is considered not a recurring issue.
The United Kingdom has not exchanged information on new assets of existing taxpayers benefitting from the grandfathered IP regime, as this information was still not available. The United Kingdom is currently evaluating ways to collect alternative information on new IP assets for the purpose of exchanging under the transparency framework (ToR I.4.1.3). This is a continuing recommendation from the prior year peer review.	The United Kingdom is recommended to identify and exchange alternative information on new assets of existing taxpayers benefitting from the grandfathered IP regime.
United States	
	No recommendations are made.
Viet Nam	
Viet Nam is currently putting in place a process for completion of templates and exchange of information on rulings (ToR II.5).	Viet Nam is recommended to continue to put in place a process to complete the templates for all relevant rulings and to ensure the timely exchange of information on rulings in the form required by the transparency framework.

Note

1. The Action 5 Report, *Countering Harmful Tax Practices More Effectively, Taking Into Account Transparency and Substance* (OECD, 2015) also provides that additional types of rulings could be added to the scope of the transparency framework in the future, where the FHTP and the Inclusive Framework agree that such a ruling could lead to BEPS concerns in the absence of spontaneous information exchange.

Reference

OECD (2015), *Countering Harmful Tax Practices More Effectively, Taking into Account Transparency and Substance, Action 5 - 2015 Final Report*, OECD/G20 Base Erosion and Profit Shifting Project, OECD Publishing, Paris. http://dx.doi.org/10.1787/9789264241190-en.

Chapter 1. The review of the BEPS Action 5 standard on the exchange of information on certain tax rulings

Overview of the peer review on the exchange of information on tax rulings

1. The 2015 Action 5 Report, *Countering Harmful Tax Practices More Effectively, Taking Into Account Transparency and Substance* (Action 5 Report, OECD, 2015) is one of the four BEPS minimum standards. It involves two distinct aspects: a review of certain preferential tax regimes to ensure they are not harmful, and a framework for the exchange of information on tax rulings ("the transparency framework"). Each of the four BEPS minimum standards is subject to peer review in order to ensure timely and accurate implementation and thus safeguard the level playing field. All members of the Inclusive Framework on BEPS commit to implementing the Action 5 minimum standard and to participating in the peer review, on an equal footing. The peer review of the Action 5 minimum standard is undertaken by the Forum on Harmful Tax Practices ("FHTP") and approved by the Inclusive Framework on BEPS.

2. The purpose of a peer review is to ensure the effective and consistent implementation of an agreed standard and to recognise progress made by jurisdictions in this regard. The peer review evaluates the implementation of the standard against an agreed set of criteria. These criteria are set out in terms of reference, which include each of the elements that a jurisdiction needs to demonstrate it has fulfilled in order to show proper implementation of the standard.[1]

3. The peer review has been conducted in accordance with the agreed methodology. The methodology sets out the process for undertaking the peer review, including the process for collecting the relevant data, the preparation and approval of annual reports, the outputs of the review and the follow up process.

4. The terms of reference and agreed methodology do not alter the Action 5 minimum standard. Any terms used in the terms of reference or methodology take their meaning from the language and context of the Action 5 Report (OECD, 2015) and the references therein. Any terms in this report which are not included in the glossary take their meaning from the language and context of the Action 5 Report (OECD, 2015).

Outline of the key aspects assessed in the annual report

5. This annual report contains the findings of the second annual peer review of jurisdictions' compliance with the transparency framework, conducted over the course of 2018. Where the first annual peer review covered 44 jurisdictions (i.e. OECD and G20 countries and the countries that were in the OECD accession process throughout the BEPS project), this second review covers 92 jurisdictions, including 48 Inclusive Framework members and Jurisdictions of Relevance identified by the Inclusive Framework which have undergone the peer review process for the first time. The second

annual peer review process assesses the implementation of the transparency framework during the 1 January 2017 – 31 December 2017 period.

6. One of the terms of reference is related to confidentiality (ToR III). Each jurisdiction that receives information on rulings under the transparency framework should ensure that the information received is kept confidential. The confidentiality aspect is reviewed by making sure that the international information exchange mechanisms being used by the jurisdictions include a confidentiality provision that restricts the use of information on rulings and there is the necessary domestic law and information security practices in place to give effect to such restrictions. Given its expertise in this area, the reviews of confidentiality in connection with the transparency framework defer to the work of the Global Forum on Transparency and Exchange of Information for Tax Purposes ("Global Forum") in connection with the standard on Automatic Exchange of Financial Account Information for Tax Purposes. The outcomes of that work are not published and no further references to the review of confidentiality are made in this peer review document.

7. Where a jurisdiction has not been assessed by the Global Forum, they have been requested to complete the standard confidentiality and data safeguards questionnaire used as the basis of those assessments, and this has been made available to FHTP members to inform their decision as to which jurisdictions it should exchange with.

8. The reports on each reviewed jurisdiction published herein cover each of the aspects of the terms of reference, except for confidentiality, which are broken down into three elements. A fourth element applies to jurisdictions which offer IP regimes. These capture the key elements of the transparency framework which are briefly described below.

A. The information gathering process

9. This involves assessing the processes in place in each of the jurisdictions for identifying past and future rulings that fall within the scope of the transparency framework, and for each of these rulings, identifying the jurisdictions with which the information should be exchanged. With respect to past rulings which do not contain information to identify those jurisdictions for which the tax rulings would be relevant, the jurisdiction issuing the ruling should apply the "best efforts approach" to try to identify this information. The review of the information gathering process also covers any supervision mechanism that the jurisdiction has in place to ensure that all relevant information is captured adequately.

B. The exchange of information

10. The exchange of information requires the legal and administrative framework to be in place to allow spontaneous exchange of information on the relevant tax rulings and subsequent exchange of the relevant rulings where a valid exchange of information request is received. Information on past rulings was to be spontaneously exchanged pursuant to the relevant deadline outlined in each jurisdiction's report. Information on future rulings is to be spontaneously exchanged as soon as possible and no later than three months after the date on which the ruling becomes available to the Competent Authority for exchange of information. The exchange of information should occur in the agreed standardised form, either using the template contained in Annex C of the Action 5 Report (OECD, 2015), or the OECD XML Schema. Adequate completion of the summary section in the Annex C template or the OECD XML Schema should be ensured through

adherence to the instruction sheet to the summary section or the internal FHTP suggested guidance, or an alternate process that allows the summary section to contain sufficient detail for the receiving jurisdiction's tax administration to appropriately assess the potential base erosion and profit shifting risks posed by the ruling where applicable.

11. The peer review includes reviewing (i) that there is a sufficient domestic and international legal framework for the exchange information related to rulings; (ii) that the templates for information on rulings being exchanged are complete and in the appropriate form; and (iii) that the systems are in place to ensure that information on rulings is transmitted to the jurisdiction's Competent Authority for exchange of information without undue delay and exchanged with relevant jurisdictions in accordance with the appropriate timelines.

12. The Action 5 Report (OECD, 2015) acknowledged that some jurisdictions may need to put in place the domestic or international legal framework in order to comply with the obligations under Action 5. In such cases the timelines for exchange of information on rulings are subject to a jurisdiction's legal framework.

13. With respect to the international exchange of information, the terms of reference required jurisdictions to exchange information with Inclusive Framework members being reviewed for the same year, to the extent that an exchange of information agreement was in force for such exchanges and subject to the recipient jurisdiction demonstrating that it would keep the information received confidential.[2]

C. Statistics

14. Each jurisdiction is required to report statistics on the exchange of information under the transparency framework including (i) the total number of spontaneous exchanges sent, (ii) the number of spontaneous exchanges under each category of ruling and (iii) a list of jurisdictions with which the information was exchanged for each type of ruling.

D. Exchange of information on IP regimes

15. The review of the transparency framework also includes a review of the spontaneous exchanges of information which are required to occur in respect of certain features of IP regimes, as set out in the Action 5 "nexus approach." This includes identifying and exchanging information on new entrants benefitting from grandfathered IP regimes (regardless of whether a ruling is provided), taxpayers which benefit from the third category of IP assets, and taxpayers making use of the option to treat the nexus ratio as a rebuttable presumption. This aspect of the review is only relevant for those jurisdictions which offer IP regimes, and the minimum standard does not require any jurisdiction to introduce such a regime.

Response to the report

16. Jurisdictions had the option to include a response to the report and update on recent developments which occurred after the 2017 year in review. Where included, this reflects the individual jurisdiction's views, and not those of the FHTP or the OECD Secretariat.

Notes

[1] Terms of Reference and Methodology for the review as approved by the Inclusive Framework on 20 January 2017 (OECD, 2017).

[2] Where a ruling related only to tax years which were not covered by the relevant exchange of information agreement, no exchange of information would be required to occur in respect of that ruling. No negative inference is drawn in the peer review where an exchange was not permitted to occur because of the absence of, or the tax years covered by, an exchange of information agreement.

References

OECD (2017), *BEPS Action 5 on Harmful Tax Practices – Terms of Reference and Methodology for the Conduct of the Peer Reviews of the Action 5 Transparency Framework*, OECD/G20 Base Erosion and Profit Shifting Project, OECD, Paris. www.oecd.org/tax/beps/beps-action-5-harmful-tax-practices-peer-review-transparencyframework.pdf.

OECD (2015), *Countering Harmful Tax Practices More Effectively, Taking into Account Transparency and Substance, Action 5 - 2015 Final Report*, OECD/G20 Base Erosion and Profit Shifting Project, OECD Publishing, Paris. https://doi.org/10.1787/9789264241190-en.

Chapter 2. Country Profiles

Andorra

Andorra has met all aspects of the terms of reference (ToR) for the calendar year 2017 (year in review), except for identifying potential exchange jurisdictions for past rulings (ToR I.4.2.2) and for future rulings (ToR I.4.2.1) and for undertaking spontaneous exchange of information on tax rulings (ToR II.5). Andorra is recommended to continue to apply the "best efforts approach" to identify potential exchange jurisdictions for all past rulings and to ensure that all potential exchange jurisdictions are identified swiftly for all future rulings. Andorra has introduced the necessary legal basis for spontaneous exchange of information on rulings, which took effect from 10 June 2017. However, Andorra did not undertake spontaneous exchange of information on tax rulings within scope of the transparency framework during the year in review. Andorra is recommended to complete the templates for all relevant rulings and to ensure that the exchanges of information on rulings occur as soon as possible.

Andorra can legally issue five types of rulings within the scope of the transparency framework.

In practice, Andorra issued 177 past rulings; and for the year in review, Andorra issued 44 future rulings within the scope of the transparency framework.

As no exchange of information on rulings was conducted, no peer input was received in respect of the exchanges of information on rulings received from Andorra.

Introduction

1. This peer review covers Andorra's implementation of the BEPS Action 5 transparency framework for the year 2017. The report has four parts, each relating to a key part of the ToR. Each part is discussed in turn. A summary of recommendations is included at the end of this report.

A. The information gathering process

2. Andorra can legally issue the five following type of rulings within the scope of the transparency framework: (i) rulings related to preferential regimes;[1] (ii) cross-border unilateral advance pricing arrangements (APAs) and any other cross-border unilateral tax rulings (such as an advance tax ruling) covering transfer pricing or the application of transfer pricing principles; (iii) unilateral downward adjustments; (iv) permanent establishment rulings; and (v) conduit rulings. These rulings are referred to as written tax inquiries, special agreements, preferential regime rulings or previous valuation agreements. The Andorran Tax Administration ("ATA") is responsible for issuing rulings through a centralised office. Rulings issued under the form of written inquiries (binding consultations) are published online in anonymised form.[2] Rulings under the form of special agreements are published in the Andorran official gazette. Previous valuation agreements are not published.

Past rulings (ToR I.4.1.1, I.4.1.2, I.4.2.1, I.4.2.2)

3. For Andorra, past rulings are any tax rulings within scope that are issued either: (i) on or after 1 January 2015 but before 1 April 2017; or (ii) on or after 1 January 2012 but before 1 January 2015, provided they were still in effect as at 1 January 2015.

4. The process for identifying past rulings was conducted as follows. Rulings were maintained in a database and a review for past rulings was performed. The specific files were reviewed for the cases in which the rulings were not saved in the database. The Andorran Tax Administration has been in charge of the research, identification and review of the existing past rulings, with support of staff within the international financial matters division.

5. Andorra had difficulties to identify potential exchange jurisdictions, as this information was not required as part of the process for issuing past rulings. Andorra used internal information contained in the ruling request itself, in the company organisation chart or in the different contracts eventually annexed to the request. Andorra was not able to obtain information on potential exchange jurisdictions. Andorra is recommended to apply the "best efforts approach" to identify potential exchange jurisdictions for all past rulings. Andorra notes that it is currently working on the information gathering process and identifying the potential exchange jurisdictions.

Future rulings (ToR I.4.1.1, I.4.1.2, I.4.2.1)

6. For Andorra, future rulings are any tax rulings within scope that are issued on or after 1 April 2017.

7. As was the case for past rulings issued since 2015, rulings are maintained in a database and identified by manual verification by the respective division, which checks all rulings as soon as they are issued against the obligations for spontaneous exchange. A

brief review is also done on an annual basis to detect any eventual remaining cases to be issued.

8. In order to identify all potential exchange jurisdictions, the ruling application process will be amended and the taxpayer will be required to identify all relevant jurisdictions when requesting the ruling, including the immediate parent company and ultimate parent company. Andorra is planning to introduce these amendments by the end of 2018. However, during the year in review, this information was not requested in the ruling process and as such Andorra has not yet started the process to capture the relevant information. In the meantime, Andorra is applying the "best efforts approach" to identify potential exchange jurisdictions for future rulings.

Review and supervision mechanism (ToR I.4.3)

9. Andorra centralised the procedure to collect information with regard to the tax rulings that are in the scope of the transparency framework, appointing the Director of the Tax Administration as having responsibility, with support of staff in the international financial matters division. The EOI division also performs a quality control check in relation to each ruling identified as subject to exchange. This includes checking that the ruling is categorised correctly and that all relevant information has been provided.

Conclusion on section A

10. Andorra has met all of the ToR for the information gathering process except for identifying all potential exchange jurisdictions for past rulings (ToR I.4.2.2) and for future rulings (ToR I.4.2.1). Andorra is recommended to apply the "best efforts approach" to identify potential exchange jurisdictions for all past rulings and to ensure that all potential exchange jurisdictions are identified swiftly for all future rulings.

B. The exchange of information

Legal basis for spontaneous exchange of information (ToR II.5.1, II.5.2)

11. Andorra did not previously have the necessary domestic legal basis to exchange information spontaneously for rulings. The Andorran domestic Law that enables spontaneous exchange of information has been introduced and entered into force on 10 June 2017. However, the *Multilateral Convention on Mutual Administrative Assistance in Tax Matters: Amended by the 2010 Protocol* (OECD/Council of Europe, 2011) ("the Convention") allows Andorra to exchange information on rulings issued as of 1 January 2012, provided they were still in effect on 1 January 2017 (after the date of entry into effect of the Convention) [3]. Andorra explained that this limitation of the possibility to exchange information on past rulings was necessary, as Andorra's legal framework does not foresee the possibility of introducing legislation with retrospective effect. Due to this limitation, only information concerning periods after the entry into force of the legal basis on spontaneous exchange of information can be exchanged, regardless of the date on which the ruling was issued.[4]

12. Andorra notes that apart from the restriction to exchange information on past rulings there are no legal or practical impediments that prevent the spontaneous exchange of information on rulings as contemplated in the Action 5 minimum standard after the date of entry into effect of the Convention.

13. Andorra is a party to international agreements permitting spontaneous exchange of information, including (i) the Convention and (ii) double tax agreements in force with 28 jurisdictions.[5]

Completion and exchange of templates (ToR II.5.3, II.5.4, II.5.5, II.5.6, II.5.7)

14. Andorra noted that it will exchange future rulings as soon as all the potential exchange jurisdictions of the rulings issued are identified.

15. With respect to future rulings, Andorra will educate its tax officers to ensure that rulings are submitted to the Competent Authority for exchange of information within three months of the ruling being issued. The EOI unit will also ensure that the necessary administrative and practical measures (such as IT, process descriptions, professional training, etc.) are taken by the Tax Administration, in order to ensure that spontaneous exchange of information is implemented effectively.

16. As there were no exchanges for the year in review, no data on the timeliness of exchanges can be reported.

Conclusion on section B

17. Andorra has introduced the necessary legal basis for spontaneous exchange of information on rulings, which took effect from 10 June 2017. However, the Convention allows Andorra to exchange information on rulings issued as of 1 January 2012, provided they were still in effect on 1 January 2017 (after the date of entry into effect of the Convention). Andorra did not undertake spontaneous exchange of information on tax rulings within scope of the transparency framework during the year in review. Andorra is recommended to complete the templates for all relevant rulings and to ensure that the exchanges of information on rulings occur as soon as possible.

C. Statistics (ToR IV)

18. As there were no exchanges for the year in review, no statistics data can be reported.

D. Matters related to intellectual property regimes (ToR I.4.1.3)

19. Andorra offers an intellectual property regime ("IP regime").[6] However, for the year in review no transparency requirements under the Action 5 Report (OECD, 2015) were relevant, as follows:

- ***New entrants benefitting from the grandfathered IP regime***: not applicable for the year in review, because Andorra was in the process of amending the regime (draft legislation under parliament procedure) and had not taken a decision yet on whether it will provide grandfathering to existing taxpayers. Should Andorra provide grandfathering to taxpayers for which IP income benefits and that entered the regimes after the publication of the 2017 Progress Report (OECD, 2017b) which occurred on 16 October 2017, transparency requirements will apply and this will be taken into account during the 2018 peer review.
- ***Third category of IP assets***: not applicable to this regime, which in 2017 was in the process of being amended.

- ***Taxpayers making the use of the option to treat the nexus ratio as a rebuttable presumption***: not applicable to this regime, which in 2017 was in the process of being amended.

Summary of recommendations on implementation of the transparency framework

Aspect of implementation of the transparency framework that should be improved	Recommendation for improvement
Andorra experienced difficulties in identifying all potential exchange jurisdictions for past rulings.	Andorra is recommended to continue to apply the "best efforts approach" to identify potential exchange jurisdictions for all past rulings.
Andorra experienced difficulties in identifying all potential exchange jurisdictions for future rulings.	Andorra is recommended to ensure that all potential exchange jurisdictions are identified swiftly for all future rulings.
Andorra did not undertake spontaneous exchange of information on tax rulings within scope of the transparency framework during the year in review.	Andorra is recommended to continue its efforts to complete the templates for all relevant rulings and to ensure that the exchanges of information on rulings occur as soon as possible.

Notes

[1] These are: 1) Holding company regime, 2) Intercompany and financing regime, 3) Companies involved in international trade and 4) Companies involved in the international exploitation of intangible assets regime. The rulings related to these preferential regimes are not published.

[2] These rulings are published at www.impostos.ad/comunicats-tecnics-i-consultes-vinculants. Rulings (issued by means of articles 65, 66 and 67 of the Andorran Law on General Taxation - Written inquiries, Previous valuation agreements and Special agreements) can be included in more than one of the transparency framework categories according to the specific demand the taxpayer has requested.

[3] Andorra is a signatory to the Convention, which is in effect as of 1 January 2017 and permits Andorra to spontaneously exchange information from 1 January 2017.

[4] The Action 5 Report (OECD, 2015) notes that jurisdictions which do not currently have the necessary legal framework in place for spontaneous exchange of information on rulings will need to put in place such a framework in order to comply with the obligations under the transparency framework, but that in such cases the timelines are subject to a country's legal framework.

[5] Parties to the Convention are available here: www.oecd.org/tax/exchange-of-tax-information/convention-on-mutual-administrative-assistance-in-tx-matters.htm. Andorra also has bilateral agreements in force with Argentina, Australia, Austria, Belgium, Czech Republic, Denmark, Faroe Islands, Finland, France, Germany, Greenland, Iceland, Italy, Korea, Liechtenstein, Luxembourg, Malta, Monaco, Netherlands, Norway, Poland, Portugal, San Marino, Spain, Sweden, Switzerland and United Arab Emirates.

[6] This regime is the Companies involved in the international exploitation of intangible assets regime, to be amended by Law 6/2018.

References

OECD (2017a), *BEPS Action 5 on Harmful Tax Practices – Terms of Reference and Methodology for the Conduct of the Peer Reviews of the Action 5 Transparency Framework*, OECD/G20 Base Erosion and Profit Shifting Project, OECD, Paris. www.oecd.org/tax/beps/beps-action-5-harmful-tax-practices-peer-review-transparencyframework.pdf.

OECD (2017b), *Harmful Tax Practices - 2017 Progress Report on Preferential Regimes: Inclusive Framework on BEPS: Action 5*, OECD/G20 Base Erosion and Profit Shifting Project, OECD Publishing, Paris. http://dx.doi.org/10.1787/9789264283954-en.

OECD (2015), *Countering Harmful Tax Practices More Effectively, Taking into Account Transparency and Substance, Action 5 - 2015 Final Report*, OECD/G20 Base Erosion and Profit Shifting Project, OECD Publishing, Paris. https://doi.org/10.1787/9789264241190-en.

OECD/Council of Europe (2011), *The Multilateral Convention on Mutual Administrative Assistance in Tax Matters: Amended by the 2010 Protocol*, OECD Publishing, Paris. http://dx.doi.org/10.1787/9789264115606-en.

Angola

Angola is taking steps to implement the legal basis for the transparency framework and to commence administrative preparations to ensure that information on rulings will be exchanged in a timely manner. Angola is recommended to finalise its information gathering process to identify all past and future rulings and potential exchange jurisdictions, with a review and supervision mechanism, as soon as possible (ToR I.4). Angola is recommended to continue to put in place a domestic legal framework allowing spontaneous exchange of information on rulings and to continue its efforts to complete the templates for all relevant rulings and to ensure that the exchanges of information on rulings occur as soon as possible (ToR II.5).

Angola can legally issue five types of rulings within the scope of the transparency framework.

In practice, Angola has not identified during the calendar year 2017 (year in review) any past rulings; and for the year in review, Angola issued one future ruling within the scope of the transparency framework.

As no exchanges of information on rulings were conducted, no peer input was received in respect of the exchanges of information on rulings received from Angola.

Introduction

20. This peer review covers Angola's implementation of the BEPS Action 5 transparency framework for the year 2017. The report has four parts, each relating to a key part of the ToR. Each part is discussed in turn. A summary of recommendations is included at the end of this report.

A. The information gathering process

21. Angola can legally issue the five following types of rulings within the scope of the transparency framework: (i) rulings related to preferential regimes; (ii) cross-border unilateral advance pricing agreements (APAs) and any other cross-border unilateral tax rulings (such as an advance tax ruling) covering transfer pricing or the application of transfer pricing principles; (iii) rulings providing a downward adjustment of taxable profits; (iv) permanent establishment rulings; and (v) related party conduit rulings. Certain rulings are issued local by different tax offices around Angola and "binding information requests" are issued by the legal directorate, office of fiscal services, large taxpayers' directorate and directorate for natural resources of the *Administração Geral Tributária* ("AGT"). These are the rulings related to the oil, gas and mining sectors. Angola is currently starting a process to request information from all branches and directorates that issue decisions on taxpayer complaints and appeals in order to identify whether other rulings in scope were issued during the year in review. Angola acknowledges that a transfer pricing unit has been recently created and legislation and procedures are being developed.

Past rulings (ToR I.4.1.1, I.4.1.2, I.4.2.1, I.4.2.2)

22. For Angola, past rulings are any tax rulings within scope that are issued either: (i) on or after 1 January 2015 but before 1 April 2017; or (ii) on or after 1 January 2012 but before 1 January 2015, provided they were still in effect as at 1 January 2015.

23. AGT has contacted the areas responsible for issuing rulings and have instructed staff to search their files to identify rulings issued as required by the transparency framework. However, AGT acknowledges that it has not recorded the information on the tax rulings issued with the necessary level of detail to meet the standard of the transparency framework.

24. Angola acknowledges that the necessary information on past rulings is unlikely to be found on the available records. Angola notes that it will seek to apply the "best efforts approach" once all past rulings have been identified.

Future rulings (ToR I.4.1.1, I.4.1.2, I.4.2.1)

25. For Angola, future rulings are any tax rulings within scope that are issued on or after 1 April 2017.

26. AGT has read and verified all rulings issued ("binding information requests"). AGT has contacted the areas responsible for issuing rulings and have instructed staff that it is necessary to keep record of details of rulings issued as required by the transparency framework.

27. Angola affirms it is currently following guidelines covering which rulings fall in the scope of the transparency framework and what information on the rulings should be

kept in order to meet the level of detail required by the transparency framework. AGT is also developing a system to record and track all future rulings in order to be able to conduct an effective analysis of future rulings issued.

Review and supervision mechanism (ToR I.4.3)

28. Angola did not yet have an information gathering process for past rulings under the transparency framework for the year in review. Angola started to put in place a revision and supervision mechanism for future rulings to be issued by requiring that the information on tax rulings is recorded in hard copy and electronically in spreadsheets in Excel format with the name, date and topic of the information requested or issue being complained or appealed.

Conclusion on section A

29. Angola is recommended to finalise its information gathering process for identifying all past and future rulings and potential exchange jurisdictions, with a review and supervision mechanism, as soon as possible (ToR I.4).

B. The exchange of information

Legal basis for spontaneous exchange of information (ToR II.5.1, II.5.2)

30. Angola is currently working to have in place the necessary domestic legal basis to exchange information spontaneously.

31. Angola does not have currently in effect an agreement that would allow for spontaneous exchange of information under the transparency framework. Angola is not a Party to the *Multilateral Convention on Mutual Administrative Assistance in Tax Matters: Amended by the 2010 Protocol* (OECD/Council of Europe, 2011) ("the Convention"). Angola is encouraged to continue its efforts to expand its international exchange of information instruments to be able to exchange rulings. It is however noted that jurisdictions are assessed on their compliance with the transparency framework in respect of the exchange of information network in effect for the year of the particular annual review.

Completion and exchange of templates (ToR II.5.3, II.5.4, II.5.5, II.5.6, II.5.7)

32. Angola is still developing a process to complete the templates on relevant rulings, to make them available to the Competent Authority for exchange of information and to exchange them with relevant jurisdictions. Angola acknowledges that an information exchange unit has been recently created to assume the role of the Competent Authority and legislation and procedures for the functioning of the unit are being developed.

33. For the year in review, Angola had not undertaken any exchanges of information.

Conclusion on section B

34. Angola is recommended to continue to put in place a domestic legal framework allowing spontaneous exchange of information on rulings and to continue its efforts to complete the templates for all relevant rulings and to ensure that the exchanges of information on rulings occur as soon as possible (ToR II.5).

C. Statistics (ToR IV)

35. As no information on rulings was exchanged for the year in review, no statistical data can be reported.

D. Matters related to intellectual property regimes (ToR I.4.1.3)

36. Angola does not offer an intellectual property regime for which transparency requirements under the Action 5 Report (OECD, 2015) were imposed.

Summary of recommendations on implementation of the transparency framework

Aspect of implementation of the transparency framework that should be improved	Recommendation for improvement
Angola has not yet finalised the steps to have in place its necessary information and gathering process.	Angola is recommended to finalise its information gathering process for identifying all past and future rulings and potential exchange jurisdictions, with a review and supervision mechanism, as soon as possible.
Angola has not yet finalised the steps to have effective compulsory spontaneous exchange of information on the tax rulings within the scope of the transparency framework.	Angola is recommended to continue to put in place a domestic legal framework allowing spontaneous exchange of information on rulings and to continue its efforts to complete the templates for all relevant rulings and to ensure that the exchanges of information on rulings occur as soon as possible.

References

OECD (2017), *BEPS Action 5 on Harmful Tax Practices – Terms of Reference and Methodology for the Conduct of the Peer Reviews of the Action 5 Transparency Framework*, OECD/G20 Base Erosion and Profit Shifting Project, OECD, Paris. www.oecd.org/tax/beps/beps-action-5-harmful-tax-practices-peer-review-transparencyframework.pdf.

OECD (2015), *Countering Harmful Tax Practices More Effectively, Taking into Account Transparency and Substance, Action 5 - 2015 Final Report*, OECD/G20 Base Erosion and Profit Shifting Project, OECD Publishing, Paris. https://doi.org/10.1787/9789264241190-en.

OECD/Council of Europe (2011), *The Multilateral Convention on Mutual Administrative Assistance in Tax Matters: Amended by the 2010 Protocol*, OECD Publishing, Paris. http://dx.doi.org/10.1787/9789264115606-en.

Argentina

Argentina has met all aspects of the terms of reference (ToR) for the calendar year 2017 (year in review) except that Argentina had difficulties in identifying future rulings (ToR I.4.1.2). Argentina is recommended to provide any necessary interpretive guidance and continue its efforts to ensure that there is an effective system for identifying all future rulings in a timely way.

Argentina can legally issue five types of rulings within the scope of the transparency framework.

In practice, Argentina has issued two past rulings; for the period 1 April 2016 - 31 December 2016, Argentina issued no future rulings; and for the year in review, Argentina issued one future ruling within the scope of the transparency framework.

No peer input was received in respect of the exchanges of information on rulings received from Argentina.

Introduction

37. This peer review covers Argentina's implementation of the BEPS Action 5 transparency framework for the year 2017. The report has four parts, each relating to a key part of the ToR. Each part is discussed in turn. A summary of recommendations is included at the end of this report.

A. The information gathering process

38. This section relates to the adequacy of the process used to collect information relating to the tax rulings that are in the scope of the transparency framework, both past and future rulings, as well as the jurisdictions with which information on rulings should be exchanged.

39. Argentina can legally issue the five following types of rulings within the scope of the transparency framework: (i) rulings related to preferential regimes;[1] (ii) cross-border unilateral advance pricing agreements (APAs) and any other cross-border unilateral tax rulings (such as an advance tax ruling) covering transfer pricing or the application of transfer pricing principles; (iii) cross-border rulings giving a unilateral downward adjustment to the taxpayer's taxable profits in the country giving the ruling; (iv) permanent establishment rulings; and (v) related party conduit rulings. These rulings are referred to as individual binding consultations. Argentina notes that it does not issue APAs and that although the binding consultation regime does not explicitly exclude any of these categories of issues from its scope, the legal tax framework would not allow for a downward adjustment ruling. Argentina also notes that the preferential regime is not granted by tax ruling and there would not be expected to be any reason for a binding consultation on the interpretation of the regime to be given in practice. In addition, Argentina notes that it is highly unlikely that a conduit ruling would be issued given the structure of Argentina's tax laws which make it unlikely to be a jurisdiction of choice for a taxpayer using such arrangements. In Argentina, a specific unit (the Deputy General Direction for Technical and Legal Tax Matters) within the tax administration, the Federal Administration of Public Revenues (AFIP), is in charge of issuing the tax rulings. Rulings are published in anonymized form.[2]

Past rulings (ToR I.4.1.1, I.4.1.2, I.4.2.1, I.4.2.2)

40. For Argentina, past rulings are any tax rulings within scope that are issued either: (i) on or after 1 January 2014 but before 1 April 2016; or (ii) on or after 1 January 2010 but before 1 January 2014, provided they were still in effect as at 1 January 2014.

41. In the prior year peer review report, it was determined that AFIP's undertakings to identify past rulings and all potential exchange jurisdictions were sufficient to meet the minimum standard.

42. AFIP's implementation in this regard remains unchanged, and therefore continues to meet the minimum standard.

Future rulings (ToR I.4.1.1, I.4.1.2, I.4.2.1)

43. For Argentina, future rulings are any tax rulings within scope that are issued on or after 1 April 2016.

44. In the prior year peer review report, it was determined that AFIP's process for identifying the rulings and potential exchange jurisdictions was sufficient to meet the minimum standard. This process was that the Deputy General Direction for Technical and Legal Tax Matters (which is responsible for issuing rulings) would alert the Directorate for International Affairs in case a relevant tax ruling is issued. The Directorate for International Affairs would analyse the ruling to verify whether the ruling is within the scope of the transparency framework, and also consult the public repository of rulings on a quarterly basis to double check that all relevant rulings have been identified. Information on potential exchange jurisdictions would be identified from information from the ruling itself or where this was not sufficient, by AFIP exercising its discretionary powers to request additional information from the taxpayer.

45. During the information gathering process for future rulings for the year in review, there was a delay in the identification process of one future ruling. The application for the future ruling issued occurred prior to the publication of Action 5 Report and the ruling was issued in February 2017 and published in October 2017. While checking the public repository of anonymised consultations by the end of November 2017, it was noted that this consultation had been issued and that it potentially fell within the scope of the transparency framework. In late 2017, measures were taken to obtain the details of the full technical report in order to determine if this ruling was subject to exchange and whether there were legal instruments which allow spontaneous exchange of information for the period referred in the ruling in force with the relevant jurisdictions. As a result of the analysis of the ruling, Argentina confirmed that the future ruling was within the scope of the transparency framework, and the relevant exchange was made. Argentina notes it is a temporary circumstance related to the issuance of the particular future ruling.

46. AFIP is working on modifications to its internal regulations to expressly contemplate the process currently in place and to require the taxpayer to provide the relevant information when submitting an application for a ruling which could potentially fall within the scope of the transparency framework, as well as to have a clearer process on the steps taken to identify those tax rulings. Argentina expects to have these modifications in force by the end of 2018.

Review and supervision mechanism (ToR I.4.3)

47. In the prior year peer review report, it was determined that AFIP's review and supervision mechanisms were sufficient to meet the minimum standard. AFIP's implementation in this regard remains unchanged, and therefore continues to meet the minimum standard.

Conclusion on section A

48. Argentina has met all of the ToR for the information gathering process except that Argentina had difficulties in identifying one future ruling (ToR I.4.1.2). Argentina is finalising modifications to the internal regulations to make sure the identification of future rulings occurs in all cases, the effectiveness of which will be reviewed in the 2019 peer review. Argentina is recommended to provide any necessary interpretive guidance and continue its efforts to ensure that there is an effective system for identifying all future rulings in a timely way.

B. The exchange of information

Legal basis for spontaneous exchange of information (ToR II.5.1, II.5.2)

49. Argentina has the necessary domestic legal basis to exchange information spontaneously. Argentina notes that there are no legal or practical impediments that prevent the spontaneous exchange of information on rulings as contemplated in the Action 5 minimum standard.

50. Argentina is a party to international agreements permitting spontaneous exchange of information, including the (i) *Multilateral Convention on Mutual Administrative Assistance in Tax Matters: Amended by the 2010 Protocol* (OECD/Council of Europe, 2011) ("the Convention") and (ii) double tax agreements in force with 16 jurisdictions and (iii) tax information exchange agreements with seven jurisdictions.[3]

Completion and exchange of templates (ToR II.5.3, II.5.4, II.5.5, II.5.6, II.5.7)

51. In the prior year peer review report, it was determined that AFIP's completion and exchange of templates were sufficient to meet the minimum standard. AFIP's implementation in this regard remains unchanged, and therefore continues to meet the minimum standard. As there were no relevant rulings to be exchanged in the prior year, this was the first year in which the process was used in practice. The processes in relation to the completion of the summary section for the AFIP are as follows: The information required by the template of Annex C is filled in manually by the Directorate of International Affairs after analysing the full technical report of the binding consultation. The information of that report is summarised in order to produce a short summary of the issue covered by the ruling in English or in Spanish, if it is the language bilaterally agreed. Furthermore, Argentina has confirmed that their approach to the completion of the summary section in section 7 of Annex C of the 2015 Action 5 Report (OECD, 2015) conforms to the prescribed instructions for the section. Where relevant, Argentina also utilises the internal FHTP suggested guidance.

52. With respect to the one ruling within the scope of the transparency framework which was issued in the 2017 year of review, this was identified as being within scope only in early 2018, for the reasons noted in section A above. The ruling was exchanged in February 2018, as soon confirmed that it was subject to exchange and that there was a legal instrument in force which allows spontaneous exchange of information for the covered period.

53. The timeliness of exchanges is as follows:

Past rulings in the scope of the transparency framework	Number of exchanges transmitted by 31 December 2017	Delayed exchanges		
		Number of exchanges not transmitted by 31 December 2017	Reasons for the delays	Any other comments
	N/A	N/A	N/A	
Future rulings in the scope of the transparency framework	**Number of exchanges transmitted within three months of the information becoming available to the competent authority or immediately after legal impediments have been lifted**	**Delayed exchanges**		
		Number of exchanges transmitted later than three months of the information on rulings becoming available to the competent authority	Reasons for the delays	Any other comments
	0	2	Date of submission of the binding consultation	See paragraph 16 above.
Total	0	2		

Follow up requests received for exchange of the ruling	Number	Average time to provide response	Number of requests not answered
	0	N/A	N/A

Conclusion on section B

54. Argentina has the necessary legal basis for spontaneous exchange of information, and a process for completing the templates in a timely way. A delay in the timeliness of exchanges occurred due to a problem in the identification process and once identified, the information on this future ruling was exchanged within one month of the deadline. As this was not an issue related to the exchange of information process itself, no recommendation in this section is made. Argentina has met all of the ToR for the exchange of information process.

C. Statistics (ToR IV)

55. As no information on rulings was exchanged for the year in review, no statistical data can be reported.

D. Matters related to intellectual property regimes (ToR I.4.1.3)

56. Argentina does not offer an intellectual property regime for which transparency requirements under the Action 5 Report (OECD, 2015) were imposed.

Summary of recommendations on implementation of the transparency framework

Aspect of implementation of the transparency framework that should be improved	Recommendation for improvement
Argentina experienced difficulties on the identification of information on future rulings.	Argentina is recommended to provide any necessary interpretive guidance and continue its efforts to ensure that there is an effective system for identifying all future rulings in a timely way.

Notes

[1] With respect to the following preferential regime: Promotional Regime for Software Industry.

[2] Available at http://biblioteca.afip.gob.ar/search/query/BoletinesDGI.aspx (accessed 20 November 2018) and http://biblioteca.afip.gob.ar/estaticos/consultasVinculantes/index.aspx (accessed 20 November 2018).

[3] Parties to the Convention are available here: www.oecd.org/tax/exchange-of-tax-information/convention-on-mutual-administrative-assistance-in-tax-matters.htm. Argentina has in force Double Tax Agreements permitting spontaneous exchange of information with: Australia, Belgium, Bolivia, Brazil, Canada, Chile, Denmark, Finland, France, Italy, Netherlands, Norway, Russia, Spain, Sweden and United Kingdom. In addition, Argentina has agreements permitting spontaneous exchange of information with Aruba, Azerbaijan, Brazil, Ecuador, Italy, Peru, and Venezuela.

References

OECD (2017), *BEPS Action 5 on Harmful Tax Practices – Terms of Reference and Methodology for the Conduct of the Peer Reviews of the Action 5 Transparency Framework*, OECD/G20 Base Erosion and Profit Shifting Project, OECD, Paris. www.oecd.org/tax/beps/beps-action-5-harmful-tax-practices-peer-review-transparencyframework.pdf.

OECD (2015), *Countering Harmful Tax Practices More Effectively, Taking into Account Transparency and Substance, Action 5 - 2015 Final Report*, OECD/G20 Base Erosion and Profit Shifting Project, OECD Publishing, Paris. https://doi.org/10.1787/9789264241190-en.

OECD/Council of Europe (2011), *The Multilateral Convention on Mutual Administrative Assistance in Tax Matters: Amended by the 2010 Protocol*, OECD Publishing, Paris. http://dx.doi.org/10.1787/9789264115606-en.

Australia

Australia has met all aspects of the terms of reference (ToR) for the calendar year 2017 (year in review) and no recommendations are made.

Australia can legally issue four types of rulings within the scope of the transparency framework.

In practice, Australia has issued 208 past rulings. For the period 1 April 2016 - 31 December 2016, Australia issued nine future rulings. For the year in review, Australia issued 22 future rulings within the scope of the transparency framework.

Peer input was received from two jurisdictions in respect of the exchanges of information on rulings received from Australia. It was positive, noting that information was complete in the correct format and indicating that co-operation with Australia had been positive.

Introduction

57. This peer review covers Australia's implementation of the BEPS Action 5 transparency framework for the year 2017. The report has four parts, each relating to a key part of the ToR. Each part is discussed in turn. A summary of recommendations is included at the end of this report.

A. The information gathering process

58. Australia can legally issue the four following types of rulings within the scope of the transparency framework: (i) rulings related to preferential regimes;[1] (ii) cross-border unilateral advance pricing arrangements (APAs) and any other cross-border unilateral tax rulings (such as an advance tax ruling) covering transfer pricing or the application of transfer pricing principles; (iii) permanent establishment rulings; and (iv) related party conduit rulings. Rulings are issued by different interpretative areas of the Australian Taxation Office (ATO). Australia publishes edited anonymised versions of written binding advice in the Register of Private Binding Rulings (PBRs) for all categories (excluding the unilateral APA's which are not published due to privacy reasons).[2]

Past rulings (ToR I.4.1.1, I.4.1.2, I.4.2.1, I.4.2.2)

59. For Australia, past rulings are any tax rulings within scope that are issued either: (i) on or after 1 January 2014 but before 1 April 2016; or (ii) on or after 1 January 2010 but before 1 January 2014, provided they were still in effect as at 1 January 2014.

60. In the prior year peer review report, it was determined that the ATO's undertakings to identify past rulings and all potential exchange jurisdictions were sufficient to meet the minimum standard. The ATO's implementation in this regard remains unchanged, and therefore continues to meet the minimum standard.

Future rulings (ToR I.4.1.1, I.4.1.2, I.4.2.1)

61. For Australia, future rulings are any tax rulings within scope that are issued on or after 1 April 2016.

62. In the prior year peer review report, it was determined that the ATO's undertakings to identify future rulings and all potential exchange jurisdictions were sufficient to meet the minimum standard. The ATO's implementation in this regard remains unchanged, and therefore continues to meet the minimum standard.

Review and supervision mechanism (ToR I.4.3)

63. In the prior year peer review report, it was determined that the ATO's review and supervision mechanism was sufficient to meet the minimum standard. The ATO's implementation in this regard remains unchanged, and therefore continues to meet the minimum standard.

Conclusion on section A

64. Australia has met all of the ToR for the information gathering process and no recommendations are made.

B. The exchange of information

Legal basis for spontaneous exchange of information (ToR II.5.1, II.5.2)

65. Australia has the necessary domestic legal basis to exchange information spontaneously. Australia notes that there are no legal or practical impediments that prevent the spontaneous exchange of information on rulings as contemplated in the Action 5 minimum standard.

66. Australia is a party to international agreements permitting spontaneous exchange of information, including (i) the *Multilateral Convention on Mutual Administrative Assistance in Tax Matters: Amended by the 2010 Protocol* (OECD/Council of Europe, 2011) ("the Convention") and (ii) double tax agreements in force with 43 jurisdictions.[3]

Completion and exchange of templates (ToR II.5.3, II.5.4, II.5.5, II.5.6, II.5.7)

67. In the prior year peer review report, it was determined that the ATO's completion and exchange of templates were sufficient to meet the minimum standard. The ATO's implementation in this regard remains unchanged, and therefore continues to meet the minimum standard.

68. Australia has guidance material in place to assist tax officers to complete the template in Annex C of the 2015 Action 5 Report (OECD, 2015). This guidance includes instructions on how to complete the summary section (section 7) of the template. Whilst Australia's current guidance on the summary section do not specifically refer to the internal FHTP's suggested guidance, it is based on and contains key elements of the suggested guidance in order to ensure that the summaries contain sufficient detail to allow the receiving tax administration to risk-assess the potential BEPS risks.

69. For the year in review, the timeliness of exchanges is as follows:

Past rulings in the scope of the transparency framework	Number of exchanges transmitted by 31 December 2017	Delayed exchanges		
		Number of exchanges not transmitted by 31 December 2017	Reasons for the delays	Any other comments
	12	50	See below	See below
Future rulings in the scope of the transparency framework	**Number of exchanges transmitted within three months of the information becoming available to the competent authority or immediately after legal impediments have been lifted**	**Delayed exchanges**		
		Number of exchanges transmitted later than three months of the information on rulings becoming available to the competent authority	**Reasons for the delays**	**Any other comments**
	16	0	N/A	
Total	28	50		

Follow up requests received for exchange of the ruling	Number	Average time to provide response	Number of requests not answered
	0	N/A	N/A

70. Australia provides the following explanations for the transmission delay:

- Australia indicates that it has reached out to some partner jurisdictions which Australia knew did not yet have their system in place to receive the XML Schemas in the agreed format and from whom they had not received any rulings to ensure both the confidentiality of the information and that the countries received the rulings in a format that they could use. Upon receipt of a response, the ATO exchanged the rulings and in several cases sent them in a different format to the XML Schema. Thus, some exchanges were delayed due to receipt of the response occurring after 31 December 2017. These were exchanged during 2018 except where the recipient jurisdiction does not yet have the legal frameworks in place or the ATO could not confirm the format to be sent.
- Australia indicates it also experienced delays due to the movement of personnel handling the exchanges. Of the 50 past ruling exchanges not transmitted by 31 December 2017, 31 exchanges were sent on 27 February 2018. This is within a relatively short period of the due date. The balance of 19 exchanges pertain to those jurisdictions which the ATO has not yet confirmed whether they have legal frameworks in place or to confirm the appropriate format of exchange.
- There are a further 40 exchanges on past rulings which were not required to take place during the year of review, which are in respect of jurisdictions with which Australia did not have an agreement in force permitting spontaneous exchange of information, or developing countries which requested a deferral under the Action 5 transparency framework and it was agreed that Australia is not required to exchange with until 31 December 2018.

Conclusion on section B

71. Australia has the necessary legal basis for spontaneous exchange of information and a process for completing the templates in a timely way. Australia explained that the delay in exchanging past rulings is mostly on account of seeking to ensure effective co-operation rather than from any difficulty with the process itself, although some delays could also be attributed to movement of personnel in 2017 and these delays were remedied within three months of the deadline. In addition, some of the exchanges which are considered as delayed are with developing countries with which Australia is not required to exchange before 31 December 2018 and these are not considered to be a deficiency in Australia's implementation of the transparency framework. Australia has met all of the ToR for the exchange of information process and no recommendations are made.

C. Statistics (ToR IV)

72. The statistics for the year in review are as follows:

Category of ruling	Number of exchanges	Jurisdictions exchanged with
Rulings related to preferential regimes	0	N/A
Cross-border unilateral advance pricing agreements (APAs) and any other cross-border unilateral tax rulings (such as an advance tax ruling) covering transfer pricing or the application of transfer pricing principles	19	Belgium, Canada, Ireland, Italy, Japan, Netherlands, New Zealand, Sweden, United Kingdom, Unites States
Cross-border rulings providing for a unilateral downward adjustment to the taxpayer's taxable profits that is not directly reflected in the taxpayer's financial / commercial accounts	N/A	N/A
Permanent establishment rulings	9	Ireland, Luxembourg, Netherlands, New Zealand, South Africa, United Kingdom, Unites States
Related party conduit rulings	0	N/A
De minimis rule	N/A	N/A
IP regimes: total exchanges on taxpayers benefitting from the third category of IP assets, new entrants benefitting from grandfathered IP regimes; and taxpayers making use of the option to treat the nexus ratio as a rebuttable presumption	N/A	N/A
Total	28	

D. Matters related to intellectual property regimes (ToR I.4.1.3)

73. Australia does not offer an intellectual property regime for which transparency requirements under the Action 5 Report (OECD, 2015) were imposed.

Summary of recommendations on implementation of the transparency framework

Aspect of implementation of the transparency framework that should be improved	Recommendation for improvement
	No recommendations are made.

Notes

1 With respect to the following preferential regimes: 1) Offshore banking unit regime and 2) Conduit foreign income regime.

2 Available at: www.ato.gov.au/law/#Law (accessed 20 November 2018).

3 Parties to the Convention are available here: www.oecd.org/tax/exchange-of-tax-information/convention-on-mutual-administrative-assistance-in-tax-matters.htm. Australia also has bilateral agreements with Argentina, Austria, Belgium, Canada, Chile, China (People's Republic of), Czech Republic, Denmark, Fiji, Finland, France, Germany, Hungary, India, Indonesia, Ireland, Italy, Japan, Kiribati, Korea, Malaysia, Malta, Mexico, Netherlands, New Zealand, Norway, Papua New Guinea, Philippines, Poland, Romania, Russia, Singapore, Slovak Republic, South Africa, Spain, Sri Lanka, Sweden, Switzerland, Chinese Taipei, Thailand, Turkey, United Kingdom, United States and Viet Nam.

References

OECD (2017), *BEPS Action 5 on Harmful Tax Practices – Terms of Reference and Methodology for the Conduct of the Peer Reviews of the Action 5 Transparency Framework*, OECD/G20 Base Erosion and Profit Shifting Project, OECD, Paris. www.oecd.org/tax/beps/beps-action-5-harmful-tax-practices-peer-review-transparencyframework.pdf.

OECD (2015), *Countering Harmful Tax Practices More Effectively, Taking into Account Transparency and Substance, Action 5 - 2015 Final Report*, OECD/G20 Base Erosion and Profit Shifting Project, OECD Publishing, Paris. https://doi.org/10.1787/9789264241190-en.

OECD/Council of Europe (2011), *The Multilateral Convention on Mutual Administrative Assistance in Tax Matters: Amended by the 2010 Protocol*, OECD Publishing, Paris. http://dx.doi.org/10.1787/9789264115606-en.

Austria

Austria has met all aspects of the terms of reference (ToR) for the calendar year 2017 (year in review) except for the timely exchange of information on past and future rulings (ToR II.5.6). As such, the recommendation made in the prior year peer review report remains in place. Austria is recommended to ensure that all information on past and future rulings is exchanged as soon as possible. In the prior year review report, Austria was recommended to ensure that information on all potential exchange jurisdictions is obtained. Austria has now put in place the process and was able to identify information on all potential exchange jurisdictions and as such the recommendation is removed.

Austria can legally issue one type of rulings within the scope of the transparency framework.

In practice, Austria has issued 59 past rulings;[1] for the period 1 April 2016 – 31 December 2016, Austria issued 13 future rulings; and for the year in review, Austria issued 10 future rulings within the scope of the transparency framework.

No peer input was received in respect of the exchanges of information on rulings received from Austria.

Introduction

74. This peer review covers Austria's implementation of the BEPS Action 5 transparency framework for the year 2017. The report has four parts, each relating to a key part of the ToR. Each part is discussed in turn. A summary of recommendations is included at the end of this report.

A. The information gathering process

75. Austria can legally issue one type of rulings within the scope of the transparency framework: cross-border unilateral advance pricing arrangements (APAs) and any other cross-border unilateral tax rulings (such as an advance tax ruling) covering transfer pricing or the application of transfer pricing principles. In Austria, 39 competent local tax offices are authorised to issue opinions.

Past rulings (ToR I.4.1.1, I.4.1.2, I.4.2.1, I.4.2.2)

76. For Austria, past rulings are any tax rulings within scope that are issued either: (i) on or after 1 January 2014 but before 1 April 2016; or (ii) on or after 1 January 2010 but before 1 January 2014, provided they were still in effect as at 1 January 2014.

77. In the prior year peer review report, it was determined that the Austrian tax administration's undertakings to identify past rulings and all potential exchange jurisdictions were sufficient to meet the minimum standard. The Austrian tax administration's implementation in this regard remains unchanged except that for the year in review, the Audit Unit for Large Traders is now responsible for the collection of all past rulings from the local tax offices as well as verification for exchange purposes.

78. Austria reported that there was an error in counting the past rulings in the prior year peer review. The error was detected during a review process carried out by Austria. Austria had reported that there were 63 past rulings, which was counted based on the number of files, whereas after a review the correct number of 59 past rulings was confirmed. The four over-reported cases appeared on account of ruling requests, which were withdrawn, test files or not subject to exchange. The review process has verified that there are no additional errors in the identification of past rulings, and therefore continues to meet the minimum standard.

Future rulings (ToR I.4.1.1, I.4.1.2, I.4.2.1)

79. For Austria, future rulings are any tax rulings within scope that are issued on or after 1 April 2016.

80. In the prior year peer review report, it was determined that the Austrian tax administration's undertakings to identify future rulings were sufficient to meet the minimum standard except that it was not certain that information on all potential exchange jurisdictions were able to be identified in all cases. The Austrian tax administration was recommended to continue with its plan to ensure information on all potential exchange jurisdictions is obtained as part of the ruling process.

81. Internal ministerial guidance[2] was issued in late 2016, making the process of gathering information on all potential exchange jurisdictions mandatory for all Austrian tax offices. The guidance refers explicitly to information required by the template of Annex C of the 2015 Action 5 Report (OECD, 2015) including the details of the entities

in recipient jurisdiction. Accordingly, during the year in review, the local tax office and Large Taxpayer Audit Units already carried out the information gathering process on all potential exchange jurisdictions using information in the taxpayer file and other databases. Austria reports that in all cases, information on all potential exchange jurisdictions was identified.

Review and supervision mechanism (ToR I.4.3)

82. In the prior year peer review report, it was determined that the Austrian tax administration's review and supervision mechanism was sufficient to meet the minimum standard. In addition, Austria carried out a review process, as a result of which the errors in respect of four past rulings were identified. This review process involved checking every case on the basis of its content and confirmed that the identification of all rulings was otherwise undertaken accurately. The Austrian tax administration's implementation meets the minimum standard.

Conclusion on section A

83. For the year in review, Austria strengthened its internal guidance and improved its review process, as explained above, and therefore Austria has met all of the ToR for the information gathering process and no recommendations are made.

B. The exchange of information

Legal basis for spontaneous exchange of information (ToR II.5.1, II.5.2)

84. Austria has the necessary domestic legal basis to exchange information spontaneously. Austria notes that there are no legal or practical impediments that prevent the spontaneous exchange of information on rulings as contemplated in the Action 5 minimum standard.

85. Austria is a party to international agreements permitting spontaneous exchange of information, including (i) the *Multilateral Convention on Mutual Administrative Assistance in Tax Matters: Amended by the 2010 Protocol* (OECD/Council of Europe, 2011) ("the Convention"), (ii) double tax agreements in force with 70 jurisdictions and (iii) tax information exchange agreements with seven jurisdictions.[3]

Completion and exchange of templates (ToR II.5.3, II.5.4, II.5.5, II.5.6, II.5.7)

86. In the prior year peer review report, it was noted that the Austrian tax administration's completion and exchange of templates were sufficient to meet the minimum standard except for the timely exchange of information on past and future rulings (ToR II.5.6). With respect to the completion of the summary section of the template, Austria confirms that it uses the suggested FHTP internal guidance.

87. For the year in review, the timeliness of exchanges is as follows:

Past rulings in the scope of the transparency framework	Number of exchanges transmitted by 31 December 2017	Delayed exchanges		
		Number of exchanges not transmitted by 31 December 2017	Reasons for the delays	Any other comments
	23	36	See below	This includes past rulings that needed to be exchanged with new members of the IF that joined in 2017
Future rulings in the scope of the transparency framework	Number of exchanges transmitted within three months of the information becoming available to the competent authority or immediately after legal impediments have been lifted	Delayed exchanges		
		Number of exchanges transmitted later than three months of the information on rulings becoming available to the competent authority	Reasons for the delays	Any other comments
	0	23	See below	This includes exchanges on 13 future rulings issued in 2016 and all 23 were exchanged in 2018.
Total	23	59		

Follow up requests received for exchange of the ruling	Number	Average time to provide response	Number of requests not answered
	0	0	N/A

88. Austria provided the following explanation for the transmission delay regarding past and future rulings during 2017. Austria experienced some issues in relation to a technical incompatibility between the European Commission IT module and the domestic Austrian IT systems. These problems were continuing from 2016, as a result of which the prior year peer review report noted that no exchanges of information on past and future rulings occurred in 2016 and made a recommendation to continue efforts to remedy the issue.

89. The technical issues were resolved in late 2017. Austria notes that once the European Commission's transmission tool was received, the local tax offices and large taxpayers unit was informed and provided with training at the end of November 2017. In December 2017, Austria was able to initiate the exchange process. Due to the time constraints, the Austrian tax administration was not able to transmit all rulings in 2017. The remaining rulings were transmitted in 2018.

Conclusion on section B

90. Austria has the necessary legal basis for spontaneous exchange of information, a process for completing the templates in a timely way. In respect of both past and future rulings, Austria did not complete any exchanges until late 2017 and early 2018. This includes information on rulings that were otherwise due to be exchanged in 2016. Austria has met all of the ToR except for the timely exchange of information on past and future

rulings (ToR II.5.6). Austria is recommended to ensure that all information on past and future rulings is exchanged as soon as possible.

C. Statistics (ToR IV)

91. The statistics for the year in review are as follows:

Category of ruling	Number of exchanges	Jurisdictions exchanged with
Rulings related to preferential regimes	N/A	N/A
Cross-border unilateral advance pricing arrangement (APAs) and any other cross-border unilateral tax rulings (such as an advance tax ruling) covering transfer pricing or the application of transfer pricing principles	23	Germany, Bulgaria, Singapore, Brazil, Russia, Netherlands, Belgium, Ireland, Italy, Korea, Malta, Switzerland
Cross-border rulings providing for a unilateral downward adjustment to the taxpayer's taxable profits that is not directly reflected in the taxpayer's financial / commercial accounts	N/A	N/A
Permanent establishment rulings	N/A	N/A
Related party conduit rulings	N/A	N/A
De minimis rule	N/A	N/A
IP regimes: total exchanges on taxpayers benefitting from the third category of IP assets, new entrants benefitting from grandfathered IP regimes; and taxpayers making use of the option to treat the nexus ratio as a rebuttable presumption	N/A	N/A
Total	23	

D. Matters related to intellectual property regimes (ToR I.4.1.3)

92. Austria does not offer an intellectual property regime for which transparency requirements under the Action 5 Report (OECD, 2015) were imposed.

Summary of recommendations on implementation of the transparency framework

Aspect of implementation of the transparency framework that should be improved	Recommendation for improvement
Austria encountered delays in the timely exchange of information on past and future rulings. This is a continuing recommendation from the prior year peer review.	Austria is recommended to ensure that all information on past and future rulings is exchanged as soon as possible.

Jurisdiction's response and recent developments

93. Austria has taken steps to remedy the above recommendation and confirms that the remaining rulings not transmitted in 2017 were transmitted in 2018.

Notes

[1] In the prior year peer review, Austria reported that it had issued 63 past rulings, however subsequent analysis clarified that this incorrectly included cases such as withdrawn ruling request and test files.

[2] BMF-280000/0214-IV/2/2016 and BMF-010221/0708-VI/8/2016.

[3] Parties to the Convention are available here: www.oecd.org/tax/exchange-of-tax-information/convention-on-mutual-administrative-assistance-in-tax-matters.htm. Austria also has bilateral agreements in force with Algeria, Armenia, Bahamas, Bahrain, Belarus, Bosnia and Herzegovina, Brunei Darussalam, Burkina Faso, Dominican Republic, Egypt, El Salvador, Former Yugoslav Republic of Macedonia, Gabon, Guatemala, Hong Kong (China), Jamaica, Kenya, Kuwait, Montenegro, Morocco, Peru, Philippines, Qatar, Serbia, Chinese Taipei, Tajikistan, Thailand, Turkey, Turkmenistan, United Arab Emirates, United States, Venezuela and Viet Nam.

References

OECD (2017), *BEPS Action 5 on Harmful Tax Practices – Terms of Reference and Methodology for the Conduct of the Peer Reviews of the Action 5 Transparency Framework*, OECD/G20 Base Erosion and Profit Shifting Project, OECD, Paris. www.oecd.org/tax/beps/beps-action-5-harmful-tax-practices-peer-review-transparencyframework.pdf.

OECD (2015), *Countering Harmful Tax Practices More Effectively, Taking into Account Transparency and Substance, Action 5 - 2015 Final Report*, OECD/G20 Base Erosion and Profit Shifting Project, OECD Publishing, Paris. https://doi.org/10.1787/9789264241190-en.

OECD/Council of Europe (2011), *The Multilateral Convention on Mutual Administrative Assistance in Tax Matters: Amended by the 2010 Protocol*, OECD Publishing, Paris. http://dx.doi.org/10.1787/9789264115606-en.

Barbados

Barbados' implementation of the transparency framework is still in the early stages of development. Barbados is recommended to finalise its information gathering process for identifying all past and future rulings and potential exchange jurisdictions, with a review and supervision mechanism, as soon as possible (ToR I.4). Barbados is recommended to continue its efforts to complete the templates for all relevant rulings and to ensure that the exchanges of information on rulings occur as soon as possible (ToR II.5).

Barbados can legally issue five types of rulings within the scope of the transparency framework.

In practice, Barbados has issued two past rulings; and for the year in review, Barbados issued no future rulings within scope of the transparency framework.

As no exchanges of information on rulings were conducted during the year in review, no peer input was received in respect of the exchanges of information on rulings received from Barbados.

Introduction

94. This peer review covers Barbados' implementation of the BEPS Action 5 transparency framework for the year 2017. The report has four parts, each relating to a key part of the ToR. A summary of recommendations is included at the end of this report.

A. The information gathering process

95. Barbados can legally issue the five following types of rulings within the scope of the transparency framework: (i) rulings related to preferential regimes;[1] (ii) cross-border unilateral advance pricing arrangements (APAs) and any other cross-border unilateral tax rulings (such as an advance tax ruling) covering transfer pricing or the application of transfer pricing principles; (iii) cross-border rulings giving a unilateral downward adjustment to the taxpayer's taxable profits in the country giving the ruling; (iv) permanent establishment rulings; and (v) related party conduit rulings. The Legal Department of the Barbados Revenue Authority ("BRA") is authorised to issue rulings.

Past rulings (ToR I.4.1.1, I.4.1.2, I.4.2.1, I.4.2.2)

96. For Barbados, past rulings are any tax rulings within scope that are issued either: (i) on or after 1 January 2015 but before 1 September 2017; or (ii) on or after 1 January 2012 but before 1 January 2015, provided they were still in effect as at 1 January 2015.

97. Barbados acknowledges that it did not implement the information gathering process during the year in review. As a result, no past rulings were identified. However, Barbados has implemented new processes to identify past rulings in 2018.

98. The process for identifying past rulings in 2018 was conducted as follows. The BRA is constituted as one centralised office. Rulings are not recorded on any database, but all physical files relating to rulings are maintained within one area of the Legal Department. Due to the small number of rulings issued by Barbados, the Legal Department staff members therefore conducted a manual review of all files pertaining to tax rulings to identify past rulings in scope. Each physical file was manually read and reviewed to determine whether it fell into any of the five rulings categories.

99. In order to identify potential exchange jurisdictions, the BRA reviewed the available information in the taxpayer's files. As there were only two past rulings in scope, Barbados was able to ascertain the relevant exchange jurisdiction from the information on file. Barbados reports that the "best efforts approach" was not utilised as all the information regarding relevant exchange jurisdictions was contained within the ruling request in the file.

Future rulings (ToR I.4.1.1, I.4.1.2, I.4.2.1)

100. For Barbados, future rulings are any tax rulings within scope that are issued on or after 1 September 2017.

101. Barbados acknowledges that it did not implement the information gathering process during the year in review. As a result, no future rulings were identified. However, Barbados has implemented new processes to identify future rulings in 2018, and has identified that BRA did not issue any future rulings during the year in review.

102. Barbados' information gathering process for future rulings is identical to the process for past rulings. For future rulings, information regarding potential exchange

jurisdictions is to be acquired during the ruling request process. A rulings request would not be processed without the relevant information being obtained from the taxpayer.

Review and supervision mechanism (ToR I.4.3)

103. The BRA is a small, centralised office that also serves as Competent Authority of Barbados. The rulings information compiled by the legal officers within the BRA Legal Department is thereafter reviewed by the Senior Manager of the Policy, Planning and Governance Department who has the ultimate responsibility for matters of international taxation.

Conclusion on section A

104. Barbados is recommended to finalise its information gathering process for identifying all past and future rulings and potential exchange jurisdictions, with a review and supervision mechanism, as soon as possible (ToR I.4). It is recognised that Barbados has made efforts to rectify their information gathering process in 2018, and Barbados' implementation of the information gathering process during 2018 will be assessed in the next annual peer review.

B. The exchange of information

Legal basis for spontaneous exchange of information (ToR II.5.1, II.5.2)

105. Barbados has the necessary domestic legal basis to exchange information spontaneously. Barbados notes that there are no legal or practical impediments that prevent the spontaneous exchange of information on rulings as contemplated in the Action 5 minimum standard.

106. Barbados is a party to international agreements permitting spontaneous exchange of information, including (i) the *Multilateral Convention on Mutual Administrative Assistance in Tax Matters: Amended by the 2010 Protocol* (OECD/Council of Europe, 2011) ("the Convention") and (ii) double tax agreements in force with 32 jurisdictions.[2]

Completion and exchange of templates (ToR II.5.3, II.5.4, II.5.5, II.5.6, II.5.7)

107. For the year in review, Barbados had not identified any rulings in scope of the transparency framework and therefore no exchanges were undertaken.

108. Barbados is still developing a process to complete the templates on relevant rulings, to make them available to the Competent Authority for exchange of information and to exchange them with relevant jurisdictions.

109. The BRA has indicated, in the event of an exchange, that the information would be provided via the template in Annex C of the 2015 Action 5 Report (OECD, 2015). The Legal Department of the BRA would be responsible for completing the template, and this process would be supervised by the Senior Manager of the Policy, Planning and Governance Department.

Conclusion on section B

110. Barbados has the necessary legal basis to undertake spontaneous exchange of information. Barbados is recommended to continue its efforts to complete the templates

for all relevant rulings and to ensure that the exchanges of information on rulings occur as soon as possible (ToR II.5).

C. Statistics (ToR IV)

111. As no information on rulings was exchanged for the year in review, no statistical data can be reported.

D. Matters related to intellectual property regimes (ToR I.4.1.3)

112. Barbados offers two preferential regimes, which also offer benefits to income from intellectual property ("IP regime").[3] However for the year in review no transparency requirements were relevant, as follows:

- ***New entrants benefitting from the grandfathered IP regime***: not applicable for the year in review, because Barbados is currently amending both regimes and in the process of implementing grandfathering for the International business companies regime. The enhanced transparency requirements will apply to Barbados' regimes that provide grandfathering to taxpayers that entered the regimes after the publication of the 2017 Progress Report (OECD, 2017b), which occurred on 16 October 2017, and this will be taken into account during the subsequent peer review.
- ***Third category of IP assets***: not applicable to these regimes, which in 2017 were in the process of being amended.
- ***Taxpayers making the use of the option to treat the nexus ratio as a rebuttable presumption***: not applicable to these regimes, which in 2017 were in the process of being amended.

Summary of recommendations on implementation of the transparency framework

Aspect of implementation of the transparency framework that should be improved	Recommendation for improvement
Barbados did not complete the information gathering process during the year in review.	Barbados is recommended to finalise its information gathering process for identifying all past and future rulings and potential exchange jurisdictions, with a review and supervision mechanism, as soon as possible.
Barbados did not undertake spontaneous exchange of information on tax rulings within scope of the transparency framework during the year in review.	Barbados is recommended to continue its efforts to complete the templates for all relevant rulings and to ensure that the exchanges of information on rulings occur as soon as possible.

Notes

[1] Credit for foreign currency earnings.

[2] Antigua, Austria, Bahrain, Belize, Botswana, Canada, China (People's Republic of), Cyprus, Cuba, Czech Republic, Dominica, Iceland, Italy, Finland, Grenada, Guyana, Jamaica, Luxembourg, Malta, Mauritius, Mexico, Netherlands, Norway, Panama, Portugal, Singapore, Spain, Sweden, United Arab Emirates, Singapore, Saint Kitts and Nevis, Saint Vincent and the Grenadines, San Marino, Seychelles, Switzerland, Qatar, United Kingdom, United States and Venezuela.

Note by Turkey: The information in this document with reference to "Cyprus" relates to the southern part of the Island. There is no single authority representing both Turkish and Greek Cypriot people on the Island. Turkey recognises the Turkish Republic of Northern Cyprus (TRNC). Until a lasting and equitable solution is found within the context of the United Nations, Turkey shall preserve its position concerning the "Cyprus issue".

Note by all the European Union Member States of the OECD and the European Union. The Republic of Cyprus is recognised by all members of the United Nations with the exception of Turkey. The information in this document relates to the area under the effective control of the Government of the Republic of Cyprus.

[3] These regimes are: 1) International business companies and 2) International societies with restricted liability.

References

OECD (2017a), *BEPS Action 5 on Harmful Tax Practices – Terms of Reference and Methodology for the Conduct of the Peer Reviews of the Action 5 Transparency Framework*, OECD/G20 Base Erosion and Profit Shifting Project, OECD, Paris. www.oecd.org/tax/beps/beps-action-5-harmful-tax-practices-peer-review-transparencyframework.pdf.

OECD (2017b), *Harmful Tax Practices - 2017 Progress Report on Preferential Regimes: Inclusive Framework on BEPS: Action 5*, OECD/G20 Base Erosion and Profit Shifting Project, OECD Publishing, Paris. http://dx.doi.org/10.1787/9789264283954-en.

OECD (2015), *Countering Harmful Tax Practices More Effectively, Taking into Account Transparency and Substance, Action 5 - 2015 Final Report*, OECD/G20 Base Erosion and Profit Shifting Project, OECD Publishing, Paris. https://doi.org/10.1787/9789264241190-en.

OECD/Council of Europe (2011), *The Multilateral Convention on Mutual Administrative Assistance in Tax Matters: Amended by the 2010 Protocol*, OECD Publishing, Paris. http://dx.doi.org/10.1787/9789264115606-en.

Belgium

Belgium has met all aspects of the terms of reference (ToR) for the calendar year 2017 (year in review), except for the timely exchange of information on new entrants benefitting from grandfathered IP regime (ToR I.4.1.3). Belgium is recommended to continue its efforts to identify and exchange information on new entrants to the grandfathered IP regime.

Belgium can legally issue four types of rulings within the scope of the transparency framework.

In practice, Belgium issued 586 past rulings; for the period 1 April 2016 - 31 December 2016, Belgium issued 57 future rulings; and for the year in review, Belgium issued 107 future rulings.

Peer input was received from four jurisdictions in respect of the exchanges of information on rulings received from Belgium. The input noted that information was in the correct format, complete and timely. One peer noted technical issues experienced in the format of attachments to information received. Belgium indicated that they have attempted to resolve this issue on a bilateral basis.

Introduction

113. This peer review covers Belgium's implementation of the BEPS Action 5 transparency framework for the year 2017. The report has four parts, each relating to a key part of the ToR. Each part is discussed in turn. A summary of recommendations is included at the end of this report.

A. The information gathering process

114. Belgium can legally issue the following four types of rulings within the scope of the transparency framework: (1) rulings related to preferential regimes;[1] (2) cross-border unilateral advance pricing agreements (APAs) and any other cross-border unilateral tax rulings (such as an advance tax ruling) covering transfer pricing or the application of transfer pricing principles; (3) downward adjustments; and (4) permanent establishment rulings. These rulings are published in an anonymised way.[2]

115. In Belgium, there are four services that issue rulings within the scope of the transparency framework: the international relations department, two non-resident taxpayers services offices (a centralised and specialised division in Brussels, Centrum Buitenland, and the Polyvalent Center Eupen), the Ruling Commission and the transfer pricing unit of the tax audit and compliance management office.

Past rulings (ToR I.4.1.1, I.4.1.2, I.4.2.1, I.4.2.2)

116. For Belgium, past rulings are any tax rulings within scope that are issued either: (i) on or after 1 January 2014 but before 1 April 2016; or (ii) on or after 1 January 2010 but before 1 January 2014, provided they were still in effect as at 1 January 2014.

117. In the prior year peer review report, it was determined that the Belgian tax administration's undertakings to identify past rulings and all potential exchange jurisdictions were sufficient to meet the minimum standard. The Belgian tax administration's implementation in this regard remains unchanged, and therefore continues to meet the minimum standard.

Future rulings (ToR I.4.1.1, I.4.1.2, I.4.2.1)

118. For Belgium, future rulings are any tax rulings within scope that are issued on or after 1 April 2016.

119. In the prior year peer review report, it was determined that the Belgian Tax Administration's implementation of a new system to identify future rulings and all potential exchange jurisdictions was sufficient to meet the minimum standard. The Belgian Tax Administration's implementation in this regard remains unchanged, and therefore continues to meet the minimum standard.

Review and supervision mechanism (ToR I.4.3)

120. In the prior year peer review report, it was determined that the Belgian Tax Administration's review and supervision mechanism was sufficient to meet the minimum standard. The Belgian Tax Administration's implementation in this regard remains unchanged, and therefore continues to meet the minimum standard.

Conclusion on section A

121. Belgium has met all of the ToR for the information gathering process and no recommendations are made.

B. The exchange of information

Legal basis for spontaneous exchange of information (ToR II.5.1, II.5.2)

122. Belgium has the necessary domestic legal basis to exchange information spontaneously. Belgium notes that there are no legal or practical impediments that prevent the spontaneous exchange of information on rulings as contemplated in the Action 5 minimum standard.

123. Belgium is a party to international agreements permitting spontaneous exchange of information, including (i) the *Multilateral Convention on Mutual Administrative Assistance in Tax Matters: Amended by the 2010 Protocol* (OECD/Council of Europe, 2011) ("the Convention"), (ii) the Directive 2011/16/EU with all other European Union Member States and (iii) double tax agreements in force with 43 jurisdictions.[3]

Completion and exchange of templates (ToR II.5.3, II.5.4, II.5.5, II.5.6, II.5.7)

124. In the prior year peer review report, it was determined that the Belgian Tax Administration's completion and exchange of templates was sufficient to meet the minimum standard. Belgium therefore continues to meet the minimum standard in this regard. Furthermore, in February 2018, Belgium enhanced the link between the XML tool and the application used for the international exchange, so that rulings are now instantaneously transmitted to the Competent Authority for exchange as soon as they are registered. This ensures a faster transmission of rulings to the Competent Authority and therefore swifter exchanges with partner jurisdictions in the future. Belgium does not currently use the internal FHTP suggested guidance in the completion of the summary section of the template, but provides information for a country to evaluate the possible impact of the ruling. For transfer pricing rulings, this includes information on the transaction(s), the transfer pricing method use, the mark up and the function of the Belgian taxpayer. For other rulings, a summary of the facts and information regarding how the taxpayer will be treated for tax purposes in Belgium is provided.

125. For the year in review, the timeliness of exchanges is as follows:

Past rulings in the scope of the transparency framework	Number of exchanges transmitted by 31 December 2017	Delayed exchanges		
		Number of exchanges not transmitted by 31 December 2017	Reasons for the delays	Any other comments
	248	0	N/A	These 248 exchanges include 246 delayed exchanges from the previous year peer review and 2 exchanges with new Inclusive Framework members that joined in 2017.
Future rulings in the scope of the transparency framework	Number of exchanges transmitted within three months of the information becoming available to the competent authority or immediately after legal impediments have been lifted	Delayed exchanges		
		Number of exchanges transmitted later than three months of the information on rulings becoming available to the competent authority	Reasons for the delays	Any other comments
	554	0	N/A	
Total	802	0		

Follow up requests received for exchange of the ruling	Number	Average time to provide response	Number of requests not answered
	14	28 days	N/A

Conclusion on section B

126. Belgium has the necessary legal basis for spontaneous exchange of information, a process for completing the templates in a timely way and has completed all exchanges on time. Belgium has met all of the ToR for the exchange of information process and no recommendations are made.

C. Statistics (ToR IV)

127. The statistics for the year in review are as follows:

Category of ruling	Number of exchanges	Jurisdictions exchanged with
Rulings related to preferential regimes	13	Canada, China (People's Republic of), Denmark, France, Italy, Japan, Luxembourg, Netherlands, Sweden, Singapore, United Kingdom
Cross-border unilateral advance pricing arrangements (APAs) and any other cross-border unilateral tax rulings (such as an advance tax ruling) covering transfer pricing or the application of transfer pricing principles	757	Argentina, Australia, Austria, Brazil, Bulgaria, Canada, Chile, China (People's Republic of), Colombia, Czech Republic, Denmark, Estonia, Finland, France, Gabon, Germany, Greece, Hong Kong (China), Hungary, India, Indonesia, Ireland, Israel, Italy, Japan, Kazakhstan, Korea, Latvia, Lithuania, Luxembourg, Mexico, Netherlands, New Zealand, Norway, Poland, Portugal, Romania, Russia, Singapore, Slovak Republic, Slovenia, South Africa, Sweden, Tunisia, Turkey, United Kingdom, United States, Viet Nam
Cross-border rulings providing for a unilateral downward adjustment to the taxpayer's taxable profits that is not directly reflected in the taxpayer's financial / commercial accounts	0	N/A
Permanent establishment rulings	117	Australia, Austria, Bulgaria, Canada, Denmark, Estonia, Finland, France, Germany, Greece, Ireland, Israel, India, Italy, Japan, Luxembourg, Norway, Poland, Portugal, Romania, Singapore, Sweden, United Kingdom, United States
Related party conduit rulings	N/A	N/A
De minimis rule	N/A	N/A
IP regimes: total exchanges on taxpayers benefitting from the third category of IP assets, new entrants benefitting from grandfathered IP regimes; and taxpayers making use of the option to treat the nexus ratio as a rebuttable presumption	1	N/A
Total	888[4]	

D. Matters related to intellectual property regimes (ToR I.4.1.3)

128. Belgium has an intellectual property regime that is subject to transparency requirements under the Action 5 Report (OECD, 2015) (the Innovation Income Deduction). It states that the identification of the benefitting taxpayers will occur as follows:

- ***New entrants benefitting from the grandfathered IP regime***: For taxpayers filing tax returns in calendar year 2017 (regarding tax year 2016), Belgium introduced a new requirement in the tax return form for taxpayers to identify as new taxpayers not previously benefitting from the regime. This requirement involves a simple check-the-box election that allows the tax administration to conduct further analysis after the tax assessment procedure. The 2017 tax return is able to identify all new taxpayers that entered the regime between 1 January 2016 - 30 June 2016.

The 2017 return is also able identify new taxpayers that entered the regime in between 6 February 2015 - 31 December 2015, and continued to remain in the regime in 2016. However, due to administrative and time constraints, the 2016 tax return was not amended in time to include the check-the-box election, and therefore taxpayers that entered and exited the regime between 6 February 2015 - 31 December 2015 are not be reflected in the 2017 tax return. However, it is recognised that the likelihood of taxpayers entering the regime to enjoy benefits for a period of less than 10 months is low and the benefit to be obtained from such a limited period would be minimal. Therefore, the majority of taxpayers benefitting from the grandfathered regime would be continuing to benefit in 2016 and identified in the 2017 tax return. Belgium is recommended to continue its efforts to identify and exchange information on new entrants to the grandfathered IP regime, specifically with respect to taking mitigating steps to exchange relevant information on taxpayers entering and exiting the regime in 2015, should it become aware of such new entrants in the course of tax audits or investigations.

- However, new assets of existing claimants benefitting from the grandfathered IP regime from 6 February 2015 - 30 June 2016 were not identified in the same way via the tax return process, and therefore Belgium is currently examining alternative approaches to capture this information. Belgium cites difficulty in obtaining this information absent a formal investigation, but is intending to instruct tax auditors currently conducting investigations to collect the necessary information in relation to new assets in order to appropriately exchange for new entrants benefitting from the grandfathered IP regime. Belgium further notes that assets obtained from related parties were prohibited from entering the grandfathered regime from 1 January 2016 onwards. Belgium is recommended to continue its efforts to identify and exchange information on new entrants to the grandfathered IP regime, specifically with respect to new IP assets of existing taxpayers.

- Information regarding new taxpayers benefitting from the grandfathered regime was required to be filed in the 2017 tax return by the annual due date of 30 September 2017. The Belgian tax assessment procedure for the 2017 tax returns was finalised by the annual due date of 30 June 2018, whereby 155 taxpayers were identified as having made the check-the-box election as new taxpayers to the grandfathered regime between 6 February 2015 - 30 June 2016. The Belgian Tax Administration will subsequently analyse and verify the accuracy of the taxpayers' self-elections by conducting further investigations and seeking information regarding relevant exchange jurisdictions as necessary. Once this verification procedure is completed, Belgium will be able to exchange information on new taxpayers benefitting from the grandfathered regime. It is noted that the timeframe in which Belgium will conduct these exchanges is likely to exceed the timeframes required under the transparency framework. Belgium is recommended to continue its efforts to identify and exchange information on new entrants to the grandfathered IP regime, specifically with respect to the timely exchange of information on new entrants.

- Furthermore, there were four rulings granted in 2017 for new entrants benefitting from the grandfathered IP regime. Two of these four rulings were cross-border and exchanged with the relevant exchange jurisdictions, one in in 2017 and one in 2018.

- ***Third category of assets***: not applicable, as this option has not been incorporated into Belgium's IP regime.
- ***Taxpayers making use of the option to treat the nexus ratio as a rebuttable presumption***: Belgium confirms that no taxpayer elected to treat the nexus approach as a rebuttable presumption.

129. Belgium is recommended to continue its efforts to identify and exchange information on new entrants to the grandfathered IP regime (ToR I.4.1.3).

Summary of recommendations on implementation of the transparency framework

Aspect of implementation of the transparency framework that should be improved	Recommendation for improvement
Belgium has not exchanged all information on new taxpayers benefitting from the grandfathered IP regime, and new assets of existing taxpayers benefitting from the grandfathered regime as this information was not able to be collected during the year in review.	Belgium is recommended to continue its efforts to identify and exchange information on new entrants to the grandfathered IP regime.

Notes

[1] Patent income deduction, tax shelter regime for maritime exploitation and excess profits.

[2] Available at: www.ruling.be/telechargement/decisions (accessed 19 November 2018).

[3] Andorra, Argentina, Australia, Brazil, Belize, Canada, Chile, China (People's Republic of), Congo, Democratic Republic of the Congo, Egypt, Gabon, Georgia, Hong Kong (China), Iceland, India, Indonesia, Israel, Japan, Korea, Kazakhstan, Malaysia, Mauritius, Mexico, Mongolia, New Zealand, Nigeria, Norway, Pakistan, Russia, San Marino, Senegal, Singapore, Seychelles, South Africa, Sri Lanka, Thailand, Tunisia, Turkey, Ukraine, United States, Uruguay and Viet Nam.

[4] There were 802 exchanges as defined under footnote 13 of the Terms of Reference. The total of number of exchanges given in this table is higher than 802 due to the fact that some exchanges fall under more than one category of ruling.

References

OECD (2017), *BEPS Action 5 on Harmful Tax Practices – Terms of Reference and Methodology for the Conduct of the Peer Reviews of the Action 5 Transparency Framework*, OECD/G20 Base Erosion and Profit Shifting Project, OECD, Paris. www.oecd.org/tax/beps/beps-action-5-harmful-tax-practices-peer-review-transparencyframework.pdf.

OECD (2015), *Countering Harmful Tax Practices More Effectively, Taking into Account Transparency and Substance, Action 5 - 2015 Final Report*, OECD/G20 Base Erosion and Profit Shifting Project, OECD Publishing, Paris. https://doi.org/10.1787/9789264241190-en.

OECD/Council of Europe (2011), *The Multilateral Convention on Mutual Administrative Assistance in Tax Matters: Amended by the 2010 Protocol*, OECD Publishing, Paris. http://dx.doi.org/10.1787/9789264115606-en.

Belize

Belize has met all aspects of the terms of reference (ToR) for the calendar year 2017 (year in review) that can be met in the absence of rulings being issued.

Belize indicates that it cannot legally issue any type of rulings within the scope of the transparency framework.

As no rulings were issued, no exchange of information was required. No peer input was received in respect of the exchanges of information on rulings received from Belize.

Introduction

130. This peer review covers Belize's implementation of the BEPS Action 5 transparency framework for the year 2017. The report has four parts, each relating to a key part of the ToR. Each part is discussed in turn. A summary of recommendations is included at the end of this report.

A. The information gathering process

131. As no rulings are issued, this section is not assessed.

B. The exchange of information

132. As no rulings are issued, this section is not assessed.

C. Statistics (ToR IV)

133. As no rulings are issued, no statistical data can be reported.

D. Matters related to intellectual property regimes (ToR I.4.1.3)

134. Belize offers a preferential regime, the International business companies regime, which also offer benefits to income from intellectual property ("IP regime"). However for the year in review no transparency requirements under the Action 5 Report (OECD, 2015) were relevant, as follows:

- ***New entrants benefitting from the grandfathered IP regime***: not applicable for the year in review, because Belize is currently in the process of amending the regime and has not taken a decision yet on whether it will provide grandfathering to existing taxpayers. Should Belize provide grandfathering to taxpayers that entered the regime after the publication of the 2017 Progress Report, which occurred on 16 October 2017, then the enhanced transparency requirements will apply and this will be taken into account during the subsequent peer review.
- ***Third category of IP assets***: not applicable to this regime, which in 2017 was in the process of being amended..
- ***Taxpayers making the use of the option to treat the nexus ratio as a rebuttable presumption***: not applicable to this regime, which in 2017 was in the process of being amended.

Summary of recommendations on implementation of the transparency framework

Aspect of implementation of the transparency framework that should be improved	Recommendation for improvement
	No recommendations are made.

References

OECD (2017), *BEPS Action 5 on Harmful Tax Practices – Terms of Reference and Methodology for the Conduct of the Peer Reviews of the Action 5 Transparency Framework*, OECD/G20 Base Erosion and Profit Shifting Project, OECD, Paris. www.oecd.org/tax/beps/beps-action-5-harmful-tax-practices-peer-review-transparencyframework.pdf.

OECD (2015), *Countering Harmful Tax Practices More Effectively, Taking into Account Transparency and Substance, Action 5 - 2015 Final Report*, OECD/G20 Base Erosion and Profit Shifting Project, OECD Publishing, Paris. https://doi.org/10.1787/9789264241190-en.

Benin

Benin has met the terms of reference (ToR) for the calendar year 2017 (year in review) that can be met in the absence of rulings being issued.[1]

Benin does not issue any type of rulings within the scope of the transparency framework. Benin only issues interpretative rulings. These tax rulings are not binding for the tax authorities and are therefore not considered rulings as defined in the Action 5 report (OECD, 2015). In the event that Benin puts in place the administrative process to issue rulings within the scope of the transparency framework, Benin notes that it would implement the transparency framework obligations.

As there were no rulings issued, no exchange of information was required. Therefore no peer input was received in respect of exchanges of information on rulings received from Benin.

Introduction

135. This peer review covers Benin's implementation of the BEPS Action 5 transparency framework for the year 2017. The report has four parts, each relating to a key part of the ToR. Each part is discussed in turn. A summary of recommendations is included at the end of this report.

A. The information gathering process

136. As no rulings are issued, this section is not assessed.

B. The exchange of information

137. As no rulings are issued, this section is not assessed.

C. Statistics (ToR IV)

138. As no rulings are issued, no statistical data can be reported.

D. Matters related to intellectual property regimes (ToR I.4.1.3)

139. Benin does not offer an intellectual property regime for which transparency requirements under the Action 5 Report (OECD, 2015) were imposed.

Summary of recommendations on implementation of the transparency framework

Aspect of implementation of the transparency framework that should be improved	Recommendation for improvement
	No recommendations are made.

Note

[1] Benin did not provide written comments on this peer review report.

References

OECD (2017), *BEPS Action 5 on Harmful Tax Practices – Terms of Reference and Methodology for the Conduct of the Peer Reviews of the Action 5 Transparency Framework*, OECD/G20 Base Erosion and Profit Shifting Project, OECD, Paris. www.oecd.org/tax/beps/beps-action-5-harmful-tax-practices-peer-review-transparencyframework.pdf.

OECD (2015), *Countering Harmful Tax Practices More Effectively, Taking into Account Transparency and Substance, Action 5 - 2015 Final Report*, OECD/G20 Base Erosion and Profit Shifting Project, OECD Publishing, Paris. https://doi.org/10.1787/9789264241190-en.

Brazil

Brazil has met all aspects of the terms of reference (ToR) for the calendar year 2017 (year in review) and no recommendations are made. Brazil has implemented amendments to the process for granting rulings, which requires taxpayers to submit the information necessary for ensuring that all relevant related parties are identified. Brazil also affirms that when issuing future rulings it will provide them in a timely manner to the competent authority for exchange in accordance with the transparency framework requirements.

Brazil can legally issue two types of rulings within the scope of the transparency framework.

In practice, Brazil has issued ten past rulings; for the period 1 April 2016 - 31 December 2016; and for the year in review, Brazil issued no future rulings within the scope of the transparency framework.

No peer input was received in respect of the exchanges of information on rulings received from Brazil.

Introduction

140. This peer review covers Brazil's implementation of the BEPS Action 5 transparency framework for the year 2017. The report has four parts, each relating to a key part of the ToR. Each part is discussed in turn. A summary of recommendations is included at the end of this report.

A. The information gathering process

141. Brazil can legally issue the two following types of rulings within the scope of the transparency framework: (i) rulings related to preferential regimes[1] and (ii) cross-border unilateral advance pricing arrangement (APAs) and any other cross-border unilateral tax rulings (such as an advance tax ruling) covering transfer pricing or the application of transfer pricing principles. In Brazil, rulings are currently issued by the General Coordination of Taxation, an office of RFB. Since 2013, rulings are published on the *Receita Federal do Brazil* ("RFB")'s website in a redacted form.[2]

Past rulings (ToR I.4.1.1, I.4.1.2, I.4.2.1, I.4.2.2)

142. For Brazil, past rulings are any tax rulings within scope that are issued either: (i) on or after 1 January 2014 but before 1 April 2016; or (ii) on or after 1 January 2010 but before 1 January 2014, provided they were still in effect as at 1 January 2014.

143. In the prior year peer review report, it was determined that RFB's undertakings to identify past rulings and all potential exchange jurisdictions were sufficient to meet the minimum standard. RFB's implementation in this regard remains unchanged and therefore continues to meet the minimum standard.

Future rulings (ToR I.4.1.1, I.4.1.2, I.4.2.1)

144. For Brazil, future rulings are any tax rulings within scope that are issued on or after 1 April 2016.

145. In the prior year peer review report, it was determined that RFB's undertakings to identify future rulings were sufficient to meet the minimum standard. The prior year peer review report noted that it was necessary to make use of the "best efforts approach" to collect information on all potential exchange jurisdictions. Since all the necessary information was collected, the RFB's process for identifying the rulings and potential exchange jurisdictions was sufficient to meet the minimum standard. In the year in review, Brazil has implemented amendments to the process for granting rulings, which requires taxpayers to submit the information necessary for ensuring that all related parties to a taxpayer are identified in accordance with the transparency framework. In addition, RFB informs to taxpayers that the summary of the ruling will be exchanged with the tax administration of the related parties' countries, among others changes aiming to facilitate the identification of the rulings in the scope of the minimum standard.[3] RFB's implementation meets the minimum standard.

Review and supervision mechanism (ToR I.4.3)

146. In the prior year peer review report, it was determined that RFB's review and supervisions mechanisms were sufficient to meet the minimum standard. RFB affirms that the amendments to the process for granting rulings helped on the identification of the

relevant tax administration with whom to exchange information. RFB's implementation continues to meet the minimum standard.

Conclusion on section A

147. Brazil has met all of the ToR for the information gathering process and no recommendations are made.

B. The exchange of information

Legal basis for spontaneous exchange of information (ToR II.5.1, II.5.2)

148. Brazil has the necessary domestic legal basis to exchange information spontaneously. Brazil notes that there are no legal or practical impediments that prevent the spontaneous exchange of information on rulings as contemplated in the Action 5 minimum standard.

149. Brazil is a party to international agreements permitting spontaneous exchange of information, including the (i) *Multilateral Convention on Mutual Administrative Assistance in Tax Matters: Amended by the 2010 Protocol* (OECD/Council of Europe, 2011) ("the Convention") and (ii) Double Tax Agreements with 33 jurisdictions.

Completion and exchange of templates (ToR II.5.3, II.5.4, II.5.5, II.5.6, II.5.7)

150. In the prior year peer review report, it was determined that RFB's completion and exchange of templates were sufficient to meet the minimum standard. RFB's implementation in this regard remains unchanged, and therefore continues to meet the minimum standard. Furthermore, Brazil has confirmed that their approach to the completion of the summary section in section 7 of Annex C of the Action 5 Report (OECD, 2015) conforms with the internal FHTP suggested guidance to the section.

151. As no rulings within the scope of the transparency framework have been issued during the year in review and Brazil has exchanged all its past rulings in 2016, including exchanges with all relevant members of the Inclusive Framework, Brazil was not required to complete any exchanges of information and there is no data to report on the timeliness of exchanges. Brazil has not identified any other past rulings to be exchanged during the year in review.

152. Brazil affirms it is aware that when rulings are issued in the future they have to be identified and then timely provided to the competent authority to meet the transparency framework requirements.

Conclusion on section B

153. Brazil has the necessary legal basis for spontaneous exchange of information on rulings. Brazil has met all of the ToR for the exchange of information process that can be met in the absence of rulings being issued and exchanged in practice for the year in review and no recommendations are made.

C. Statistics (ToR IV)

154. As there were no rulings required to be exchanged by Brazil for the year in review, no statistics can be reported.

D. Matters related to intellectual property regimes (ToR I.4.1.3)

155. Brazil does not offer an intellectual property regime for which transparency requirements under the Action 5 Report (OECD, 2015) were imposed.

Summary of recommendations on implementation of the transparency framework

Aspect of implementation of the transparency framework that should be improved	Recommendation for improvement
No recommendations are made	

Notes

1 With respect to the following preferential regime: PADIS – Semiconductors Industry.

2 Available at: https://idg.receita.fazenda.gov.br/acesso-rapido/legislacao (accessed 20 November 2018).

3 See Article 3-A of the Normative Instruction No. 1396/2013, available at: http://normas.receita.fazenda.gov.br/sijut2consulta/link.action?visao=anotado&idAto=46030 (accessed 20 November 2018).

References

OECD (2017), *BEPS Action 5 on Harmful Tax Practices – Terms of Reference and Methodology for the Conduct of the Peer Reviews of the Action 5 Transparency Framework*, OECD/G20 Base Erosion and Profit Shifting Project, OECD, Paris. www.oecd.org/tax/beps/beps-action-5-harmful-tax-practices-peer-review-transparencyframework.pdf.

OECD (2015), *Countering Harmful Tax Practices More Effectively, Taking into Account Transparency and Substance, Action 5 - 2015 Final Report*, OECD/G20 Base Erosion and Profit Shifting Project, OECD Publishing, Paris. https://doi.org/10.1787/9789264241190-en.

OECD/Council of Europe (2011), *The Multilateral Convention on Mutual Administrative Assistance in Tax Matters: Amended by the 2010 Protocol*, OECD Publishing, Paris. http://dx.doi.org/10.1787/9789264115606-en.

Brunei Darussalam

Brunei Darussalam's implementation of the transparency framework is still in the early stages of development. Brunei Darussalam introduced legislation in February 2017 that allows the Collector of Income Tax to issue taxpayer-specific tax rulings. However, for the year in review, no rulings have been issued by Brunei Darussalam under this new framework, and no rulings requests have been received by Brunei Darussalam.

Brunei Darussalam has met all the terms of reference (ToR) for the calendar year 2017 (year in review) that can be met in the absence of rulings being issued in practice.

Brunei Darussalam can legally issue five types of rulings within the scope of the transparency framework. In practice, Brunei Darussalam has not issued any rulings within the scope of the transparency framework.

As no rulings were issued, no exchange of information was required. Therefore no peer input was received in respect of the exchanges of information on rulings received from Brunei Darussalam.

Introduction

156. This peer review covers Brunei Darussalam's implementation of the BEPS Action 5 transparency framework for the year 2017. The report has four parts, each relating to a key part of the ToR. Each part is discussed in turn. A summary of recommendations is included at the end of this report.

A. The information gathering process

157. Brunei Darussalam can legally issue the following types of ruling within the scope of the transparency framework: (i) rulings related to preferential regimes;[1] (ii) cross-border unilateral advance pricing arrangements (APAs) and any other cross-border unilateral tax rulings (such as an advance tax ruling) covering transfer pricing or the application of transfer pricing principles; (iii) cross-border rulings giving a unilateral downward adjustment; (iv) permanent establishment rulings; and (v) related party conduit rulings. Rulings are issued by the Revenue Division in the Ministry of Finance with the approval of the Collector of Income Tax.

Past rulings (ToR I.4.1.1, I.4.1.2, I.4.2.1, I.4.2.2)

158. For Brunei Darussalam, past rulings are any tax rulings within scope that are issued either: (i) on or after 1 January 2015 but before 1 April 2017; or (ii) on or after 1 January 2012 but before 1 January 2015, provided they were still in effect as at 1 January 2015.

159. Brunei Darussalam introduced legislation in February 2017 that allows the Collector of Income Tax to issue taxpayer-specific tax rulings. Prior to February 2017, Brunei Darussalam did not have a framework by which to issue tax rulings. For the year in review, no rulings have been issued by Brunei Darussalam under this new framework, and no rulings requests have been received by Brunei Darussalam.

160. Brunei Darussalam has not issued any rulings during the past rulings period. As no rulings were issued, it was not relevant to identify any exchange jurisdictions for past rulings.

Future rulings (ToR I.4.1.1, I.4.1.2, I.4.2.1)

161. For Brunei Darussalam, future rulings are any tax rulings within scope that are issued on or after 1 September 2017.

162. No rulings were issued by Brunei Darussalam during the future rulings period in the year of review. However, Brunei Darussalam indicates that there are processes in place for the issuance and physical record keeping of rulings.

163. The International Unit under the Revenue Division in the Ministry of Finance is tasked to review and establish whether any rulings issued fall in scope of the transparency framework. Currently, all rulings issued are manually reviewed to establish whether it is in scope of the transparency framework. Although in practice Brunei Darussalam did not issue any future rulings during the year in review, Brunei Darussalam has indicated that potential exchange jurisdictions will be identified in the future via the following process. Information on relevant exchange jurisdiction will be sought from the taxpayer during the ruling application process, prior to the issuance of the ruling. The Revenue Division will

also review taxpayer files and consult the Registrar of Companies and Business Names where necessary.

Review and supervision mechanism (ToR I.4.3)

164. The accuracy of the information gathering process and the identification of rulings in scope of the transparency framework is supervised by the senior management within the Revenue Division.

Conclusion on section A

165. Brunei Darussalam has met all of the ToR for the information gathering process and no recommendations are made.

B. The exchange of information

Legal basis for spontaneous exchange of information (ToR II.5.1, II.5.2)

166. Brunei Darussalam has the necessary domestic legal basis to exchange information spontaneously. Brunei Darussalam notes that there are no legal or practical impediments that prevent the spontaneous exchange of information on rulings as contemplated in the Action 5 minimum standard.

167. Brunei Darussalam is a party to international agreements permitting spontaneous exchange of information, including (i) double tax agreements in force with 16 jurisdictions.[2] Brunei Darussalam signed the *Multilateral Convention on Mutual Administrative Assistance in Tax Matters: Amended by the 2010 Protocol* (OECD/Council of Europe, 2011) ("the Convention") on 12 September 2017 and is currently in the process of ratifying the Convention. Once the Convention is ratified and enters into force, the spontaneous exchange of information can also be made with all the jurisdictions that are covered by the Convention.

Completion and exchange of templates (ToR II.5.3, II.5.4, II.5.5, II.5.6, II.5.7)

168. Brunei Darussalam notes that the Revenue Division in the Ministry of Finance will be responsible for the completion and quality check of the information required in the template contained in Annex C of the Action 5 Report (OECD, 2015). This would include providing a detailed summary of the ruling following the instructions in Annex C. Brunei Darussalam is also considering using the OECD XML Schema in the future.

169. The Revenue Division in the Ministry of Finance is the Competent Authority in Brunei Darussalam responsible for the identification, analysis and exchange of information on rulings. As the Revenue Division in the Ministry of Finance is also responsible for the issuance of rulings, all tax rulings will be readily available to the Competent Authority and no delays are expected.

170. As Brunei Darussalam did not issue any past or future rulings in scope of the transparency framework in the relevant periods, Brunei Darussalam was not required to exchange any information on rulings in the year in review and no data on the timeliness of exchanges can be reported.

Conclusion on section B

171. Brunei Darussalam has the necessary legal basis to undertake spontaneous exchange of information. Brunei Darussalam has met all of the ToR for the exchange of information process that can be met in the absence of rulings being issued and exchanged in practice and no recommendations are made.

C. Statistics (ToR IV)

172. As no information on rulings was exchanged for the year in review, no statistical data can be reported.

D. Matters related to intellectual property regimes (ToR I.4.1.3)

173. Brunei Darussalam does not offer an intellectual property regime for which transparency requirements under the Action 5 Report (OECD, 2015) were imposed.

Summary of recommendations on implementation of the transparency framework

Aspect of implementation of the transparency framework that should be improved	Recommendation for improvement
	No recommendations are made.

Notes

1 Investment Incentive Order.

2 Double tax agreements with Bahrain, China (People's Republic of), Indonesia, Japan, Kuwait, Lao People's Democratic Republic, Luxembourg, Malaysia, Oman, Pakistan, Qatar, Singapore, Korea, United Arab Emirates, United Kingdom and Viet Nam.

References

OECD (2017), *BEPS Action 5 on Harmful Tax Practices – Terms of Reference and Methodology for the Conduct of the Peer Reviews of the Action 5 Transparency Framework*, OECD/G20 Base Erosion and Profit Shifting Project, OECD, Paris. www.oecd.org/tax/beps/beps-action-5-harmful-tax-practices-peer-review-transparencyframework.pdf.

OECD (2015), *Countering Harmful Tax Practices More Effectively, Taking into Account Transparency and Substance, Action 5 - 2015 Final Report*, OECD/G20 Base Erosion and Profit Shifting Project, OECD Publishing, Paris. https://doi.org/10.1787/9789264241190-en.

OECD/Council of Europe (2011), *The Multilateral Convention on Mutual Administrative Assistance in Tax Matters: Amended by the 2010 Protocol*, OECD Publishing, Paris. http://dx.doi.org/10.1787/9789264115606-en.

Bulgaria

Bulgaria has met all aspects of the terms of reference (ToR) for the calendar year 2017 (year in review) that can be met in the absence of rulings being issued and no recommendations are made.

Bulgaria cannot legally issue any type of rulings within the scope of the transparency framework. Bulgaria issues "tax opinions" to individual taxpayers which give a general clarification with respect the interpretation and application of the tax legislation. Since these documents are very general and not legally binding on the tax administration, these tax opinions are not rulings as defined in the Action 5 report (OECD, 2015).

As no rulings were issued, no exchange of information was required. No peer input was received in respect of the exchanges of information on rulings received from Bulgaria.

Introduction

174. This peer review covers Bulgaria's implementation of the BEPS Action 5 transparency framework for the year 2017. The report has four parts, each relating to a key part of the ToR. Each part is discussed in turn. A summary of recommendations is included at the end of this report.

A. The information gathering process

175. As no rulings are issued, this section is not assessed.

B. The exchange of information

176. As no rulings are issued, this section is not assessed.

C. Statistics (ToR IV)

177. As no rulings are issued, no statistical data can be reported.

D. Matters related to intellectual property regimes (ToR I.4.1.3)

178. Bulgaria does not offer an intellectual property regime for which transparency requirements under the Action 5 Report (OECD, 2015) were imposed.

Summary of recommendations on implementation of the transparency framework

Aspect of implementation of the transparency framework that should be improved	Recommendation for improvement
	No recommendations are made.

References

OECD (2017), *BEPS Action 5 on Harmful Tax Practices – Terms of Reference and Methodology for the Conduct of the Peer Reviews of the Action 5 Transparency Framework*, OECD/G20 Base Erosion and Profit Shifting Project, OECD, Paris. www.oecd.org/tax/beps/beps-action-5-harmful-tax-practices-peer-review-transparencyframework.pdf.

OECD (2015), *Countering Harmful Tax Practices More Effectively, Taking into Account Transparency and Substance, Action 5 - 2015 Final Report*, OECD/G20 Base Erosion and Profit Shifting Project, OECD Publishing, Paris. https://doi.org/10.1787/9789264241190-en.

Burkina Faso

Burkina Faso has met the terms of reference (ToR) for the calendar year 2017 (year in review) that can be met in the absence of rulings being issued.[1]

Burkina Faso does not issue any type of rulings within the scope of the transparency framework. Burkina Faso only issues interpretative rulings. These tax rulings are not binding for the tax authorities and are therefore not considered rulings as defined in the Action 5 report (OECD, 2015). In the event that Burkina Faso put in place the administrative process to issue rulings within the scope of the transparency framework, Burkina Faso notes that it would implement the transparency framework obligations.

As there were no rulings issued, no exchange of information was required. Therefore no peer input was received in respect of exchanges of information on rulings received from Burkina Faso.

Introduction

179. This peer review covers Burkina Faso's implementation of the BEPS Action 5 transparency framework for the year 2017. The report has four parts, each relating to a key part of the ToR. Each part is discussed in turn. A summary of recommendations is included at the end of this report.

A. The information gathering process

180. As no rulings are issued, this section is not assessed.

B. The exchange of information

181. As no rulings are issued, this section is not assessed.

C. Statistics (ToR IV)

182. As no rulings are issued, no statistical data can be reported.

D. Matters related to intellectual property regimes (ToR I.4.1.3)

183. Burkina Faso does not offer an intellectual property regime for which transparency requirements under the Action 5 Report (OECD, 2015) were imposed.

Summary of recommendations on implementation of the transparency framework

Aspect of implementation of the transparency framework that should be improved	Recommendation for improvement
	No recommendations are made.

Note

[1] Burkina Faso did not provide written comments on this peer review report.

References

OECD (2017), *BEPS Action 5 on Harmful Tax Practices – Terms of Reference and Methodology for the Conduct of the Peer Reviews of the Action 5 Transparency Framework*, OECD/G20 Base Erosion and Profit Shifting Project, OECD, Paris. www.oecd.org/tax/beps/beps-action-5-harmful-tax-practices-peer-review-transparencyframework.pdf.

OECD (2015), *Countering Harmful Tax Practices More Effectively, Taking into Account Transparency and Substance, Action 5 - 2015 Final Report*, OECD/G20 Base Erosion and Profit Shifting Project, OECD Publishing, Paris. https://doi.org/10.1787/9789264241190-en.

Cameroon

Cameroon[1] did not provide a completed peer review questionnaire to the Secretariat. It is not known whether Cameroon has implemented the transparency framework. Cameroon is recommended to ensure that it has put in place an effective information gathering process to identify all relevant past and future rulings and all potential exchange jurisdictions and to implement a review and supervision mechanism, as soon as possible, (ToR I.4). Cameroon is recommended to put in place a domestic legal framework allowing spontaneous exchange of information on rulings if needed and to ensure the timely exchange of information on rulings in the form required by the transparency framework (ToR II.5).

It is not known whether Cameroon can legally issue any types of ruling within the scope of the transparency framework,[2] or whether in practice Cameroon issued any such rulings.

As no exchange of information on rulings was conducted, no peer input was received in respect of the exchanges of information on rulings received from Cameroon.

Introduction

184. This peer review covers Cameroon's implementation of the BEPS Action 5 transparency framework for the calendar year 2017 (year in review). The report has four parts, each relating to a key part of the ToR. Each part is discussed in turn. A summary of recommendations is included at the end of this report.

A. The information gathering process

185. Cameroon was not yet able to complete the peer review questionnaire. It is not known whether Cameroon has implemented the transparency framework.

Conclusion on section A

186. Cameroon is recommended to ensure that it has put in place an effective information gathering process to identify all relevant past and future rulings and all potential exchange jurisdictions and to implement a review and supervision mechanism, as soon as possible (ToR I.4).

B. The exchange of information

Legal basis for spontaneous exchange of information (ToR II.5.1, II.5.2)

187. It is not known whether Cameroon has the necessary domestic legal basis to exchange information spontaneously. Cameroon is recommended to put in place a domestic legal framework allowing spontaneous exchange of information on rulings if needed (ToR II.5.1).

188. Cameroon party to international agreements permitting spontaneous exchange of information, including (i) the *Multilateral Convention on Mutual Administrative Assistance in Tax Matters: Amended by the 2010 Protocol* (OECD/Council of Europe, 2011) ("the Convention") and (ii) double tax agreements in force with 12 jurisdictions.[3]

Completion and exchange of templates (ToR II.5.3, II.5.4, II.5.5, II.5.6, II.5.7)

189. It is not known whether Cameroon has put in place a process to exchange information on rulings in accordance with the form and timelines required by the transparency framework. Cameroon is recommended to ensure the timely exchange of information on rulings in the form required by the transparency framework.

Conclusion on section B

190. Cameroon is recommended to put in place a domestic legal framework allowing spontaneous exchange of information on rulings if needed and to ensure the timely exchange of information on rulings in the form required by the transparency framework (ToR II.5).

C. Statistics (ToR IV)

191. Cameroon did not provide statistical data for the year in review. In the absence of this information, no statistics can be reported.

D. Matters related to intellectual property regimes (ToR I.4.1.3)

192. Cameroon does not offer an intellectual property regime for which transparency requirements under the Action 5 Report (OECD, 2015) were imposed.

Summary of recommendations on implementation of the transparency framework

Aspect of implementation of the transparency framework that should be improved	Recommendation for improvement
It is not known whether Cameroon has an information gathering process in place.	Cameroon is recommended to ensure that it has put in place an effective information gathering process to identify all relevant past and future rulings and all potential exchange jurisdictions and to implement a review and supervision mechanism, as soon as possible.
It is not known whether Cameroon has a domestic legal framework allowing spontaneous exchange of information on rulings if needed and has a process in place to ensure the timely exchange of information on rulings in the form required by the transparency framework.	Cameroon is recommended to put in place a domestic legal framework allowing spontaneous exchange of information on rulings if needed and to ensure the timely exchange of information on rulings in the form required by the transparency framework.

Notes

[1] Cameroon did not provide written comments on this peer review report.

[2] Note: According to publicly available information, it appears that Cameroon can legally issue advanced tax rulings.

[3] Cameroon has Double Tax Agreements with: Belgium, Canada, Czech Republic, Egypt, France, Morocco, Romania, South Africa, Tunisia, Turkey, United Arab Emirates and Viet Nam.

References

OECD (2017), *BEPS Action 5 on Harmful Tax Practices – Terms of Reference and Methodology for the Conduct of the Peer Reviews of the Action 5 Transparency Framework*, OECD/G20 Base Erosion and Profit Shifting Project, OECD, Paris. www.oecd.org/tax/beps/beps-action-5-harmful-tax-practices-peer-review-transparencyframework.pdf.

OECD (2015), *Countering Harmful Tax Practices More Effectively, Taking into Account Transparency and Substance, Action 5 - 2015 Final Report*, OECD/G20 Base Erosion and Profit Shifting Project, OECD Publishing, Paris. https://doi.org/10.1787/9789264241190-en.

OECD/Council of Europe (2011), *The Multilateral Convention on Mutual Administrative Assistance in Tax Matters: Amended by the 2010 Protocol*, OECD Publishing, Paris. http://dx.doi.org/10.1787/9789264115606-en.

Canada

Canada has met all aspects of the terms of reference (ToR) for the calendar year 2017 (year in review) and no recommendations are made.

Canada can legally issue four types of rulings within the scope of the transparency framework.

In practice, Canada has issued 12 past rulings; for the period 1 April 2016 - 31 December 2016, Canada issued two future rulings; and for the year in review, Canada issued two future rulings within the scope of the transparency framework.

Peer input was received from one jurisdiction in respect of the exchanges of information on rulings received from Canada. It was positive, noting that information was complete, in the correct format and received in a timely manner with the summary provided a good overview of the ruling.

Introduction

193. This peer review covers Canada's implementation of the BEPS Action 5 transparency framework for the year 2017. The report has four parts, each relating to a key part of the ToR. Each part is discussed in turn. A summary of recommendations is included at the end of this report.

A. The information gathering process

194. Canada can legally issue the four following types of rulings within the scope of the transparency framework: (i) rulings related to preferential regimes;[1] (ii) cross-border unilateral advance pricing arrangements (APAs) and any other cross-border unilateral tax rulings (such as an advance tax ruling) covering transfer pricing or the application of transfer pricing principles; (iii) permanent establishment rulings; and (iv) related party conduit rulings. In Canada, the Competent Authority Services Division (CASD) for APAs, and the Income Tax Rulings Directorate (ITRD) for the other categories are two services part of the CRA that are authorised to issue opinions. With the exception of APAs, Canada's rulings are published in redacted form by third-party publishers, who provide access to the documents to their subscribers and redacted rulings are available from the Canada Revenue Agency ("CRA") upon request.

Past rulings (ToR I.4.1.1, I.4.1.2, I.4.2.1, I.4.2.2)

195. For Canada, past rulings are any tax rulings within scope that are issued either: (i) on or after 1 January 2014 but before 1 April 2016; or (ii) on or after 1 January 2010 but before 1 January 2014, provided they were still in effect as at 1 January 2014.

196. In the prior year peer review report, it was determined that the CRA's undertakings to identify past rulings and all potential exchange jurisdictions were sufficient to meet the minimum standard. The CRA's implementation in this regard remains unchanged, and therefore continues to meet the minimum standard.

Future rulings (ToR I.4.1.1, I.4.1.2, I.4.2.1)

197. For Canada, future rulings are any tax rulings within scope that are issued on or after 1 April 2016.

198. In the prior year peer review report, it was determined that the CRA's implementation of a new system to identify future rulings and all potential exchange jurisdictions was sufficient to meet the minimum standard. The CRA's implementation in this regard remains unchanged, and therefore continues to meet the minimum standard.

Review and supervision mechanism (ToR I.4.3)

199. In the prior year peer review report, it was determined that the CRA's review and supervision mechanism was sufficient to meet the minimum standard. The CRA's implementation in this regard remains unchanged, and therefore continues to meet the minimum standard.

Conclusion on section A

200. Canada has met all of the ToR for the information gathering process and no recommendations are made.

B. The exchange of information

Legal basis for spontaneous exchange of information (ToR II.5.1, II.5.2)

201. Canada has the necessary domestic legal basis to exchange information spontaneously. Canada notes that there are no legal or practical impediments that prevent the spontaneous exchange of information on rulings as contemplated in the Action 5 minimum standard.

202. Canada is a party to international agreements permitting spontaneous exchange of information, including (i) the *Multilateral Convention on Mutual Administrative Assistance in Tax Matters: Amended by the 2010 Protocol* (OECD/Council of Europe, 2011) ("the Convention") and (ii) double tax agreements in force with 93 jurisdictions.[2]

Completion and exchange of templates (ToR II.5.3, II.5.4, II.5.5, II.5.6, II.5.7)

203. In the prior year peer review report, it was determined that the CRA's completion and exchange of templates were sufficient to meet the minimum standard. The CRA's implementation in this regard remains unchanged, and therefore continues to meet the minimum standard.

204. With respect to the completion of the summary section of the template, Canada confirms that it uses the suggested FHTP internal guidance.

205. For the year in review, the timeliness of exchanges is as follows:

Past rulings in the scope of the transparency framework	Number of exchanges transmitted by 31 December 2017	Delayed exchanges		
		Number of exchanges not transmitted by 31 December 2017	Reasons for the delays	Any other comments
	0	0	N/A	See below
Future rulings in the scope of the transparency framework	Number of exchanges transmitted within three months of the information becoming available to the competent authority or immediately after legal impediments have been lifted	Delayed exchanges		
		Number of exchanges transmitted later than three months of the information on rulings becoming available to the competent authority	Reasons for the delays	Any other comments
	2	0	N/A	
Total	2	0		

Follow up requests received for exchange of the ruling	Number	Average time to provide response	Number of requests not answered
	0	0	N/A

206. For the year in review, no past rulings had to be exchanged with new members of the Inclusive Framework that joined in 2017 and as such no additional exchanges on past rulings were required.

Conclusion on section B

207. Canada has the necessary legal basis for spontaneous exchange of information, a process for completing the templates in a timely way and has completed all exchanges on

time. Canada has met all of the ToR for the exchange of information process and no recommendations are made.

C. Statistics (ToR IV)

208. The statistics for the year in review are as follows:

Category of ruling	Number of exchanges	Jurisdictions exchanged with
Rulings related to preferential regimes	0	N/A
Cross-border unilateral advance pricing arrangement (APAs) and any other cross-border unilateral tax rulings (such as an advance tax ruling) covering transfer pricing or the application of transfer pricing principles	Included in *de minimis*	N/A
Cross-border rulings providing for a unilateral downward adjustment to the taxpayer's taxable profits that is not directly reflected in the taxpayer's financial / commercial accounts	N/A	N/A
Permanent establishment rulings	0	N/A
Related party conduit rulings	0	N/A
De minimis rule	2	N/A
IP regimes: total exchanges on taxpayers benefitting from the third category of IP assets, new entrants benefitting from grandfathered IP regimes; and taxpayers making use of the option to treat the nexus ratio as a rebuttable presumption	N/A	N/A
Total	2	

D. Matters related to intellectual property regimes (ToR I.4.1.3)

209. Canada does not offer an intellectual property regime for which transparency requirements under the Action 5 Report (OECD, 2015) were imposed.

Summary of recommendations on implementation of the transparency framework

Aspect of implementation of the transparency framework that should be improved	Recommendation for improvement
	No recommendations are made.

Notes

1 Life insurance business and international shipping.

2 Parties to the Convention are available here: www.oecd.org/tax/exchange-of-tax-information/convention-on-mutual-administrative-assistance-in-tax-matters.htm. Canada also has bilateral agreements in force with Algeria, Armenia, Bangladesh, Cote d'Ivoire, Dominican Republic, Ecuador, Egypt, Gabon, Guyana, Hong Kong (China), Jamaica, Jordan, Kenya, Kuwait, Kyrgyzstan, Mongolia, Morocco, Oman, Papua New Guinea, Peru, Philippines, Serbia, Sri Lanka, Chinese Taipei, Tanzania, Thailand, Trinidad & Tobago, Turkey, United Arab Emirates, United States, Uzbekistan, Venezuela, Viet Nam, Zambia and Zimbabwe. The TIEA with Aruba also permits spontaneous exchange of information.

References

OECD (2017), *BEPS Action 5 on Harmful Tax Practices – Terms of Reference and Methodology for the Conduct of the Peer Reviews of the Action 5 Transparency Framework*, OECD/G20 Base Erosion and Profit Shifting Project, OECD, Paris. www.oecd.org/tax/beps/beps-action-5-harmful-tax-practices-peer-review-transparencyframework.pdf.

OECD (2015), *Countering Harmful Tax Practices More Effectively, Taking into Account Transparency and Substance, Action 5 - 2015 Final Report*, OECD/G20 Base Erosion and Profit Shifting Project, OECD Publishing, Paris. https://doi.org/10.1787/9789264241190-en.

OECD/Council of Europe (2011), *The Multilateral Convention on Mutual Administrative Assistance in Tax Matters: Amended by the 2010 Protocol*, OECD Publishing, Paris. http://dx.doi.org/10.1787/9789264115606-en.

Chile

Chile has met all aspects of the terms of reference (ToR) for the calendar year 2017 (year in review) that can be met in the absence of rulings being issued.

Chile can legally issue two types of rulings within the scope of the transparency framework.

In practice, Chile issued no rulings within the scope of the transparency framework.

As there were no rulings issued, no exchange of information was required. Therefore no peer input was received in respect of exchanges of information on rulings received from Chile.

Introduction

210. This peer review covers Chile's implementation of the BEPS Action 5 transparency framework for the year 2017. The report has four parts, each relating to a key part of the ToR. Each part is discussed in turn. A summary of recommendations is included at the end of this report.

A. The information gathering process

211. Chile can legally issue the two following types of rulings within the scope of the transparency framework: (i) cross-border unilateral advance pricing arrangements (APAs) and any other cross-border unilateral tax rulings (such as an advance tax ruling) covering transfer pricing or the application of transfer pricing principles; and (ii) related party conduit rulings. In Chile, a specific unit within SII, the National Directorate, considers all ruling requests. A few requests for unilateral APAs have been received from taxpayers and those requests are still under consideration by the Servicio de Impuestos Internos ("SII").

Past rulings (ToR I.4.1.1, I.4.1.2, I.4.2.1, I.4.2.2)

212. For Chile, past rulings are any tax rulings within scope that are issued either: (i) on or after 1 January 2014 but before 1 April 2016; or (ii) on or after 1 January 2010 but before 1 January 2014, provided they were still in effect as at 1 January 2014.

213. In the prior year peer review report, it was determined that SII's undertakings to identify past rulings and all potential exchange jurisdictions were sufficient to meet the minimum standard if any rulings were such to be issued. SII's implementation in this regard remains unchanged, and therefore continues to meet the minimum standard.

Future rulings (ToR I.4.1.1, I.4.1.2, I.4.2.1)

214. For Chile, future rulings are any tax rulings within scope that are issued on or after 1 April 2016.

215. In the prior year peer review report, it was determined that SII's implementation of a new system to identify future rulings and all potential exchange jurisdictions, if any such rulings are issued was sufficient to meet the minimum standard. SII's implementation in this regard remains unchanged, and therefore continues to meet the minimum standard.

Review and supervision mechanism (ToR I.4.3)

216. In the prior year peer review report, it was determined that SII's review and supervision mechanisms currently in place and the procedure to be implemented once a larger number of rulings are issued were sufficient to meet the minimum standard. SII's implementation in this regard remains unchanged, and therefore continues to meet the minimum standard.

Conclusion on section A

217. Chile has met all of the ToR for the information gathering process and no recommendations are made.

B. The exchange of information

Legal basis for spontaneous exchange of information (ToR II.5.1, II.5.2)

218. Chile has the necessary domestic legal basis to exchange information spontaneously. Chile notes that there are no legal or practical impediments that prevent the spontaneous exchange of information on rulings as contemplated in the Action 5 minimum standard.

219. Chile is a party to international agreements permitting spontaneous exchange of information, including (i) the *Multilateral Convention on Mutual Administrative Assistance in Tax Matters: Amended by the 2010 Protocol* (OECD/Council of Europe, 2011) ("the Convention") and (ii) Double Tax Agreements with 32 jurisdictions.[1]

Completion and exchange of templates (ToR II.5.3, II.5.4, II.5.5, II.5.6, II.5.7)

220. In the prior year peer review report, it was determined that SII's completion and exchange of templates procedure to be applicable once rulings are actually issued was sufficient to meet the minimum standard. SII's implementation in this regard remains unchanged, and therefore continues to meet the minimum standard.

221. Even though it is not currently issuing rulings in practice, SII affirms that when rulings are issued, the required information will be shared in a template based on Annex C of the Action 5 Report (OECD, 2015). SII also commits to complete the summary section in Annex C with the prescribed instructions to the section. Where relevant, Chile will also apply the internal FHTP suggested guidance.

222. As no rulings within the scope of the transparency framework have been issued in practice, Chile was not required to complete any exchanges of information and there is no data to report on the timeliness of exchanges.

Conclusion on section B

223. Chile has the necessary legal framework and administrative process in place for exchanging information on rulings. Chile has met all of the ToR for the exchange of information process that can be met in the absence of rulings being issued and exchanged in practice and no recommendations are made.

C. Statistics (ToR IV)

224. As there were no rulings required to be exchanged by Chile for the year in review, no statistics can be reported.

D. Matters related to intellectual property regimes (ToR I.4.1.3)

225. Chile does not offer an intellectual property regime for which transparency requirements under the Action 5 Report (OECD, 2015) were imposed.

Summary of recommendations on implementation of the transparency framework

Aspect of implementation of the transparency framework that should be improved	Recommendation for improvement
	No recommendations are made.

Note

1 Parties to the Convention are available here: www.oecd.org/tax/exchange-of-tax-information/convention-on-mutual-administrative-assistance-in-tax-matters.htm. Chile also has bilateral agreements in force with Argentina, Australia, Austria, Belgium, Brazil, Canada, China (People's Republic of), Colombia, Croatia, Czech Republic, Denmark, Ecuador, France, Ireland, Italy, Japan, Korea, Malaysia, Mexico, Norway, New Zealand, Paraguay, Peru, Poland, Portugal, Russia, Spain, South Africa, Sweden, Switzerland, Thailand and United Kingdom.

References

OECD (2017), *BEPS Action 5 on Harmful Tax Practices – Terms of Reference and Methodology for the Conduct of the Peer Reviews of the Action 5 Transparency Framework*, OECD/G20 Base Erosion and Profit Shifting Project, OECD, Paris. www.oecd.org/tax/beps/beps-action-5-harmful-tax-practices-peer-review-transparencyframework.pdf.

OECD (2015), *Countering Harmful Tax Practices More Effectively, Taking into Account Transparency and Substance, Action 5 - 2015 Final Report*, OECD/G20 Base Erosion and Profit Shifting Project, OECD Publishing, Paris. https://doi.org/10.1787/9789264241190-en.

OECD/Council of Europe (2011), *The Multilateral Convention on Mutual Administrative Assistance in Tax Matters: Amended by the 2010 Protocol*, OECD Publishing, Paris. http://dx.doi.org/10.1787/9789264115606-en.

China (People's Republic of)

The People's Republic of China ("China") has met all aspects of the terms of reference (ToR) for the calendar year 2017 (year in review), except for the timely provision of information on rulings to the Competent Authority for exchange of information (ToR II.5.5). China is recommended to reduce the timelines for providing the information on future rulings to the Competent Authority. In the prior year's peer review report, China received two recommendations regarding the identification of future rulings (ToR I.4.1.2) and timely exchange of information on future rulings (ToR II.5.6). China has addressed the issues and these recommendations are removed.

China can legally issue one type of rulings within the scope of the transparency framework.

In practice, China issued 11 past rulings; for the period 1 April 2016 - 31 December 2016, China issued six future rulings; and for the year in review, China issued three future rulings within the scope of the transparency framework.

Peer input was received from one jurisdiction in respect of the exchanges of information on rulings received from China. It was positive, noting that the information was complete, in the correct format and received in a timely manner.

Introduction

226. This peer review covers China's implementation of the BEPS Action 5 transparency framework for the year 2017. The report has four parts, each relating to a key part of the ToR. Each part is discussed in turn. A summary of recommendations is included at the end of this report.

A. The information gathering process

227. China can legally issue one type of rulings within the scope of the transparency framework: cross-border unilateral advance pricing agreements (APAs) covering transfer pricing or the application of transfer pricing principles. The local in-charge tax administration offices are responsible for issuing rulings, with relevant consultation with the Chinese Tax Administration (SAT). Where an APA involves two or more local offices or both the state tax and local tax bureau, the APA process is organised and co-ordinated by the SAT.

Past rulings (ToR I.4.1.1, I.4.1.2, I.4.2.1, I.4.2.2)

228. There is a legal barrier to the exchange of information on rulings on China, which does not allow the exchange of past rulings. The legal framework in China has now been amended to allow exchanges on future rulings. As such, the balance of this report relates only to future rulings.

Future rulings (ToR I.4.1.1, I.4.1.2, I.4.2.1)

229. For China, future rulings are any tax rulings within scope that are issued on or after 1 April 2016. In the prior year peer review report, China had not completed the process to collect information on all future APAs and all potential exchange jurisdictions, and therefore received a recommendation to complete the identification of all future rulings as soon as possible (ToR I.4.1.2). China has now addressed this recommendation, and completed the identification and exchange of future rulings for the calendar year 2016 and the year in review.

230. For the year in review, local tax authorities identify APAs for exchange at the point of issuance. The information on APAs is collected by the SAT from the local tax administration offices which have issued the ruling. In order to identify all potential relevant jurisdictions with which the information on rulings should be exchanged, this information is taken from the APA request. During the process of submitting an APA application, taxpayers are requested to provide detailed information about related parties. Specifically, applicants are required to provide a list to the local tax administration, consisting of the jurisdictions of its ultimate parent company, immediate parent company, and related parties with whom it enters into a transaction covered by the APA.

Review and supervision mechanism (ToR I.4.3)

231. In the prior year peer review report, it was determined that the Chinese Tax Administration's review and supervision mechanism was sufficient to meet the minimum standard. The Chinese Tax Administration's implementation in this regard remains unchanged, and therefore continues to meet the minimum standard.

Conclusion on section A

232. For the year in review, China has met all of the ToR for the information gathering process and no recommendations are made.

B. The exchange of information

Legal basis for spontaneous exchange of information (ToR II.5.1, II.5.2)

233. China has implemented the necessary domestic legal basis to exchange information spontaneously in place. The legal framework in place does not allow the exchange of past rulings but does allow the exchange of information on future rulings, as from 1 April 2016.[1]

234. China is a party to international agreements permitting spontaneous exchange of information, including (i) the *Multilateral Convention on Mutual Administrative Assistance in Tax Matters: Amended by the 2010 Protocol* (OECD/Council of Europe, 2011) ("the Convention"), and (ii) double tax agreements in force with 102 jurisdictions.[2]

Completion and exchange of templates (ToR II.5.3, II.5.4, II.5.5, II.5.6, II.5.7)

235. For the year in review, the SAT completed the templates in the form of Annex C of the 2015 Action 5 Report (OECD, 2015). The SAT has issued internal instructions to streamline the process for completing the information required in the Annex C template. The summary section of the template is completed with reference to the aspects of the internal FHTP suggested guidance which relate to unilateral APAs, including providing a summary of the transaction or activity covered by the unilateral APA, and identification of which transfer pricing methodology has been applied. The template is completed by local tax administration officers, and reviewed for approval at the local tax administration level. The template is then transmitted to the Competent Authority in SAT for final review and approval before the template is exchanged.

236. For the year in review, China collected all relevant templates from the local in-charge authorities in January 2018 and such information was exchanged with the relevant jurisdictions in February 2018. However, in March 2018, China finalised testing to incorporate the issuance of unilateral APAs into their holistic information system for all anti-avoidance measures. The new system allows the SAT to identify and process information relating to unilateral APAs, and receive unilateral APAs via the system within 10 days after an APA is issued rather than receiving future rulings from the local in-charge tax administration offices once a year.

237. In the prior year peer review report, China had not completed the timely exchange of information on future rulings (ToR II.5.6). For future rulings issued in 2016, China collected all relevant templates from the local in-charge tax authorities in September 2017 and such information was then exchanged with relevant jurisdictions in October 2017. China has now completed the exchange of information on future rulings and this recommendation is removed.

238. For the year in review, the timeliness of exchanges is as follows:

Past rulings in the scope of the transparency framework	Number of exchanges transmitted by 31 December 2017	Delayed exchanges		
		Number of exchanges not transmitted by 31 December 2017	Reasons for the delays	Any other comments
	N/A	N/A	N/A	
Future rulings in the scope of the transparency framework	**Number of exchanges transmitted within three months of the information becoming available to the competent authority or immediately after legal impediments have been lifted**	**Delayed exchanges**		
		Number of exchanges transmitted later than three months of the information on rulings becoming available to the competent authority	**Reasons for the delays**	**Any other comments**
	11	0	N/A	These 11 exchanges are a result of the delayed exchanges from the prior year. No exchanges were undertaken in 2017 for rulings issued in 2017, as templates were not provided to the Competent Authority until January 2018.
Total	11	0		

Follow up requests received for exchange of the ruling	Number	Average time to provide response	Number of requests not answered
	0	N/A	0

Conclusion on section B

239. China has in place the necessary legal basis for exchanging information on future rulings. China has met all the ToR for the exchange of information process except for the timely provision of information on rulings to the Competent Authority for exchange of information (ToR II.5.5). China is recommended to reduce the timelines for providing the information on future rulings to the Competent Authority.

C. Statistics (ToR IV)

240. The statistics for the year in review are as follows:

Category of ruling	Number of exchanges	Jurisdictions exchanged with
Rulings related to preferential regimes	N/A	N/A
Cross-border unilateral advance pricing arrangements (APAs) and any other cross-border unilateral tax rulings (such as an advance tax ruling) covering transfer pricing or the application of transfer pricing principles	11	Hong Kong (China), Macao (China), Germany, Indonesia, the Netherlands, United States
Cross-border rulings providing for a unilateral downward adjustment to the taxpayer's taxable profits that is not directly reflected in the taxpayer's financial / commercial accounts	N/A	N/A
Permanent establishment rulings	N/A	N/A
Related party conduit rulings	N/A	N/A
De minimis rule	N/A	N/A
IP regimes: total exchanges on taxpayers benefitting from the third category of IP assets, new entrants benefitting from grandfathered IP regimes; and taxpayers making use of the option to treat the nexus ratio as a rebuttable presumption	N/A	N/A
Total	11	

D. Matters related to intellectual property regimes (ToR I.4.1.3)

241. In the prior year's peer review report, it was determined that the transparency requirements were not relevant for China's intellectual property regime (Reduced rate for high & new tech enterprises).

Summary of recommendations on implementation of the transparency framework

Aspect of implementation of the transparency framework that should be improved	Recommendation for improvement
During the year in review, China's Competent Authority collected information on future rulings on an annual basis, which is longer than necessary.	China is recommended to reduce the timelines for providing the information on future rulings to the Competent Authority.

Jurisdiction's response and recent development

242. In March 2018, China finalised testing to incorporate the issuance of unilateral APAs into their holistic information system for all anti-avoidance measures. The new system allows the SAT to identify and process information relating to unilateral APAs, and receive unilateral APAs via the system within 10 days after an APA is issued.

Notes

1 Public Notice on Matters Regarding Enhancing the Administration of Advance Pricing Arrangements (SAT Public Notice [2016] No. 64).

2 China has Double Tax Agreements with Albania, Algeria, Armenia, Australia, Austria, Azerbaijan, Bahrein, Bangladesh, Barbados, Belarus, Belgium, Bosnia and Herzegovina, Botswana, Brazil, Brunei Darussalam, Bulgaria, Cambodia, Canada, Chile, Croatia, Cuba, Cyprus, Czech Republic, Denmark, Ecuador, Egypt, Estonia, Ethiopia, Finland, Former Yugoslav Republic of Macedonia, France, Georgia, Germany, Greece, Hungary, Iceland, India, Indonesia, Iran, Ireland, Israel, Italy, Jamaica, Japan, Kazakhstan, Korea, Kuwait, Kyrgyzstan, Lao People's Democratic Republic, Latvia, Lithuania, Luxembourg, Malaysia, Malta, Mauritius, Mexico, Moldova, Mongolia, Montenegro, Morocco, Nepal, Netherlands, New Zealand, Nigeria, Norway, Oman, Pakistan, Papua New Guinea, Philippines, Poland, Portugal, Qatar, Romania, Russia, Saudi Arabia, Serbia, Seychelles, Singapore, Slovenia, South Africa, Spain, Sri Lanka, Sudan, Sweden, Switzerland, Syria, Tajikistan, Thailand, Trinidad and Tobago, Tunisia, Turkey, Turkmenistan, Uganda, Ukraine, United Arab Emirates, United Kingdom, United States, Uzbekistan, Venezuela, Viet Nam, Zambia and Zimbabwe.

Note by Turkey: The information in this document with reference to "Cyprus" relates to the southern part of the Island. There is no single authority representing both Turkish and Greek Cypriot people on the Island. Turkey recognises the Turkish Republic of Northern Cyprus (TRNC). Until a lasting and equitable solution is found within the context of the United Nations, Turkey shall preserve its position concerning the "Cyprus issue".

Note by all the European Union Member States of the OECD and the European Union. The Republic of Cyprus is recognised by all members of the United Nations with the exception of Turkey. The information in this document relates to the area under the effective control of the Government of the Republic of Cyprus.

References

OECD (2017), *BEPS Action 5 on Harmful Tax Practices – Terms of Reference and Methodology for the Conduct of the Peer Reviews of the Action 5 Transparency Framework*, OECD/G20 Base Erosion and Profit Shifting Project, OECD, Paris. www.oecd.org/tax/beps/beps-action-5-harmful-tax-practices-peer-review-transparencyframework.pdf.

OECD (2015), *Countering Harmful Tax Practices More Effectively, Taking into Account Transparency and Substance, Action 5 - 2015 Final Report*, OECD/G20 Base Erosion and Profit Shifting Project, OECD Publishing, Paris. https://doi.org/10.1787/9789264241190-en.

OECD/Council of Europe (2011), *The Multilateral Convention on Mutual Administrative Assistance in Tax Matters: Amended by the 2010 Protocol*, OECD Publishing, Paris. http://dx.doi.org/10.1787/9789264115606-en.

Colombia

Colombia has met all aspects of the terms of reference (ToR) for the calendar year 2017 (year in review) except for completing exchanges of information on past rulings in accordance with the timelines (ToR II.5.6). This recommendation was also included in the prior year peer review report as such, the recommendation remains in place. Colombia is recommended to ensure that all information on past rulings is exchanged as soon as possible. In the prior year peer review report, Colombia also received recommendations regarding the identification of future rulings and the timely exchange of information on rulings in the form required by the transparency framework. Colombia has addressed the issues and these recommendations are removed.

Colombia can legally issue one type of rulings within the scope of the transparency framework.

In practice, Colombia issued one past ruling; and for the year in review, Colombia issued no future rulings within the scope of the transparency framework.

No peer input was received in respect of the exchanges of information on rulings received from Colombia.

Introduction

243. This peer review covers Colombia's implementation of the BEPS Action 5 transparency framework for the year 2017. The report has four parts, each relating to a key part of the ToR. Each part is discussed in turn. A summary of recommendations is included at the end of this report.

A. The information gathering process

244. Colombia can legally issue one type of rulings within the scope of the transparency framework: cross-border unilateral advance pricing agreements (APAs) and any other cross-border unilateral tax rulings (such as an advance tax ruling) covering transfer pricing or the application of transfer pricing principles. In Colombia, The International Tax Auditing team ("ITAT") is responsible for negotiating APAs and the General Director of the National Tax and Customs Administration ("DIAN") is authorised to sign and approve APAs requests.

Past rulings (ToR I.4.1.1, I.4.1.2, I.4.2.1, I.4.2.2)

245. For Colombia, past rulings are any tax rulings within scope that are issued either: (i) on or after 1 January 2014 but before 1 April 2016; or (ii) on or after 1 January 2010 but before 1 January 2014, provided they were still in effect as at 1 January 2016.

246. In the prior year peer review report, it was determined that the Colombian tax administration's undertakings to identify past rulings and all potential exchange jurisdictions were sufficient to meet the minimum standard. The Colombian tax administration's implementation in this regard remains unchanged, and therefore continues to meet the minimum standard.

Future rulings (ToR I.4.1.1, I.4.1.2, I.4.2.1)

247. For Colombia, future rulings are any tax rulings within scope that are issued on or after 1 April 2016.

248. In the prior year peer review report, Colombia did not have an information gathering process for the transparency framework and therefore Colombia was recommended to ensure that any future rulings within the scope of the transparency framework and all potential exchange jurisdictions are swiftly identified (ToR I.4.1.2).

249. For the year in review, the Colombian tax administration has adopted a process similar to that used to identify past rulings according to which ITAT is responsible for gathering all information on future rulings and potential exchange jurisdictions during the APAs' technical negotiations. This involves the team responsible for negotiating the APA to identify it at the point it is issued. Information on all potential exchange jurisdictions would be collected in the course of negotiating the APA. As such the prior year recommendation has been removed.

Review and supervision mechanism (ToR I.4.3)

250. In the prior year peer review report, it was determined that the Colombian tax administration's review and supervision mechanisms were sufficient to meet the minimum standard. In addition, all members of the team responsible for negotiating APAs are aware of the transparency framework obligations.

Conclusion on section A

251. Colombia has met all of the ToR for the information gathering process and no recommendations are made.

B. The exchange of information

Legal basis for spontaneous exchange of information (ToR II.5.1, II.5.2)

252. Colombia has the necessary domestic legal basis to exchange information spontaneously. Colombia notes that there are no legal or practical impediments that prevent the spontaneous exchange of information on rulings as contemplated in the Action 5 minimum standard.

253. Colombia is a party to international agreements permitting spontaneous exchange of information, including (i) the Multilateral Convention on Mutual Administrative Assistance in Tax Matters: Amended by the 2010 Protocol (OECD/Council of Europe, 2011) ("the Convention"), (ii) double tax agreements in force with 12 jurisdictions and (iii) tax information exchange agreements with one jurisdictions.[1]

Completion and exchange of templates (ToR II.5.3, II.5.4, II.5.5, II.5.6, II.5.7)

254. In the prior year peer review report, it was determined that the Colombian tax administration's completion and exchange of templates were sufficient to meet the minimum standard except for the timely exchange of information on rulings (ToR II.5.5, II.5.6) in the form required by the transparency framework (ToR II.5.3, II.5.4). For the year in review, Colombia notes that the Competent Authority is one of the parties involved in the APAs' negotiations and all relevant information related to the ruling and potential exchange jurisdictions is immediately available to the Competent Authority at the time the ruling is issued. As such, the prior year recommendation (ToR II.5.5) is removed.

255. Currently Colombia does not have any APAs in place and does not have a specific process to fill in the information required in the template contained in Annex C of the 2015 Action 5 Report (OECD, 2015). However, Colombia indicates that if future rulings are issued, the Competent Authority would require information on the ruling to be completed in accordance with the Annex C template. This would include providing a detailed summary of the transactions covered by the ruling and the transfer pricing methodology used. As such, the prior year recommendations (ToR II.5.3, II.5.4) are removed.

256. For the year in review, the timeliness of exchanges is as follows:

Past rulings in the scope of the transparency framework	Number of exchanges transmitted by 31 December 2017	Delayed exchanges		
		Number of exchanges not transmitted by 31 December 2017	Reasons for the delays	Any other comments
	N/A	1	N/A	Colombia exchanged information on the past ruling with the relevant Competent Authorities of two jurisdictions on 24 July 2018.
Future rulings in the scope of the transparency framework	Number of exchanges transmitted within three months of the information becoming available to the competent authority or immediately after legal impediments have been lifted	Delayed exchanges		
		Number of exchanges transmitted later than three months of the information on rulings becoming available to the competent authority	Reasons for the delays	Any other comments
	N/A	N/A	N/A	N/A
Total	N/A	1		

Follow up requests received for exchange of the ruling	Number	Average time to provide response	Number of requests not answered
	N/A	N/A	N/A

Conclusion on section B

257. Colombia has the necessary legal basis to undertake spontaneous exchange of information and a process for completing the templates for exchange. Colombia has met all of the ToR for the exchange of information except for completing exchanges of information on past rulings in accordance with the timelines (ToR II.5.6). Colombia is recommended to ensure that all information on past rulings is exchanged as soon as possible.

C. Statistics (ToR IV)

258. As no information on rulings was exchanged for the year in review, no statistical data can be reported.

D. Matters related to intellectual property regimes (ToR I.4.1.3)

259. Colombia does not offer an intellectual property regime for which transparency requirements under the Action 5 Report (OECD, 2015) were imposed.

Summary of recommendations on implementation of the transparency framework

Aspect of implementation of the transparency framework that should be improved	Recommendation for improvement
Colombia did not complete exchanges of information on past rulings in accordance with the timelines (ToR II.5.6). This is a continuing recommendation from the prior year peer review.	Colombia is recommended to ensure that all information on past rulings is exchanged as soon as possible.

Note

[1] Parties to the Convention are available here: www.oecd.org/tax/exchange-of-tax-information/convention-on-mutual-administrative-assistance-in-tax-matters.htm. Colombia also has bilateral agreements in force Bolivia, Canada, Chile, Czech Republic, Ecuador, India, Korea, Mexico, Peru, Portugal, Spain and Switzerland and a tax information exchange agreement with the United States.

References

OECD (2017), *BEPS Action 5 on Harmful Tax Practices – Terms of Reference and Methodology for the Conduct of the Peer Reviews of the Action 5 Transparency Framework*, OECD/G20 Base Erosion and Profit Shifting Project, OECD, Paris. www.oecd.org/tax/beps/beps-action-5-harmful-tax-practices-peer-review-transparencyframework.pdf.

OECD (2015), *Countering Harmful Tax Practices More Effectively, Taking into Account Transparency and Substance, Action 5 - 2015 Final Report*, OECD/G20 Base Erosion and Profit Shifting Project, OECD Publishing, Paris. https://doi.org/10.1787/9789264241190-en.

OECD/Council of Europe (2011), *The Multilateral Convention on Mutual Administrative Assistance in Tax Matters: Amended by the 2010 Protocol*, OECD Publishing, Paris. http://dx.doi.org/10.1787/9789264115606-en.

Congo

Congo[1] did not provide a completed peer review questionnaire to the Secretariat. It is not known whether Congo has implemented the transparency framework. Congo is recommended to ensure that it has put in place an effective information gathering process to identify all relevant past and future rulings and all potential exchange jurisdictions and to implement a review and supervision mechanism, as soon as possible (ToR I.4). Congo is recommended to put in place a domestic legal framework allowing spontaneous exchange of information on rulings if needed and to ensure the timely exchange of information on rulings in the form required by the transparency framework (ToR II.5).

It is not known whether Congo can legally issue any types of ruling within the scope of the transparency framework, [2] or whether in practice Congo issued any such rulings.

As no exchange of information on rulings was conducted, no peer input was received in respect of the exchanges of information on rulings received from Congo.

Introduction

260. This peer review covers Congo's implementation of the BEPS Action 5 transparency framework for the calendar year 2017 (year in review). The report has four parts, each relating to a key part of the ToR. Each part is discussed in turn. A summary of recommendations is included at the end of this report.

A. The information gathering process

261. Congo was not yet able to complete the peer review questionnaire. It is not known whether Congo has implemented the transparency framework.

Conclusion on section A

262. Congo is recommended to ensure that it has put in place an effective information gathering process to identify all relevant past and future rulings and all potential exchange jurisdictions and to implement a review and supervision mechanism as soon as possible (ToR I.4).

B. The exchange of information

Legal basis for spontaneous exchange of information (ToR II.5.1, II.5.2)

263. It is not known whether Congo has the necessary domestic legal basis to exchange information spontaneously. Congo is recommended to put in place a domestic legal framework allowing spontaneous exchange of information on rulings if needed (ToR II.5.1).

264. Congo currently has three agreements[3] in effect which would allow for spontaneous exchange of information under the transparency framework. Congo is not a Party to the *Multilateral Convention on Mutual Administrative Assistance in Tax Matters: Amended by the 2010 Protocol* (OECD/Council of Europe, 2011) ("the Convention"). Congo is encouraged to continue its efforts to expand its international exchange of information instruments to be able to exchange rulings. It is however noted that jurisdictions are assessed on their compliance with the transparency framework in respect of the exchange of information network in effect for the year of the particular annual review.

Completion and exchange of templates (ToR II.5.3, II.5.4, II.5.5, II.5.6, II.5.7)

265. It is not known whether Congo has put in place a process to exchange information on rulings in accordance with the form and timelines required by the transparency framework. Congo is recommended to ensure the timely exchange of information on rulings in the form required by the transparency framework.

Conclusion on section B

266. Congo is recommended to put in place a domestic legal framework allowing spontaneous exchange of information on rulings if needed and to ensure the timely exchange of information on rulings in the form required by the transparency framework (ToR II.5).

C. Statistics (ToR IV)

267. Congo did not provide statistical data for the year in review. In the absence of this information, no statistics can be reported.

D. Matters related to intellectual property regimes (ToR I.4.1.3)

268. Congo does not offer an intellectual property regime for which transparency requirements under the Action 5 Report (OECD, 2015) were imposed.

Summary of recommendations on implementation of the transparency framework

Aspect of implementation of the transparency framework that should be improved	Recommendation for improvement
It is not known whether Congo has an information gathering process in place.	Congo is recommended to ensure that it has put in place an effective information gathering process to identify all relevant past and future rulings and all potential exchange jurisdictions and to implement a review and supervision mechanism, as soon as possible.
It is not known whether Congo has a domestic legal framework allowing spontaneous exchange of information on rulings if needed and a process in place to ensure the timely exchange of information on rulings in the form required by the transparency framework.	Congo is recommended to put in place a domestic legal framework allowing spontaneous exchange of information on rulings if needed and to ensure the timely exchange of information on rulings in the form required by the transparency framework.

Notes

[1] Congo did not provide written comments on this peer review report.

[2] Note: According to publicly available information, it appears that Congo can legally issue APAs.

[3] Congo has Double Tax Agreements with France, Italy and Mauritius.

References

OECD (2017), *BEPS Action 5 on Harmful Tax Practices – Terms of Reference and Methodology for the Conduct of the Peer Reviews of the Action 5 Transparency Framework*, OECD/G20 Base Erosion and Profit Shifting Project, OECD, Paris. www.oecd.org/tax/beps/beps-action-5-harmful-tax-practices-peer-review-transparencyframework.pdf.

OECD (2015), *Countering Harmful Tax Practices More Effectively, Taking into Account Transparency and Substance, Action 5 - 2015 Final Report*, OECD/G20 Base Erosion and Profit Shifting Project, OECD Publishing, Paris. https://doi.org/10.1787/9789264241190-en.

OECD/Council of Europe (2011), *The Multilateral Convention on Mutual Administrative Assistance in Tax Matters: Amended by the 2010 Protocol*, OECD Publishing, Paris. http://dx.doi.org/10.1787/9789264115606-en.

Costa Rica

Costa Rica has met the terms of reference (ToR) for the calendar year 2017 (year in review), except for applying the "best efforts approach" for the year in review to identify all potential exchange jurisdictions for all past rulings (ToR I.4.2.2), ensuring that information on all potential exchange jurisdictions is obtained for future rulings (ToR I.4.2.1) and having in place a process to complete the templates in the form required by the transparency framework and submit them to the Competent Authority and completing exchanges of information on rulings in accordance with the timelines (ToR II.5). Costa Rica is recommended to continue to apply the "best efforts approach" to identify potential exchange jurisdictions for all past rulings, to continue its efforts to ensure that all potential exchange jurisdictions are identified swiftly for all future rulings, to continue its efforts to complete the templates for all relevant rulings and to ensure that the exchanges of information on rulings occur as soon as possible.

Costa Rica can legally issue two types of rulings within the scope of the transparency framework.

In practice, Costa Rica has issued two past rulings; and for the year in review, Costa Rica issued no future rulings within the scope of the transparency framework.

No peer input was received in respect of the exchanges of information on rulings received from Costa Rica.

Introduction

269. This peer review covers Costa Rica's implementation of the BEPS Action 5 transparency framework for the year 2017. The report has four parts, each relating to a key part of the ToR. Each part is discussed in turn. A summary of recommendations is included at the end of this report.

A. The information gathering process

270. Costa Rica can legally issue the two following types of rulings within the scope of the transparency framework: (i) cross-border unilateral advance pricing arrangements (APAs) and any other cross-border unilateral tax rulings (such as an advance tax ruling) covering transfer pricing or the application of transfer pricing principles; and (ii) permanent establishment (PE) rulings. The resolution to authorise the issuing of APAs is pending. As no APAs have been issued to date, no determination has been made as to who would be responsible for issuing them. PE rulings are issued by each local tax administration and the Large Business Directorate, following prior coordination with and based on drafting provided by the transfer pricing unit. To date, Costa Rica has issued only PE rulings.

Past rulings (ToR I.4.1.1, I.4.1.2, I.4.2.1, I.4.2.2)

271. For Costa Rica, past rulings are any tax rulings within scope that are issued either: (i) on or after 1 January 2015 but before 1 April 2017; or (ii) on or after 1 January 2012 but before 1 January 2015, provided they were still in effect as at 1 January 2015.

272. The process for identifying past rulings was conducted as follows. Rulings were maintained in separate rulings files. In the case of PE rulings, they are kept by the local tax administrations or the Large Business Directorate, which send a copy of the ruling to the transfer pricing unit. In the case of APA rulings, they are going to be kept by the transfer pricing unit. Rulings were identified according to their name, as the title of each ruling (APA or PE) matches with the categories in the transparency framework. In order to identify past rulings, the transfer pricing unit manually analysed the files and searched for the date of issuance to determine if it was within the period of validity for past rulings.

273. In order to identify potential exchange jurisdictions, information was obtained from the ruling. Information related to the jurisdiction of the head office (since Costa Rica only issued PE rulings) was already required to be provided by the taxpayer when applying for the ruling and was available to the tax administration. Information on the immediate parent company and ultimate parent company was not required to be provided in the ruling application. Costa Rica used the "best efforts approach" in order to identify these jurisdictions, which involved searching the taxpayer's file. This file contained information on the immediate parent company, but not on the ultimate parent company. Costa Rica still needs to use the "best efforts approach" to identify information on the jurisdiction of the ultimate parent company.

Future rulings (ToR I.4.1.1, I.4.1.2, I.4.2.1)

274. For Costa Rica, future rulings are any tax rulings within scope that are issued on or after 1 April 2017.

275. As was the case for past rulings, rulings are maintained in separate rulings files and identified according to their name. In order to identify future rulings, the transfer

pricing unit, which is in charge of collecting both PE and APA rulings, analyses the files and searches for the date of issuance. A new procedure is being put in place, according to which this process is undertaken as soon as any new ruling is issued. In the year in review, as no future rulings were issued, the fact that this process was not in place has not had an impact in practice.

276. In order to identify all potential exchange jurisdictions, the ruling application process will be amended together with the resolutions that regulate the issuance of APAs and PE rulings currently under review. The information on the immediate parent company and ultimate parent company will be obtained from the register of shareholders to be hold by the Central Bank. However, since this register is not yet in place, in the meantime the taxpayer will be required to provide this information when requesting the ruling. This process will be amended by the end of 2018.

Review and supervision mechanism (ToR I.4.3)

277. Senior officers were instructed on the requirements of the transparency framework and supervised the process to ensure the relevant information was captured accurately.

278. Costa Rica is currently putting in place a more formal procedure according to which the Exchange of Information (EOI) unit will be in charge of the review and supervision mechanism, including senior officers having oversight of the issuance of the tax rulings to ensure the relevant information is captured accurately.

Conclusion on section A

279. Costa Rica has met the ToR for the information gathering process, except that Costa Rica did not apply the "best efforts approach" for the year in review to identify all potential exchange jurisdictions for all past rulings (ToR I.4.2.2) and does not yet ensure all potential exchange jurisdictions would be identified for future rulings (ToR I.4.2.1). Costa Rica is recommended to continue to apply the "best efforts approach" to identify potential exchange jurisdictions for all past rulings and to continue its efforts to ensure that all potential exchange jurisdictions are identified swiftly for all future rulings. It is noted that Costa Rica identified the jurisdictions of the ultimate parent company in July 2018, by using the "best efforts approach".

B. The exchange of information

Legal basis for spontaneous exchange of information (ToR II.5.1, II.5.2)

280. Costa Rica has the necessary domestic legal basis to exchange information spontaneously. Costa Rica notes that there are no legal or practical impediments that prevent the spontaneous exchange of information on rulings as contemplated in the Action 5 minimum standard.

281. Costa Rica is a party to international agreements permitting spontaneous exchange of information, including (i) the *Multilateral Convention on Mutual Administrative Assistance in Tax Matters: Amended by the 2010 Protocol* (OECD/Council of Europe, 2011) ("the Convention") and (ii) double tax agreements in force with two jurisdictions.[1]

Completion and exchange of templates (ToR II.5.3, II.5.4, II.5.5, II.5.6, II.5.7)

282. For the year in review, the procedure to fill in the information was under revision. According to the new procedure, the transfer pricing unit will be in charge of filling in the template for both APA and PE rulings. The officers of the transfer pricing unit will be trained in order for them to deliver the templates already in the form of the XML schema to the EOI unit. Costa Rica has confirmed that their approach to the completion of the summary section of the template will use the internal FHTP suggested guidance, which will be an Annex to the new procedure.

283. Costa Rica is working on a procedure to establish a time limit for the unit that issues the ruling to send the relevant information to the EOI unit. With respect to past rulings, the information was provided to the EOI unit in mid-2018, and which sent the templates to relevant jurisdictions via e-mail. With respect to future rulings, every time a new ruling is issued the transfer pricing unit will inform the EOI Unit.

284. The EOI unit will revise the templates and send them to the Competent Authority for its signature, receive the signed templates from the Competent Authority and finally perform the exchanges via encrypted email with the relevant jurisdictions. The new procedure also envisages designating the head of the tax treaties unit to review the templates before the exchange. The EOI Unit will process the XML in the system and then have three months to send the information to the relevant jurisdictions.

285. For the year in review, the timeliness of exchanges is as follows:

Past rulings in the scope of the transparency framework	Number of exchanges transmitted by 31 December 2017	Delayed exchanges		
		Number of exchanges not transmitted by 31 December 2017	Reasons for the delays	Any other comments
	0	2	See below	Costa Rica exchanged information on the past rulings in July 2018.
Future rulings in the scope of the transparency framework	Number of exchanges transmitted within three months of the information becoming available to the competent authority or immediately after legal impediments have been lifted	Delayed exchanges		
		Number of exchanges transmitted later than three months of the information on rulings becoming available to the competent authority	Reasons for the delays	Any other comments
	N/A	N/A	N/A	N/A
Total	0	2		

Follow up requests received for exchange of the ruling	Number	Average time to provide response	Number of requests not answered
	N/A	N/A	N/A

286. Costa Rica explained that the transmission delay for exchanges of information on the two past rulings is due to the implementation of the new procedure for the exchange of information process, and the time take to apply the "best efforts approach" to complete the missing information. Costa Rica confirmed that the identified rulings were exchanged in July 2018 and the two rulings were processed in the template format for the exchange of information.

Conclusion on section B

287. Costa Rica has the necessary legal basis to undertake spontaneous exchange of information. In the year in review, Costa Rica was putting in place procedures to perform exchange of information, including filling the templates with the necessary information required on relevant rulings in the form of Annex C of the Action 5 Report (OECD, 2015) or the XML Schema, to provide them to the EOI unit without undue delay and to exchange them within the timelines required by the transparency framework. Costa Rica is recommended to continue its efforts to complete the templates for all relevant rulings and to ensure that the exchanges of information on rulings occur as soon as possible (ToR II.5).

C. Statistics (ToR IV)

288. As no information on rulings was exchanged for the year in review, no statistical data can be reported.

D. Matters related to intellectual property regimes (ToR I.4.1.3)

289. Costa Rica does not offer an intellectual property regime for which transparency requirements under the Action 5 Report (OECD, 2015) were imposed.

Summary of recommendations on implementation of the transparency framework

Note

Aspect of implementation of the transparency framework that should be improved	Recommendation for improvement
For the year in review, Costa Rica did not apply the "best efforts approach" to identify all potential exchange jurisdictions for all past rulings.	Costa Rica is recommended to continue to apply the "best efforts approach" to identify potential exchange jurisdictions for all past rulings.
Costa Rica does not yet ensure that information on all potential exchange jurisdictions is always obtained for future rulings.	Costa Rica is recommended to continue its efforts to ensure that all potential exchange jurisdictions are identified swiftly for all future rulings.
In the year in review, Costa Rica had not yet finalised the process to complete the templates and submit them to the Competent Authority and had not undertaken any exchanges of information.	Costa Rica is recommended to continue its efforts to complete the templates for all relevant rulings and to ensure that the exchanges of information on rulings occur as soon as possible.

References

OECD (2017), *BEPS Action 5 on Harmful Tax Practices – Terms of Reference and Methodology for the Conduct of the Peer Reviews of the Action 5 Transparency Framework*, OECD/G20 Base Erosion and Profit Shifting Project, OECD, Paris. www.oecd.org/tax/beps/beps-action-5-harmful-tax-practices-peer-review-transparencyframework.pdf.

OECD (2015), *Countering Harmful Tax Practices More Effectively, Taking into Account Transparency and Substance, Action 5 - 2015 Final Report*, OECD/G20 Base Erosion and Profit Shifting Project, OECD Publishing, Paris. https://doi.org/10.1787/9789264241190-en.

OECD/Council of Europe (2011), *The Multilateral Convention on Mutual Administrative Assistance in Tax Matters: Amended by the 2010 Protocol*, OECD Publishing, Paris. http://dx.doi.org/10.1787/9789264115606-en.

Côte d'Ivoire

Côte d'Ivoire has met the terms of reference (ToR) for the calendar year 2017 (year in review) that can be met in the absence of rulings being issued.[1]

Côte d'Ivoire does not issue any type of rulings within the scope of the transparency framework. Côte d'Ivoire only issues interpretative rulings. These tax rulings are not binding for the tax authorities and are therefore not considered rulings as defined in the Action 5 report (OECD, 2015). In the event that Côte d'Ivoire put in place the administrative process to issue rulings within the scope of the transparency framework, Côte d'Ivoire notes that it would implement the transparency framework obligations.

As there were no rulings issued, no exchange of information was required. Therefore no peer input was received in respect of exchanges of information on rulings received from Côte d'Ivoire.

Introduction

290. This peer review covers Côte d'Ivoire's implementation of the BEPS Action 5 transparency framework for the year 2017. The report has four parts, each relating to a key part of the ToR. Each part is discussed in turn. A summary of recommendations is included at the end of this report.

A. The information gathering process

291. As no rulings are issued, this section is not assessed.

B. The exchange of information

292. As no rulings are issued, this section is not assessed.

C. Statistics (ToR IV)

293. As no rulings are issued, no statistical data can be reported.

D. Matters related to intellectual property regimes (ToR I.4.1.3)

294. Côte d'Ivoire does not offer an intellectual property regime for which transparency requirements under the Action 5 Report (OECD, 2015) were imposed.

Summary of recommendations on implementation of the transparency framework

Aspect of implementation of the transparency framework that should be improved	Recommendation for improvement
	No recommendations are made.

Note

[1] Côte d'Ivoire did not provide written comments on this peer review report.

Reference

OECD (2017), *BEPS Action 5 on Harmful Tax Practices – Terms of Reference and Methodology for the Conduct of the Peer Reviews of the Action 5 Transparency Framework*, OECD/G20 Base Erosion and Profit Shifting Project, OECD, Paris. www.oecd.org/tax/beps/beps-action-5-harmful-tax-practices-peer-review-transparencyframework.pdf.

OECD (2015), *Countering Harmful Tax Practices More Effectively, Taking into Account Transparency and Substance, Action 5 - 2015 Final Report*, OECD/G20 Base Erosion and Profit Shifting Project, OECD Publishing, Paris. https://doi.org/10.1787/9789264241190-en.

Croatia

Croatia has met all aspects of the terms of reference (ToR) for the calendar year 2017 (year in review) and no recommendations are made.

Croatia can legally issue four types of rulings within the scope of the transparency framework.

In practice, Croatia issued no rulings within the scope of the transparency framework. For the year in review, there was one APA request which was under negotiation.

As there were no rulings issued, no exchange of information was required. Therefore no peer input was received in respect of the exchanges of information on rulings received from Croatia.

Introduction

295. This peer review covers Croatia's implementation of the BEPS Action 5 transparency framework for the year 2017. The report has four parts, each relating to a key part of the ToR. Each part is discussed in turn. A summary of recommendations is included at the end of this report.

A. The information gathering process

296. Croatia can legally issue the four following type of rulings within the scope of the transparency framework: (i) cross-border unilateral advance pricing arrangements (APAs) and any other cross-border unilateral tax rulings (such as an advance tax ruling) covering transfer pricing or the application of transfer pricing principles, (ii) unilateral downward adjustments; (iii) permanent establishment rulings; and (iv) conduit rulings. The tax administration is responsible for issuing rulings.

Past rulings (ToR I.4.1.1, I.4.1.2, I.4.2.1, I.4.2.2)

297. For Croatia, past rulings are any tax rulings within scope that are issued either: (i) on or after 1 January 2015 but before 1 April 2017; or (ii) on or after 1 January 2012 but before 1 January 2015, provided they were still in effect as at 1 January 2015.

298. Croatia can only issue advance tax rulings since 1 January 2016 and APAs since 1 January 2017. Before that date, Croatia did not have the relevant domestic legal framework in place which would authorise the issuance of any taxpayer specific rulings.

299. Croatia does not have a separate unit responsible for the rulings but forms a different expert team with officers from the Tax Administration, Head Office, Regional Offices and the Office for Large Taxpayers each time a taxpayer requests a ruling. The team usually consists of a profit tax advisor, an audit advisor and a legal advisor.

300. The expert teams were responsible for identifying past rulings. After a ruling is issued, it is electronically stored on the "share portal" and is made available to the members of the expert teams that have participated in the issuing of the ruling, the management and with the particular team working on the risk analysis for audit purposes. The expert teams reviewed the share portal and identified rulings within the scope of the transparency framework that fell into the period of validity for past rulings.

301. In order to identify potential exchange jurisdictions with respect to the past rulings, the expert team checked the available data in the taxpayer's internal file and the data from the tax administration information system. When a taxpayer requests a ruling, the request has to include all information on relevant exchange jurisdictions, which would cover all potential exchange jurisdictions for the purposes of the transparency framework. This information was gathered by the expert team.

302. If necessary, the taxpayer is required to submit additional information. In addition, a preliminary interview is held with the taxpayer upon starting the ruling process. However, as in practice, Croatia did not issue any past rulings, it was not relevant to identify the potential exchange jurisdictions.

Future rulings (ToR I.4.1.1, I.4.1.2, I.4.2.1)

303. For Croatia, future rulings are any tax rulings within scope that are issued on or after 1 April 2017.

304. The information gathering process for future rulings is identical to the process for past rulings.

Review and supervision mechanism (ToR I.4.3)

305. The accuracy of the information-gathering process is ensured by the Competent Authority that supervises the process for all of the issued rulings.

Conclusion on section A

306. Croatia has met all of the ToR for the information gathering process and no recommendations are made.

B. The exchange of information

Legal basis for spontaneous exchange of information (ToR II.5.1, II.5.2)

307. Croatia has the necessary domestic legal basis to exchange information spontaneously. Croatia notes that there are no legal or practical impediments that prevent the spontaneous exchange of information on rulings as contemplated in the Action 5 minimum standard.

308. Croatia is a party to international agreements permitting spontaneous exchange of information, including (i) the *Multilateral Convention on Mutual Administrative Assistance in Tax Matters: Amended by the 2010 Protocol* (OECD/Council of Europe, 2011) ("the Convention"), (ii) the Directive 2011/16/EU with all other European Union Member States and (iii) double tax agreements in force with 62 jurisdictions.[1]

Completion and exchange of templates (ToR II.5.3, II.5.4, II.5.5, II.5.6, II.5.7)

309. The expert teams that are responsible for issuing the tax rulings are obliged to complete the template contained in Annex C of the Action 5 Report (OECD, 2015) and to send this template to the Competent Authority within one month after the date of issuing. When completing the summary section of the template, the expert teams use the internal FHTP suggested guidance. Croatia has indicated that if a relevant ruling were issued in the future, it would be exchanged within three months with the relevant exchange jurisdictions after it is received by the Competent Authority.

310. As no rulings within the scope of the transparency framework have been issued in practice, Croatia was not required to complete any exchanges of information and there is no data to report on the timeliness of exchanges.

Conclusion on section B

311. Croatia has the necessary legal basis for spontaneous exchange of information, and a process for completing the templates in a timely way. As no rulings in the scope of the transparency framework have been issued, no exchanges were required for the year in review. Croatia has met all of the ToR for the exchange of information process and no recommendations are made.

C. Statistics (ToR IV)

312. As there were no rulings required to be exchanged by Croatia in the year of review, no statistics can be reported.

D. Matters related to intellectual property regimes (ToR I.4.1.3)

313. Croatia does not offer an intellectual property regime for which transparency requirements under the Action 5 Report (OECD, 2015) were imposed.

Summary of recommendations on implementation of the transparency framework

Aspect of implementation of the transparency framework that should be improved	Recommendation for improvement
	No recommendations are made.

Note

1 Parties to the Convention are available here: www.oecd.org/tax/exchange-of-tax-information/convention-on-mutual-administrative-assistance-in-tax-matters.htm. Croatia also has bilateral agreements in force with Albania, Armenia, Austria, Azerbaijan, Belarus, Belgium, Bosnia and Herzegovina, Bulgaria, Canada, Chile, China (People's Republic of), Czech Republic, Denmark, Estonia, Finland, Former Yugoslav Republic of Macedonia, France, Georgia, Germany, Greece, Hungary, Iceland, India, Indonesia, Iran, Ireland, Israel, Italy, Jordan, Korea, Kosovo, Kuwait, Latvia, Lithuania, Luxembourg, Malaysia, Malta, Mauritius, Morocco, Moldova, Montenegro, Netherlands, Norway, Oman, Poland, Portugal, Qatar, Romania, Russia, San Marino, Serbia, Slovak Republic, Slovenia, South Africa, Spain, Syrian Arab Republic, Sweden, Switzerland, Turkey, Turkmenistan, Ukraine and United Kingdom.

References

OECD (2017), *BEPS Action 5 on Harmful Tax Practices – Terms of Reference and Methodology for the Conduct of the Peer Reviews of the Action 5 Transparency Framework*, OECD/G20 Base Erosion and Profit Shifting Project, OECD, Paris. www.oecd.org/tax/beps/beps-action-5-harmful-tax-practices-peer-review-transparencyframework.pdf.

OECD (2015), *Countering Harmful Tax Practices More Effectively, Taking into Account Transparency and Substance, Action 5 - 2015 Final Report*, OECD/G20 Base Erosion and Profit Shifting Project, OECD Publishing, Paris. https://doi.org/10.1787/9789264241190-en.

OECD/Council of Europe (2011), *The Multilateral Convention on Mutual Administrative Assistance in Tax Matters: Amended by the 2010 Protocol*, OECD Publishing, Paris. http://dx.doi.org/10.1787/9789264115606-en.

Curaçao

Curaçao has met the terms of reference (ToR) for the calendar year 2017 (year in review), except for identifying which category each ruling falls into (ToR I.4.1.2) and completing exchanges of information on rulings in accordance with the timelines (ToR II.5.6). Curaçao is recommended to continue to finalise its information gathering process identifying all past and future rulings as soon as possible and to continue its efforts to ensure all information on past and future rulings is exchanged as soon as possible.

Curaçao can legally issue five types of rulings within the scope of the transparency framework.

In practice, Curaçao has issued an estimated number of 3 630 past rulings; and for the year in review, Curaçao issued an estimated number of 320 future rulings within the scope of the transparency framework.

No peer input was received in respect of the exchanges of information on rulings received from Curaçao.

Introduction

314. This peer review covers Curaçao's implementation of the BEPS Action 5 transparency framework for the year 2017. The report has four parts, each relating to a key part of the ToR. Each part is discussed in turn. A summary of recommendations is included at the end of this report.

A. The information gathering process

315. Curaçao can legally issue the five following types of rulings within the scope of the transparency framework: i) taxpayer specific rulings related to preferential regimes;[1] ii) cross-border unilateral advance pricing arrangements (APAs) and any other cross-border unilateral tax rulings (such as an advance tax ruling) covering transfer pricing or the application of transfer pricing principles; iii) cross-border rulings giving a unilateral downward adjustment to the taxpayer's taxable profits in the country giving the ruling; iv) permanent establishment (PE) rulings; and v) related conduit rulings. In Curaçao, the ruling office in the tax administration, which is an agency of the Ministry of Finance of Curaçao, is in charge of issuing the tax rulings.

316. The process for gathering information about past rulings is explained first, followed by the process for gathering information about future rulings.

Past rulings (ToR I.4.1.1, I.4.1.2, I.4.2.1, I.4.2.2)

317. For Curaçao, past rulings are any tax rulings within scope that are issued either: (i) on or after 1 January 2015 but before 1 April 2017; or (ii) on or after 1 January 2012 but before 1 January 2015, provided they were still in effect as at 1 January 2015.

318. The process for identifying past rulings was conducted as follows. The tax rulings are stored in a database on the basis of the issuance date. The database also contains the ruling reference number and the name of the taxpayer. The rulings team used the database to identify all possibly relevant rulings, and then checked the content of the ruling. This included reading each ruling to conduct an analysis of the requested benefits, the review of the issuance date to determine the period of validity for past rulings, as well as an examination of the structure charts of the company to determine if there were likely to be cross-border aspects. The ruling team additionally matched the text of the granted tax rulings with the tax returns of the taxpayers. Where relevant, the ruling was identified and registered according to its corresponding category under the transparency framework.

319. By the end of 2017 Curaçao completed its review process and identified the rulings issued in the past. Currently Curacao is in the process of reviewing the past rulings in order to confirm that they are cross border rulings and therefore within the scope of the transparency framework. This process also entails identifying which category each ruling falls into, as there has been a large number of rulings, and many of these fall into more than one category. This process, including the exchange of the rulings under the transparency agenda, will be completed by the first quarter of 2019.

320. In order to identify the exchange jurisdictions, the same review process was used as this information is usually included in each ruling. Curaçao has used the "best efforts approach" in cases where information on all the relevant jurisdictions was not contained in the ruling, whereby Curaçao approached the relevant taxpayers and tax advisors to assist with completing the templates and to provide the structure chart to identify all relevant jurisdictions.

Future rulings (ToR I.4.1.1, I.4.1.2, I.4.2.1)

321. For Curaçao, future rulings are any tax rulings within scope that are issued on or after 1 April 2017.

322. As is the case for past rulings, the tax rulings are stored in a database on the basis of the issuance date. The database also contains the ruling reference number and the name of the taxpayer. The rulings team checks the database each month and then reviews the content of the ruling, including an analysis of the requested benefits as well as of the structure charts of the company. The ruling team additionally matches the text of the granted tax rulings with the tax returns of the taxpayers. Consequently, the ruling is identified and registered as such in its corresponding category within the transparency framework scope.

323. The same review process is used to identify the exchange jurisdictions. In respect of some future rulings for the year in review, information was not available to identify all relevant jurisdictions. In these cases, the taxpayer has been requested to provide an updated structure chart in order for the Curaçao tax administration to identify all the necessary potential exchange jurisdictions. This enabled the Curaçao tax administration to identify all potential exchange jurisdictions.

324. Curaçao has designed a new streamlined ruling practice, and taxpayers have been informed that the procedure will apply for a ruling issued in 2018. The new prerequisites were published in February 2018, which provide that in order to obtain a ruling the taxpayer must provide an updated structure chart and a completed template when submitting a request for a tax ruling. Information regarding the type of rulings and the jurisdictions with which the rulings have to be exchanged will be captured from this template and thoroughly checked by the Ruling Team. No ruling will be issued if these prerequisites are not provided or information is found to be incorrect following the verification by the Curacao Tax Authority and therefore it is ensured that all information is always obtained. In addition Curaçao is currently in the process to digitalise the ruling request procedure through an electronic online system which is expected to be implemented in the year 2019. The new procedure will affect the information gathering process and the exchanges activities performed in 2018 and will be reviewed in the subsequent peer reviews.

Review and supervision mechanism (ToR I.4.3)

325. Curaçao had a review and supervision mechanism in place for the year in review. Officials in charge of complying with the transparency framework both within the rulings team in the tax administration and the Ministry of Finance/Directorate of Fiscal Affairs have received internal guidance about the transparency framework requirements. One senior officer is in charge of providing oversight on the process and a review board within the rulings team will ensure that the relevant information is captured accurately.

Conclusion on section A

326. Curaçao completed its review process and identified all of the past and future rulings issued. However Curaçao has not yet completed the process of reviewing the remaining templates of past and future rulings in order to confirm that they are cross border rulings and therefore within the scope of the transparency framework and to identify which category each ruling falls into (ToR I.4.1.2). Curaçao is recommended to

continue to finalise its information gathering process identifying all past and future rulings as soon as possible.

B. The exchange of information

Legal basis for spontaneous exchange of information (ToR II.5.1, II.5.2)

327. Curaçao has the necessary domestic legal basis to exchange information spontaneously. Curaçao notes that there are no legal or practical impediments that prevent the spontaneous exchange of information on rulings as contemplated in the Action 5 minimum standard.

328. Curaçao is a party to international agreements permitting spontaneous exchange of information, including: (i) *Multilateral Convention on Mutual Administrative Assistance in Tax Matters:* Amended *by the 2010 Protocol* (OECD/Council of Europe, 2011) ("the Convention") and (ii) double tax agreements in force with two jurisdictions.[2]

Completion and exchange of templates (ToR II.5.3, II.5.4, II.5.5, II.5.6, II.5.7)

329. The tax administration (i.e. the ruling team) is in charge of completing the templates, using Annex C of the BEPS Action 5 Report. Templates are sent to the Directorate of Fiscal Affairs of the Ministry of Finance together with a copy of the ruling, the structure chart and the analysis by the Curaçao tax administration. The Directorate of Fiscal Affairs compares the information contained in the template with the information contained in the ruling and the structure chart. If the information is correct, the template is sent to the Competent Authority to be exchanged. If not, corrections are made by the Directorate of Fiscal Affairs in dialogue with the Curaçao tax administration and the revised template is then sent to the Competent Authority to be exchanged. Currently a postal courier service is used to securely deliver the templates to the exchange jurisdictions. A digitalised system for the spontaneous exchange of information on tax rulings will be operational in the year 2019.

330. For past and future rulings, the templates were sent to the Directorate of Fiscal Affairs in November and December 2017. According to the new procedure under development, the completion of the template by the rulings team is part of the ruling request procedure to ensure that the information can be sent to the Directorate of Fiscal Affairs very shortly after the ruling is issued. At the end of each month, the tax administration provides the Directorate of Fiscal Affairs with the templates, the structure charts and a copy of the rulings issued that month. With regard to the completion of the summary section, the templates provide a summary of the applicable regime and a summary of the specific agreements made between the Tax Inspectorate and the taxpayer with respect to how certain income and costs will be treated in Curaçao.

331. For the year in review, the timeliness of exchanges is as follows:

Past rulings in the scope of the transparency framework	Number of exchanges transmitted by 31 December 2017	Delayed exchanges		
		Number of exchanges not transmitted by 31 December 2017	Reasons for the delays	Any other comments
	146	3 505	Curaçao has a large amount of rulings. Curaçao is currently identifying the rulings to be able to exchange all the cross border rulings.	
Future rulings in the scope of the transparency framework	Number of exchanges transmitted within three months of the information becoming available to the competent authority or immediately after legal impediments have been lifted	Delayed exchanges		
		Number of exchanges transmitted later than three months of the information on rulings becoming available to the competent authority	Reasons for the delays	Any other comments
	12	296	See below	
Total	158	3 801		

Follow up requests received for exchange of the ruling	Number	Average time to provide response	Number of requests not answered
	N/A	N/A	N/A

332. Curaçao explained that the delays originated from the analysis of the tax rulings required to classify and categorise them as well as the determination of the relevant exchange jurisdictions. These delays will be remedied by training additional staff at the Curaçao tax administration and with the application of the new procedures when issuing a ruling, supported by monthly monitoring of progress. Curaçao expects to complete the exchange of remaining past and future rulings by the first quarter of 2019.

Conclusion on section B

333. Curaçao has the necessary legal basis for spontaneous exchange of information and a process for completing the templates in a timely way. Curaçao experienced significant delays in exchanging past and future rulings mostly due to the administrative burden which stems from the issuance of a large number of rulings within the scope of the transparency framework. Curaçao has met all of the ToR for the exchange of information other than the timely exchange of information on past and future rulings (ToR II.5.6). Curaçao is recommended to continue its efforts to ensure all information on past and future rulings is exchanged as soon as possible.

C. Statistics (ToR IV)

334. The statistics for the year in review are as follows:[3]

Category of ruling	Number of exchanges	Jurisdictions exchanged with
Ruling related to a preferential regime	306	Andorra, Australia, Barbados, Belgium, Belize, Brazil, Canada, China (People's Republic of), Denmark, France, Germany, Hungary, Isle of Man, Israel, Italy, Jersey, Liechtenstein, Luxembourg, Malta, Mauritius, Mexico, Netherlands, Nigeria, Norway, Portugal, Russia, Singapore, Spain, Switzerland, United Kingdom, United States
Cross-border unilateral advance pricing arrangements (APAs) and any other cross-border unilateral tax rulings (such as an advance tax ruling) covering transfer pricing or the application of transfer pricing principles	4	Andorra, Netherlands
Cross-border rulings providing for a unilateral downward adjustment to the taxpayer's taxable profits that is not directly reflected in the taxpayer's financial / commercial accounts	4	Guernsey, Luxembourg
Permanent establishment rulings	2	Netherlands, United States
Related party conduit rulings	N/A	N/A
De minimis rule	N/A	N/A
IP regimes: total exchanges on taxpayers benefitting from the third category of IP assets, new entrants benefitting from grandfathered IP regimes; and taxpayers making use of the option to treat the nexus ratio as a rebuttable presumption	N/A	N/A
Total	316	

D. Matters related to intellectual property regimes (ToR I.4.1.3)

335. Curaçao offers two preferential regimes, which also offer benefits to income from intellectual property ("IP regime").[4] However no transparency requirements were relevant, as follows:

- ***New entrants benefitting from the grandfathered IP regime***: not applicable for the year in review, because during the year in review, Curaçao was in the process of amending/abolishing the two regimes and had not taken a decision yet on whether it would provide grandfathering to existing taxpayers. Should Curaçao provide grandfathering to taxpayers that entered the regime after the publication of the 2017 Progress Report, which occurred on 16 October 2017, then the enhanced transparency requirements will apply and this will be taken into account during the subsequent peer review.
- ***Third category of IP assets***: not applicable to these regimes, which in 2017 were in the process of being amended.
- ***Taxpayers making use of the option to treat the nexus ratio as a rebuttable presumption***: not applicable to these regimes, which in 2017 were in the process of being amended.

Summary of recommendations on implementation of the transparency framework

Aspect of implementation of the transparency framework that should be improved	Recommendation for improvement
The information gathering process is still underway in Curaçao with respect to past and future rulings and the classification of these rulings under each category.	Curaçao is recommended to continue to finalise its information gathering process identifying all past and future rulings as soon as possible.
Curaçao experienced delays in exchanging information on past and future rulings.	Curaçao is recommended to continue its efforts to ensure all information on past and future rulings is exchanged as soon as possible.

Notes

1 With respect to the following preferential regimes: 1) export facility; 2) tax exempt entity; 3) free zone; and 4) offshore regimes. The offshore regime has been abolished in 2001 and is grandfathered for fiscal years preceding 30 June 2019.

2 Parties to the Convention are available here: www.oecd.org/tax/exchange-of-tax-information/convention-on-mutual-administrative-assistance-in-tax-matters.htm. Curaçao also has bilateral agreements with the Netherlands and Norway.

3 Curaçao issues dual category which have as main element a preferential regime but can also contain one of the other four categories mentioned above. In terms of counting, these dual category ruling have been included into the "preferential regime" category. Only when a ruling relates exclusively to one of the categories mentioned above, it is counted in that category.

4 These regimes are: 1) Export facility and 2) Tax exempt entity.

References

OECD (2017), *BEPS Action 5 on Harmful Tax Practices – Terms of Reference and Methodology for the Conduct of the Peer Reviews of the Action 5 Transparency Framework*, OECD/G20 Base Erosion and Profit Shifting Project, OECD, Paris. www.oecd.org/tax/beps/beps-action-5-harmful-tax-practices-peer-review-transparencyframework.pdf.

OECD (2015), *Countering Harmful Tax Practices More Effectively, Taking into Account Transparency and Substance, Action 5 - 2015 Final Report*, OECD/G20 Base Erosion and Profit Shifting Project, OECD Publishing, Paris. https://doi.org/10.1787/9789264241190-en.

OECD/Council of Europe (2011), *The Multilateral Convention on Mutual Administrative Assistance in Tax Matters: Amended by the 2010 Protocol*, OECD Publishing, Paris. http://dx.doi.org/10.1787/9789264115606-en.

Czech Republic

The Czech Republic has met the all aspects of the terms of reference (ToR) for the calendar year 2017 (year in review) except for the timely exchange of information on past and future rulings (ToR II.5.6). This issue is continuing from the prior year peer review report. The Czech Republic is recommended to ensure that all information on past and future rulings is exchanged as soon as possible.

In the year of review[1] the Czech Republic could legally issue one type of rulings within the scope of the transparency framework.

In practice, the Czech Republic has issued 48 past rulings; for the period 1 April 2016 - 31 December 2016, the Czech Republic issued five future rulings; and for the year in review, the Czech Republic issued 11 future rulings within the scope of the transparency framework.

Peer input was received from one jurisdiction in the respect of the exchanges of information on rulings from the Czech Republic. The input was positive, noting that the information was in a correct format and received in a timely manner.

Introduction

336. This peer review covers the Czech Republic's implementation of the BEPS Action 5 transparency framework for the year 2017. The report has four parts, each relating to a key part of the ToR. Each part is discussed in turn. A summary of recommendations is included at the end of this report.

A. The information gathering process

337. In the year of review the Czech Republic could legally issue one type of rulings within the scope of the transparency framework: cross-border unilateral advance pricing agreements (APAs) and any other cross-border unilateral tax rulings (such as an advance tax ruling) covering transfer pricing or the application of transfer pricing principles. Rulings are issued by the General Financial Directorate, with rulings issued to large taxpayers being issued by a special office and other rulings being issued by local tax administrators.

Past rulings (ToR I.4.1.1, I.4.1.2, I.4.2.1, I.4.2.2)

338. For the Czech Republic, past rulings are any tax rulings within scope that are issued either: (i) on or after 1 January 2014 but before 1 April 2016; or (ii) on or after 1 January 2010 but before 1 January 2014, provided they were still in effect as at 1 January 2014.

339. In the prior year peer review report, it was determined that the Czech Republic tax administration's undertakings to identify past rulings and all potential exchange jurisdictions were sufficient to meet the minimum standard. In the course of exchanging information on certain past rulings in 2017, the Competent Authority detected that for some past rulings, information had to be exchanged with additional jurisdictions than had been indicated in the database.

340. After detecting this issue, the Czech Republic conducted a complete review of all past rulings and amended the information gathering procedures. The subsequent revision of the rulings in scope led to the identification of eight more exchanges with on past rulings that had to be transmitted, including two exchanges with new Inclusive Framework members. In order to ensure that this issue does not occur in the future, the Czech Republic amended its identification process. As a standard procedure the ruling is now forwarded to the Competent Authority to double check the correct identification of all potential exchange jurisdictions. This issue has therefore been resolved and is therefore considered not a recurring issue. It is determined that the Czech Republic tax administration's implementation meets the minimum standard.

Future rulings (ToR I.4.1.1, I.4.1.2, I.4.2.1)

341. For the Czech Republic, future rulings are any tax rulings within scope that are issued on or after 1 April 2016.

342. In the prior year peer review report, it was determined that the Czech Republic's process to identify future rulings and all potential exchange jurisdictions was sufficient to meet the minimum standard. After amending the information gathering process to identify all potential exchange jurisdictions as noted above, it is determined that the Czech Republic's implementation meets the minimum standard.

Review and supervision mechanism (ToR I.4.3)

343. In the prior year peer review report, it was determined that the Czech Republic's review and supervision mechanisms were sufficient to meet the minimum standard. This was enhanced with the additional review process conducted in the year of review. The Czech Republic's implementation therefore meets the minimum standard.

Conclusion on section A

344. The Czech Republic has met all of the ToR for the information gathering process and no recommendations are made.

B. The exchange of information

Legal basis for spontaneous exchange of information (ToR II.5.1, II.5.2)

345. The Czech Republic has the necessary domestic legal basis to exchange information spontaneously. The Czech Republic notes that there are no legal or practical impediments that prevent the spontaneous exchange of information on rulings as contemplated in the Action 5 minimum standard.

346. The Czech Republic is a party to international agreements permitting spontaneous exchange of information, including (i) *the Multilateral Convention on Mutual Administrative Assistance in Tax Matters; Amended by the 2010 Protocol* (OECD/Council of Europe, 2011) ("the Convention"), (ii) the Directive 2011/16/EU with all other European Union Member States and (iii) double tax agreements in force with 87 jurisdictions.[2]

Completion and exchange of templates (ToR II.5.3, II.5.4, II.5.5, II.5.6, II.5.7)

347. In the prior year peer review report, it was determined that the Czech Republic's completion of the templates were sufficient to meet the minimum standard. In the prior year report, it was noted that the exchanges with EU member states were planned to take place in accordance with timelines under the EU Directive, and for non-EU member states in accordance with the timelines set out in the transparency framework. As such, the Czech Republic was recommended to exchange all information on past rulings as soon as possible, and to apply the timelines for future rulings as set out in the transparency framework.

348. It is noted that the Czech Republic continues to apply the EU timelines, i.e. the exchanges of information on past rulings took place by 31 December 2017, and the exchanges of information on future rulings are carried out within three months after the end of the calendar half-year in which these rulings were issued, regardless whether the exchange is transmitted to EU Member States or other jurisdictions. The Czech Republic notes that it prefers to have a single timeline system in order to avoid delays.

349. The Czech Republic confirms that it uses the internal FHTP suggested guidance for completing the summary section for information exchanged under the transparency framework. The summary section therefore contains a description of the case with information including the subject the transfer pricing method applied and where is appropriate the value of the transaction.

350. The timeliness of exchanges in the year of review is as follows:

Past rulings in the scope of the transparency framework	Number of exchanges transmitted by 31 December 2017	Delayed exchanges		
		Number of exchanges not transmitted by 31 December 2017	Reasons for the delays	Any other comments
	29	45	Delays occurred due to an one-time additional review process noted in section A, and the time taken for manual review in complicated cases.	Two past rulings had to be exchanged with new Inclusive Framework members; of the delayed exchanges 43 were sent by June 2018, and the remaining two exchanges are expected to be sent before the end of 2018.
Future rulings in the scope of the transparency framework	Number of exchanges transmitted within three months of the information becoming available to the competent authority or immediately after legal impediments have been lifted	Delayed exchanges		
		Number of exchanges transmitted later than three months of the information on rulings becoming available to the competent authority	Reasons for the delays	Any other comments
	4	30	The Czech Republic continues to apply the EU timeline for the exchange of information; in complicated cases the delay also exceeds the EU timelines.	All delayed exchanges were sent by May 2018.
Total	33	75		

Follow up requests received for exchange of the ruling	Number	Average time to provide response	Number of requests not answered
	0	N/A	N/A

351. The Czech Republic experienced significant delays in exchanging information on past rulings and is experiencing delays in the exchange of information on future rulings, not only due to the application of the EU timelines but in more complex cases also exceeding those timelines. The Czech Republic points out that it amended its processes in the year of review in order to identify all potential exchange jurisdictions which led to an increase of work for the Competent Authority, which is now not only transferring information from the database into the template but manually reviewing each ruling itself. The Czech Republic is currently improving this process in order to become more effective and to comply with the EU timelines.

Conclusion on section B

352. The Czech Republic has the necessary legal basis for spontaneous exchange of information and a process for completing the templates for exchange. However, the Czech Republic has still not exchanged information on all past rulings and experienced

significant delays in the exchange of information on future rulings (ToR II.5.6). The recommendation from the prior year peer review report is therefore retained, and the Czech Republic is recommended to ensure that all information on past and future rulings is exchanged as soon as possible.

C. Statistics (ToR IV)

353. The statistics for the year in review are as follows:

Category of ruling	Number of exchanges	Jurisdictions exchanged with
Rulings related to preferential regimes	N/A	N/A
Cross-border unilateral advance pricing agreements (APAs) and any other cross-border unilateral tax rulings (such as an advance tax ruling) covering transfer pricing or the application of transfer pricing principles	33	Belgium, Bosnia and Herzegovina, Croatia, Cyprus[3], Denmark, Former Yugoslav Republic of Macedonia, Germany, Hungary, Italy, Luxembourg, Netherlands, Poland, Serbia, Slovak Republic, Sweden, Switzerland, Turkey, United Kingdom, United States
Cross-border rulings providing for a unilateral downward adjustment to the taxpayer's taxable profits that is not directly reflected in the taxpayer's financial / commercial accounts	N/A	N/A
Permanent establishment rulings	N/A	N/A
Related party conduit rulings	N/A	N/A
De minimis rule	N/A	N/A
IP regimes: total exchanges on taxpayers benefitting from the third category of IP assets, new entrants benefitting from grandfathered IP regimes; and taxpayers making use of the option to treat the nexus ratio as a rebuttable presumption	N/A	N/A
Total	33	

D. Matters related to intellectual property regimes (ToR I.4.1.3)

354. The Czech Republic does not offer an intellectual property regime for which transparency requirements under the Action 5 Report (OECD, 2015) were imposed.

Summary of recommendations on implementation of the transparency framework

Aspect of implementation of the transparency framework that should be improved	Recommendation for improvement
The Czech Republic has not completed the exchange of information on past rulings and is experiencing significant delays in the exchange of information on future rulings due to the application of the timelines set out in the EU Directive 2011/16/EU, but also exceeding those timelines in complex cases. This is a continuing recommendation from the prior year peer review.	The Czech Republic is recommended to ensure that all information on future rulings is exchanged as soon as possible.

Notes

[1] Since 1 January 2018 the Czech Republic can also issues rulings on permanent establishments. This will be reviewed in the subsequent year peer review report.

[2] Parties to the Convention are available here: www.oecd.org/tax/exchange-of-tax-information/convention-on-mutual-administrative-assistance-in-tax-matters.htm. Czech Republic also has bilateral agreements in force with: Albania, Armenia, Australia, Austria, Bahrain, Barbados, Belarus, Belgium, Bosnia and Herzegovina, Brazil, Bulgaria, Canada, Chile, China (People's Republic of), Colombia, Croatia, Cyprus, Democratic People's Republic of Korea, Denmark, Egypt, Estonia, Ethiopia, Finland, Former Yugoslav Republic of Macedonia, France, Georgia, Germany, Greece, Hong Kong, Hungary, Iceland, India, Indonesia, Iran, Ireland, Israel, Italy, Japan, Jordan, Kazakhstan, Korea, Kuwait, Latvia, Lebanon, Liechtenstein, Lithuania, Luxembourg, Malaysia, Malta, Mexico, Moldovia, Mongolia, Montenegro, Morocco, Netherlands, New Zealand, Nigeria, Norway, Pakistan, Panama, Philippines, Poland, Portugal, Romania, Russia, Saudi Arabia, Serbia, Singapore, Slovak Republic, Slovenia, South Africa, Spain, Sri Lanka, Sweden, Switzerland, Syria, Tajikistan, Thailand, Tunisia, Turkey, Ukraine, United Arab Emirates, United Kingdom, United States, Uzbekistan, Venezuela and Viet Nam.

[3] Note by Turkey: The information in this document with reference to "Cyprus" relates to the southern part of the Island. There is no single authority representing both Turkish and Greek Cypriot people on the Island. Turkey recognises the Turkish Republic of Northern Cyprus (TRNC). Until a lasting and equitable solution is found within the context of the United Nations, Turkey shall preserve its position concerning the "Cyprus issue".

Note by all the European Union Member States of the OECD and the European Union. The Republic of Cyprus is recognised by all members of the United Nations with the exception of Turkey. The information in this document relates to the area under the effective control of the Government of the Republic of Cyprus.

References

OECD (2017), *BEPS Action 5 on Harmful Tax Practices – Terms of Reference and Methodology for the Conduct of the Peer Reviews of the Action 5 Transparency Framework*, OECD/G20 Base Erosion and Profit Shifting Project, OECD, Paris. www.oecd.org/tax/beps/beps-action-5-harmful-tax-practices-peer-review-transparencyframework.pdf.

OECD (2015), *Countering Harmful Tax Practices More Effectively, Taking into Account Transparency and Substance, Action 5 - 2015 Final Report*, OECD/G20 Base Erosion and Profit Shifting Project, OECD Publishing, Paris. https://doi.org/10.1787/9789264241190-en.

OECD/Council of Europe (2011), *The Multilateral Convention on Mutual Administrative Assistance in Tax Matters: Amended by the 2010 Protocol*, OECD Publishing, Paris. http://dx.doi.org/10.1787/9789264115606-en.

Democratic Republic of the Congo

Democratic Republic of the Congo has met all aspects of the terms of reference (ToR) for the calendar year 2017 (year in review) that can be met in the absence of rulings being issued.[1]

Democratic Republic of the Congo indicates that it does not issue any type of rulings within the scope of the transparency framework. Theoretically, there is no impediment for Democratic Republic of the Congo to issue rulings, but in practice Democratic Republic of the Congo does not issue any rulings. In the event that Democratic Republic of the Congo put in place the administrative process or develop the administrative capacity to issue rulings, Democratic Republic of the Congo would be asked to implement the transparency framework obligations.

As no rulings were issued, no exchange of information was required. Therefore, no peer input was received in respect of the exchanges of information on rulings received from Democratic Republic of the Congo.

Introduction

355. This peer review covers Democratic Republic of the Congo's implementation of the BEPS Action 5 transparency framework for the year 2017. The report has four parts, each relating to a key part of the ToR. Each part is discussed in turn. A summary of recommendations is included at the end of this report.

A. The information gathering process

356. As no rulings are issued, this section is not assessed.

B. The exchange of information

357. As no rulings are issued, this section is not assessed.

C. Statistics (ToR IV)

358. As no rulings are issued, no statistical data can be reported.

D. Matters related to intellectual property regimes (ToR I.4.1.3)

359. Democratic Republic of the Congo does not offer an intellectual property regime for which transparency requirements under the Action 5 Report (OECD, 2015) were imposed.

Summary of recommendations on implementation of the transparency framework

Aspect of implementation of the transparency framework that should be improved	Recommendation for improvement
	No recommendations are made.

Note

[1] Democratic Republic of the Congo did not provide written comments on this peer review report.

References

OECD (2017), *BEPS Action 5 on Harmful Tax Practices – Terms of Reference and Methodology for the Conduct of the Peer Reviews of the Action 5 Transparency Framework*, OECD/G20 Base Erosion and Profit Shifting Project, OECD, Paris. www.oecd.org/tax/beps/beps-action-5-harmful-tax-practices-peer-review-transparencyframework.pdf.

OECD (2015), *Countering Harmful Tax Practices More Effectively, Taking into Account Transparency and Substance, Action 5 - 2015 Final Report*, OECD/G20 Base Erosion and Profit Shifting Project, OECD Publishing, Paris. https://doi.org/10.1787/9789264241190-en.

Denmark

Denmark has met all aspects of the terms of reference (ToR) for the calendar year 2017 (year in review) and no recommendations are made.

Denmark can legally issue five types of rulings within the scope of the transparency framework.

In practice, Denmark has issued 43 past rulings; for the period 1 April 2016 - 31 December 2016, Denmark issued seven future rulings; and for the year in review, Denmark issued 17 future rulings within the scope of the transparency framework.

Peer input was received from three jurisdictions in respect of the exchanges of information on rulings received from Denmark. The input was generally positive, noting that information was complete in the correct format. One peer noted one exchange delay with respect to future rulings.

Introduction

360. This peer review covers Denmark's implementation of the BEPS Action 5 transparency framework for the year 2017. The report has four parts, each relating to a key part of the ToR. Each part is discussed in turn. A summary of recommendations is included at the end of this report.

A. The information gathering process

361. Denmark can legally issue the five following types of rulings within the scope of the transparency framework: (i) rulings related to preferential regimes (tonnage tax); (ii) cross-border unilateral advance pricing agreements (APAs) and any other cross-border unilateral tax rulings (such as an advance tax ruling) covering transfer pricing or the application of transfer pricing principles; (iii) downward adjustments; (iv) permanent establishment rulings; and (v) conduit rulings. Rulings are issued by the tax administration and, in cases where the matter is of general public interest, by the Tax Assessment Council as referred by the tax administration. These rulings are published in anonymised form on the tax administration's website when they are deemed of general public interest.[1] Denmark notes that in practice downward adjustments are rarely issued as such rulings are conditional on a corresponding upward adjustment being made in the other jurisdiction.

Past rulings (ToR I.4.1.1, I.4.1.2, I.4.2.1, I.4.2.2)

362. For Denmark, past rulings are any tax rulings within scope that are issued either: (i) on or after 1 January 2014 but before 1 April 2016; or (ii) on or after 1 January 2010 but before 1 January 2014, provided they were still in effect as at 1 January 2014.

363. In the prior year peer review report, it was determined that the Danish tax administration's undertakings to identify past rulings and all potential exchange jurisdictions were sufficient to meet the minimum standard. The Danish tax administration's implementation in this regard remains unchanged, and therefore continues to meet the minimum standard.

Future rulings (ToR I.4.1.1, I.4.1.2, I.4.2.1)

364. For Denmark, future rulings are any tax rulings within scope that are issued on or after 1 April 2016.

365. In the prior year peer review report, it was determined that the Danish tax administration's system to identify future rulings and all potential exchange jurisdictions was sufficient to meet the minimum standard. The Danish tax administration's implementation in this regard remains unchanged, and therefore continues to meet the minimum standard.

Review and supervision mechanism (ToR I.4.3)

366. In the prior year peer review report, it was determined that the Danish tax administration's review and supervision mechanism was sufficient to meet the minimum standard. The Danish tax administration's implementation in this regard remains unchanged, and therefore continues to meet the minimum standard.

Conclusion on section A

367. Denmark has met all of the ToR for the information gathering process and no recommendations are made.

B. The exchange of information

Legal basis for spontaneous exchange of information (ToR II.5.1, II.5.2)

368. Denmark has the necessary domestic legal basis to exchange information spontaneously. Denmark notes that there are no legal or practical impediments that prevent the spontaneous exchange of information on rulings as contemplated in the Action 5 minimum standard. Although there is a legal requirement to notify all concerned taxpayers before the exchange of information, Denmark notes that such notification process does not prevent exchange, but implies that exchange of information has to await the time by which it can be expected that the notification is received by the taxpayer.

369. Denmark is a party to international agreements permitting spontaneous exchange of information, including (i) the *Multilateral Convention on Mutual Administrative Assistance in Tax Matters: Amended by the 2010 Protocol* (OECD/Council of Europe, 2011) ("the Convention"), (ii) the Directive 2011/16/EU with all other European Union Member States and (iii) double tax agreements in force with 69 jurisdictions.[2]

Completion and exchange of templates (ToR II.5.3, II.5.4, II.5.5, II.5.6, II.5.7)

370. In the prior year peer review report, Denmark's process for the completion and exchange of templates was described. Since then, Denmark has made a separation of duties so that the employees responsible for processing the rulings are not involved in the process of exchange of information on the rulings. In addition, for the year in review Denmark commenced using the OECD XML Schema for exchanges. The process is substantially the same as it was for the completion of the template in Annex C of the 2015 Action 5 Report (OECD, 2015). The appointed employees responsible for the exchange of information will, instead of filling in the template, enter the data in the OECD XML Schema by use of the European Commission's Central Directory (CD) database. The Schema will not be saved in the CD but will be exported and saved as an XML file in the filing system at the tax administration. Immediately thereafter, the XML file will be sent to the Competent Authority.

371. Denmark notes that the summary section contains a translation of the summary sent to the National Tax Board, such as the key conclusions reached by the tax authority in issuing the ruling and the tax administration's view of the interpretation of the tax law if it is different from the taxpayer's interpretation. It is noted that the internal FHTP suggested guidance will be incorporated into the process in the future.

372. For the year in review, the timeliness of exchanges is as follows:

Past rulings in the scope of the transparency framework	Number of exchanges transmitted by 31 December 2017	Delayed exchanges		
		Number of exchanges not transmitted by 31 December 2017	Reasons for the delays	Any other comments
	32	0	N/A	These relate to the delayed exchanges reported in the prior year peer review report, and which were exchanged by February 2017
Future rulings in the scope of the transparency framework	**Number of exchanges transmitted within three months of the information becoming available to the competent authority or immediately after legal impediments have been lifted**	**Delayed exchanges**		
		Number of exchanges transmitted later than three months of the information on rulings becoming available to the competent authority	Reasons for the delays	Any other comments
	25	0	N/A	One exchange concerns a future ruling issued in 2016 occurred in February 2017 – within about four months of the ruling being issued but within three months of the information becoming available to the competent authority
Total	57	0		

Follow up requests received for exchange of the ruling	Number	Average time to provide response	Number of requests not answered
	0	N/A	N/A

373. Denmark notes that one exchange concerns a future ruling issued in 2016 and for which the exchange occurred in February 2017. This was within about four months of the ruling being issued but within three months of the information becoming available to the competent authority. Information on this ruling should have been transmitted to two jurisdictions and the exchange was made only to one by mistake initially. The information on this ruling was re-submitted to the additional jurisdiction in February 2017. As such, this is a minor error which was remedied quickly.

Conclusion on section B

374. Denmark has the necessary legal basis for spontaneous exchange of information, a process for completing the templates in a timely way and has completed all exchanges on time. Denmark has met all of the ToR for the exchange of information process and no recommendations are made.

C. Statistics (ToR IV)

375. The statistics for the year in review are as follows:

Category of ruling	Number of exchanges	Jurisdictions exchanged with
Rulings related to preferential regimes	Included in *de minimis*	N/A
Cross-border unilateral advance pricing agreements (APAs) and any other cross-border unilateral tax rulings (such as an advance tax ruling) covering transfer pricing or the application of transfer pricing principles	7	Canada, Iceland, Lithuania, Luxembourg, Norway, Sweden, United Kingdom
Cross-border rulings providing for a unilateral downward adjustment to the taxpayer's taxable profits that is not directly reflected in the taxpayer's financial / commercial accounts	0	N/A
Permanent establishment rulings	43	Austria, Canada, France, Germany, Ireland, Italy, Jersey, Lithuania, Luxembourg, Malta, Netherlands, Norway, Poland, Sweden, United Kingdom, United States
Related party conduit rulings	Included in *de minimis*	N/A
De minimis rule	7	N/A
IP regimes: total exchanges on taxpayers benefitting from the third category of IP assets, new entrants benefitting from grandfathered IP regimes; and taxpayers making use of the option to treat the nexus ratio as a rebuttable presumption	N/A	N/A
Total	57	

D. Matters related to intellectual property regimes (ToR I.4.1.3)

376. Denmark does not offer an intellectual property regime for which transparency requirements under the Action 5 Report (OECD, 2015) were imposed.

Summary of recommendations on implementation of the transparency framework

Aspect of implementation of the transparency framework that should be improved	Recommendation for improvement
	No recommendations are made.

Notes

[1] Available at www.skat.dk/skat.aspx?oid=80859&ik_navn=transport (accessed 20 November 2018).

[2] Parties to the Convention are available here: www.oecd.org/tax/exchange-of-tax-information/convention-on-mutual-administrative-assistance-in-tax-matters.htm. Denmark also has bilateral agreements in force with Argentina, Australia, Austria, Bangladesh, Belarus, Belgium, Brazil, , Bulgaria, Canada, Chile, China (People's Republic of), Croatia, Cyprus, Czech Republic, Egypt, Estonia, Former Yugoslav Republic of Macedonia, Georgia, Germany, Ghana, Greece, Hungary, India, Indonesia, Ireland, Israel, Italy, Jamaica, Japan, Kenya, Korea, Kuwait, Kyrgyzstan, Latvia, Lithuania, Luxembourg, Malaysia, Malta, Mexico, Montenegro, Morocco, Netherlands, New Zealand, Pakistan, Philippines, Poland, Portugal, Romania, Russia, Serbia, Singapore, Slovak Republic, Slovenia, South Africa, Sri Lanka, Switzerland, Chinese Taipei, Tanzania, Thailand, Trinidad and Tobago, Tunisia, Turkey, Uganda, Ukraine, United Kingdom, United States, Venezuela, Viet Nam and Zambia. Denmark also has a Tax Information Exchange Agreement permitting spontaneous exchange of information with Aruba.

Note by Turkey: The information in this document with reference to "Cyprus" relates to the southern part of the Island. There is no single authority representing both Turkish and Greek Cypriot people on the Island. Turkey recognises the Turkish Republic of Northern Cyprus (TRNC). Until a lasting and equitable solution is found within the context of the United Nations, Turkey shall preserve its position concerning the "Cyprus issue".

Note by all the European Union Member States of the OECD and the European Union. The Republic of Cyprus is recognised by all members of the United Nations with the exception of Turkey. The information in this document relates to the area under the effective control of the Government of the Republic of Cyprus.

References

OECD (2017), *BEPS Action 5 on Harmful Tax Practices – Terms of Reference and Methodology for the Conduct of the Peer Reviews of the Action 5 Transparency Framework*, OECD/G20 Base Erosion and Profit Shifting Project, OECD, Paris. www.oecd.org/tax/beps/beps-action-5-harmful-tax-practices-peer-review-transparencyframework.pdf.

OECD (2015), *Countering Harmful Tax Practices More Effectively, Taking into Account Transparency and Substance, Action 5 - 2015 Final Report*, OECD/G20 Base Erosion and Profit Shifting Project, OECD Publishing, Paris. https://doi.org/10.1787/9789264241190-en.

OECD/Council of Europe (2011), *The Multilateral Convention on Mutual Administrative Assistance in Tax Matters: Amended by the 2010 Protocol*, OECD Publishing, Paris. http://dx.doi.org/10.1787/9789264115606-en.

Djibouti

Djibouti has met all aspects of the terms of reference (ToR) for the calendar year 2017 (year in review) that can be met in the absence of rulings being issued.[1]

Djibouti indicates that it cannot legally issue any type of rulings within the scope of the transparency framework.

As no rulings were issued, no exchange of information was required. No peer input was received in respect of the exchanges of information on rulings received from Djibouti.

Introduction

377. This peer review covers Djibouti's implementation of the BEPS Action 5 transparency framework for the year 2017. The report has four parts, each relating to a key part of the ToR. Each part is discussed in turn. A summary of recommendations is included at the end of this report.

A. The information gathering process

378. As no rulings are issued, this section is not assessed.

B. The exchange of information

379. As no rulings are issued, this section is not assessed.

C. Statistics (ToR IV)

380. As no rulings are issued, no statistical data can be reported.

D. Matters related to intellectual property regimes (ToR I.4.1.3)

381. Djibouti does not offer an intellectual property regime for which transparency requirements under the Action 5 Report (OECD, 2015) were imposed.

Summary of recommendations on implementation of the transparency framework

Aspect of implementation of the transparency framework that should be improved	Recommendation for improvement
	No recommendations are made.

Note

[1] Djibouti did not provide written comments on this peer review report.

References

OECD (2017), *BEPS Action 5 on Harmful Tax Practices – Terms of Reference and Methodology for the Conduct of the Peer Reviews of the Action 5 Transparency Framework*, OECD/G20 Base Erosion and Profit Shifting Project, OECD, Paris. www.oecd.org/tax/beps/beps-action-5-harmful-tax-practices-peer-review-transparencyframework.pdf.

OECD (2015), *Countering Harmful Tax Practices More Effectively, Taking into Account Transparency and Substance, Action 5 - 2015 Final Report*, OECD/G20 Base Erosion and Profit Shifting Project, OECD Publishing, Paris. https://doi.org/10.1787/9789264241190-en.

Estonia

Estonia has met all aspects of the terms of reference (ToR) for the calendar year 2017 (year in review) and no recommendations are made. In the prior year peer review report, Estonia was recommended to ensure information is obtained on all potential exchange jurisdictions for future rulings and to exchange information on all rulings as soon as possible. Estonia has now put in place a procedure that requires the applicant to disclose information in the ruling application and all exchange of information has been completed, the recommendation is removed.

Estonia can legally issue two types of rulings within the scope of the transparency framework.

In practice, Estonia has issued 20 past rulings; for the period 1 April 2016 - 31 December 2016, Estonia issued eight future rulings; and for the year in review, Estonia issued 11 future rulings within the scope of the transparency framework.

Peer input was received from one jurisdiction in respect of the exchanges of information on rulings received from Estonia. It was positive, noting that information was complete, in the correct format and received in a timely manner.

Introduction

382. This peer review covers Estonia's implementation of the BEPS Action 5 transparency framework for the year 2017. The report has four parts, each relating to a key part of the ToR. Each part is discussed in turn. A summary of recommendations is included at the end of this report.

A. The information gathering process

383. Estonia can legally issue the following two types of rulings within the scope of the transparency framework: (i) permanent establishment rulings; and (ii) related party conduit rulings. In Estonia, the legal department is responsible for preparing the rulings within the scope of the transparency framework in co-operation with the Tax Department of the ETCB, which are then signed by the Director General of ETCB. Estonia publishes anonymised summaries of tax rulings on the Estonian Tax and Customs Board (ETCB) website.[1]

Past rulings (ToR I.4.1.1, I.4.1.2, I.4.2.1, I.4.2.2)

384. For Estonia, past rulings are any tax rulings within scope that are issued either: (i) on or after 1 January 2014 but before 1 April 2016; or (ii) on or after 1 January 2010 but before 1 January 2014, provided they were still in effect as at 1 January 2014.

385. In the prior year peer review report, it was determined that The ECTB's undertakings to identify past rulings and all potential exchange jurisdictions were sufficient to meet the minimum standard. The ECTB's implementation in this regard remains unchanged, and therefore continues to meet the minimum standard.

Future rulings (ToR I.4.1.1, I.4.1.2, I.4.2.1)

386. For Estonia, future rulings are future rulings are any tax rulings within scope that are issued on or after 1 April 2016.

387. In the prior year peer review report, it was noted that the information on the ultimate parent company is not always obtained. In the year in review, Estonia notes that ETCB has been explaining to the intermediaries (usually law firms) the need to provide information on the whole structure on the enterprise group and on the beneficial owners for the past year and a half. There is a procedure in place that requires the applicant to disclose information in the ruling application. The ETCB has the right to ask for any additional information if needed. The ECTB's implementation in this regard remains unchanged, and therefore continues to meets the minimum standard.

Review and supervision mechanism (ToR I.4.3)

388. In the prior year peer review report, it was determined that the ECTB's review and supervision mechanism was sufficient to meet the minimum standard. The ECTB's implementation in this regard remains unchanged, and therefore continues to meet the minimum standard.

Conclusion on section A

389. Estonia has a procedure in place that requires the applicant to disclose information in the ruling application, especially the ultimate parent company. Estonia has met all of the ToR for the information gathering process and no recommendations are made.

B. The exchange of information

Legal basis for spontaneous exchange of information (ToR II.5.1, II.5.2)

390. Estonia has the necessary domestic legal basis to exchange information spontaneously. Estonia notes that there are no legal or practical impediments that prevent the spontaneous exchange of information on rulings as contemplated in the Action 5 minimum standard.

391. Estonia is a party to international agreements permitting spontaneous exchange of information, including (i) the *Multilateral Convention on Mutual Administrative Assistance in Tax Matters: Amended by the 2010 Protocol* (OECD/Council of Europe, 2011) ("the Convention"), (ii) the Directive 2011/16/EU with all other European Union Member States and (iii) double tax agreements in force with 57 jurisdictions.[2]

Completion and exchange of templates (ToR II.5.3, II.5.4, II.5.5, II.5.6, II.5.7)

392. In the prior year peer review report, it was determined that the ECTB's completion and exchange of templates were sufficient to meet the minimum standard. The ECTB's implementation in this regard remains unchanged, and therefore continues to meet the minimum standard.

393. Estonia has exchanged all past rulings before 31 December 2017. For the eight exchanges transmitted in 2017, Estonia notes that it is due to the misunderstanding on the use of European Commission's Database.

394. With respect to the completion of the summary section in the template, the ETCB uses the suggested internal guidance. The summary consists of 2 000 – 3 500 characters and gives descriptions of the arrangements with ETCB's assessment (including indications for possible cross-border impact). All summaries are translated into English.

395. For the year in review, the timeliness of exchanges is as follows:

Past rulings in the scope of the transparency framework	Number of exchanges transmitted by 31 December 2017	Delayed exchanges		
		Number of exchanges not transmitted by 31 December 2017	Reasons for the delays	Any other comments
	8	0	N/A	These relate to the delayed exchanges reported in the prior year peer review report.
Future rulings in the scope of the transparency framework	Number of exchanges transmitted within three months of the information becoming available to the competent authority or immediately after legal impediments have been lifted	Delayed exchanges		
		Number of exchanges transmitted later than three months of the information on rulings becoming available to the competent authority	Reasons for the delays	Any other comments
	8	3	N/A	The three delayed exchanges are the delayed exchanges reported in the prior year peer review report and which were exchanged in 2017.
Total	16	3		

Follow up requests received for exchange of the ruling	Number	Average time to provide response	Number of requests not answered
	0	N/A	N/A

Conclusion on section B

396. Estonia has the necessary legal basis for spontaneous exchange of information, a process for completing the templates in a timely way and has completed all exchanges. Estonia has met all of the ToR for the exchange of information process and no recommendations are made.

C. Statistics (ToR IV)

397. The statistics for the year in review are as follows:

Category of ruling	Number of exchanges	Jurisdictions exchanged with
Rulings related to preferential regimes	N/A	N/A
Cross-border unilateral advance pricing arrangements (APAs) and any other cross-border unilateral tax rulings (such as an advance tax ruling) covering transfer pricing or the application of transfer pricing principles	N/A	N/A
Cross-border rulings providing for a unilateral downward adjustment to the taxpayer's taxable profits that is not directly reflected in the taxpayer's financial / commercial accounts	N/A	N/A
Permanent establishment rulings	8	Finland, Ireland, Latvia, Netherlands, Sweden, Switzerland
Related party conduit rulings	11	Denmark, Finland, Latvia, Luxembourg, Netherlands, Norway, United Kingdom, United States
De minimis rule	N/A	N/A
IP regimes: total exchanges on taxpayers benefitting from the third category of IP assets, new entrants benefitting from grandfathered IP regimes; and taxpayers making use of the option to treat the nexus ratio as a rebuttable presumption	N/A	N/A
Total	19	

D. Matters related to intellectual property regimes (ToR I.4.1.3)

398. Estonia does not offer an intellectual property regime for which transparency requirements under the Action 5 Report (OECD, 2015) were imposed.

Summary of recommendations on implementation of the transparency framework

Aspect of implementation of the transparency framework that should be improved	Recommendation for improvement
	No recommendations are made.

Notes

1 Available at www.emta.ee/et/ariklient/maksukorraldus-maksude-tasumine/siduvad-eelotsused/siduvate-eelotsuste-kokkuvotted (accessed 19 November 2018).

2 Parties to the Convention are available here: www.oecd.org/tax/exchange-of-tax-information/convention-on-mutual-administrative-assistance-in-tax-matters.htm. Estonia also has bilateral agreements in force with Albania, Armenia, Azerbaijan, Austria, Bahrein, Belarus, Belgium, Bulgaria, Canada, China (People's Republic of), Croatia, Cyprus, Czech Republic, Denmark, Finland, Former Yugoslav Republic of Macedonia, France, Georgia, Germany, Greece, Hungary, Iceland, India, Ireland, Isle of Man, Israel, Italy, Jersey, Kazakhstan, Korea, Latvia, Lithuania, Luxembourg, Malta, Mexico, Moldova, Netherlands, Norway, Poland, Portugal, Romania, Serbia, Singapore, Slovak Republic, Slovenia, Spain, Sweden, Switzerland, Thailand, Turkey, Turkmenistan, Ukraine, United Arab Emirates, United Kingdom, United States, Uzbekistan and Viet Nam.

Note by Turkey: The information in this document with reference to "Cyprus" relates to the southern part of the Island. There is no single authority representing both Turkish and Greek Cypriot people on the Island. Turkey recognises the Turkish Republic of Northern Cyprus (TRNC). Until a lasting and equitable solution is found within the context of the United Nations, Turkey shall preserve its position concerning the "Cyprus issue".

Note by all the European Union Member States of the OECD and the European Union. The Republic of Cyprus is recognised by all members of the United Nations with the exception of Turkey. The information in this document relates to the area under the effective control of the Government of the Republic of Cyprus.

References

OECD (2017), *BEPS Action 5 on Harmful Tax Practices – Terms of Reference and Methodology for the Conduct of the Peer Reviews of the Action 5 Transparency Framework*, OECD/G20 Base Erosion and Profit Shifting Project, OECD, Paris. www.oecd.org/tax/beps/beps-action-5-harmful-tax-practices-peer-review-transparencyframework.pdf.

OECD (2015), *Countering Harmful Tax Practices More Effectively, Taking into Account Transparency and Substance, Action 5 - 2015 Final Report*, OECD/G20 Base Erosion and Profit Shifting Project, OECD Publishing, Paris. https://doi.org/10.1787/9789264241190-en.

OECD/Council of Europe (2011), *The Multilateral Convention on Mutual Administrative Assistance in Tax Matters: Amended by the 2010 Protocol*, OECD Publishing, Paris. http://dx.doi.org/10.1787/9789264115606-en.

Finland

Finland has met all aspects of the terms of reference (ToR) for the calendar year 2017 (year in review) and no recommendations are made. In the prior year peer review report, Finland was recommended to ensure that information on all past and future rulings is exchanged as soon as possible. Finland has now exchanged all past and future rulings by 31 December 2017, and the recommendation is removed.

Finland can legally issue four types of rulings within the scope of the transparency framework.

In practice, Finland has issued 42 past rulings; for the period 1 April 2016 - 31 December 2016, Finland issued 13 future ruling; and for the year in review, Finland issued 19 future rulings within the scope of the transparency framework.

No peer input was received in respect of the exchanges of information on rulings received from Finland.

Introduction

399. This peer review covers Finland's implementation of the BEPS Action 5 transparency framework for the year 2017. The report has four parts, each relating to a key part of the ToR. Each part is discussed in turn. A summary of recommendations is included at the end of this report.

A. The information gathering process

400. Finland can legally issue the four following types of rulings within the scope of the transparency framework: (i) rulings related to preferential regimes (shipping regime); (ii) cross-border unilateral advance pricing arrangements (APAs) and any other cross-border unilateral tax rulings (such as an advance tax ruling) covering transfer pricing or the application of transfer pricing principles; (iii) permanent establishment rulings and (iv) conduit rulings. In Finland, rulings within the scope of the transparency framework are issued mainly by the Corporate Taxation Unit. Rulings are also issued by the Central Tax Board, which is an autonomous body within the tax administration, except for rulings relating to transfer pricing (that can be issued only by the Corporate Taxation Unit). Rulings issued by the Corporate Taxation Unit are issued either nationally by the large taxpayers' office or locally by one of the six regional corporate tax offices. Some rulings are published on the tax administration's website, at the discretion of the Central Tax Board.[1]

Past rulings (ToR I.4.1.1, I.4.1.2, I.4.2.1, I.4.2.2)

401. For Finland, past rulings are any tax rulings within scope that are issued either: (i) on or after 1 January 2014 but before 1 April 2016; or (ii) on or after 1 January 2010 but before 1 January 2014, provided they were still in effect as at 1 January 2014.

402. In the prior year peer review report, it was determined that the Finnish tax administration's undertakings to identify past rulings and all potential exchange jurisdictions were sufficient to meet the minimum standard. The Finnish tax administration's implementation in this regard remains unchanged, and therefore continues to meet the minimum standard.

Future rulings (ToR I.4.1.1, I.4.1.2, I.4.2.1)

403. For Finland, future rulings are any tax rulings within scope that are issued on or after 1 April 2016.

404. In the prior year peer review report, it was determined that the Finnish tax administration's implementation of a new system to identify future rulings and all potential exchange jurisdictions was sufficient to meet the minimum standard. The Finnish tax administration's implementation in this regard remains unchanged, and therefore continues to meet the minimum standard.

Review and supervision mechanism (ToR I.4.3)

405. In the prior year peer review report, it was determined that the Finnish tax administration's review and supervision mechanism was sufficient to meet the minimum standard. The Finnish tax administration's implementation in this regard remains unchanged, and therefore continues to meet the minimum standard.

Conclusion on section A

406. Finland has met all of the ToR for the information gathering process and no recommendations are made.

B. The exchange of information

Legal basis for spontaneous exchange of information (ToR II.5.1, II.5.2)

407. Finland has the necessary domestic legal basis to exchange information spontaneously. Finland notes that there are no legal or practical impediments that prevent the spontaneous exchange of information on rulings as contemplated in the Action 5 minimum standard.

408. Finland is a party to international agreements permitting spontaneous exchange of information, including (i) the *Multilateral Convention on Mutual Administrative Assistance in Tax Matters: Amended by the 2010 Protocol* (OECD/Council of Europe, 2011) ("the Convention"), (ii) the Directive 2011/16/EU with all other European Union Member States and (iii) double tax agreements in force with 85 jurisdictions.[2]

Completion and exchange of templates (ToR II.5.3, II.5.4, II.5.5, II.5.6, II.5.7)

409. In the prior year peer review report, it was determined that Finland had met all of the ToR for the exchange of information process except for the timely exchange of information on future rulings (ToR II.5.6) and Finland is recommended to ensure that information on all past and future rulings is exchanged as soon as possible. In the year in review, since Finland has exchanged all past and future rulings by 31 December 2017, the recommendation is removed.

410. With respect to the completion of the summary section of the templates, Finland has guided the officials who are working with advance rulings to summarise the main content and the actual decision of the ruling. The officials are instructed that these summaries should provide all the necessary information in order for the receiving tax administration to risk-assess the issues raised by the ruling.

411. For the year in review, the timeliness of exchanges is as follows:

Past rulings in the scope of the transparency framework	Number of exchanges transmitted by 31 December 2017	Delayed exchanges		
		Number of exchanges not transmitted by 31 December 2017	Reasons for the delays	Any other comments
	42	0	N/A	These 42 exchanges relate to the delayed exchanges reported in the prior year peer review report.
Future rulings in the scope of the transparency framework	Number of exchanges transmitted within three months of the information becoming available to the competent authority or immediately after legal impediments have been lifted	Delayed exchanges		
		Number of exchanges transmitted later than three months of the information on rulings becoming available to the competent authority	Reasons for the delays	Any other comments
	14	18		The 18 delayed exchanges are the delayed exchanges reported in the prior year peer review report and which were exchanged in 2017.
Total	56	18		

Follow up requests received for exchange of the ruling	Number	Average time to provide response	Number of requests not answered
	0	N/A	N/A

Conclusion on section B

412. Finland has the necessary legal basis for spontaneous exchange of information, a process for completing the templates in a timely way and has completed all exchanges on future rulings. Finland has met all of the ToR for the exchange of information process and no recommendations are made.

C. Statistics (ToR IV)

413. The statistics for the year in review are as follows:

Category of ruling	Number of exchanges	Jurisdictions exchanged with
Rulings related to preferential regimes	0	
Cross-border unilateral advance pricing arrangements (APAs) and any other cross-border unilateral tax rulings (such as an advance tax ruling) covering transfer pricing or the application of transfer pricing principles	29	China (People's Republic of), Denmark, Estonia, Germany, India, Latvia, Luxembourg, Norway, Poland, Sweden, United Kingdom, United States
Cross-border rulings providing for a unilateral downward adjustment to the taxpayer's taxable profits that is not directly reflected in the taxpayer's financial / commercial accounts	N/A	N/A
Permanent establishment rulings	45	Croatia, Estonia, Germany, Italy, Luxembourg, Netherlands, Poland, Sweden, United Kingdom
Related party conduit rulings	0	N/A
De minimis rule	0	N/A
IP regimes: total exchanges on taxpayers benefitting from the third category of IP assets, new entrants benefitting from grandfathered IP regimes; and taxpayers making use of the option to treat the nexus ratio as a rebuttable presumption	N/A	N/A
Total	74	

D. Matters related to intellectual property regimes (ToR I.4.1.3)

414. Finland does not offer an intellectual property regime for which transparency requirements under the Action 5 Report (OECD, 2015) were imposed.

Summary of recommendations on implementation of the transparency framework

Aspect of implementation of the transparency framework that should be improved	Recommendation for improvement
	No recommendations are made.

Notes

[1] Available at: www.vero.fi/syventavat-vero-ohjeet/ennakkoratkaisut/ (accessed 20 November 2018).

[2] Parties to the Convention are available here: www.oecd.org/tax/exchange-of-tax-information/convention-on-mutual-administrative-assistance-in-tax-matters.htm. Finland also has bilateral agreements in force with Argentina, Armenia, Aruba, Australia, Austria, Azerbaijan, Bailiwick of Jersey, Barbados, Belarus, Belgium, Bermuda, Bosnia and Herzegovina, Brazil, British Virgin Islands, Bulgaria, Canada, Cayman Islands, China (People's Republic of), Croatia, Cyprus, Czech Republic, Denmark, Egypt, Estonia, Faroe Islands, Former Yugoslav Republic of Macedonia, France, Georgia, Germany, Greece, Guernsey, Hungary, India, Indonesia, Ireland, Isle of Man, Israel, Italy, Japan, Kazakhstan, Korea, Kosovo, Kyrgyzstan, Latvia, Lebanon, Lithuania, Luxembourg, Malaysia, Malta, Mexico, Moldova, Montenegro, Morocco, Netherlands, Netherlands Antilles, New Zealand, Norway, Pakistan, Philippines, Poland, Portugal, Romania, Russia, Serbia, Singapore, Slovak Republic, Slovenia, South Africa, Spain, Sri Lanka, Sweden, Switzerland, Tajikistan, Tanzania, Thailand, Turkey, Turkmenistan, Ukraine, United Arab Emirates, United Kingdom, United States, Uruguay, Uzbekistan, Viet Nam and Zambia.

Note by Turkey: The information in this document with reference to "Cyprus" relates to the southern part of the Island. There is no single authority representing both Turkish and Greek Cypriot people on the Island. Turkey recognises the Turkish Republic of Northern Cyprus (TRNC). Until a lasting and equitable solution is found within the context of the United Nations, Turkey shall preserve its position concerning the "Cyprus issue".

Note by all the European Union Member States of the OECD and the European Union. The Republic of Cyprus is recognised by all members of the United Nations with the exception of Turkey. The information in this document relates to the area under the effective control of the Government of the Republic of Cyprus.

References

OECD (2017), *BEPS Action 5 on Harmful Tax Practices – Terms of Reference and Methodology for the Conduct of the Peer Reviews of the Action 5 Transparency Framework*, OECD/G20 Base Erosion and Profit Shifting Project, OECD, Paris. www.oecd.org/tax/beps/beps-action-5-harmful-tax-practices-peer-review-transparencyframework.pdf.

OECD (2015), *Countering Harmful Tax Practices More Effectively, Taking into Account Transparency and Substance, Action 5 - 2015 Final Report*, OECD/G20 Base Erosion and Profit Shifting Project, OECD Publishing, Paris. https://doi.org/10.1787/9789264241190-en.

OECD/Council of Europe (2011), *The Multilateral Convention on Mutual Administrative Assistance in Tax Matters: Amended by the 2010 Protocol*, OECD Publishing, Paris. http://dx.doi.org/10.1787/9789264115606-en.

France

France has met all aspects of the terms of reference (ToR) for the calendar year 2017 (year in review) except that France experienced some delays in exchanging information on future rulings (ToR II.5.6) and France did not identify or exchange information on new entrants to the IP regime or taxpayers benefitting from the third category of IP assets (ToR I.4.1.3). This latter recommendation was also included in the prior year peer review report. France is recommended to ensure that all information on future rulings is exchanged as soon as possible, to identify and exchange information on all new entrants to the IP regime, and to identify and exchange information on taxpayers benefitting from the third category of IP assets.

France can legally issue three types of rulings within the scope of the transparency framework.

In practice, France has issued 45 past rulings; for the period 1 April 2016 - 31 December 2016, France issued four future rulings; and for the year in review, France issued six future rulings within the scope of the transparency framework.

Peer input was received from one jurisdiction in respect of the exchanges of information on rulings received from France. The input was positive, noting that information was complete and in the correct format.

Introduction

415. This peer review covers France's implementation of the BEPS Action 5 transparency framework for the year 2017. The report has four parts, each relating to a key part of the ToR.

416. Each part is discussed in turn. A summary of recommendations is included at the end of this report.

A. The information gathering process

417. France can legally issue the three following types of rulings within the scope of the transparency framework: (i) rulings related to preferential regimes;[1] (ii) cross-border unilateral advance pricing agreements (APAs) and any other cross-border unilateral tax rulings (such as an advance tax ruling) covering transfer pricing or the application of transfer pricing principles; and (iii) permanent establishment rulings. Rulings related to preferential regimes are issued by a specialised service in the legal department of the French tax administration. APAs are delivered by a specialised legal and economic expertise department in the legal department of the French tax administration.

Past rulings (ToR I.4.1.1, I.4.1.2, I.4.2.1, I.4.2.2)

418. For France, past rulings are any tax rulings within scope that are issued either: (i) on or after 1 January 2014 but before 1 April 2016; or (ii) on or after 1 January 2010 but before 1 January 2014, provided they were still in effect as at 1 January 2014.

419. In the prior year peer review report, it was determined that the French Tax Administration's undertakings to identify past rulings and all potential exchange jurisdictions were sufficient to meet the minimum standard. The French Tax Administration's implementation in this regard remains unchanged, and therefore continues to meet the minimum standard.

Future rulings (ToR I.4.1.1, I.4.1.2, I.4.2.1)

420. For France, future rulings are any tax rulings within scope that are issued on or after 1 April 2016.

421. In the prior year peer review report, it was determined that the French Tax Administration's implementation of a new system to identify future rulings and all potential exchange jurisdictions was sufficient to meet the minimum standard. The French Tax Administration's implementation in this regard remains unchanged, and therefore continues to meet the minimum standard.

Review and supervision mechanism (ToR I.4.3)

422. In the prior year peer review report, it was determined that the French tax administration's review and supervisions mechanisms were sufficient to meet the minimum standard. The French tax administration's implementation in this regard remains unchanged, and therefore continues to meet the minimum standard.

Conclusion on section A

423. France has met all of the ToR for the information gathering process and no recommendations are made.

B. The exchange of information

Legal basis for spontaneous exchange of information (ToR II.5.1, II.5.2)

424. France has the necessary domestic legal basis to exchange information spontaneously. France notes that there are no legal or practical impediments that prevent the spontaneous exchange of information on rulings as contemplated in the Action 5 minimum standard.

425. France is a party to international agreements permitting spontaneous exchange of information, including (i) the *Multilateral Convention on Mutual Administrative Assistance in Tax Matters: Amended by the 2010 Protocol* (OECD/Council of Europe, 2011) ("the Convention"), (ii) the Directive 2011/16/EU with all other European Union Member States and (iii) double tax agreements in force with 125 jurisdictions.[2]

Completion and exchange of templates (ToR II.5.3, II.5.4, II.5.5, II.5.6, II.5.7)

426. In the prior year peer review report, it was determined that the French Tax Administration's completion and exchange of templates were sufficient to meet the minimum standard. Furthermore, France has confirmed that their approach to the completion of the summary section in section 7 of Annex C of the 2015 Action 5 Report (OECD, 2015) conforms with the internal FHTP suggested guidance to the section.

427. The timeliness of exchanges is as follows:

Past rulings in the scope of the transparency framework	Number of exchanges transmitted by 31 December 2017	Delayed exchanges		
		Number of exchanges not transmitted by 31 December 2017	Reasons for the delays	Any other comments
	45	0		These relate to the delayed exchanges reported in the prior year peer review report and were exchanged in early 2017.
Future rulings in the scope of the transparency framework	Number of exchanges transmitted within three months of the information becoming available to the competent authority or immediately after legal impediments have been lifted	Delayed exchanges		
		Number of exchanges transmitted later than three months of the information on rulings becoming available to the competent authority	Reasons for the delays	Any other comments
	0	3	Incorrect validation of records in the European Commission Central Directory.	Transmission occurred within 7 months of receipt by the Competent Authority.
Total	45	3		

Follow up requests received for exchange of the ruling	Number	Average time to provide response	Number of requests not answered
	0	N/A	N/A

428. France notes that during the prior year review, exchanges were performed with all relevant members of the Inclusive Framework and France has not identified any other past rulings to be additionally exchanged during the year in review.

429. France notes that the reason for the delay in exchanging future rulings was due to an incorrect validation of records in the European Commission Central Directory. The exchanges were then transmitted within seven months of receipt by the Competent Authority, instead of within three months as required under the transparency framework. To address this issue, France has promoted training to staff to make them aware of the functioning of the European Commission Central Directory to avoid any further delays in the future. The result of this procedure will be assessed during the subsequent peer review process.

430. Although six future rulings were issued, information was exchanged with respect to only three of these rulings as the other three were issued towards the end of 2017. France notes that information on these rulings was exchanged in early 2018 and within the timeframes set out in the transparency framework and this will be reviewed in the subsequent peer review.

Conclusion on section B

431. France has the necessary legal framework and administrative process in place for exchanging information on rulings. France was not able to exchange all information on future rulings by the timelines set out in the transparency framework. France has met all of the ToR for the exchange of information process except with respect to delays in the timeliness of exchanges (ToR II.5.6). France is recommended to ensure that all information on future rulings is exchanged as soon as possible.

C. Statistics (ToR IV)

432. The statistics for the 2017 review are as follows:

Category of ruling	Number of exchanges	Jurisdictions exchanged with
Rulings related to preferential regimes	N/A	N/A
Cross-border unilateral advance pricing agreements (APAs) and any other cross-border unilateral tax rulings (such as an advance tax ruling) covering transfer pricing or the application of transfer pricing principles	12	India, Ireland, Japan, Luxembourg, Spain, Switzerland, United Kingdom, United States
Cross-border rulings providing for a unilateral downward adjustment to the taxpayer's taxable profits that is not directly reflected in the taxpayer's financial / commercial accounts	N/A	N/A
Permanent establishment rulings	36	Belgium, Bulgaria, Germany, Ireland, Italy, Lebanon, Luxembourg, Monaco, the Netherlands, Portugal, Spain, Switzerland, Tunisia, United Kingdom, United States.
Related party conduit rulings	N/A	N/A
De minimis rule	0	N/A
IP regimes: total exchanges on taxpayers benefitting from the third category of IP assets, new entrants benefitting from grandfathered IP regimes; and taxpayers making use of the option to treat the nexus ratio as a rebuttable presumption	0	
Total	48	

D. Matters related to intellectual property regimes (ToR I.4.1.3)

433. France offers an intellectual property regime ("IP regime").[3] During the prior year peer review, France did not identify or exchange information on new entrants to the IP regime or taxpayers benefitting from the third category of IP asset. France was recommended to put in place a mechanism to ensure that it can identify and exchange information on all new entrants to the IP regime as soon as possible, and to identify and exchange information on taxpayers benefitting from the third category of IP asset as soon as possible.

- ***New entrants benefitting from the grandfathered regime:*** as France has not amended its IP regime to conform to the Action 5 "nexus approach" and the regime is considered to be harmful, there is no grandfathering. However, France should have information available to it on new entrants after 6 February 2015 to the existing IP regime. France has not exchanged information on new entrants to the existing IP regime in 2016. This remains unchanged from the prior year peer review.

- ***Third category of IP assets:*** France's IP regime provides benefits to income from patentable inventions, which appear to be a type of the "third category of IP asset" described in paragraph 37 of the Action 5 report (OECD, 2015). France has not implemented all of the requirements associated with this category of IP assets, thus the transparency requirements described in paragraph 37 would still apply to this case. France did not identify yet taxpayers benefitting from the third category of IP asset, and as such has not exchanged information on these taxpayers. This remains unchanged from the prior year peer review.

- ***Taxpayers making use of the option to treat the nexus ratio as a rebuttable presumption:*** not applicable to this regime, which in 2017 did not comply with the nexus approach and has considered to be harmful.

434. In the year of review, France did not undertake any improvements in relation to the identification or the exchange of information on new entrants to the IP regime or taxpayers benefitting from the third category of IP asset. As such, the recommendation has not been addressed and remains in place. France is recommended to identify and exchange information on all new entrants to the IP regime, and to identify and exchange information on taxpayers benefitting from the third category of IP assets.

435. However, in 2018 France announced its intention to amend the IP regime by the end of 2018. France affirms that it will make the necessary changes together with the requirements of the transparency framework in respect of this regime.

Summary of recommendations on implementation of the transparency framework

Aspect of implementation of the transparency framework that should be improved	Recommendation for improvement
France has experienced delays in exchanging information on future rulings. This is a continuing recommendation from the prior year peer review.	France is recommended to ensure that all information on future rulings is exchanged as soon as possible
France did not identify or exchange information on new entrants to the IP regime or taxpayers benefitting from the third category of IP asset. This is a continuing recommendation from the prior year peer review.	France is recommended to identify and exchange information on all new entrants to the IP regime, and to identify and exchange information on taxpayers benefitting from the third category of IP assets.

Notes

[1] With respect to the following preferential regime: shipping regime.

[2] Parties to the Convention are available here: www.oecd.org/tax/exchange-of-tax-information/convention-on-mutual-administrative-assistance-in-tax-matters.htm. France also has bilateral agreements in force with: Albania, Algeria, Andorra, Argentina, Armenia, Australia, Austria, Azerbaijan, Bahrain, Bangladesh, Belarus, Belgium, Benin, Bolivia, Bosnia and Herzegovina, Botswana, Brazil, Bulgaria, Burkina Faso, Cameroon, Canada, Central African Republic, Chile, China (People's Republic of), Chinese Taipei, Congo, Côte d'Ivoire, Croatia, Cyprus, Czech Republic, Ecuador, Egypt, Estonia, Ethiopia, Finland, Former Yugoslav Republic of Macedonia, French Polynesia, Gabon, Georgia, Germany, Ghana, Greece, Guinea, Hong Kong (China), Hungary, Iceland, India, Indonesia, Iran, Ireland, Israel, Italy, Jamaica, Japan, Jordan, Kazakhstan, Kenya, Korea, Kosovo, Kuwait, Kyrgyzstan, Latvia, Lebanon, Libya, Lithuania, Luxembourg, Madagascar, Malawi, Malaysia, Mali, Malta, Mauritania, Mauritius, Mexico, Monaco, Mongolia, Montenegro, Morocco, Namibia, Netherlands, New Caledonia, New Zealand, Niger, Nigeria, Norway, Oman, Pakistan, Panama, Philippines, Poland, Portugal, Qatar, Quebec, Romania, Russia, Saudi Arabia, Senegal, Serbia, Singapore, Slovak Republic, Slovenia, South Africa, Spain, Sri Lanka, Saint Martin, Saint Pierre and Miquelon, Sweden, Switzerland, Syrian Arab Republic, Thailand, Togo, Trinidad and Tobago, Tunisia, Turkey, Turkmenistan, Ukraine, United Arab Emirates, United Kingdom, United States, Uzbekistan, Venezuela, Viet Nam, Zambia and Zimbabwe.

Note by Turkey: The information in this document with reference to "Cyprus" relates to the southern part of the Island. There is no single authority representing both Turkish and Greek Cypriot people on the Island. Turkey recognises the Turkish Republic of Northern Cyprus (TRNC). Until a lasting and equitable solution is found within the context of the United Nations, Turkey shall preserve its position concerning the "Cyprus issue".

Note by all the European Union Member States of the OECD and the European Union. The Republic of Cyprus is recognised by all members of the United Nations with the exception of Turkey. The information in this document relates to the area under the effective control of the Government of the Republic of Cyprus.

[3] This regime is the reduced rate for long term capital gains and profits from the licensing of IP rights.

References

OECD (2017), *BEPS Action 5 on Harmful Tax Practices – Terms of Reference and Methodology for the Conduct of the Peer Reviews of the Action 5 Transparency Framework*, OECD/G20 Base Erosion and Profit Shifting Project, OECD, Paris. www.oecd.org/tax/beps/beps-action-5-harmful-tax-practices-peer-review-transparencyframework.pdf.

OECD (2015), *Countering Harmful Tax Practices More Effectively, Taking into Account Transparency and Substance, Action 5 - 2015 Final Report*, OECD/G20 Base Erosion and Profit Shifting Project, OECD Publishing, Paris. https://doi.org/10.1787/9789264241190-en.

OECD/Council of Europe (2011), *The Multilateral Convention on Mutual Administrative Assistance in Tax Matters: Amended by the 2010 Protocol*, OECD Publishing, Paris. http://dx.doi.org/10.1787/9789264115606-en.

Germany

Germany has met all aspects of the terms of reference (ToR) for the calendar year 2017 (year in review) and no recommendations are made.

Germany can legally issue five types of rulings within the scope of the transparency framework.

In practice, Germany has issued 30 past rulings;[1] for the period 1 April 2016 - 31 December 2016, Germany issued seven future rulings; and for the year in review, Germany issued ten future rulings within the scope of the transparency framework.

Peer input was received from one jurisdiction in respect of the exchanges of information on rulings received from Germany. The input was positive, noting that information was complete, in the correct format and received in a timely manner.

Introduction

436. This peer review covers Germany's implementation of the BEPS Action 5 transparency framework for the year 2017. The report has four parts, each relating to a key part of the ToR. Each part is discussed in turn. A summary of recommendations is included at the end of this report.

A. The information gathering process

437. Germany can legally issue the following four types of rulings within the scope of the transparency framework: (i) rulings related to preferential regimes;[2] (ii) cross-border unilateral advance pricing agreements (APAs) and any other cross-border unilateral tax rulings (such as an advance tax ruling) covering transfer pricing or the application of transfer pricing principles; (iii) rulings providing for a downward adjustments of taxable profits; (iv) permanent establishment rulings; and (v) related party conduit rulings. In Germany, rulings within the scope of the transparency framework can be issued by the local tax officers within the tax administrations at state level or for certain rulings by certain authorities within the Federal Central Tax Office at federal level ("FCTO").

Past rulings (ToR I.4.1.1, I.4.1.2, I.4.2.1, I.4.2.2)

438. For Germany, past rulings are any tax rulings within scope that are issued either: (i) on or after 1 January 2014 but before 1 April 2016; or (ii) on or after 1 January 2010 but before 1 January 2014, provided they were still in effect as at 1 January 2014.

439. In the prior year peer review report, it was determined that the German tax administration's undertakings to identify past rulings and all potential exchange jurisdictions were sufficient to meet the minimum standard. However, Germany notes that it identified 12[3] additional past rulings since the prior year peer report due to a misunderstanding of the "still in effect at 1 January 2014" requirement. The shortcoming was detected during the exchange process of APAs according to the EU timelines in November 2017. The past rulings were forwarded to the Competent Authority and exchanged within the same month. Germany addressed the issue by providing further training to the tax officers responsible to identify the rulings. As Germany completed the process of identifying and exchanging the past rulings within the year of review and took measures to remedy the issue it is determined that Germany's implementation in this regard continues to meet the minimum standard.

Future rulings (ToR I.4.1.1, I.4.1.2, I.4.2.1)

440. For Germany, future rulings are any tax rulings within scope that are issued on or after 1 April 2016.

441. In the prior year peer review report, it was determined that Germany's implementation of a new system to identify future rulings and all potential exchange jurisdictions was sufficient to meet the minimum standard. Germany's implementation in this regard remains unchanged, and therefore continues to meet the minimum standard.

Review and supervision mechanism (ToR I.4.3)

442. In the prior year peer review report, it was determined that the German tax administration's review and supervision mechanism was sufficient to meet the minimum standard. As a consequence of the delayed identification of 12 additional past rulings the

German tax administration all officers involved in the identification process received another training, in which the approach and the common understanding of the definition of "past ruling" was communicated again. It is therefore not expected to be a recurring issue and therefore Germany continues to meet the minimum standard.

Conclusion on section A

443. Germany has met all of the ToR for the information gathering process and no recommendations are made.

B. The exchange of information

Legal basis for spontaneous exchange of information (ToR II.5.1, II.5.2)

444. Germany has the necessary domestic legal basis to exchange information spontaneously. Germany notes that there are no legal or practical impediments that prevent the spontaneous exchange of information on rulings as contemplated in the Action 5 minimum standard.

445. Germany is a party to international agreements permitting spontaneous exchange of information, including (i) the *Multilateral Convention on Mutual Administrative Assistance in Tax Matters: Amended by the 2010 Protocol* (OECD/Council of Europe, 2011) ("the Convention"), (ii) the Directive 2011/16/EU with all other European Union Member States and (iii) double tax agreements in force with 95 jurisdictions.[4]

Completion and exchange of templates (ToR II.5.3, II.5.4, II.5.5, II.5.6, II.5.7)

446. In the prior year peer review report, Germany experienced minor delays in the exchange of information on past rulings, but did not receive any recommendations as the exchange process was completed within a relatively short period of the deadline. The German tax administration incorporated most of the suggested internal guidance to complete the summary section of the template in Annex C of the 2015 Action 5 Report (OECD, 2015), which is quality checked by the FCTO.

447. Germany identified 12 additional past rulings in the year of review and forwarded and exchanged information on those past rulings within the same month the rulings were discovered. Therefore no recommendations are made in this regard as it is not considered to be a recurring issue.

448. For the year in review, the timeliness of exchanges is as follows:

Past rulings in the scope of the transparency framework	Number of exchanges transmitted by 31 December 2017	Delayed exchanges		
		Number of exchanges not transmitted by 31 December 2017	Reasons for the delays	Any other comments
	19	0	N/A	The 19 exchanges include the seven exchanges which were not transmitted before 31 December 2016; the other 12 exchanges refer to the past rulings which were only identified in the course of 2017 and partly relate to exchanges with new Inclusive Framework members.
Future rulings in the scope of the transparency framework	**Number of exchanges transmitted within three months of the information becoming available to the Competent Authority or immediately after legal impediments have been lifted**	**Delayed exchanges**		
		Number of exchanges transmitted later than three months of the information on rulings becoming available to the Competent Authority	Reasons for the delays	Any other comments
	9	1	The delayed exchanged was transmitted in May 2017 after four months and occurred due to uncertainties within the FCTO regarding the handling of the identification and exchange requirements.	Germany revised its processes in May 2017 to ensure a timely exchange in the future.
Total	28	1		

Follow up requests received for exchange of the ruling	Number	Average time to provide response	Number of requests not answered
	0	N/A	N/A

Conclusion on section B

449. Germany has the necessary legal basis for spontaneous exchange of information, a process for completing the templates in a timely way and has completed all exchanges but one on time, and the cause of this issue has been resolved. Germany has met all of the ToR for the exchange of information process and no recommendations are made.

C. Statistics (ToR IV)

450. The statistics for the year in review are as follows:

Category of ruling	Number of exchanges	Jurisdictions exchanged with
Rulings related to preferential regimes	0	N/A
Cross-border unilateral advance pricing agreements (APAs) and any other cross-border unilateral tax rulings (such as an advance tax ruling) covering transfer pricing or the application of transfer pricing principles	8[5]	Belgium, Ireland, Luxembourg, Netherlands, Romania, Switzerland, United States
Cross-border rulings providing for a unilateral downward adjustment to the taxpayer's taxable profits that is not directly reflected in the taxpayer's financial / commercial accounts	Included in *de minimis*	N/A
Permanent establishment rulings	19	Austria, Canada, Finland, France, India, Korea, Liechtenstein, Luxembourg, Netherlands, Poland, United States
Related party conduit rulings	0	N/A
De minimis rule	2	N/A
IP regimes: total exchanges on taxpayers benefitting from the third category of IP assets, new entrants benefitting from grandfathered IP regimes; and taxpayers making use of the option to treat the nexus ratio as a rebuttable presumption	N/A	N/A
Total	29	

D. Matters related to intellectual property regimes (ToR I.4.1.3)

451. Germany does not offer an intellectual property regime for which transparency requirements under the Action 5 Report (OECD, 2015) were imposed.

Summary of recommendations on implementation of the transparency framework

Aspect of implementation of the transparency framework that should be improved	Recommendation for improvement
Germany identified 12 additional past rulings during the year of review and therefore after the timeline of 31 December 2016 due to a misunderstanding of the "still in effect at 1 January 2014" requirement.	No recommendation is made because Germany addressed the problem and completed the exchanges of information on all past rulings within the month the rulings were identified and this is not a recurring issue.

Notes

[1] Of which 12 were only identified during the year of review, including one that fell into more than one category under the BEPS Action 5 report.

[2] The preferential regime relates to the Tonnage tax regime.

[3] One ruling counted as an APA as well as a ruling on PE.

[4] Parties to the Convention are available here: www.oecd.org/tax/exchange-of-tax-information/convention-on-mutual-administrative-assistance-in-tax-matters.htm. Germany also has bilateral agreements in force with Albania, Algeria, Argentina, Armenia, Australia, Austria, Bangladesh, Belarus, Belgium, Bolivia, Bosnia and Herzegovina, Bulgaria, Canada, China (People's Republic of), Costa Rica, Côte d'Ivoire, Croatia, Cyprus, Czech Republic, Denmark, Ecuador, Egypt, Estonia, Finland, Former Yugoslav Republic of Macedonia, France, Georgia, Ghana, Greece, Hungary, Iceland, India, Indonesia, Iran, Ireland, Israel, Italy, Jamaica, Japan, Jersey, Kazakhstan, Kenia, Korea, Kosovo, Kuwait, Kyrgyzstan, Latvia, Liberia, Liechtenstein, Lithuania, Luxemburg, Malaysia, Malta, Morocco, Mauritius, Mexico, Moldavia, Mongolia, Montenegro, Namibia, Netherlands, New Zealand, Norway, Pakistan, Philippines, Poland, Portugal, Romania, Russia, Serbia, Singapore, Slovak Republic, Slovenia, South Africa, Spain, Sri Lanka, Sweden, Switzerland, Syria, Tajikistan, Thailand, Trinidad and Tobago, Tunisia, Turkey, Turkmenistan, Ukraine, United Arab Emirates, United Kingdom, United States, Uruguay, Uzbekistan, Venezuela, Viet Nam, Zambia, Zimbabwe.

Note by Turkey: The information in this document with reference to "Cyprus" relates to the southern part of the Island. There is no single authority representing both Turkish and Greek Cypriot people on the Island. Turkey recognises the Turkish Republic of Northern Cyprus (TRNC). Until a lasting and equitable solution is found within the context of the United Nations, Turkey shall preserve its position concerning the "Cyprus issue".

Note by all the European Union Member States of the OECD and the European Union. The Republic of Cyprus is recognised by all members of the United Nations with the exception of Turkey. The information in this document relates to the area under the effective control of the Government of the Republic of Cyprus.

[5] One of these rulings is also a PE ruling; it is only counted once in these statistics.

References

OECD (2017), *BEPS Action 5 on Harmful Tax Practices – Terms of Reference and Methodology for the Conduct of the Peer Reviews of the Action 5 Transparency Framework*, OECD/G20 Base Erosion and Profit Shifting Project, OECD, Paris. www.oecd.org/tax/beps/beps-action-5-harmful-tax-practices-peer-review-transparencyframework.pdf.

OECD (2015), *Countering Harmful Tax Practices More Effectively, Taking into Account Transparency and Substance, Action 5 - 2015 Final Report*, OECD/G20 Base Erosion and Profit Shifting Project, OECD Publishing, Paris. https://doi.org/10.1787/9789264241190-en.

OECD/Council of Europe (2011), *The Multilateral Convention on Mutual Administrative Assistance in Tax Matters: Amended by the 2010 Protocol*, OECD Publishing, Paris. http://dx.doi.org/10.1787/9789264115606-en.

Greece

Greece has met all aspects of the terms of reference (ToR) for the calendar year 2017 (year in review) and no recommendations are made. In the prior year peer review report, Greece received one recommendation. Greece has addressed the issue and the recommendation is removed.

Greece can legally issue one type of rulings within the scope of the transparency framework.

In practice, Greece has issued one past ruling; for the period 1 April 2016 - 31 December 2016; and for the year in review, Greece issued no future rulings within the scope of the transparency framework.

No peer input was received in respect of the exchanges of information on rulings received from Greece.

Introduction

452. This peer review covers Greece's implementation of the BEPS Action 5 transparency framework for the year 2017. The report has four parts, each relating to a key part of the ToR. Each part is discussed in turn. A summary of recommendations is included at the end of this report.

A. The information gathering process

453. Greece can legally issue one type of rulings within the scope of the transparency framework: cross-border unilateral advance pricing arrangements (APAs) and any other cross-border unilateral tax rulings (such as an advance tax ruling) covering transfer pricing or the application of transfer pricing principles. Rulings are issued by a specific department within the Directorate of Audits of the Independent Authority for Public Revenue (Greek tax administration, "IAPR"), the Department of Special Tax Audits (the issuing department, "DSTA").

Past rulings (ToR I.4.1.1, I.4.1.2, I.4.2.1, I.4.2.2)

454. For Greece, past rulings are any tax rulings within scope that are issued either: (i) on or after 1 January 2014 but before 1 April 2016; or (ii) on or after 1 January 2010 but before 1 January 2014, provided they were still in effect as at 1 January 2014.

455. In the prior year peer review report, it was determined that the IAPR's undertakings to identify past rulings and all potential exchange jurisdictions were sufficient to meet the minimum standard. The IAPR's implementation in this regard remains unchanged, and therefore continues to meet the minimum standard.

Future rulings (ToR I.4.1.1, I.4.1.2, I.4.2.1)

456. For Greece, future rulings are any tax rulings within scope that are issued on or after 1 April 2016.

457. In the prior year peer review report, it was determined that the IAPR's implementation of a new system to identify future rulings and all potential exchange jurisdictions was sufficient to meet the minimum standard. The IAPR's implementation in this regard remains unchanged, and therefore continues to meet the minimum standard.

Review and supervision mechanism (ToR I.4.3)

458. In the prior year peer review report, it was determined that the IAPR's review and supervision mechanism was sufficient to meet the minimum standard. The Head of the DSTA verifies that every unilateral APA issued by its department is identified. The IAPR's implementation in this regard remains unchanged, and therefore continues to meet the minimum standard.

Conclusion on section A

459. Greece has met all of the ToR for the information gathering process and no recommendations are made.

B. The exchange of information

Legal basis for spontaneous exchange of information (ToR II.5.1, II.5.2)

460. Greece has the necessary domestic legal basis to exchange information spontaneously. Greece notes that there are no legal or practical impediments that prevent the spontaneous exchange of information on rulings as contemplated in the Action 5 minimum standard.

461. Greece is a party to international agreements permitting spontaneous exchange of information, including (i) the *Multilateral Convention on Mutual Administrative Assistance in Tax Matters: Amended by the 2010 Protocol* (OECD/Council of Europe, 2011) ("the Convention"), (ii) the Directive 2011/16/EU with all other European Union Member States and (iii) double tax agreements in force with 57 jurisdictions.[1]

Completion and exchange of templates (ToR II.5.3, II.5.4, II.5.5, II.5.6, II.5.7)

462. In the prior year peer review report, it was determined that the IAPR's completion of the templates was sufficient to meet the minimum standard. Greece noted that three tax officers in the Department of Special Tax Audits are responsible to negotiate APAs, to update information in the database and to forward the information to the Department of International Administrative Co-operation of International Economic Relations Directorate (Greek Competent Authority). Greece confirmed that they will complete the summary section in the template in Annex C of the 2015 Action 5 Report (OECD, 2015) for future rulings as prescribed in the internal FHTP suggested guidance. It is therefore determined that the IAPR's implementation regarding the completion and exchange procedure continues to meet the minimum standard.

463. For the year in review, the timeliness of exchanges is as follows:

Past rulings in the scope of the transparency framework	Number of exchanges transmitted by 31 December 2017	Delayed exchanges		
		Number of exchanges not transmitted by 31 December 2017	Reasons for the delays	Any other comments
	1	0	N/A	The exchange refers to the delayed exchange of the past ruling mentioned in the prior year report.
Future rulings in the scope of the transparency framework	Number of exchanges transmitted within three months of the information becoming available to the competent authority or immediately after legal impediments have been lifted	Delayed exchanges		
		Number of exchanges transmitted later than three months of the information on rulings becoming available to the competent authority	Reasons for the delays	Any other comments
	N/A	N/A	N/A	N/A
Total	1	0		

Follow up requests received for exchange of the ruling	Number	Average time to provide response	Number of requests not answered
	0	N/A	N/A

464. In prior year peer review report Greece was recommended to ensure that future rulings are exchanged according to the timelines set out in the transparency framework with respect to all other members of the Inclusive Framework, rather than on a timeline aligning with the EU Directive. As noted in the prior year peer review, the one exchange on the past ruling noted above was required to occur in 2016, and – as intended by Greece – was exchanged in 2017 under the EU Directive timelines. With respect to future rulings, this recommendation would mean exchanging on a faster timeline than the EU Directive would require. However, Greece has not issued any future rulings during the year of review and so this issue has not arisen in practice for the year in review. Greece is considering last year's recommendation and will apply the timelines set out in the transparency framework for the exchange of information on future rulings, and the recommendation is removed.

Conclusion on section B

465. Greece has the necessary legal basis for spontaneous exchange of information, a process for completing the templates in a timely way and has completed all exchanges on time. Greece has met all of the ToR for the exchange of information process and no recommendations are made.

C. Statistics (ToR IV)

466. The statistics for the year in review are as follows:

Category of ruling	Number of exchanges	Jurisdictions exchanged with
Rulings related to preferential regimes	N/A	N/A
Cross-border unilateral advance pricing arrangements (APAs) and any other cross-border unilateral tax rulings (such as an advance tax ruling) covering transfer pricing or the application of transfer pricing principles	Included in *de minimis*	N/A
Cross-border rulings providing for a unilateral downward adjustment to the taxpayer's taxable profits that is not directly reflected in the taxpayer's financial / commercial accounts	N/A	N/A
Permanent establishment rulings	N/A	N/A
Related party conduit rulings	N/A	N/A
De minimis rule	1	N/A
IP regimes: total exchanges on taxpayers benefitting from the third category of IP assets, new entrants benefitting from grandfathered IP regimes; and taxpayers making use of the option to treat the nexus ratio as a rebuttable presumption	N/A	N/A
Total	1	

D. Matters related to intellectual property regimes (ToR I.4.1.3)

467. Greece does not offer an intellectual property regime for which transparency requirements under the Action 5 Report (OECD, 2015) were imposed.

Summary of recommendations on implementation of the transparency framework

Aspect of implementation of the transparency framework that should be improved	Recommendation for improvement
	No recommendations are made.

Notes

[1] Parties to the Convention are available here: www.oecd.org/tax/exchange-of-tax-information/convention-on-mutual-administrative-assistance-in-tax-matters.htm. Greece also has bilateral agreements in force with Albania, Armenia, Austria, Azerbaijan, Belgium, Bosnia and Herzegovina, Bulgaria, Canada, China (People's Republic of), Qatar, Croatia, Cyprus, Czech Republic, Denmark, Egypt, Estonia, Finland, France, Germany, Georgia, Hungary, Iceland, India, Ireland, Israel, Italy, Korea, Kuwait, Latvia, Lithuania, Luxembourg, Malta, Mexico, Moldova, Morocco, Netherlands, Norway, Poland, Portugal, Romania, Russian Federation, San Marino, Saudi Arabia, Serbia, Slovakia, Slovenia, Spain, South Africa, Sweden, Swiss Federation, Tunisia, Turkey, Ukraine, United Arab Emirates, United Kingdom, Uzbekistan and United States.

Note by Turkey: The information in this document with reference to "Cyprus" relates to the southern part of the Island. There is no single authority representing both Turkish and Greek Cypriot people on the Island. Turkey recognises the Turkish Republic of Northern Cyprus (TRNC). Until a lasting and equitable solution is found within the context of the United Nations, Turkey shall preserve its position concerning the "Cyprus issue".

Note by all the European Union Member States of the OECD and the European Union. The Republic of Cyprus is recognised by all members of the United Nations with the exception of Turkey. The information in this document relates to the area under the effective control of the Government of the Republic of Cyprus.

References

OECD (2017), *BEPS Action 5 on Harmful Tax Practices – Terms of Reference and Methodology for the Conduct of the Peer Reviews of the Action 5 Transparency Framework*, OECD/G20 Base Erosion and Profit Shifting Project, OECD, Paris. www.oecd.org/tax/beps/beps-action-5-harmful-tax-practices-peer-review-transparencyframework.pdf.

OECD (2015), *Countering Harmful Tax Practices More Effectively, Taking into Account Transparency and Substance, Action 5 - 2015 Final Report*, OECD/G20 Base Erosion and Profit Shifting Project, OECD Publishing, Paris. https://doi.org/10.1787/9789264241190-en.

OECD/Council of Europe (2011), *The Multilateral Convention on Mutual Administrative Assistance in Tax Matters: Amended by the 2010 Protocol*, OECD Publishing, Paris. http://dx.doi.org/10.1787/9789264115606-en.

Guernsey

Guernsey has met all aspects of the terms of reference (ToR) for the calendar year 2017 (year in review) and no recommendations are made.

Guernsey can legally issue five types of rulings within the scope of the transparency framework.

In practice, Guernsey issued five past rulings; and for the year in review, Guernsey issued three future rulings within the scope of the transparency framework.

No peer input was received in respect of the exchanges of information on rulings received from Guernsey.

Introduction

468. This peer review covers Guernsey's implementation of the BEPS Action 5 transparency framework for the year 2017. The report has four parts, each relating to a key part of the ToR. Each part is discussed in turn. A summary of recommendations is included at the end of this report.

A. The information gathering process

469. Guernsey can legally issue the following five types of rulings within the scope of the transparency framework: (i) rulings related to preferential regimes; (ii) cross-border unilateral advance pricing agreements (APAs) and any other cross-border unilateral tax rulings (such as an advance tax ruling) covering transfer pricing or the application of transfer pricing principles; (iii) cross-border rulings giving a unilateral downward adjustment to the taxpayer's taxable profits in the country giving the ruling; (iv) permanent establishment rulings; and (v) related party conduit rulings. In Guernsey, the Director of Income Tax, Deputy Director, Assistant Deputy Director and Senior Technical Inspector at the Guernsey Income Tax Office ("ITO"), which is a centralised office, are authorised to issue rulings.

Past rulings (ToR I.4.1.1, I.4.1.2, I.4.2.1, I.4.2.2)

470. For Guernsey, past rulings are any tax rulings within scope that are issued either: (i) on or after 1 January 2015 but before 1 April 2017; or (ii) on or after 1 January 2012 but before 1 January 2015, provided they were still in effect as at 1 January 2015.

471. The process for identifying past rulings was conducted as follows: All records of past rulings are kept in one centralised office in the ITO since Guernsey has no separate field offices. All tax rulings are maintained in physical files (management control file and taxpayer's physical file) as well as in electronic form (document management system).

472. In order to identify all past rulings in scope issued by the Director of Income Tax, a Deputy Director, the Assistant Deputy Director or the Senior Technical Inspector, a three-tier review process was developed. For stage one, senior officers in the Exchange of Information (EOI) team, known as the International Co-operation Unit, would manually review the management control files to verify the dates and whether the rulings are within scope of Action 5 by reading each of the issued rulings. In stage two, the Compliance and Investigation Manager would then further review the analysis conducted in stage one to ensure that the rulings identified were in fact a ruling within the scope of the transparency framework. The third and final review was jointly conducted by the Deputy Director (Compliance and International) and the Assistant Deputy Director to ensure accuracy.

473. For rulings pertaining to companies carrying on a banking business, rulings are stored in separate banking control files, and these rulings are issued by the Senior Technical Inspector (unlike other types of activity which are issued by the Senior Management Team). The Senior Technical Inspector responsible for issuing such rulings conducted a manual search of all of the files for taxpayers carrying out a banking business in order to identify any potential past rulings in the scope of Action 5 for stage one of the review process. Stages two and three of the review process were then conducted as detailed in paragraph 8.

474. In order to identify all potential exchange jurisdictions, the rulings themselves were reviewed firstly. In certain cases, Guernsey adopted the "best efforts approach" by

reviewing the documents and correspondence of the relevant tax ruling. The relevant taxpayer's file (both electronic and physical) would be subject to further review in order to determine all potential exchange jurisdictions. The information was verified in the three-tier checking process at increasing levels of seniority. Guernsey was able to identify the potential exchange jurisdictions in all cases.

Future rulings (ToR I.4.1.1, I.4.1.2, I.4.2.1)

475. For Guernsey, future rulings are any tax rulings within scope that are issued on or after 1 April 2017.

476. In 2017, Guernsey introduced a tax ruling template to be used by taxpayers for all future tax rulings applications. The template is available in electronic form on the ITO's website.

477. Guernsey indicates that the completion of the template is mandatory for all ruling applications. The template requires the taxpayer to provide their identification details (name, tax reference number and address), accounting period, category of ruling, summary of issues, details of jurisdictions of residence of related parties and details of jurisdictions of residence of both the immediate parent and ultimate parent of the taxpayer. The applicant also has the option to provide details of the taxpayer's main business activities and include group structure diagrams or any other documentation in support of their application. New applications for a tax ruling will not be considered unless information concerning potential exchange jurisdictions is included by the taxpayer.

478. As part of the rulings process in place, all tax ruling applications are subject to a two-tier review process. A senior tax officer/inspector will review the template submitted by the taxpayer to determine if it is complete. If any information is lacking, the taxpayer is requested to provide the additional information. A second reviewer (Director, a Deputy Director or Assistant Deputy Director) will review the analysis and decision conducted by the first reviewer. At this stage, the potential exchange jurisdictions in the future rulings issued and ruling category are identified.

Review and supervision mechanism (ToR I.4.3)

479. Guernsey notes that training on the transparency framework was provided to all Senior Assessor and Tax Inspectors taking part in the process of identifying the relevant rulings. An internal procedure with regards to the application process for future tax rulings was introduced to ensure all rulings are identified and all necessary information is obtained.

480. Guernsey developed a three-tier review process at increasing levels of seniority. The final-tier review under the information-gathering process to identify potential past ruling and categories of tax rulings is carried out by the Deputy Director (Compliance and International) and the Assistant Deputy Director.

Conclusion on section A

481. Guernsey has met all of the ToR for the information gathering process and no recommendations are made.

B. The exchange of information

Legal basis for spontaneous exchange of information (ToR II.5.1, II.5.2)

482. Guernsey has the necessary domestic legal basis to exchange information spontaneously. Guernsey notes that there are no legal or practical impediments that prevent the spontaneous exchange of information on rulings as contemplated in the Action 5 minimum standard.

483. Guernsey is a party to international agreements permitting spontaneous exchange of information, including (i) the *Multilateral Convention on Mutual Administrative Assistance in Tax Matters: Amended by the 2010 Protocol* (OECD/Council of Europe, 2011) ("the Convention"), (ii) double tax agreements and (iii) tax information exchange agreements. In total, this network covers 120 jurisdictions[1] (although for some jurisdictions the Convention has not yet entered into force).

Completion and exchange of templates (ToR II.5.3, II.5.4, II.5.5, II.5.6, II.5.7)

484. Guernsey notes that the team responsible for issuing tax rulings (both past and future rulings) is also responsible for identifying those rulings which are to be exchanged under Action 5. With respect to past rulings, the team fills in the template in PDF format as contained in Annex C of the Action 5 report (OECD, 2015).

485. With respect to future rulings, Guernsey made it mandatory for taxpayers seeking a ruling to complete a template setting out all of the required information, which is subject to review by the relevant officer dealing with the case, followed by authorisation by either the Director, Deputy Director or Assistant Deputy Director. Once a ruling has been authorised, the case is sent to the International Compliance Unit where one of the officers will complete the Annex C template. The file will be re-submitted to the Director, Deputy Director or Assistant Deputy Director for the review of the accuracy of the documents before sending. For past and future rulings, Guernsey confirms that it uses the internal FHTP suggested guidance to complete the summary section of the template under Annex C.

486. Guernsey indicates that the process for making the information available to the Competent Authority is immediate, as the same office that issues rulings is also responsible for exchanging the rulings. The past rulings that were within scope were all exchanged before the deadline of 31 December 2017. Information on future rulings is generally exchanged within three months after a particular ruling is issued.

487. The timeliness of exchanges is as follows:

Past rulings in the scope of the transparency framework	Number of exchanges transmitted by 31 December 2017	Delayed exchanges		
		Number of exchanges not transmitted by 31 December 2017	Reasons for the delays	Any other comments
	6	0	N/A	N/A
Future rulings in the scope of the transparency framework	**Number of exchanges transmitted within three months of the information becoming available to the competent authority or immediately after legal impediments have been lifted**	**Delayed exchanges**		
		Number of exchanges transmitted later than three months of the information on rulings becoming available to the competent authority	Reasons for the delays	Any other comments
	3	2	See below	See below
Total	9	2		

Follow up requests received for exchange of the ruling	Number	Average time to provide response	Number of requests not answered
	0	N/A	N/A

488. Guernsey explained that the transmission delay regarding future rulings during 2017 occurred due to an internal incorrect classification as past rulings, so they inadvertently were subjected to the internal review and exchange timetable put in place for past rulings. The affected future rulings were in any case completed during the year in review.

489. Guernsey has explained that procedures are now in place where officers in the International Co-operation Unit maintain a spreadsheet that contains a list of all tax ruling applications, which are monitored regularly. The Line Manager of International Co-operation Unit requires weekly updates of all exchange of information statistics including rulings in order to ensure close monitoring to enable the Line Manager to deploy adequate resources accordingly. The introduction of these procedures ensures that information on tax rulings are exchanged in a timely manner.

Conclusion on section B

490. Guernsey has the necessary legal basis for spontaneous exchange of information and completing the templates for exchange. There were some delays for exchanging information on future rulings, however the explanation given by Guernsey indicates that this was due to a one-off classification error. Monitoring mechanisms are now place ensuring the timely exchange of all future rulings. Guernsey has met all of the ToR for the exchange of information process and no recommendations are made.

C. Statistics (ToR IV)

491. The statistics for the year in review are as follows:

Category of ruling	Number of exchanges	Jurisdictions exchanged with
Rulings related to preferential regimes	0	N/A
Cross-border unilateral advance pricing agreements (APAs) and any other cross-border unilateral tax rulings (such as an advance tax ruling) covering transfer pricing or the application of transfer pricing principles	Included in *de minimis*	N/A
Cross-border rulings providing for a unilateral downward adjustment to the taxpayer's taxable profits that is not directly reflected in the taxpayer's financial / commercial accounts	Included in *de minimis*	N/A
Permanent establishment rulings	6	Cyprus, Jersey, United Kingdom, United States
Related party conduit rulings	0	N/A
De minimis rule	5	N/A
IP regimes: total exchanges on taxpayers benefitting from the third category of IP assets, new entrants benefitting from grandfathered IP regimes; and taxpayers making use of the option to treat the nexus ratio as a rebuttable presumption	N/A	N/A
Total	11	

D. Matters related to intellectual property regimes (ToR I.4.1.3)

492. Guernsey does not offer an intellectual property regime for which transparency requirements under the Action 5 Report (OECD, 2015) were imposed.

Summary of recommendations on implementation of the transparency framework

Aspect of implementation of the transparency framework that should be improved	Recommendation for improvement
No recommendations are made.	

Notes

1 Parties to the Convention are available here: www.oecd.org/tax/exchange-of-tax-information/convention-on-mutual-administrative-assistance-in-tax-matters.htm. Guernsey also has bilateral agreements in force with Bahamas, British Virgin Islands, Cayman Islands, Cyprus, Gibraltar, Hong Kong, Isle of Man, Jersey, Liechtenstein, Luxembourg, Malta, Mauritius, Monaco, Qatar, Seychelles, Singapore, Turks and Caicos Islands, United Kingdom and United States permitting spontaneous exchange of information.

Note by Turkey: The information in this document with reference to "Cyprus" relates to the southern part of the Island. There is no single authority representing both Turkish and Greek Cypriot people on the Island. Turkey recognises the Turkish Republic of Northern Cyprus (TRNC). Until a lasting and equitable solution is found within the context of the United Nations, Turkey shall preserve its position concerning the "Cyprus issue".

Note by all the European Union Member States of the OECD and the European Union. The Republic of Cyprus is recognised by all members of the United Nations with the exception of Turkey. The information in this document relates to the area under the effective control of the Government of the Republic of Cyprus.

References

OECD (2017), *BEPS Action 5 on Harmful Tax Practices – Terms of Reference and Methodology for the Conduct of the Peer Reviews of the Action 5 Transparency Framework*, OECD/G20 Base Erosion and Profit Shifting Project, OECD, Paris. www.oecd.org/tax/beps/beps-action-5-harmful-tax-practices-peer-review-transparencyframework.pdf.

OECD (2015), *Countering Harmful Tax Practices More Effectively, Taking into Account Transparency and Substance, Action 5 - 2015 Final Report*, OECD/G20 Base Erosion and Profit Shifting Project, OECD Publishing, Paris. https://doi.org/10.1787/9789264241190-en.

OECD/Council of Europe (2011), *The Multilateral Convention on Mutual Administrative Assistance in Tax Matters: Amended by the 2010 Protocol*, OECD Publishing, Paris. http://dx.doi.org/10.1787/9789264115606-en.

Haiti

Haiti has met all aspects of the terms of reference (ToR) for the calendar year 2017 (year in review) that can be met in the absence of rulings being issued.[1]

Haiti cannot legally issue any type of rulings within the scope of the transparency framework.

As no rulings were issued, no exchange of information was required. No peer input was received in respect of the exchanges of information on rulings received from Haiti.

Introduction

493. This peer review covers Haiti's implementation of the BEPS Action 5 transparency framework for the year 2017. The report has four parts, each relating to a key part of the ToR. Each part is discussed in turn. A summary of recommendations is included at the end of this report.

A. The information gathering process

494. As no rulings are issued, this section is not assessed.

B. The exchange of information

495. As no rulings are issued, this section is not assessed.

C. Statistics (ToR IV)

496. As no rulings are issued, no statistical data can be reported.

D. Matters related to intellectual property regimes (ToR I.4.1.3)

497. Haiti does not offer an intellectual property regime for which transparency requirements under the Action 5 Report (OECD, 2015) were imposed.

Summary of recommendations on implementation of the transparency framework

Aspect of implementation of the transparency framework that should be improved	Recommendation for improvement
No recommendations are made.	

Note

[1] Haiti did not provide written comments on this peer review report.

References

OECD (2017), *BEPS Action 5 on Harmful Tax Practices – Terms of Reference and Methodology for the Conduct of the Peer Reviews of the Action 5 Transparency Framework*, OECD/G20 Base Erosion and Profit Shifting Project, OECD, Paris. www.oecd.org/tax/beps/beps-action-5-harmful-tax-practices-peer-review-transparencyframework.pdf.

OECD (2015), *Countering Harmful Tax Practices More Effectively, Taking into Account Transparency and Substance, Action 5 - 2015 Final Report*, OECD/G20 Base Erosion and Profit Shifting Project, OECD Publishing, Paris. https://doi.org/10.1787/9789264241190-en.

Chapter 3. Hong Kong (China)

Hong Kong (China) ("Hong Kong") has met all of the terms of reference (ToR) for the calendar year 2017 (year in review) and no recommendations are made.

Hong Kong can legally issue four types of rulings within the scope of the transparency framework.

In practice, Hong Kong issued one past ruling; and for the year in review, Hong Kong issued no future rulings within the scope of the transparency framework.

No peer input was received in respect of the exchanges of information on rulings received from Hong Kong.

Introduction

498. This peer review covers Hong Kong's implementation of the BEPS Action 5 transparency framework for the year 2017. The report has four parts, each relating to a key part of the ToR. Each part is discussed in turn. A summary of recommendations is included at the end of this report.

A. The information gathering process

499. Hong Kong can legally issue the following four types of rulings within the scope of the transparency framework: (i) rulings related to preferential regimes;[1] (ii) cross-border unilateral APAs and any other cross-border unilateral tax rulings (such as an AR) covering transfer pricing or the application of transfer pricing principles; (iii) permanent establishment rulings; and (iv) conduit rulings. The IRD is responsible for issuing rulings. The Tax Treaty Section is responsible for issuing APAs and the Profits Tax Unit and the Commissioner's Unit are responsible for issuing ARs within the other three categories of tax rulings. The Inland Revenue Department of Hong Kong ("IRD") may publish some ARs on its website in redacted form.[2]

Past rulings (ToR I.4.1.1, I.4.1.2, I.4.2.1, I.4.2.2)

500. For Hong Kong, past rulings are any tax rulings within scope that are issued either: (i) on or after 1 January 2015 but before 1 April 2017; or (ii) on or after 1 January 2012 but before 1 January 2015, provided they were still in effect as at 1 January 2015.

501. A dedicated APA register and AR register are maintained to record the details of the rulings issued, including the category and a brief description of the case, as well as the date of issue and duration of the APA/AR issued. Such details will be entered into the registers in the course of processing the APA/AR. The registers contain the details of all rulings issued since the introduction of the statutory AR regime (1998) and the administrative APA regime (2012).

502. Officers in the Tax Treaty Section were responsible for identifying past rulings, by consulting the details in the APA register and the AR register. In addition, the paper files of the identified cases were manually reviewed to verify whether the rulings fell within the past ruling period. One ruling was identified to be within the scope of the transparency framework during this review process.

503. In order to identify potential exchange jurisdictions with respect to the past ruling, the "best efforts approach" was used. The officers first examined the paper file of the relevant AR case, the tax file of the taxpayer and the annual report of the taxpayer's ultimate parent entity available from the internet to identify the relevant related parties and their jurisdictions of tax residence. All information on potential exchange jurisdictions was identified.

Future rulings (ToR I.4.1.1, I.4.1.2, I.4.2.1)

504. For Hong Kong, future rulings are any tax rulings within scope that are issued on or after 1 April 2017.

505. The rulings are identified at the moment that applications for APAs/ARs are received from the taxpayer.

506. With respect to ARs, applicants are now required to state whether the requested ARs fall within the four categories in the scope of the transparency framework, and if so, to which categories the ARs belong. This information will be registered in the AR register and updated in the course of processing the ARs after verification by senior officers. For controlling purposes, a monthly report will be generated from the AR register to identify all the issued ARs which are not classified as Action 5 rulings. If they appear to fall within the scope, the AR register will be amended.

507. In order to identify potential exchange jurisdictions, the taxpayer is required to provide this information in the AR application. This information is verified by senior officers by checking the supporting documents, and consulting the profits tax file of the taxpayer and the annual report of the taxpayer's ultimate parent entity available from internet. Upon the finalisation of the AR, the case officer is required to double check the available information to ensure that all relevant related parties and their jurisdictions of residence are correctly identified.

508. In the year of review, Hong Kong only considered applications for unilateral APAs in exceptional circumstances and no such APA was issued. The information gathering process for future APA rulings was the same as for past APA rulings. Following the enactment of the Inland Revenue (Amendment) (No. 6) Ordinance 2018 on 13 July 2018, Hong Kong's APA regime has been codified and applications for unilateral APAs will generally be considered. The information gathering process for APA applications has now been revised along the same line as the amended process for ARs as described in the previous paragraphs.

Review and supervision mechanism (ToR I.4.3)

509. The IRD has issued internal guidance to explain the five categories of Action 5 rulings and the requirement to exchange such rulings spontaneously with the jurisdictions in which the related parties are resident. In addition, training has been held for relevant AR and APA officers. Taxpayers have been informed of the need for exchanging information on ARs through information included on the amended AR application form. The APA application form will be amended accordingly.

Conclusion on section A

510. Hong Kong has met all of the ToR for the information gathering process and no recommendations are made. Hong Kong is encouraged to continue its work on revising the APA application procedure in order to identify the relevant information with respect to future APAs.

B. The exchange of information

Legal basis for spontaneous exchange of information (ToR II.5.1, II.5.2)

511. Hong Kong has the necessary domestic legal basis to exchange information spontaneously. Hong Kong notes that there are no legal or practical impediments that prevent the spontaneous exchange of information on rulings as contemplated in the Action 5 minimum standard.

512. Hong Kong is party to international agreements permitting spontaneous exchange of information, including double tax agreements in force with 29 jurisdictions.[3]

513. In addition, the Inland Revenue (Amendment) Ordinance 2018 was enacted to empower the Chief Executive-in-Council ("CE-in-C") to make an order for giving effect to multilateral tax arrangements in Hong Kong. By a declaration deposited with the OECD on 29 May 2018, China extended the application of the *Multilateral Convention on Mutual Administrative Assistance in Tax Matters: Amended by the 2010 Protocol* (OECD/Council of Europe, 2011) ("the Convention") to Hong Kong. The order made by the CE-in-C for giving effect to the Convention came into operation on 13 July 2018, and the Convention entered into force in Hong Kong on 1 September 2018.

Completion and exchange of templates (ToR II.5.3, II.5.4, II.5.5, II.5.6, II.5.7)

514. With respect to the one past ruling, the Tax Treaty Section completed the relevant template, which was in the form of Annex C of the 2015 Action 5 Report (OECD, 2015). Internal guidance has been issued by the IRD to explain the information required in the template. The officer in charge of the AR or APA case is required to follow the internal FHTP suggested guidance by including a description of the relevant transaction or activity covered by the AR/APA, the agreed tax treatment and any other relevant information. This template was submitted for review and approval by the Deputy Commissioner of the IRD (who is also the Competent Authority). The information was exchanged with the relevant jurisdiction in December 2017.

515. For future rulings, the AR and APA officers are required to complete the relevant templates and send them to the Tax Treaty Section immediately after issuing the rulings. The template is currently in Word format but based on the OECD *XML Schema and User Guide* (OECD, 2017b). The head of the Tax Treaty Section reviews if the relevant templates are accurate and complete before submitting them to the Competent Authority for exchange within two months of issue of the ruling. In addition there is a separate register, the "Outgoing Spontaneous Exchange of Information Register", which will generate a monthly report showing the position of all Action 5 rulings issued. The cases with respect to which exchange of relevant templates have not been conducted within two months after the date of issue of the rulings will be referred to the head of the Tax Treaty Section. This register will also be reconciled with the APA register and the AR register to ensure that all Action 5 rulings issued are monitored.

516. The IRD is currently developing a computer program to enable officers to convert the relevant templates into XML schema format (in accordance with the OECD XML Schema). All validation elements that are required in the OECD *XML Schema and User Guide* (OECD, 2017) will be incorporated in this computer program.

517. For the year in review, the timeliness of exchanges is as follows:

Past rulings in the scope of the transparency framework	Number of exchanges transmitted by 31 December 2017	Delayed exchanges		
		Number of exchanges not transmitted by 31 December 2017	Reasons for the delays	Any other comments
	1	0	N/A	N/A
Future rulings in the scope of the transparency framework	Number of exchanges transmitted within three months of the information becoming available to the competent authority or immediately after legal impediments have been lifted	Delayed exchanges		
		Number of exchanges transmitted later than three months of the information on rulings becoming available to the competent authority	Reasons for the delays	Any other comments
	0	0	N/A	
Total	1	0		

Follow up requests received for exchange of the ruling	Number	Average time to provide response	Number of requests not answered
	0	N/A	N/A

Conclusion on section B

518. Hong Kong has the necessary legal framework and administrative process in place for exchanging information on rulings. Hong Kong has timely exchanged the information on the ruling within scope of the transparency framework. Hong Kong has met all of the ToR for the exchange of information process and no recommendations are made.

C. Statistics (ToR IV)

519. The statistics for the year in review are as follows:

Category of ruling	Number of exchanges	Jurisdictions exchanged with
Rulings related to preferential regimes	Included in *de minimis*	N/A
Cross-border unilateral advance pricing agreements (APAs) and any other cross-border unilateral tax rulings (such as an advance tax ruling) covering transfer pricing or the application of transfer pricing principles	0	N/A
Cross-border rulings providing for a unilateral downward adjustment to the taxpayer's taxable profits that is not directly reflected in the taxpayer's financial / commercial accounts	N/A	N/A
Permanent establishment rulings	0	N/A
Related party conduit rulings	0	N/A
De minimis rule	1	N/A
IP regimes: total exchanges on taxpayers benefitting from the third category of IP assets, new entrants benefitting from grandfathered IP regimes; and taxpayers making use of the option to treat the nexus ratio as a rebuttable presumption	N/A	N/A
Total	1	

D. Matters related to intellectual property regimes (ToR I.4.1.3)

520. Hong Kong does not offer an intellectual property regime for which transparency requirements under the Action 5 Report (OECD, 2015) were imposed.

Summary of recommendations on implementation of the transparency framework

Aspect of implementation of the transparency framework that should be improved	Recommendation for improvement
	No recommendations are made.

Notes

1 With respect to the following preferential regimes: 1) Profits tax concession for corporate treasury centres, 2) Profits tax concession for professional reinsurers, 3) Profits tax concession for captive insurers, 4) Profits tax exemptions for ship operators and 5) Profits tax concessions for aircraft lessors and aircraft leasing managers.

2 www.ird.gov.hk/eng/ppr/arc.htm (accessed 19 November 2018).

3 Hong Kong has bilateral agreements with Austria, Bailiwick of Guernsey, Belarus, Belgium, Canada, China (People's Republic of), France, Hungary, Indonesia, Ireland, Italy, Japan, Jersey, Korea, Latvia, Malta, Mexico, Netherlands, Pakistan, Portugal, Qatar, Romania, South Africa, Spain, Switzerland, Thailand, United Arab Emirates, United Kingdom and Viet Nam.

References

OECD (2017a), *BEPS Action 5 on Harmful Tax Practices – Terms of Reference and Methodology for the Conduct of the Peer Reviews of the Action 5 Transparency Framework*, OECD/G20 Base Erosion and Profit Shifting Project, OECD, Paris. www.oecd.org/tax/beps/beps-action-5-harmful-tax-practices-peer-review-transparencyframework.pdf.

OECD (2017b), Country-by-Country Reporting XML Schema: User Guide for Tax Administrations, OECD, Paris. www.oecd.org/tax/country-by-country-reporting-xmlschema-user-guide-for-tax-administrations.pdf.

OECD (2015), *Countering Harmful Tax Practices More Effectively, Taking into Account Transparency and Substance, Action 5 - 2015 Final Report*, OECD/G20 Base Erosion and Profit Shifting Project, OECD Publishing, Paris. https://doi.org/10.1787/9789264241190-en.

OECD/Council of Europe (2011), *The Multilateral Convention on Mutual Administrative Assistance in Tax Matters: Amended by the 2010 Protocol*, OECD Publishing, Paris. http://dx.doi.org/10.1787/9789264115606-en.

Hungary

Hungary has met all aspects of the terms of reference (ToR) for the calendar year 2017 (year in review) except for applying the "best efforts approach" for past rulings by using all information accessible to the tax administration (ToR I.4.2.2), to identify all potential exchange jurisdictions for future rulings before the new application process took effect (ToR I.4.2.1), to timely exchange information on past and future rulings (ToR II.5.6); and to identify and exchange information on new entrants to the grandfathered IP regime (ToR I.4.1.3) Hungary received four recommendations in the prior year report. Hungary has addressed one recommendation relating to the submission of information to the Competent Authority without undue delay, which is removed. One new recommendation is made. Hungary is recommended to continue to apply the "best efforts approach" to identify potential exchange jurisdictions for all past rulings, to ensure that all potential exchange jurisdictions are identified swiftly for all future rulings, to ensure that all information on future rulings is exchanged as soon as possible, and to identify and exchange information on new entrants to the grandfathered IP regime.

Hungary can legally issue four types of rulings within the scope of the transparency framework.

In practice, Hungary has issued 77 past rulings; for the period 1 April 2016 - 31 December 2016, Hungary issued four future rulings; and for the year in review Hungary issued nine future rulings within the scope of the transparency framework.

Peer input was received from one jurisdiction in respect of the exchanges of information on rulings from Hungary. The input was positive, noting that the information was complete, in the correct format and received in a timely manner.

Introduction

521. This peer review covers the Hungary's implementation of the BEPS Action 5 transparency framework for the year 2017. The report has four parts, each relating to a key part of the ToR. Each part is discussed in turn. A summary of recommendations is included at the end of this report.

A. The information gathering process

522. In the year of review the Hungary could legally issue the four following types of rulings within the scope of the transparency framework: (i) rulings related to preferential regimes (IP regime for royalties and capital gains); (ii) cross-border unilateral advance pricing agreements (APAs) and any other cross-border unilateral tax rulings (such as an advance tax ruling) covering transfer pricing or the application of transfer pricing principles; (iii) permanent establishment rulings; and (iv) related party conduit rulings. Unilateral APAs are issued by the APA unit in the National Tax and Customs Administration (NTCA) and all other types of rulings are issued by the Ministry for National Economy.

Past rulings (ToR I.4.1.1, I.4.1.2, I.4.2.1, I.4.2.2)

523. For Hungary, past rulings are any tax rulings within scope that are issued either: (i) on or after 1 January 2014 but before 1 April 2016; or (ii) on or after 1 January 2010 but before 1 January 2014, provided they were still in effect as at 1 January 2014.

524. In the prior year peer review report, it was determined that the Hungarian tax administration's undertakings to identify past rulings and all potential exchange jurisdictions were sufficient to meet the minimum standard. Hungary states that for APAs it was able to identify most of the potential exchange information as the information was usually included in the ruling itself, even though the taxpayer is not required to provide information on the ultimate parent company. For other rulings, Hungary was only able to identify about half of the potential exchange jurisdictions as those rulings usually did not include information on the immediate and ultimate parent companies. So far the tax administration was primarily consulting the ruling itself and was not using other sources that may contain further information on the taxpayer, including through access to company incorporation databases.

525. In order to identify further potential Hungary is recommended to continue to apply the "best efforts approach" to identify potential exchange jurisdictions for all past rulings.

Future rulings (ToR I.4.1.1, I.4.1.2, I.4.2.1)

526. For Hungary, future rulings are any tax rulings within scope that are issued on or after 1 April 2016.

527. In the prior year peer review report, it was determined that Hungary's process to identify future rulings was sufficient to meet the minimum standard except for identifying all potential exchange jurisdictions. Hungary was recommended to amend its ruling practice to ensure that information on all potential exchange jurisdictions, particularly on the ultimate parent company, is always obtained. Hungary has amended its rulings practice with effect of 1 January 2018 requiring the taxpayer to provide information on immediate and ultimate parent company when applying for a ruling. As the new

procedure was only introduced on 1 January 2018 Hungary should try to gather information on further potential exchange information for future rulings issued before that date using all sources available to the tax administration that may contain further information on the taxpayer, including through access to company incorporation databases.

528. Hungary is therefore recommended to ensure that all potential exchange jurisdictions are identified swiftly for all future rulings.

Review and supervision mechanism (ToR I.4.3)

529. In the prior year peer review report, it was determined that Hungary's review and supervision mechanisms were sufficient to meet the minimum standard. Hungary's implementation in this regard remains unchanged, and therefore continues to meet the minimum standard.

Conclusion on section A

530. It is determined that Hungary has met all of the ToR except for identifying all potential exchange jurisdictions for past rulings (ToR I.4.2.2) and future rulings (ToR I.4.2.1). Hungary is recommended to continue to apply the "best efforts approach" to identify potential exchange jurisdictions for all past rulings and to ensure that all potential exchange jurisdictions are identified swiftly for all future rulings.

B. The exchange of information

Legal basis for spontaneous exchange of information (ToR II.5.1, II.5.2)

531. In the year of review, Hungary identified that it only had the domestic legal basis to exchange information with EU Member States and was therefore not able to exchange information with all members of the Inclusive Framework. Hungary introduced the legal basis to exchange information on rulings issued after 31 December 2017 with all members of the Inclusive Framework on 24 November 2017 and introduced the legal basis to exchange information on rulings issued between 1 January 2010 and 31 December 2017 with all members of the Inclusive Framework on 1 January 2018. Therefore, Hungary did not have the necessary domestic legal basis to exchange information on rulings with all members of the Inclusive Framework during the year of review, but has addressed the issue and is able to exchange information with all other members of the Inclusive Framework as of 1 January 2018.

532. Hungary is a party to international agreements permitting spontaneous exchange of information, including (i) *the Multilateral Convention on Mutual Administrative Assistance in Tax Matters; Amended by the 2010 Protocol* (OECD/Council of Europe, 2011) ("the Convention"), (ii) the Directive 2011/16/EU with all other European Union Member States and (iii) double tax agreements in force with 80 jurisdictions.[1]

Completion and exchange of templates (ToR II.5.3, II.5.4, II.5.5, II.5.6, II.5.7)

533. In the prior year peer review report, it was determined that Hungary's completion of the templates were sufficient to meet the minimum standard except for the timely submission of the information to the Competent Authority (ToR II.5.5) and the timely exchange of information on rulings (ToR II.5.6). In the prior year report, Hungary remarked that it intended to remedy this issue via an internal procedural regulation.

Hungary states that it now takes in average three months to forward information on rulings to the Competent Authority from the date the ruling is issued and that it is intended to further reduce the timelines to two weeks.

534. Due to the lack of the domestic legal basis to exchange information with all members of the Inclusive Framework, Hungary only exchanged information with EU Member States under the EU timelines during the year in review. After introducing the legal basis to exchange with other Inclusive framework members, Hungary was able to exchange information on all past rulings and future rulings issued until 31 December 2017 by July 2018.

535. For the year in review, the timeliness of exchanges is as follows:

Past rulings in the scope of the transparency framework	Number of exchanges transmitted by 31 December 2017	Delayed exchanges		
		Number of exchanges not transmitted by 31 December 2017	Reasons for the delays	Any other comments
	46	92	All delayed exchanges on past rulings have been transmitted until 30 June 2018 according with domestic legislation	
Future rulings in the scope of the transparency framework	Number of exchanges transmitted within three months of the information becoming available to the Competent Authority or immediately after legal impediments have been lifted	Delayed exchanges		
		Number of exchanges transmitted later than three months of the information on rulings becoming available to the Competent Authority	Reasons for the delays	Any other comments
	0	14[2]	Hungary is applying the EU timelines to exchange information with EU Member States. Regarding Non EU Member States Hungary encountered legal impediments and therefore could not transmit eight exchanges on future rulings in the year of review.	Since the introduction of the national legislation with effect of 1 January 2018, eight exchanges on future rulings have been transmitted.
Total	46	98		

Follow up requests received for exchange of the ruling	Number	Average time to provide response	Number of requests not answered
	0	N/A	N/A

536. Hungary exchanged information later than three months after the information became available to the Competent Authority. Hungary is recommended to ensure that all information on future rulings is exchanged as soon as possible.

Conclusion on section B

537. For the year in review, Hungary did not have the necessary legal basis for spontaneous exchange of information with all members of the Inclusive Framework. However, Hungary has introduced the necessary legal basis to exchange information with all members of the Inclusive Framework with effect of 1 January 2018 and has transmitted the exchanges of information on all past and future rulings with other members of the Inclusive Framework until July 2018. Hungary has also taken steps to meet the timelines for forwarding information to the Competent Authority. Hungary is recommended to ensure that all information on future rulings is exchanged as soon as possible (ToR II.5.6).

C. Statistics (ToR IV)

538. The statistics for the year in review are as follows:

Category of ruling	Number of exchanges	Jurisdictions exchanged with
Rulings related to preferential regimes	7	Germany, Ireland, Romania, United Kingdom
Cross-border unilateral advance pricing agreements (APAs) and any other cross-border unilateral tax rulings (such as an advance tax ruling) covering transfer pricing or the application of transfer pricing principles	31	Austria, Croatia Czech Republic, Cyprus[3], Germany, Ireland, Luxembourg, Netherlands, Poland, Romania, Slovak Republic, Slovenia, United Kingdom
Cross-border rulings providing for a unilateral downward adjustment to the taxpayer's taxable profits that is not directly reflected in the taxpayer's financial / commercial accounts	0	N/A
Permanent establishment rulings	14	Austria, Germany, Ireland, Luxembourg, Netherlands, Malta, Poland, United Kingdom
Related party conduit rulings	0	N/A
De minimis rule	0	N/A
IP regimes: total exchanges on taxpayers benefitting from the third category of IP assets, new entrants benefitting from grandfathered IP regimes; and taxpayers making use of the option to treat the nexus ratio as a rebuttable presumption	0	N/A
Total	52	

D. Matters related to intellectual property regimes (ToR I.4.1.3)

539. Hungary offers an intellectual property regime that is subject to transparency requirements under the Action 5 Report (OECD, 2015).[4] According to the information provided for the prior year report, the identification of the benefitting taxpayers will occur as follows:

- ***New entrants benefitting from the grandfathered regime:*** Taxpayers that are new entrants to the IP regime can be identified in the tax return. The first tax returns containing information on new entrants have been filed after 6 February 2015. Hungary is currently trying to identify new taxpayers by analysing previous tax returns of taxpayers who have opted into the grandfathered regime. However, new IP assets cannot be identified in the absence of the relevant data in the tax returns and the identification of the new IP assets requires detailed inspection of each taxpayer benefitting from the IP regime. Therefore, Hungary has not exchanged information on new entrants to the grandfathered regime yet. Hungary intends to exchange the information on a retroactive basis as soon as it has identified the new entrants (i.e. both new taxpayers and new IP assets).

- ***Third category of IP assets:*** not applicable, as this option has not been incorporated in the Hungarian IP regime.
- ***Taxpayers making use of the option to treat the nexus ratio as a rebuttable presumption:*** not applicable, as this option has not been incorporated in the Hungarian IP regime.

540. Hungary is recommended to continue its efforts to identify and exchange information on all new entrants to the IP regime as soon as possible (ToR I.4.1.3).

Summary of recommendations on implementation of the transparency framework

Aspect of implementation of the transparency framework that should be improved	Recommendation for improvement
Hungary was only able to identify potential exchange jurisdictions for around half of the past rulings issued, even though Hungary may have additional ownership information in its possession or this information is accessible to the tax administration, including through access to company incorporation databases.	Hungary is recommended to continue to apply the "best efforts approach" to identify potential exchange jurisdictions for all past rulings.
Hungary was only able to identify potential exchange jurisdictions for around half of the future rulings issued until 31 December 2017, even though Hungary may have additional ownership information in its possession or this information is accessible to the tax administration, including through access to company incorporation databases. It is noted that Hungary has amended its issuing procedure for future rulings as of 1 January 2018 requiring the taxpayers to provide information on relevant exchange jurisdictions. This is a continuing recommendation from the prior year peer review.	Hungary is recommended to ensure that all potential exchange jurisdictions are identified swiftly for all future rulings.
Hungary was not able to exchange future and past rulings in the year of review with non EU Member States as it did not have the legal basis to do so. Hungary introduced a new legal basis as of 1 January 2018 and has exchanged information on rulings with all G20 and non-EU Member States. For the exchange of information with EU Member States Hungary did not meet the timelines of the transparency framework. This is a continuing recommendation from the prior year peer review.	Hungary is recommended to ensure that all information on future rulings is exchanged as soon as possible.
Hungary has not identified and exchanged information on new entrants to the grandfathered IP regime, although information for the 2015 period should be available. This is a continuing recommendation from the prior year peer review.	Hungary is recommended to continue its efforts to identify and exchange information on new entrants to the grandfathered IP regime.

Notes

[1] Parties to the Convention are available here: www.oecd.org/tax/exchange-of-tax-information/convention-on-mutual-administrative-assistance-in-tax-matters.htm. Hungary also has bilateral agreements in force with Albania, Armenia, Australia, Austria, Azerbaijan, Bahrain, Belarus, Belgium, Bosnia and Herzegovina, Brazil, Bulgaria, Canada, China (People's Republic of), Croatia, Cyprus, Czech Republic, Denmark, Egypt, Estonia, Finland, Former Yugoslav Republic of Macedonia, France, Georgia, Germany, Greece, Hong Kong (China), Iceland, India, Indonesia, Iran, Ireland, Israel, Italy, Japan, Kazakhstan, Korea, Kosovo, Kuwait, Latvia, Liechtenstein, Lithuania, Luxembourg, Malaysia, Malta, Mexico, Moldova, Mongolia, Montenegro, Morocco, Netherlands, Norway, Oman, Pakistan, Philippines, Poland, Portugal, Qatar, Romania, Russia, San Marino, Saudi Arabia, Serbia, Singapore, Slovak Republic, Slovenia, South Africa, Spain, Sweden, Switzerland, Chinese Taipei, Thailand, Tunisia, Turkey, Turkmenistan, Ukraine, United Arab Emirates, United Kingdom, United States, Uruguay, Uzbekistan and Viet Nam.

[2] In the prior year's report the number of 20 delayed exchanges on future rulings had to be revised as Hungary notes that not all of the rulings to which the exchanges related were in scope of the transparency framework.

[3] Note by Turkey: The information in this document with reference to "Cyprus" relates to the southern part of the Island. There is no single authority representing both Turkish and Greek Cypriot people on the Island. Turkey recognises the Turkish Republic of Northern Cyprus (TRNC). Until a lasting and equitable solution is found within the context of the United Nations, Turkey shall preserve its position concerning the "Cyprus issue".

Note by all the European Union Member States of the OECD and the European Union. The Republic of Cyprus is recognised by all members of the United Nations with the exception of Turkey. The information in this document relates to the area under the effective control of the Government of the Republic of Cyprus.

[4] IP Regime for royalties and capital gains.

References

OECD (2017), *BEPS Action 5 on Harmful Tax Practices – Terms of Reference and Methodology for the Conduct of the Peer Reviews of the Action 5 Transparency Framework*, OECD/G20 Base Erosion and Profit Shifting Project, OECD, Paris. www.oecd.org/tax/beps/beps-action-5-harmful-tax-practices-peer-review-transparencyframework.pdf.

OECD (2015), *Countering Harmful Tax Practices More Effectively, Taking into Account Transparency and Substance, Action 5 - 2015 Final Report*, OECD/G20 Base Erosion and Profit Shifting Project, OECD Publishing, Paris. https://doi.org/10.1787/9789264241190-en.

OECD/Council of Europe (2011), *The Multilateral Convention on Mutual Administrative Assistance in Tax Matters: Amended by the 2010 Protocol*, OECD Publishing, Paris. http://dx.doi.org/10.1787/9789264115606-en.

Iceland

Iceland has met all aspects of the terms of reference (ToR) for the calendar year 2017 (year in review) and no recommendations are made. In the prior year peer review report, Iceland received one recommendation for not providing information in the form of the template contained in Annex C of the Action 5 Report (OECD, 2015) or the OECD XML Schema and in accordance with the OECD *XML Schema User Guide* (OECD, 2017b). Iceland has addressed the issue and the recommendation is removed.

Iceland can legally issue two types of rulings within the scope of the transparency framework.

In practice, Iceland has issued one past ruling; and for the period 1 April 2016 - 31 December 2016 and the year in review, Iceland issued no future rulings within the scope of the transparency framework.

No peer input was received in respect of the exchanges of information on rulings received from Iceland.

Introduction

541. This peer review covers Iceland's implementation of the BEPS Action 5 transparency framework for the year 2017. The report has four parts, each relating to a key part of the ToR. Each part is discussed in turn. A summary of recommendations is included at the end of this report.

A. The information gathering process

542. Iceland can legally issue the two following types of rulings within the scope of the transparency framework: (i) permanent establishment rulings; and (ii) related party conduit rulings. The Directorate of Internal Revenue (Icelandic tax administration, "IRD") has authorised around 50 persons to issue those rulings. Rulings are published on the tax administration website in anonymised form.[1]

Past rulings (ToR I.4.1.1, I.4.1.2, I.4.2.1, I.4.2.2)

543. For Iceland, past rulings are any tax rulings within scope that are issued either: (i) on or after 1 January 2014 but before 1 April 2016; or (ii) on or after 1 January 2010 but before 1 January 2014, provided they were still in effect as at 1 January 2014.

544. In the prior year peer review report, it was determined that the IRD's undertakings to identify past rulings and all potential exchange jurisdictions were sufficient to meet the minimum standard. The IRD's implementation in this regard remains unchanged, and therefore continues to meet the minimum standard.

Future rulings (ToR I.4.1.1, I.4.1.2, I.4.2.1)

545. For Iceland, future rulings are any tax rulings within scope that are issued on or after 1 April 2016.

546. In the prior year peer review report, it was determined that the IRD's implementation of a new system to identify future rulings and all potential exchange jurisdictions was sufficient to meet the minimum standard. The IRD's implementation in this regard remains unchanged, and therefore continues to meet the minimum standard.

Review and supervision mechanism (ToR I.4.3)

547. In the prior year peer review report, it was determined that the IRD's review and supervision mechanism including a dual control principle was sufficient to meet the minimum standard. On 11 May 2017 the IRD announced a new person as a Competent Authority responsible for all exchanges of information, including rulings. Therefore as of that date the person issuing the ruling is no longer the Competent Authority. The person issuing rulings is subject to the supervision of the Director General of the IRD. The Competent Authority is directly responsible to the Director of the Administrative Department, an organizational unit within the IRD, concerned with daily management of the Director General's office, organizational issues, as well as international relations and cooperation, and subject to his supervision. The supervision of the Director General and the Director of the Administrative Department includes reviewing whether rulings are correctly identified and exchanged.

548. As Iceland enhanced its review and supervision mechanism it continues to meet the minimum standard.

Conclusion on section A

549. Iceland has met all of the ToR for the information gathering process and no recommendations are made.

B. The exchange of information

Legal basis for spontaneous exchange of information (ToR II.5.1, II.5.2)

550. Iceland has the necessary domestic legal basis to exchange information spontaneously. Iceland notes that there are no legal or practical impediments that prevent the spontaneous exchange of information on rulings as contemplated in the Action 5 minimum standard.

551. Iceland is a party to international agreements permitting spontaneous exchange of information, including (i) the *Multilateral Convention on Mutual Administrative Assistance in Tax Matters: Amended by the 2010 Protocol* (OECD/Council of Europe, 2011) ("the Convention"), (ii) the Nordic Convention with Denmark, Faroe Islands, Finland, Greenland, Norway and Sweden and (iii) double tax agreements with 39 jurisdictions.[2]

Completion and exchange of templates (ToR II.5.3, II.5.4, II.5.5, II.5.6, II.5.7)

552. In the prior year peer review report, Iceland was recommended to exchange information on future rulings using the form set out in Annex C of the 2015 Action 5 Report (OECD, 2015). Iceland did not issue any new future rulings in the year of review, but will use the Annex C template for any exchanges of information on future rulings and will complete the summary section in the Annex C as prescribed in the internal FHTP suggested guidance. Therefore it is determined that the IRD's completion and exchange of templates are sufficient to meet the minimum standard and the recommendation is removed.

553. As no rulings within the scope of the transparency framework have been issued in the year of review, Iceland was not required to complete any exchanges of information and there is no data to report on the timeliness of exchanges

Conclusion on section B

554. Iceland has the necessary legal basis for spontaneous exchange of information and an administrative process in place for exchanging information. Iceland has confirmed that it will use the template in Annex C of the 2015 Action 5 Report (OECD, 2015) for the exchange of information on future rulings and the recommendation made in the prior year peer review is removed. Iceland meets all of the ToR for the exchange of information process and no recommendations are made.

C. Statistics (ToR IV)

555. As no exchanges were required to occur in the year of review, no statistics can be reported.

D. Matters related to intellectual property regimes (ToR I.4.1.3)

556. Iceland does not offer an intellectual property regime for which transparency requirements under the Action 5 Report (OECD, 2015) were imposed.

Summary of recommendations on implementation of the transparency framework

Aspect of implementation of the transparency framework that should be improved	Recommendation for improvement
	No recommendations are made.

Notes

[1] Available at: www.rsk.is/fagadilar/bindandi-alit (accessed 20 November 2018).

[2] Parties to the Convention are available here: www.oecd.org/tax/exchange-of-tax-information/convention-on-mutual-administrative-assistance-in-tax-matters.htm. Iceland also has bilateral agreements in force with Albania, Austria, Barbados, Belgium, Canada, China (People's Republic of), Croatia, Cyprus, Czech Republic, Estonia, France, Georgia, Greece, Greenland, Germany, Hungary, India, Ireland, Italy, Korea, Latvia, Liechtenstein, Lithuania, Luxembourg, Malta, Mexico, Netherlands, Poland, Portugal, Romania, Russia, Slovak Republic, Slovenia, Spain, Switzerland, Ukraine, United Kingdom, United States, Viet Nam.

Note by Turkey: The information in this document with reference to "Cyprus" relates to the southern part of the Island. There is no single authority representing both Turkish and Greek Cypriot people on the Island. Turkey recognises the Turkish Republic of Northern Cyprus (TRNC). Until a lasting and equitable solution is found within the context of the United Nations, Turkey shall preserve its position concerning the "Cyprus issue".

Note by all the European Union Member States of the OECD and the European Union. The Republic of Cyprus is recognised by all members of the United Nations with the exception of Turkey. The information in this document relates to the area under the effective control of the Government of the Republic of Cyprus.

References

OECD (2017a), *BEPS Action 5 on Harmful Tax Practices – Terms of Reference and Methodology for the Conduct of the Peer Reviews of the Action 5 Transparency Framework*, OECD/G20 Base Erosion and Profit Shifting Project, OECD, Paris. www.oecd.org/tax/beps/beps-action-5-harmful-tax-practices-peer-review-transparencyframework.pdf.

OECD (2017b), Country-by-Country Reporting XML Schema: User Guide for Tax *Administrations*, OECD, Paris. www.oecd.org/tax/country-by-country-reporting-xmlschema-user-guide-for-tax-administrations.pdf.

OECD (2015), *Countering Harmful Tax Practices More Effectively, Taking into Account Transparency and Substance, Action 5 - 2015 Final Report*, OECD/G20 Base Erosion and Profit Shifting Project, OECD Publishing, Paris. https://doi.org/10.1787/9789264241190-en.

OECD/Council of Europe (2011), *The Multilateral Convention on Mutual Administrative Assistance in Tax Matters: Amended by the 2010 Protocol*, OECD Publishing, Paris. http://dx.doi.org/10.1787/9789264115606-en.

India

India has met all aspects of the terms of reference (ToR) for the calendar year 2017 (year in review) except for applying the "best efforts approach" for past rulings by using all information accessible to the tax administration (ToR I.4.2.2), for identifying potential exchange jurisdictions for all future rulings (ToR I.4.2.1), and the timely exchange of information on past and future APAs (ToR II.5.6). Two issues are continuing from the prior year peer review report. One additional recommendation made in the prior year peer review report has been addressed and this recommendation is removed. For the year in review, India is recommended to continue to apply the "best efforts approach" to identify potential exchange jurisdictions for all past rulings, to ensure that all potential exchange jurisdictions are identified swiftly for all future rulings and to ensure that all information on past and future APAs is exchanged as soon as possible.

India can legally issue two types of rulings within the scope of the transparency framework.

In practice, India has issued 69 past rulings; for the period 1 April 2016 - 31 December 2016, India issued 55 future rulings; and for the year in review, India issued 73 future rulings within the scope of the transparency framework.[1]

Peer input was received from six jurisdictions in respect of the exchange of information on rulings. Five peers noted that the information received was complete and in the correct format. Three peers remarked that information on future rulings was received with delay, one peer noted that information on past rulings was received after 31 December 2017. One peer noted that it would be convenient to be informed about the period covered by the rulings, as India only indicated the financial year of the requesting taxpayer, which in India covers the period of 1 April to 31 March of the next year.

Introduction

557. This peer review covers India's implementation of the BEPS Action 5 transparency framework for the year 2017. The report has four parts, each relating to a key part of the ToR. Each part is discussed in turn. A summary of recommendations is included at the end of this report.

A. The information gathering process

558. India can legally issue the two following types of rulings within the scope of the transparency framework: (i) cross-border unilateral advance pricing agreements (APAs) and (ii) permanent establishment rulings. In India, two offices of the Central Board of Direct Tax (CBDT) issue APAs, and the Authority for Advance Rulings (AAR) is responsible for issuing PE rulings.PE rulings are published unless it is stated to be confidential by the Authority issuing the ruling, whereas unilateral APAs are not.[2]

Past rulings (ToR I.4.1.1, I.4.1.2, I.4.2.1, I.4.2.2)

559. For India, past rulings are any tax rulings within scope that are issued either: (i) on or after 1 January 2014 but before 1 April 2016; or (ii) on or after 1 January 2010 but before 1 January 2014, provided they were still in effect as at 1 January 2014.

560. In the prior year peer review report, it was determined that the undertakings of the CBDT and the AAR to identify future rulings were sufficient to meet the minimum standard. However, India was recommended to apply the "best efforts approach" to identify the immediate parent and ultimate parent companies for all relevant past PE rulings and past APAs. In order to address this recommendation in the year in review, India gathered information available in the public domain such as search engines on the internet. However, for 19 rulings, neither the immediate nor ultimate parent jurisdiction could be obtained, and for 23 rulings either the ultimate parent jurisdiction or the immediate parent jurisdiction could not be identified. This means that out of 69 past rulings, in more than half of those cases one or more potential exchange jurisdictions could not be identified using the "best efforts approach". As additional ownership information may be in the possession of or accessible to the tax administration, including through access to company incorporation databases and in tax return filings, India is recommended to continue to apply the "best efforts approach" to identify potential exchange jurisdictions for all past rulings (ToR I.4.2.2).

Future rulings (ToR I.4.1.1, I.4.1.2, I.4.2.1)

561. For India, future rulings are any tax rulings within scope that are issued on or after 1 April 2016.

562. In the prior year peer review report, it was determined that the undertakings of the CBDT and the AAR to identify future rulings were sufficient to meet the minimum standard regarding the identification of rulings in scope. Since last year's report, India had to correct the number of future PE rulings issued in 2016 from 77 to six. This was because 71 PE rulings were incorrectly identified as rulings in the scope of Action 5 by the field officers. The mistake was discovered in February 2017 when the Competent Authority received the templates for those rulings. In order to remedy the risk of incorrect identification in the future, the task of identifying the relevant category of the rulings together with completion of the templates has now been centralised and is now

undertaken by the departmental representative in the AAR, who is aware of the facts in each case and the criteria of rulings in scope of Action 5. It is therefore determined that India meets the minimum standard regarding the identification of future rulings.

563. In the prior year peer review report, India was recommended to proceed with the plan to amend the process for issuing future rulings in order to identify the immediate parent and the ultimate parent company, using definitions that are consistent with accounting or legal provisions in India's domestic law. India has amended the application form for APAs and for PE Rulings to capture all necessary information with effect as of 16 June 2017 and 13 July 2018 respectively.

564. For APAs and PE rulings issued before the amended application forms were introduced, India is continuing to use the "best efforts approach". For 31 rulings, neither the ultimate parent nor immediate parent jurisdiction could be identified, and for 17 rulings either the ultimate parent jurisdiction or immediate parent jurisdiction could not be identified. India is recommended to ensure that all potential exchange jurisdictions are identified swiftly for all future rulings (ToR I 4.2.1).

Review and supervision mechanism (ToR I.4.3)

565. In the prior year peer review report, it was determined that the review and supervision mechanism implemented by India was sufficient to meet the minimum standard. India strengthened its existing review process regarding PE rulings by having the Competent Authority also receive a copy of each ruling on a monthly basis so that the number of eligible rulings and the quality of the templates are cross verified to ensure accuracy. It is determined that India's supervision mechanism continues to meet the minimum standard.

Conclusion on section A

566. India has met all of the ToR for the information gathering process except for sufficiently applying the "best efforts approach" for past rulings (ToR I.4.2.2) and for identifying all potential exchange jurisdictions for future rulings (ToR I.4.2.1). India is recommended to continue to apply the "best efforts approach" to identify potential exchange jurisdictions for all past rulings and to ensure that all potential exchange jurisdictions are identified swiftly for all future rulings.

B. The exchange of information

Legal basis for spontaneous exchange of information (ToR II.5.1, II.5.2)

567. India has the necessary domestic legal basis to exchange information spontaneously. India notes that there are no legal or practical impediments that prevent the spontaneous exchange of information on rulings as contemplated in the Action 5 minimum standard.

568. India is a party to international agreements permitting spontaneous exchange of information, including (i) the *Multilateral Convention on Mutual Administrative Assistance in Tax Matters: Amended by the 2010 Protocol* (OECD/Council of Europe, 2011) ("the Convention"), (ii) double tax agreements and (iii) the South Asian Association for Regional Cooperation (SAARC) Agreement.[3]

Completion and exchange of templates (ToR II.5.3, II.5.4, II.5.5, II.5.6, II.5.7)

569. In the prior year peer review report, it was determined that India's completion of templates were sufficient to meet the minimum standard. In order to complete the summary section, India notes that it provides all information required by the template in Annex C of the 2015 Action 5 Report (OECD, 2015), and in addition is considering the internal FHTP suggested guidance to see whether it is possible to incorporate it in the processes to complete the summary section in future.

570. In the prior year peer review report it was noted that India experienced significant delays in providing information to the Competent Authority and therefore in the exchange of information on past rulings. It is noted that India exchanged information pertaining to the remaining 51 past rulings by June 2018 and experienced continuing delays in the exchange of all future APAs. To some extent, this delay is caused by the delay in identifying potential exchange jurisdictions, which is noted in Part A. Furthermore, there were delays in the centralised office in the Competent Authority due to the volume of past and future unilateral APAs that had to be verified for accuracy and exchanged. India expects that since all the past APAs have now been exchanged, it should now be possible to exchange future unilateral APA rulings within the time limit.

571. For the year in review, the timeliness of exchanges is as follows:

Past rulings in the scope of the transparency framework	Number of exchanges transmitted by 31 December 2017	Delayed exchanges		
		Number of exchanges not transmitted by 31 December 2017	Reasons for the delays	Any other comments
	141	151	This relates partly to exchanges, which were delayed in 2016 and continue to be delayed and partly to additional exchanges that have been identified using the "best efforts approach".	82 exchanges took place by May 2018; a further 22 past rulings cannot be exchanged due to confidentiality action plan/lack of exchange instruments; the 51 outstanding exchanges have been exchanged by June 2018.
Future rulings in the scope of the transparency framework	**Number of exchanges transmitted within three months of the information becoming available to the competent authority or immediately after legal impediments have been lifted**	**Delayed exchanges**		
		Number of exchanges transmitted later than three months of the information on rulings becoming available to the competent authority	**Reasons for the delays**	**Any other comments**
	5	196	11 of these exchanges relate to information which was delayed from 2016. In addition to the delays encountered identifying all potential exchange jurisdictions, additional delays were caused in the centralised office in the Competent Authority because of the volume of past and future rulings that had to be verified for accuracy and exchanged.	All outstanding 199 exchanges on future APAs were completed by 31 December 2017, four exchanges on future PE rulings have been exchanged by May 2018.
Total	146	347		

Follow up requests received for exchange of the ruling	Number	Average time to provide response	Number of requests not answered
	5	90 days	0

572. India introduced a new internal advisory for the process of issuing future APAs to ensure that all relevant information is transmitted in a timely manner to the Competent Authority. Officials issuing future APAs are advised to submit the template to the Competent Authority when the ruling is actually issued. This means that as soon as the

ruling is issued, the Competent Authority has all information necessary to complete the exchange, and India expects the exchanges to occur within the prescribed timelines. The new process was introduced on 1 April 2018. India anticipates that after the introduction of the new process it will not experience more delays in the exchange of future APAs, and this will be reviewed in the subsequent peer review.

Conclusion on section B

573. India has the necessary legal basis for spontaneous exchange of information. India experienced delays in the exchange of past rulings and in the exchange of all future APAs partly due to the time intensive identification of the potential exchange jurisdictions as noted in Part A, and partly because of the volume of past and future rulings that had to be verified for accuracy and exchanged. India amended its processes of providing information to the Competent Authority in early 2018. India is recommended to ensure that all information on past and future APAs is exchanged as soon as possible (ToR II.5.6).

C. Statistics (ToR IV)

574. The statistics for the year in review are as follows:

Category of ruling	Number of exchanges	Jurisdictions exchanged with
Rulings related to preferential regimes	N/A	N/A
Cross-border unilateral advance pricing agreements (APAs) and any other cross-border unilateral tax rulings (such as an advance tax ruling) covering transfer pricing or the application of transfer pricing principles	325	Argentina, Australia, Austria, Bangladesh, Belarus, Belgium, Brazil, Canada, Chile, China (People's Republic of), Colombia, Croatia, Czech Republic, Denmark, Estonia, Ethiopia, Finland, France, Germany, Greece, Hungary, Iceland, Indonesia, Ireland, Israel, Italy, Japan, Jersey, Kazakhstan, Kenya, Korea, Latvia, Lithuania, Luxembourg, Malaysia, Malta, Mauritius, Mexico, Morocco, Netherlands, New Zealand, Nigeria, Norway, Oman, Pakistan, Poland, Portugal, Russia, Saudi Arabia, Serbia, Singapore, Slovak Republic, Slovenia, South Africa, Spain, Sri Lanka, Sweden, Switzerland, Chinese Taipei, Thailand, Turkey, Tunisia, Ukraine, United Arab Emirates, United Kingdom, United States, Uruguay, Viet Nam
Cross-border rulings providing for a unilateral downward adjustment to the taxpayer's taxable profits that is not directly reflected in the taxpayer's financial / commercial accounts	N/A	N/A
Permanent establishment rulings	9	Australia, Brazil, Mauritius, Singapore, Sri Lanka, United Kingdom, United States
Related party conduit rulings	N/A	N/A
De minimis rule	N/A	N/A
IP regimes: total exchanges on taxpayers benefitting from the third category of IP assets, new entrants benefitting from grandfathered IP regimes; and taxpayers making use of the option to treat the nexus ratio as a rebuttable presumption	N/A	N/A
Total	345	

D. Matters related to intellectual property regimes (ToR I.4.1.3)

575. In the prior year peer review report, it was determined that the transparency requirements were not relevant for India's intellectual property regime ("IP regime") (Tax on income from patent regime):

- ***New entrants benefitting from the grandfathered regime***: not applicable, as the regime is new and comprises no grandfathering clause.
- ***Third category of IP assets***: not applicable, as this option has not been incorporated in the Indian IP regime.
- ***Taxpayers making use of the option to treat the nexus ratio as a rebuttable presumption***: not applicable, as this option has not been incorporated in the Indian IP regime.

Summary of recommendations on implementation of the transparency framework

Aspect of implementation of the transparency framework that should be improved	Recommendation for improvement
India experienced difficulties to identify immediate parent and ultimate parent companies for past rulings, even though India may have additional ownership information in its possession or this information is accessible to the tax administration, including through access to company incorporation databases and in tax return filings. This is a continuing recommendation from the prior year peer review.	India is recommended to continue to apply the "best efforts approach" to identify potential exchange jurisdictions for all past rulings.
India experienced difficulties to identify immediate parent and ultimate parent for future rulings issued between 1 April 2016 until the new issuing procedures take effect. By introducing the new issuing procedures, which requires the taxpayer to provide all necessary information on potential exchange information, India has addressed the issue for future rulings which have been issued after the new issuing procedures come into effect. The issue is therefore limited to future APAs and PE rulings, where taxpayers have applied before the amended application forms were introduced.	India is recommended to ensure that all potential exchange jurisdictions are identified swiftly for all future rulings.
India experienced delays in the exchange of information on past and future APAs. This is a continuing recommendation from the prior year peer review regarding the exchange of APAs. Subsequent to receiving this recommendation in October 2017, India has addressed the delay in the exchange of rulings by amending the issuing procedure for APAs and PE rulings as of 16 June 2017 and 13 July 2018 respectively.	India is recommended to ensure that all information on past and future APAs is exchanged as soon as possible.

Notes

[1] The number of future rulings was stated in the prior year report to have been 126, but had to be corrected as the former number contained an additional 71 rulings subsequently determined to be out of scope.

[2] Available at: www.aarrulings.in (accessed 20 November 2018).

[3] Parties to the Convention are available here: www.oecd.org/tax/exchange-of-tax-information/convention-on-mutual-administrative-assistance-in-tax-matters.htm. India has bilateral agreements in force with Albania, Armenia, Australia, Austria, Azerbaijan, Bangladesh, Belarus, Belgium, Bhutan, Botswana, Brazil, Bulgaria, Canada, China (People's Republic of), Colombia, Croatia, Cyprus, Czech Republic, Denmark, Egypt, Estonia, Ethiopia, Faroe Islands, Fiji, Finland, Former Yugoslav Republic of Macedonia, France, Georgia, Germany, Greece, Hungary, Iceland, Indonesia, Ireland, Israel, Italy, Japan, Jordan, Kazakhstan, Kenya, Korea, Kuwait, Kyrgyzstan, Latvia, Libya, Lithuania, Luxembourg, Malaysia, Malta, Mauritius, Mexico, Moldova, Mongolia, Morocco, Montenegro, Mozambique, Myanmar, Namibia, Nepal, Netherlands, New Zealand, Norway, Oman, Philippines, Poland, Portugal, Qatar, Romania, Russia, Saudi Arabia, Serbia, Sierra Leone, Singapore, Slovak Republic, Slovenia, South Africa, Spain, Sri Lanka, Sudan, Sweden, Switzerland, Syria, Chinese Taipei, Tajikistan, Tanzania, Thailand, Trinidad and Tobago, Turkey, Turkmenistan, Uganda, Ukraine, United Arab Emirates, United Kingdom, United States, Uruguay, Uzbekistan, Viet Nam and Zambia. The SAARC was entered into force on 19 May 2010 and provides for exchanges with Bangladesh, Bhutan, Maldives, Nepal, Pakistan and Sri Lanka.

Note by Turkey: The information in this document with reference to "Cyprus" relates to the southern part of the Island. There is no single authority representing both Turkish and Greek Cypriot people on the Island. Turkey recognises the Turkish Republic of Northern Cyprus (TRNC). Until a lasting and equitable solution is found within the context of the United Nations, Turkey shall preserve its position concerning the "Cyprus issue".

Note by all the European Union Member States of the OECD and the European Union. The Republic of Cyprus is recognised by all members of the United Nations with the exception of Turkey. The information in this document relates to the area under the effective control of the Government of the Republic of Cyprus.

References

OECD (2017), *BEPS Action 5 on Harmful Tax Practices – Terms of Reference and Methodology for the Conduct of the Peer Reviews of the Action 5 Transparency Framework*, OECD/G20 Base Erosion and Profit Shifting Project, OECD, Paris. www.oecd.org/tax/beps/beps-action-5-harmful-tax-practices-peer-review-transparencyframework.pdf.

OECD (2015), *Transfer Pricing Documentation and Country-by-Country Reporting, Action 13 - 2015 Final Report*, OECD/G20 Base Erosion and Profit Shifting Project, OECD Publishing, Paris. http://dx.doi.org/10.1787/9789264241480-en.

OECD/Council of Europe (2011), *The Multilateral Convention on Mutual Administrative Assistance in Tax Matters: Amended by the 2010 Protocol*, OECD Publishing, Paris. http://dx.doi.org/10.1787/9789264115606-en.

Indonesia

Indonesia has met all aspects of the terms of reference (ToR) for the calendar year 2017 (year in review) that can be met in the absence of rulings being issued and no recommendations are made.

Indonesia can legally issue one type of rulings within the scope of the transparency framework.

In practice, Indonesia issued no rulings within the scope of the transparency framework. 15 requests for unilateral APAs, including 14 requests mentioned in the prior year report, have been received from taxpayers until 31 December 2017, 12 of the requests are still under consideration by Directorate General of Taxes.[1]

As no rulings were issued, no exchange of information was required. No peer input was received in respect of the exchanges of information on rulings received from Indonesia.

Introduction

576. This peer review covers Indonesia's implementation of the BEPS Action 5 transparency framework for the year 2017. The report has four parts, each relating to a key part of the ToR. Each part is discussed in turn. A summary of recommendations is included at the end of this report.

A. The information gathering process

577. Indonesia can legally issue one type of rulings within the scope of the transparency framework: cross-border unilateral advance pricing arrangements (APAs) and any other cross-border unilateral tax rulings (such as an advance tax ruling) covering transfer pricing or the application of transfer pricing principles. In Indonesia, APAs are issued by the Directorate of International Taxation, a unit allocated within the Directorate General of Taxes (Indonesian "tax administration"), through a decree.

Past rulings (ToR I.4.1.1, I.4.1.2, I.4.2.1, I.4.2.2)

578. For Indonesia, past rulings are any tax rulings within scope that are issued either: (i) on or after 1 January 2014 but before 1 April 2016; or (ii) on or after 1 January 2010 but before 1 January 2014, provided they were still in effect as at 1 January 2014.

579. In the prior year peer review report, it was determined that the Indonesian tax administration's undertakings to identify past rulings and all potential exchange jurisdictions in the absence of any past rulings being issued were sufficient to meet the minimum standard. As the implementation in this regard remains unchanged and Indonesia did not issue any past rulings it is determined that the Indonesian tax administration's implementation continues to meet the minimum standard.

Future rulings (ToR I.4.1.1, I.4.1.2, I.4.2.1)

580. For Indonesia, future rulings are any tax rulings within scope that are issued on or after 1 April 2016.

581. In the prior year peer review report, it was determined that Indonesia's existing system to identify future rulings and all potential exchange jurisdictions was sufficient to meet the minimum standard. The implementation in this regard remains unchanged and Indonesia did not issue any future rulings. Therefore the system to identify future rulings continues to meet the minimum standard.

Review and supervision mechanism (ToR I.4.3)

582. In the prior year peer review report, it was determined that Indonesian tax administration's review and supervision mechanism was sufficient to meet the minimum standard. The Indonesian tax administration's implementation in this regard remains unchanged, and therefore continues to meet the minimum standard.

Conclusion on section A

583. Indonesia has met all of the ToR for the information gathering process and no recommendations are made.

B. The exchange of information

Legal basis for spontaneous exchange of information (ToR II.5.1, II.5.2)

584. Indonesia has the necessary domestic legal basis to exchange information spontaneously. Indonesia notes that there are no legal or practical impediments that prevent the spontaneous exchange of information on rulings as contemplated in the Action 5 minimum standard.

585. Indonesia is a party to international agreements permitting spontaneous exchange of information, including (i) the *Multilateral Convention on Mutual Administrative Assistance in Tax Matters: Amended by the 2010 Protocol* (OECD/Council of Europe, 2011) ("the Convention") and (ii) double tax agreements in force with 65 jurisdictions.[2]

Completion and exchange of templates (ToR II.5.3, II.5.4, II.5.5, II.5.6, II.5.7)

586. The prior year peer review report noted that Indonesia has put in place a process to exchange information on rulings in accordance with the form and timelines required by the transparency framework. As no rulings within the scope of the transparency framework have been issued in practice, Indonesia was not required to complete any exchanges of information and there is no data to report on the timeliness of exchanges.

Conclusion on section B

587. Indonesia has the necessary legal basis and administrative process in place for the spontaneous exchange of information on rulings. Indonesia has met all of the ToR for the exchange of information process that can be met in the absence of rulings being issued and exchanged in practice and no recommendations are made.

C. Statistics (ToR IV)

588. As there were no rulings required to be exchanged by Indonesia for the year in review, no statistics can be reported.

D. Matters related to intellectual property regimes (ToR I.4.1.3)

589. Indonesia does not offer an intellectual property regime for which transparency requirements under the Action 5 Report (OECD, 2015) were imposed.

Summary of recommendations on implementation of the transparency framework

Aspect of implementation of the transparency framework that should be improved	Recommendation for improvement
	No recommendations are made.

Notes

1 Two ruling requests have been withdrawn by the taxpayers, one ruling request was denied.

2 Parties to the Convention are available here: www.oecd.org/tax/exchange-of-tax-information/convention-on-mutual-administrative-assistance-in-tax-matters.htm. Indonesia has bilateral agreements with Algeria, Armenia, Australia, Austria, Bangladesh, Belgium, Brunei Darussalam, Bulgaria, Canada, China (People's Republic of), Croatia, Czech Republic, Democratic People's Republic of Korea, Denmark, Egypt, Finland, France, Germany, Hong Kong, Hungary, India, Iran, Italy, Japan, Jordan, Korea, Kuwait, Lao People's Democratic Republic, Luxembourg, Malaysia, Mexico, Mongolia, Morocco, Netherlands, New Zealand, Norway, Pakistan, Papua New Guinea, Philippines, Poland, Portugal, Qatar, Romania, Russia, Seychelles, Singapore, Slovak Republic, South Africa, Spain, Sri Lanka, Sudan, Suriname, Sweden, Syria, Chinese Taipei, Thailand, Tunisia, Turkey, Ukraine, United Arab Emirates, United Kingdom, United States, Uzbekistan, Venezuela, Viet Nam.

References

OECD (2017), *BEPS Action 5 on Harmful Tax Practices – Terms of Reference and Methodology for the Conduct of the Peer Reviews of the Action 5 Transparency Framework*, OECD/G20 Base Erosion and Profit Shifting Project, OECD, Paris. www.oecd.org/tax/beps/beps-action-5-harmful-tax-practices-peer-review-transparencyframework.pdf.

OECD (2015), *Countering Harmful Tax Practices More Effectively, Taking into Account Transparency and Substance, Action 5 - 2015 Final Report*, OECD/G20 Base Erosion and Profit Shifting Project, OECD Publishing, Paris. https://doi.org/10.1787/9789264241190-en.

OECD/Council of Europe (2011), *The Multilateral Convention on Mutual Administrative Assistance in Tax Matters: Amended by the 2010 Protocol*, OECD Publishing, Paris. http://dx.doi.org/10.1787/9789264115606-en.

Ireland

Ireland has met all aspects of the terms of reference (ToR) for the calendar year 2017 (year in review) and no recommendations are made.

Ireland can legally issue three types of rulings within the scope of the transparency framework.

In practice, Ireland has issued 29 past rulings; [1] for the period 1 April 2016 – 31 December 2016, Ireland issued no future rulings; and for the year in review, Ireland issued two future rulings within the scope of the transparency framework.

No peer input was received in respect of the exchanges of information on rulings received from Ireland.

Introduction

590. This peer review covers Ireland's implementation of the BEPS Action 5 transparency framework for the year 2017. The report has four parts, each relating to a key part of the ToR. Each part is discussed in turn. A summary of recommendations is included at the end of this report.

A. The information gathering process

591. Ireland can legally issue the three following types of rulings within the scope of the transparency framework: (i) rulings related to preferential regimes;[2] (ii) cross-border unilateral advance pricing agreements (APAs) and any other cross-border unilateral tax rulings (such as an advance tax ruling) covering transfer pricing or the application of transfer pricing principles; and (iii) permanent establishment rulings. In Ireland, different divisions and regions in the Irish tax administration are authorised to issue opinions, which are signed off at a senior level and in most cases after obtaining the input from the Technical Services section.

Past rulings (ToR I.4.1.1, I.4.1.2, I.4.2.1, I.4.2.2)

592. For Ireland, past rulings are any tax rulings within scope that are issued either: (i) on or after 1 January 2014 but before 1 April 2016; or (ii) on or after 1 January 2010 but before 1 January 2014, provided they were still in effect as at 1 January 2014.

593. In the prior year peer review report, it was determined that the Irish tax administration's undertakings to identify past rulings and all potential exchange jurisdictions were sufficient to meet the minimum standard. The Irish tax administration's implementation in this regard remains unchanged, and therefore continues to meet the minimum standard.

Future rulings (ToR I.4.1.1, I.4.1.2, I.4.2.1)

594. For Ireland, future rulings are any tax rulings within scope that are issued on or after 1 April 2016.

595. In the prior year peer review report, it was determined that the Irish tax administration's implementation of a new system to identify future rulings and all potential exchange jurisdictions was sufficient to meet the minimum standard. The Irish tax administration's implementation in this regard remains unchanged, and therefore continues to meet the minimum standard.

Review and supervision mechanism (ToR I.4.3)

596. In the prior year peer review report, it was determined that the Irish tax administration's review and supervision mechanism was sufficient to meet the minimum standard. The Irish tax administration's implementation in this regard remains unchanged, and therefore continues to meet the minimum standard.

Conclusion on section A

597. Ireland has met all of the ToR for the information gathering process and no recommendations are made.

B. The exchange of information

Legal basis for spontaneous exchange of information (ToR II.5.1, II.5.2)

598. Ireland has the necessary domestic legal basis to exchange information spontaneously. Ireland notes that there are no legal or practical impediments that prevent the spontaneous exchange of information on rulings as contemplated in the Action 5 minimum standard.

599. Ireland is a party to international agreements permitting spontaneous exchange of information, including (i) the *Multilateral Convention on Mutual Administrative Assistance in Tax Matters: Amended by the 2010 Protocol* (OECD/Council of Europe, 2011) ("the Convention"), (ii) the Directive 2011/16/EU with all other European Union Member States and (iii) double tax agreements in force with 73 jurisdictions, 69 of which allow for spontaneous exchange of information.[3]

Completion and exchange of templates (ToR II.5.3, II.5.4, II.5.5, II.5.6, II.5.7)

600. In the prior year peer review report, it was determined that the Irish tax administration's completion and exchange of templates were sufficient to meet the minimum standard. The Irish tax administration's implementation in this regard remains unchanged, and therefore continues to meet the minimum standard. The processes in relation to the completion of the summary section of Annex C of the 2015 Action 5 Report (OECD, 2015) for the Irish tax administration are as follows: The initial case officer will complete the summary section in accordance with the internal Revenue Operational Manual, which incorporates the internal FHTP suggested guidance. The completed template is subsequently quality checked by both senior management and the EOI Branch prior to exchange.

601. For the year in review, the timeliness of exchanges is as follows:

Past rulings in the scope of the transparency framework	Number of exchanges transmitted by 31 December 2017	Delayed exchanges		
		Number of exchanges not transmitted by 31 December 2017	Reasons for the delays	Any other comments
	0	0	N/A	
Future rulings in the scope of the transparency framework	Number of exchanges transmitted within three months of the information becoming available to the competent authority or immediately after legal impediments have been lifted	Delayed exchanges		
		Number of exchanges transmitted later than three months of the information on rulings becoming available to the competent authority	Reasons for the delays	Any other comments
	4	0	N/A	
Total	4	0		

Follow up requests received for exchange of the ruling	Number	Average time to provide response	Number of requests not answered
	0	N/A	N/A

Conclusion on section B

602. Ireland has the necessary legal basis for spontaneous exchange of information, a process for completing the templates in a timely way and has completed all exchanges on time. Ireland has met all of the ToR for the exchange of information process and no recommendations are made.

C. Statistics (ToR IV)

603. The statistics for the year in review are as follows:

Category of ruling	Number of exchanges	Jurisdictions exchanged with
Rulings related to preferential regimes	Included in *de minimis*	N/A
Cross-border unilateral advance pricing agreements (APAs) and any other cross-border unilateral tax rulings (such as an advance tax ruling) covering transfer pricing or the application of transfer pricing principles	Included in *de minimis*	N/A
Cross-border rulings providing for a unilateral downward adjustment to the taxpayer's taxable profits that is not directly reflected in the taxpayer's financial / commercial accounts	N/A	N/A
Permanent establishment rulings	Included in *de minimis*	N/A
Related party conduit rulings	N/A	N/A
De minimis rule	4	N/A
IP regimes: total exchanges on taxpayers benefitting from the third category of IP assets, new entrants benefitting from grandfathered IP regimes; and taxpayers making use of the option to treat the nexus ratio as a rebuttable presumption	0	N/A
Total	4	

D. Matters related to intellectual property regimes (ToR I.4.1.3)

604. Ireland offers an intellectual property regime ("IP regime") that is subject to transparency requirements under the Action 5 Report (OECD, 2015) (Knowledge Development Box). It states that the identification of the benefitting taxpayers will occur as follows:

- ***New entrants benefitting from the grandfathered IP regime***: as this is a new IP regime rather than a grandfathered IP regime, transparency on new entrants was not relevant.
- ***Third category of IP assets***: the corporate tax returns have been designed to allow the collection of relevant information. These corporate tax returns will be filed as of mid-2018 at the earliest for this regime. Information will be exchanged with relevant jurisdictions shortly after the submission of those returns.
- ***Taxpayers making use of the option to treat the nexus ratio as a rebuttable presumption:*** not applicable as the regime does not allow the nexus ratio to be

treated as a rebuttable presumption. Summary of recommendations on implementation of the transparency framework.

Summary of recommendations on implementation of the transparency framework

Aspect of implementation of the transparency framework that should be improved	Recommendation for improvement
	No recommendations are made.

Notes

[1] Including five that fell into more than one category under the BEPS Action 5 report.

[2] With respect to the following preferential regimes: 1) Shipping regime and 2) Knowledge development box.

[3] Ireland has Double Tax Agreements that allow for spontaneous exchange of information with Albania, Armenia, Australia, Bahrain, Belarus, Belgium, Bosnia and Herzegovina, Botswana, Bulgaria, Canada, Chile, China, Croatia, Cyprus, Czech Republic, Denmark, Egypt, Estonia, Ethiopia, Finland, France, Georgia, Germany, Greece, Hungary, Iceland, India, Israel, Italy, Japan, Kazakhstan, Korea, Kuwait, Latvia, Lithuania, Luxembourg, Macedonia, Malaysia, Malta, Mexico, Moldova, Montenegro, Morocco, Netherlands, New Zealand, Norway, Pakistan, Poland, Portugal, Qatar, Romania, Russia, Saudi Arabia, Servia, Singapore, Slovak Republic, Slovenia, South Africa, Spain, Sweden, Thailand, Turkey, United Arab Emirates, Ukraine, United Kingdom, United States, Uzbekistan, Viet Nam, and Zambia.

Note by Turkey: The information in this document with reference to "Cyprus" relates to the southern part of the Island. There is no single authority representing both Turkish and Greek Cypriot people on the Island. Turkey recognises the Turkish Republic of Northern Cyprus (TRNC). Until a lasting and equitable solution is found within the context of the United Nations, Turkey shall preserve its position concerning the "Cyprus issue".

Note by all the European Union Member States of the OECD and the European Union. The Republic of Cyprus is recognised by all members of the United Nations with the exception of Turkey. The information in this document relates to the area under the effective control of the Government of the Republic of Cyprus.

References

OECD (2017), *BEPS Action 5 on Harmful Tax Practices – Terms of Reference and Methodology for the Conduct of the Peer Reviews of the Action 5 Transparency Framework*, OECD/G20 Base Erosion and Profit Shifting Project, OECD, Paris. www.oecd.org/tax/beps/beps-action-5-harmful-tax-practices-peer-review-transparencyframework.pdf.

OECD (2015), *Countering Harmful Tax Practices More Effectively, Taking into Account Transparency and Substance, Action 5 - 2015 Final Report*, OECD/G20 Base Erosion and Profit Shifting Project, OECD Publishing, Paris. https://doi.org/10.1787/9789264241190-en.

OECD/Council of Europe (2011), *The Multilateral Convention on Mutual Administrative Assistance in Tax Matters: Amended by the 2010 Protocol*, OECD Publishing, Paris. http://dx.doi.org/10.1787/9789264115606-en.

Isle of Man

The Isle of Man has met all aspects of the terms of reference (ToR) for the calendar year 2017 (year in review) and no recommendations are made.

The Isle of Man can legally issue two types of rulings within the scope of the transparency framework.

In practice, the Isle of Man has issued two past rulings; and for the year in review, the Isle of Man did not issue any future rulings within the scope of the transparency framework.

No peer input was received in respect of the exchanges of information on rulings received from the Isle of Man.

Introduction

605. This peer review covers the Isle of Man's implementation of the BEPS Action 5 transparency framework for the year 2017. The report has four parts, each relating to a key part of the ToR. Each part is discussed in turn. A summary of recommendations is included at the end of this report.

A. The information gathering process

606. The Isle of Man can legally issue the following two types of rulings within the scope of the transparency framework: (i) cross-border giving a unilateral downward adjustment to the taxpayer's taxable profits in the country giving the ruling; and (ii) permanent establishment rulings. In the Isle of Man, the Income Tax Division is authorised to issue rulings.

Past rulings (ToR I.4.1.1, I.4.1.2, I.4.2.1, I.4.2.2)

607. For the Isle of Man, past rulings are any tax rulings within scope that are issued either: (i) on or after 1 January 2015 but before 1 April 2017; or (ii) on or after 1 January 2012 but before 1 January 2015, provided they were still in effect as at 1 January 2015.

608. The Isle of Man notes that the Income Tax Division did not maintain a central list of rulings for the "past ruling" period, so the identification process undertaken involved a manual review of the taxpayer files. A project team was established and the review was undertaken by the most senior technical officer in the Income Tax Division. This senior technical officer has been involved in technical casework, which would involve the issuing of tax rulings of any type, since 2007.

609. The senior case officer reviewed the taxpayer files of all taxpayers which were subject to the higher tax rate of 10% applicable in the relevant period (banking, real property and certain retail businesses) and considered likely to engage in cross border transactions and/or to have a related party in a foreign jurisdiction such that there would be exchange of information required under the Action 5 Report. The tax files of those taxpayers which were subject to the standard nil tax rate were not reviewed, as there would be no need for them to obtain the type of rulings from the Isle of Man in the scope of the transparency framework. The date and scope of the ruling were identified from the correspondence held in the taxpayer file. The review process was completed by 30 November 2017.

610. In order to identify potential exchange jurisdictions, the "best efforts approach" was used as the rulings process at that time did not include the gathering of all of necessary information on relevant jurisdictions required by Action 5. In all cases the information was taken from public information on the companies register and/or from the group structure or equivalent sections on the companies' own websites, and all relevant parties and potential exchange jurisdictions were able to be identified.

Future rulings (ToR I.4.1.1, I.4.1.2, I.4.2.1)

611. For the Isle of Man, future rulings are any tax rulings within scope that are issued on or after 1 April 2017.

612. For the year in review, the process for the identification of future rulings was similar to the one used for past rulings and involved a manual review of the

correspondence on each taxpayer file to verify whether rulings had been issued since 1 April 2017 that are in scope of Action 5. The review process was completed by 30 November 2017. Although the identification process was completed late in 2017, in practice there were no future rulings issued in the relevant period and therefore no adverse practical impact resulting from this process.

613. In order to identify potential exchange jurisdictions, the Isle of Man indicates that the rulings application process was updated and includes a new rulings application form published on the Income Tax Division website. All corporate taxpayers are required to submit a rulings application form if they are applying for a ruling which falls within scope of Action 5 and even for those rulings which are out of scope. The new form requires the taxpayer to provide all of the necessary information required to identify the relevant jurisdictions for exchange as required by Action 5. Rulings falling within the scope of Action 5 will not be issued without receipt of a completed application form.

614. It is noted that in 2018 the Isle of Man has established a central database of tax rulings which includes the date of issue and the type of rulings to facilitate the timely identification of future rulings within the scope of Action 5. The process for granting a ruling has also been updated to ensure that all rulings applications are referred to one of the three technical officers for initial review and allocation, then back to the senior technical officer for final sign off and notification to the Competent Authority.

Review and supervision mechanism (ToR I.4.3)

615. The Isle of Man Income Tax Division set up a project team to review all rulings issued within the scope of Action 5 and the process was supervised by the most senior technical officer in the Income Tax Division. The review process for both past and future rulings was completed by 30 November 2017 which allowed sufficient time for the past rulings identified to be exchanged by 31 December 2017. The caseworkers who form part of the project team are technically trained members of staff in relation to the income tax technical aspects of the ruling.

Conclusion on section A

616. The Isle of Man has met all of the ToR for the information gathering process and no recommendations are made.

B. The exchange of information

Legal basis for spontaneous exchange of information (ToR II.5.1, II.5.2)

617. The Isle of Man has the necessary domestic legal basis to exchange information spontaneously. The Isle of Man notes that there are no legal or practical impediments that prevent the spontaneous exchange of information on rulings as contemplated in the Action 5 minimum standard.

618. The Isle of Man is a party to international agreements permitting spontaneous exchange of information, including (i) the *Multilateral Convention on Mutual Administrative Assistance in Tax Matters: Amended by the 2010 Protocol* (OECD/Council of Europe, 2011) ("the Convention"), (ii) double tax agreements in force with 10 jurisdictions, all of which allow for spontaneous exchange of information and (iii) more than 30 Tax Information Exchange Agreements, of which four permit spontaneous exchange of information.[1]

Completion and exchange of templates (ToR II.5.3, II.5.4, II.5.5, II.5.6, II.5.7)

619. Once a ruling is identified as being in scope and is approved by the senior technical officer, the latter notifies the Competent Authority that uses a separate recording system to generate either a paper template compliant with Annex C of the 2015 Action 5 Report (OECD, 2015) or an XML Schema template for the identified ruling, depending on the recipient jurisdiction's chosen method of exchange. The Competent Authority also reviews the completed template and approves it for exchange or rejects it and requests the missing information necessary for exchange. The completion of the XML template is monitored by the XML schema validation. Both templates are supported by a guidance note with answers to basic questions. The Competent Authority deals with the more detailed questions, if necessary.

620. The Isle of Man indicates that the internal FHTP suggested guidance was not specifically utilised to complete the summary section of Annex C for the past rulings exchanged, but the notes for guidance for completion of all sections appended to Annex C were used. The Isle of Man indicates that the internal FHTP suggested guidance will be used when completing the summary sections for all future rulings as prescribed by the internal processes for completing that section of the template.

621. Annex C forms for each past ruling were completed and submitted to the Competent Authority by mid-December 2017 for exchange by 31 December 2017. As no future rulings were issued during the review period, no exchanges were required. However, in the event a future ruling is issued, the rulings process includes a step to ensure that all future rulings falling within the scope of Action 5 are notified to the Competent Authority within 30 days of the ruling application being approved or rejected. The rulings index in the central database, which contains all data necessary for the exchange, will be reviewed on a quarterly basis to ensure that all rulings approved/rejected since the last review have been or are made available to the Competent Authority.

622. For the year in review, the timeliness of exchanges is as follows:

Past rulings in the scope of the transparency framework	Number of exchanges transmitted by 31 December 2017	Delayed exchanges		
		Number of exchanges not transmitted by 31 December 2017	Reasons for the delays	Any other comments
	3	0	N/A	
Future rulings in the scope of the transparency framework	**Number of exchanges transmitted within three months of the information becoming available to the competent authority or immediately after legal impediments have been lifted**	**Delayed exchanges**		
		Number of exchanges transmitted later than three months of the information on rulings becoming available to the competent authority	**Reasons for the delays**	**Any other comments**
	0	0	N/A	
Total	3	0		

Follow up requests received for exchange of the ruling	Number	Average time to provide response	Number of requests not answered
	0	N/A	N/A

Conclusion on section B

623. The Isle of Man has the necessary legal basis for spontaneous exchange of information, a process for completing the templates in a timely way and has completed all exchanges on time. The Isle of Man has met all of the ToR for the exchange of information process and no recommendations are made.

C. Statistics (ToR IV)

624. The statistics for the year in review are as follows:

Category of ruling	Number of exchanges	Jurisdictions exchanged with
Rulings related to preferential regimes	N/A	N/A
Cross-border unilateral advance pricing agreements (APAs) and any other cross-border unilateral tax rulings (such as an advance tax ruling) covering transfer pricing or the application of transfer pricing principles	N/A	N/A
Cross-border rulings providing for a unilateral downward adjustment to the taxpayer's taxable profits that is not directly reflected in the taxpayer's financial / commercial accounts	0	N/A
Permanent establishment rulings	Included in *de minimis*	N/A
Related party conduit rulings	N/A	N/A
De minimis rule	3	N/A
IP regimes: total exchanges on taxpayers benefitting from the third category of IP assets, new entrants benefitting from grandfathered IP regimes; and taxpayers making use of the option to treat the nexus ratio as a rebuttable presumption	N/A	N/A
Total	3	

D. Matters related to intellectual property regimes (ToR I.4.1.3)

625. The Isle of Man does not offer an intellectual property regime for which transparency requirements under the Action 5 Report (OECD, 2015) were imposed.

Summary of recommendations on implementation of the transparency framework

Aspect of implementation of the transparency framework that should be improved	Recommendation for improvement
	No recommendations are made.

Note

1 Parties to the Convention are available here: www.oecd.org/tax/exchange-of-tax-information/convention-on-mutual-administrative-assistance-in-tax-matters.htm. The Isle of Man has bilateral agreements in force with Bahrain, British Virgin Islands, Cayman Islands, Estonia,

Guernsey, Jersey, Luxembourg, Malta, Qatar, Seychelles, Singapore, Turks and Caicos Islands, United Kingdom and United States.

References

OECD (2017), *BEPS Action 5 on Harmful Tax Practices – Terms of Reference and Methodology for the Conduct of the Peer Reviews of the Action 5 Transparency Framework*, OECD/G20 Base Erosion and Profit Shifting Project, OECD, Paris. www.oecd.org/tax/beps/beps-action-5-harmful-tax-practices-peer-review-transparencyframework.pdf.

OECD (2015), *Countering Harmful Tax Practices More Effectively, Taking into Account Transparency and Substance, Action 5 - 2015 Final Report*, OECD/G20 Base Erosion and Profit Shifting Project, OECD Publishing, Paris. https://doi.org/10.1787/9789264241190-en.

OECD/Council of Europe (2011), *The Multilateral Convention on Mutual Administrative Assistance in Tax Matters: Amended by the 2010 Protocol*, OECD Publishing, Paris. http://dx.doi.org/10.1787/9789264115606-en.

Israel

Israel has met all of the terms of reference (ToR) for the calendar year 2017 (year in review), except for the timely provision of information on rulings to the Competent Authority for exchange of information (ToR II.5.5), and the timely exchange of information on future rulings (ToR II.5.6). In the prior year peer review report, Israel received three recommendations regarding the identification of certain potential exchange jurisdictions for past rulings (ToR I.4.2.1), the timely exchange of information on past and future rulings (ToR II.5.6) and the exchange of information on new entrants to its IP regime (ToR I.4.1.3). Israel has addressed two of these recommendations and the recommendations for ToR I.4.2.1 and ToR I.4.1.3 have been removed, whilst the recommendation for ToR II.5.6 is retained. Israel is recommended to ensure that all information on future rulings is exchanged as soon as possible and to reduce the timelines for providing the information on future rulings to the Competent Authority.

Israel can legally issue five type of rulings within the scope of the transparency framework.

In practice, Israel issued 79 past rulings; for the period 1 April 2016 - 31 December 2016, Israel issued five future rulings; and for the year in review, Israel issued 16 future rulings within the scope of the transparency framework.[1]

Peer input received was received from one jurisdiction in respect of the exchanges of information on rulings received from Israel. The input was positive, noting that information on future rulings was complete, generally in the correct format and received in a timely manner.

Introduction

626. This peer review covers Israel's implementation of the BEPS Action 5 transparency framework for the year 2017. The report has four parts, each relating to a key part of the ToR. Each part is discussed in turn. A summary of recommendations is included at the end of this report.

A. The information gathering process

627. Israel can legally issue all five types of ruling within the scope of the transparency framework: (1) rulings related to preferential regimes;[2] (2) cross-border unilateral advance pricing agreements (APAs) and any other cross-border unilateral tax rulings (such as an advance tax ruling) covering transfer pricing or the application of transfer pricing principles; (3) cross-border rulings giving a unilateral downward adjustment to the taxpayer's taxable profits in the country giving the ruling; (4) permanent establishment rulings; and (5) related party conduit rulings. The Professional Division of the Israel Tax Authority is responsible for issuing rulings, with each department responsible for issuing a different category of ruling. Some rulings are published in anonymised form.[3]

Past rulings (ToR I.4.1.1, I.4.1.2, I.4.2.1, I.4.2.2)

628. For Israel, past rulings are any tax rulings within scope that are issued either: (i) on or after 1 January 2014 but before 1 April 2016; or (ii) on or after 1 January 2010 but before 1 January 2014, provided they were still in effect as at 1 January 2014.

629. In the prior year peer review report, it was determined that the Israel met all the ToR for the information-gathering process except for identifying all potential exchange jurisdictions for past rulings (ToR I.4.2.1). In order to address this recommendation, Israel has put in place processes to ensure the identification of jurisdictions of residence of related party counterparts to transactions covered by the ruling or which gave rise to income from related parties benefitting from a preferential treatment. Furthermore, for permanent establishment rulings the department managers are instructed to identify the jurisdiction of the head office or the permanent establishment (as the case may be), and for conduit rulings department managers were instructed to identify the ultimate beneficial owner of payments made to the conduit.

Future rulings (ToR I.4.1.1, I.4.1.2, I.4.2.1)

630. For Israel, future rulings are any tax rulings within scope that are issued on or after 1 April 2016.

631. In the prior year peer review report, it was determined that the Israel Tax Authority's process to identify future rulings and all potential exchange jurisdictions was sufficient to meet the minimum standard. The Israel Tax Authority's implementation in this regard remains unchanged, and therefore continues to meet the minimum standard.

Review and supervision mechanism (ToR I.4.3)

632. In the prior year peer review report, it was determined that the Israel tax administration's review and supervision mechanism was sufficient to meet the minimum standard. The Israel tax administration's implementation in this regard remains unchanged, and therefore continues to meet the minimum standard.

Conclusion on section A

633. Israel has met all of the ToR for the information gathering process and no recommendations are made.

B. The exchange of information

Legal basis for spontaneous exchange of information (ToR II.5.1, II.5.2)

634. Israel has the necessary domestic legal basis to exchange information spontaneously. Israel notes that there are no legal or practical impediments that prevent the spontaneous exchange of information on rulings as contemplated in the Action 5 minimum standard.

635. Israel is a party to international agreements permitting spontaneous exchange of information, including (i) the *Multilateral Convention on Mutual Administrative Assistance in Tax Matters: Amended by the 2010 Protocol* (OECD/Council of Europe, 2011) ("the Convention") and (ii) double tax agreements in force with 54 jurisdictions.[4]

Completion and exchange of templates (ToR II.5.3, II.5.4, II.5.5, II.5.6, II.5.7)

636. Israel uses a combination of the internal FHTP suggested guidance and other internal quality assurance procedures for completing the summary section for information exchanged under the transparency framework.

637. In the prior year peer review report, it was determined that the Israel Tax Authority's completion and exchange of templates was sufficient to meet the minimum standard, except for the timely exchange of information on past and future rulings (ToR II.5.6). Israel received a recommendation to ensure the speedy exchange of all past and future rulings. Israel has now completed the exchange of past and future rulings that were delayed from the prior year peer review report. However, Israel has continued to experience delays in the exchange of future rulings issued in 2017. It is not known whether 16 future rulings issued in 2017 have been exchanged. Therefore, the recommendation for the timely exchange of information on future rulings is retained (ToR II.5.6). Furthermore, Israel experienced delays in the provision of rulings to the Competent Authority during the year in review. Rulings that were issued between July and December 2017 were not transmitted to the Competent Authority for exchange until January 2018. Therefore, Israel is recommended to reduce the timelines for providing the information on future rulings to the Competent Authority (ToR II.5.5).

638. For the year in review, the timeliness of exchanges is as follows:

Past rulings in the scope of the transparency framework	Number of exchanges transmitted by 31 December 2017	Delayed exchanges		
		Number of exchanges not transmitted by 31 December 2017	Reasons for the delays	Any other comments
	50	0	N/A	These relate to the delayed exchanges reported in the prior year peer review report and were exchanged in 2017.
Future rulings in the scope of the transparency framework	Number of exchanges transmitted within three months of the information becoming available to the competent authority or immediately after legal impediments have been lifted	Delayed exchanges		
		Number of exchanges transmitted later than three months of the information on rulings becoming available to the competent authority	Reasons for the delays	Any other comments
	6	0	N/A	These relate to the delayed exchanges reported in the prior year peer review report and were exchanged in 2017. A further 16 rulings issued in 2017 have not yet been exchanged.
Total	56	0		

Follow up requests received for exchange of the ruling	Number	Average time to provide response	Number of requests not answered
	0	N/A	N/A

Conclusion on section B

639. Israel has the necessary legal framework and administrative processes in place for exchanging information on rulings. In the prior year peer review report, Israel received a recommendation regarding the timely exchange of information on past and future rulings (ToR II.5.6). Israel has continued to experience delays in the exchange of future rulings, and therefore Israel is recommended to ensure that all information on future rulings is exchanged as soon as possible. Furthermore, Israel experienced delays in the provision of rulings to the Competent Authority during the year in review, and is recommended to reduce the timelines for providing the information on future rulings to the Competent Authority (ToR II.5.5).

C. Statistics (ToR IV)

640. The statistics for the year in review are as follows:

Category of ruling	Number of exchanges	Jurisdictions exchanged with
Rulings related to preferential regimes	29	France, India, Japan, Netherlands, Singapore, Sweden, Switzerland, United Kingdom, United States
Cross-border unilateral advance pricing arrangements (APAs) and any other cross-border unilateral tax rulings (such as an advance tax ruling) covering transfer pricing or the application of transfer pricing principles	24	France, Germany, Japan, Netherlands, United Kingdom, United States
Cross-border rulings providing for a unilateral downward adjustment to the taxpayer's taxable profits that is not directly reflected in the taxpayer's financial / commercial accounts	0	N/A
Permanent establishment rulings	0	N/A
Related party conduit rulings	0	N/A
De minimis rule	3	N/A
IP regimes: total exchanges on taxpayers benefitting from the third category of IP assets, new entrants benefitting from grandfathered IP regimes; and taxpayers making use of the option to treat the nexus ratio as a rebuttable presumption	7[5]	France, Netherlands, United Kingdom, United States
Total	56	

D. Matters related to intellectual property regimes (ToR I.4.1.3)

641. Israel offers two intellectual property regimes ("IP regime") that are subject to transparency requirements under the Action 5 Report (OECD, 2015).[6] It states that the identification of the benefitting taxpayers will occur as follows:

- ***New entrants benefitting from the grandfathered IP regime***: this issue is relevant only for the grandfathering of the Preferred company regime. The benefits under this regime are only granted by way of ruling and new entrants are identified in the ruling process. New entrants for the purposes of the grandfathered Preferred company regime includes both new taxpayers not previously benefiting from the regime and new IP assets owned by taxpayers already benefiting from the regime. Up to the end of 2016, there were seven new entrants to the grandfathered IP regime. These were made available to the Competent Authority in September 2017 and exchanged immediately thereafter. Israel received a recommendation in the prior year peer review report because no information on new entrants benefitting from the grandfathered IP regime was exchanged during the year of review, although this information should have been available. Israel was recommended to ensure that information on new entrants to the grandfathered IP regime is swiftly made available to the Competent Authority for exchange of information in future. Israel notes that since the question on new entrants is relevant only to the previous version of the Preferred company regime law that was amended on 31 December 2016, there were no relevant new entrants during the year in review. Israel has now completed all exchanges of information on new entrants, and therefore this recommendation is removed.
- ***Third category of IP assets***: In Israel, a third category of asset requires certification by the Authority for Technological Innovation (the certifying agency). For the year in review, the certifying agency notes that there were no companies which benefitted from the third category of IP assets. The Israel Tax Authority receives detailed information regarding the certificates issued by the

certifying agency. Information regarding income from assets that were certified for third category assets will also be required in the company's annual returns. Israel notes that as soon as the ECIL department issues a ruling regarding the third category of IP assets, they will be shared with the Competent Authority for exchange.

- ***Taxpayers making use of the option to treat the nexus ratio as a rebuttable presumption***: not applicable as both regimes do not allow the nexus ratio to be treated as a rebuttable presumption.

Summary of recommendations on implementation of the transparency framework

Aspect of implementation of the transparency framework that should be improved	Recommendation for improvement
Israel experienced delays in the provision of rulings to the Competent Authority during the year in review.	Israel is recommended to reduce the timelines for providing the information on future rulings to the Competent Authority.
Israel encountered delays in the exchange of information for all future rulings issued in 2017 within the scope of the transparency framework issues. This is a continuing recommendation from the prior year peer review.	Israel is recommended to ensure that all information on future rulings is exchanged as soon as possible.

Notes

[1] Note: The statistical data for Israel are supplied by and under the responsibility of the relevant Israeli authorities. The use of such data by the OECD is without prejudice to the status of the Golan Heights, East Jerusalem and Israeli settlements in the West Bank under the terms of international law.

[2] Preferred company regime and Preferred technological enterprise regime

[3] Available at: https://taxes.gov.il/Pages/TaxationDecisions/TaxationDecisions.aspx (accessed 19 November 2018).

[4] Austria, Belarus, Belgium, Brazil, Bulgaria, Canada, China (People's Republic of), Croatia, Czech Republic, Denmark, Estonia, Ethiopia, Finland, France, Georgia, Germany, Greece, Hungary, India, Ireland, Italy, Jamaica, Japan, Korea, Latvia, Lithuania, Luxembourg, Malta, Mexico, Moldova, Netherlands, Norway, Panama, Philippines, Poland, Portugal, Romania, Russia, Singapore, Slovak Republic, Slovenia, South Africa, Spain, Sweden, Switzerland, Chinese Taipei, Thailand, Turkey, Ukraine, United Kingdom, United States, Uzbekistan and Viet Nam.

[5] These rulings are included in the category of preferential regime above.

[6] The Preferred company regime which is the grandfathered regime, and the Preferred technological enterprise regime which is the amended regime.

References

OECD (2017), *BEPS Action 5 on Harmful Tax Practices – Terms of Reference and Methodology for the Conduct of the Peer Reviews of the Action 5 Transparency Framework*, OECD/G20 Base Erosion and Profit Shifting Project, OECD, Paris. www.oecd.org/tax/beps/beps-action-5-harmful-tax-practices-peer-review-transparencyframework.pdf.

OECD (2015), *Countering Harmful Tax Practices More Effectively, Taking into Account Transparency and Substance, Action 5 - 2015 Final Report*, OECD/G20 Base Erosion and Profit Shifting Project, OECD Publishing, Paris. https://doi.org/10.1787/9789264241190-en.

OECD/Council of Europe (2011), *The Multilateral Convention on Mutual Administrative Assistance in Tax Matters: Amended by the 2010 Protocol*, OECD Publishing, Paris. http://dx.doi.org/10.1787/9789264115606-en.

Italy

Italy has met all aspects of the terms of reference (ToR) for the calendar year 2017 (year in review), except providing information to the Competent Authority without undue delay (ToR II.5.5) and exchanging information during the year of review on new entrants to the IP regime that obtained benefits with respect to trademarks (ToR I.4.1.3). These recommendations were also included in the prior year peer review report. In the prior peer review report, Italy received four recommendations and took steps to address each of them. Two of the recommendations referring to the swift identification of future rulings and the amendment of the ruling practice for all future rulings are therefore removed, and two recommendations (as above) are retained, as they were not yet fully addressed in the year of review. Italy is recommended to continue its efforts to reduce the timelines for providing the information on future rulings to the Competent Authority and to continue its efforts to identify and exchange information on new entrants to the grandfathered IP regime.

Italy can legally issue three types of rulings within the scope of the transparency framework.

In practice, Italy has issued 58 past rulings; for the period 1 April 2016 - 31 December 2016, Italy issued 39 future rulings;[1] and for the year in review, Italy issued 123 future rulings within the scope of the transparency framework.

Peer input was received from four jurisdictions in respect of the exchanges of information on rulings received from Italy. In general the input was positive, noting that information was complete and in the correct format.

Introduction

642. This peer review covers Italy's implementation of the BEPS Action 5 transparency framework for the year 2017. The report has four parts, each relating to a key part of the ToR. Each part is discussed in turn. A summary of recommendations is included at the end of this report.

A. The information gathering process

643. Italy can legally issue the three following types of rulings within the scope of the transparency framework: (i) rulings related to preferential regimes;[2] (ii) cross-border unilateral advance pricing arrangements (APAs) and any other cross-border unilateral tax rulings (such as an advance tax ruling) covering transfer pricing or the application of transfer pricing principles; and (iii) as of May 2016, permanent establishment rulings. Rulings related to preferential regimes (including on Patent Box applications) and permanent establishment rulings are issued by offices within the Central Directorate for Tax Regulations. APAs and Patent Box ad hoc agreements to determine the embedded IP income in accordance with transfer pricing principles are issued by the APA office within the Central Directorate for Tax Assessment. Rulings other than APAs and ad hoc Patent Box agreements may be published in anonymised form as a general ruling or "resolution" on the Italian revenue agency website, if they are of general interest.[3]

Past rulings (ToR I.4.1.1, I.4.1.2, I.4.2.1, I.4.2.2)

644. For Italy, past rulings are any tax rulings within scope that are issued either: (i) on or after 1 January 2014 but before 1 April 2016; or (ii) on or after 1 January 2010 but before 1 January 2014, provided they were still in effect as at 1 January 2014.

645. In the prior year peer review report, it was determined that the Italian tax administration's undertakings to identify past rulings and all potential exchange jurisdictions were sufficient to meet the minimum standard. The Italian tax administration's implementation in this regard remains unchanged, and therefore continues to meet the minimum standard.

Future rulings (ToR I.4.1.1, I.4.1.2, I.4.2.1)

646. For Italy, future rulings are any tax rulings within scope that are issued on or after 1 April 2016.

647. Regarding issued APA rulings and rulings on preferential regimes it was determined in the prior year peer review report that the Italian tax administration's implementation of a new system to identify future rulings and all potential exchange jurisdictions was sufficient to meet the minimum standard. Italy's implementation in this regard remains unchanged, and therefore continues to meet the minimum standard.

648. With respect to PE rulings, Italy was recommended to amend its ruling practices to ensure a swift identification of all relevant rulings and the collection of information on all potential exchange jurisdictions. Since the prior review Italy has amended its existing databases. They now include information as to whether rulings concern cross border issues and the potential exchange jurisdictions.

649. Italy also amended the procedure for collecting information relevant for the exchange of ad hoc patent box rulings. Notably, information is collected during the

process of issuing ad hoc patent box rulings. Such procedure has been introduced in November 2017 and subsequent clarifications have been issued in January 2018. The newly introduced procedure requires the competent offices to collect from taxpayers all the information necessary to identify rulings in scope and potential exchange jurisdictions. The information is then used to draft the templates for the exchange. Furthermore, this information will be gathered in a dedicated database for IP rulings that is expected to be introduced in October 2018. Potential exchange jurisdictions for ad hoc patent box rulings that were issued before November 2017 were exchanged by using the "best efforts approach", which was applied by searching the taxpayers' files and internal databases.

650. It is therefore determined that Italy's amended system to identify future rulings and all potential exchange jurisdictions is sufficient to meet the minimum standard.

Review and supervision mechanism (ToR I.4.3)

651. In the prior year peer review report, it was determined that the Italian tax administration's review and supervisions mechanisms were sufficient to meet the minimum standard. The Italian Tax Administration's implementation in this regard remains unchanged, and therefore continues to meet the minimum standard.

Conclusion on section A

652. With the amended implementation Italy is now able to identify all categories of future rulings and potential exchange jurisdictions and has therefore met all of the ToR for the information gathering process and no recommendations are made.

B. The exchange of information

Legal basis for spontaneous exchange of information (ToR II.5.1, II.5.2)

653. Italy has the necessary domestic legal basis to exchange information spontaneously. Italy notes that there are no legal or practical impediments that prevent the spontaneous exchange of information on rulings as contemplated in the Action 5 minimum standard.

654. Italy is a party to international agreements permitting spontaneous exchange of information, including (i) the *Multilateral Convention on Mutual Administrative Assistance in Tax Matters: Amended by the 2010 Protocol* (OECD/Council of Europe, 2011) ("the Convention"), (ii) the Directive 2011/16/EU with all other European Union Member States and (iii) double tax agreements in force with 93.[4]

Completion and exchange of templates (ToR II.5.3, II.5.4, II.5.5, II.5.6, II.5.7)

655. In the prior year peer review report, it was determined that the Italian tax administration's completion and exchange of templates were sufficient to meet the minimum standard except for transmitting information on future rulings to the International Co-operation Office (Italian Competent Authority) without undue delay.

656. In order to address the recommendation, Italy amended its procedure to transmit information to the Competent Authority in the year of review and reduced the timelines from every six months to every three months. In the future, Italy aims to have the information on rulings in scope to be transmitted to the Competent Authority within two months after the issuance of the ruling. However, in the year of review it took the relevant

offices an average of five months to forward the information to the Competent Authority and information on preferential regimes (including information on Patent Box rulings and ad hoc Patent Box agreements) was only transmitted to the Competent Authority in December 2017 and April 2018, and then only exchanged in January and July 2018. Italy is therefore recommended to continue its efforts to reduce the timelines for providing the information on future rulings to the Competent Authority (ToR II.5.5).

657. Italy confirms that it uses the internal FHTP suggested guidance to complete the summary section of the template in Annex C of the 2015 Action 5 Report (OECD, 2015). Currently the summary section contains a summary of the transaction or activity covered by the ruling and a summary of the transfer pricing methodology (for APA rulings) or a reference of the particular preferential regime adopted (for Patent Box rulings).

658. For the year in review, the timeliness of exchanges is as follows:

Past rulings in the scope of the transparency framework	Number of exchanges transmitted by 31 December 2017	Delayed exchanges		
		Number of exchanges not transmitted by 31 December 2017	Reasons for the delays	Any other comments
	0	0	N/A	No additional exchanges on past rulings had to be exchanged with new members of the Inclusive Framework that joined in 2017 and as such no additional exchanges on past rulings were required.
Future rulings in the scope of the transparency framework	Number of exchanges transmitted within three months of the information becoming available to the competent authority or immediately after legal impediments have been lifted	Delayed exchanges		
		Number of exchanges transmitted later than three months of the information on rulings becoming available to the competent authority	Reasons for the delays	Any other comments
	199	0	N/A	This includes information exchanged with new members of the Inclusive Framework who joined during 2017 and exchanges on future rulings that were issued in late 2016.
Total	199	0		

Follow up requests received for exchange of the ruling	Number	Average time to provide response	Number of requests not answered
	0	N/A	N/A

Conclusion on section B

659. Italy has the necessary legal basis for spontaneous exchange of information, a process for completing the templates in a timely way and has completed all exchanges on future rulings in time. In the year of review, Italy continued to experience delays in providing information on future rulings to the Competent Authority, especially with regard to rulings on preferential regimes. Italy is therefore recommended to continue its efforts to reduce the timelines for providing the information on future rulings to the Competent Authority and to ensure that information is made available to the Competent Authority without undue delay (ToR II.5.5).

C. Statistics (ToR IV)

660. The statistics for the year in review are as follows:

Category of ruling	Number of exchanges	Jurisdictions exchanged with
Rulings related to preferential regimes	0[5]	N/A
Cross-border unilateral advance pricing arrangements(APAs) and any other cross-border unilateral tax rulings (such as an advance tax ruling) covering transfer pricing or the application of transfer pricing principles	195	Argentina, Australia, Austria, Belgium, Brazil, Canada, Chile, China (People's Republic of), Colombia, Croatia, Czech Republic, Denmark, Estonia, Finland, France, Germany, Greece, Hungary, India, Ireland, Japan, Korea, Latvia, Lithuania, Luxembourg, Malaysia, Mexico, Netherlands, Pakistan, Panama, Poland, Portugal, Romania, Singapore, Slovak Republic, South Africa, Spain, Sweden, Switzerland, Thailand, Turkey, United Kingdom, United States, Viet Nam
Cross-border rulings providing for a unilateral downward adjustment to the taxpayer's taxable profits that is not directly reflected in the taxpayer's financial / commercial accounts	N/A	N/A
Permanent establishment rulings	Included in *de minimis*	N/A
Related party conduit rulings	N/A	N/A
De minimis rule	4	N/A
IP regimes: total exchanges on taxpayers benefitting from the third category of IP assets, new entrants benefitting from grandfathered IP regimes; and taxpayers making use of the option to treat the nexus ratio as a rebuttable presumption	0	N/A
Total	199	

D. Matters related to intellectual property regimes (ToR I.4.1.3)

661. Italy offers an intellectual property regime ("IP regime")[6] that was amended with effect as of 1 January 2017 to the extent it was not nexus compliant (i.e. for benefits for trademarks) but for which grandfathering was provided, and is therefore subject to transparency requirements under the Action 5 Report (OECD, 2015). It states that the identification of the benefitting taxpayers will occur as follows:

- ***New entrants benefitting from the grandfathered IP regime***: In the prior year peer review report, Italy was recommended to identify and exchange information on all new entrants to the IP regime to the extent they benefited from trademarks as soon as possible. The regime has been found to be actually harmful to the extent of extended grandfathering for taxpayers that obtained benefits with respect to trademarks. Italy released an Inter-Ministerial Decree, which came into force on 6 February 2018 and stipulates that every taxpayer who has benefitted as a new entrant from the grandfathered Italian Patent Box regime, shall indicate the option within the annual tax return. In addition, the taxpayer shall provide the following information to the Agenzia delle Entrate (competent body to issue ad hoc rulings and regime rulings relating to the Patent Box regime):
    - The type and the number of eligible assets (patent, trademarks, etc.) to which the option refers
    - the amount of the eligible income resulting from the use of the assets
    - (as regard options for trademark) information on relevant jurisdictions where related parties are fiscally resident

  These information, allow to exchange information on new entrants of the grandfathered Italian Patent Box regime who benefitted from trademarks, with the relevant exchange jurisdictions.

  As the information on the new entrants will only become available in 2018, Italy has not exchanged information on new entrants during the year of review. The recommendation from the prior year peer review report is therefore retained, and Italy is recommended to continue its efforts to identify and exchange information on new entrants to the grandfathered IP regime under the Inter-Ministerial Decree as soon as possible (ToR I.4.1.3).

662. The patent box regime is otherwise compliant with the nexus approach, however the additional transparency requirements under the Action 5 report (OECD, 2015) are not applicable because:

- ***Third category of IP assets***: not applicable as the regime does not allow the third category of IP assets to qualify for the benefits.
- ***Taxpayers making use of the option to treat the nexus ratio as a rebuttable presumption***: not applicable as the regime does not allow the nexus ratio to be treated as a rebuttable presumption.

Summary of recommendations on implementation of the transparency framework

Aspect of implementation of the transparency framework that should be improved	Recommendation for improvement
Italy amended its procedure to transmit information on future rulings to the Competent Authority on a quarterly basis. However, in practice the information was delayed in its transmission to the Competent Authority, on average within five months and particular delays were encountered with regard to rulings on preferential regimes. This is a continuing recommendation from the prior year peer review. Italy already amended its procedure to address this issue, which will be reviewed in the next peer review report.	Italy is recommended to continue its efforts to reduce the timelines for providing the information on future rulings to the Competent Authority.
Italy has introduced an Inter-Ministerial Decree to identify new entrants of the grandfathered IP regime. However, the Decree only came into force on 6 February 2018 and Italy was not able to identify all relevant information on new entrants to the IP regime that obtained benefits with respect to trademarks during the year of review. This is a continuing recommendation from the prior year peer review.	Italy is recommended to continue its efforts to identify and exchange information on new entrants to the grandfathered IP regime.

Notes

[1] Including one ruling that was only identified and exchanged during the year of review.

[2] With respect to the following preferential regimes: 1) International shipping and 2) Patent Box.

[3] Available here: www.agenziaentrate.gov.it/wps/content/Nsilib/Nsi/Normativa+e+Prassi/Risoluzioni/Archivio+risoluzioni/?page=normativa (accessed 20 November 2018).

[4] Parties to the Convention are available here: www.oecd.org/tax/exchange-of-tax-information/convention-on-mutual-administrative-assistance-in-tax-matters.htm. Italy has bilateral agreements with: Albania, Algeria, Argentina, Armenia, Australia, Austria, Azerbaijan, Bangladesh, Belarus, Belgium, Bosnia and Herzegovina, Brazil, Bulgaria, Canada, Chile, China (People's Republic of), Congo, Côte d'Ivoire, Croatia, Cyprus, Czech Republic, Denmark, Ecuador, Egypt, Estonia, Ethiopia, Finland, Former Yugoslav Republic of Macedonia, France, Georgia, Germany, Ghana, Greece, Hong Kong (China), Hungary, Iceland, India, Indonesia, Ireland, Israel, Japan, Jordan, Kazakhstan, Korea, Kuwait, Latvia, Lebanon, Lithuania, Luxembourg, Malaysia, Malta, Mauritius, Mexico, Moldova, Montenegro, Morocco, Mozambique, Netherlands, New Zealand, Norway, Oman, Pakistan, Philippines, Poland, Portugal, Qatar, Romania, Russia, San Marino, Saudi Arabia, Senegal, Serbia, Singapore, Slovak Republic, Slovenia, South Africa, Spain, Sri Lanka, Sweden, Switzerland, Syrian Arab Republic, Chinese Taipei, Tajikistan, Tanzania, Thailand, Trinidad and Tobago, Tunisia, Turkey, Turkmenistan, Uganda, Ukraine, United Arab Emirates, United Kingdom, United States, Uzbekistan, Venezuela, Viet Nam and Zambia.

Note by Turkey: The information in this document with reference to "Cyprus" relates to the southern part of the Island. There is no single authority representing both Turkish and Greek Cypriot people on the Island. Turkey recognises the Turkish Republic of Northern Cyprus (TRNC). Until a lasting and equitable solution is found within the context of the United Nations, Turkey shall preserve its position concerning the "Cyprus issue".

Note by all the European Union Member States of the OECD and the European Union. The Republic of Cyprus is recognised by all members of the United Nations with the exception of Turkey. The information in this document relates to the area under the effective control of the Government of the Republic of Cyprus.

[5] Italy notes that information on rulings related to preferential regimes was forwarded to the Competent Authority in December 2017 and April 2018 and that all such information (excluding those rulings lacking of legal basis) have therefore been exchanged by February and July 2018.

[6] Partial exemption for income/gains derived from certain IP rights.

References

OECD (2017), *BEPS Action 5 on Harmful Tax Practices – Terms of Reference and Methodology for the Conduct of the Peer Reviews of the Action 5 Transparency Framework*, OECD/G20 Base Erosion and Profit Shifting Project, OECD, Paris. www.oecd.org/tax/beps/beps-action-5-harmful-tax-practices-peer-review-transparencyframework.pdf.

OECD (2015), *Countering Harmful Tax Practices More Effectively, Taking into Account Transparency and Substance, Action 5 - 2015 Final Report*, OECD/G20 Base Erosion and Profit Shifting Project, OECD Publishing, Paris. https://doi.org/10.1787/9789264241190-en.

OECD/Council of Europe (2011), *The Multilateral Convention on Mutual Administrative Assistance in Tax Matters: Amended by the 2010 Protocol*, OECD Publishing, Paris. http://dx.doi.org/10.1787/9789264115606-en.

Jamaica

Jamaica did not provide a completed peer review questionnaire to the Secretariat. It is not known whether Jamaica has implemented the transparency framework. Jamaica is recommended to ensure that it has put in place an effective information gathering process to identify all relevant past and future rulings and all potential exchange jurisdictions and to implement a review and supervision mechanism, as soon as possible (ToR I.4). Jamaica is recommended to put in place a domestic legal framework allowing spontaneous exchange of information on rulings if needed and to ensure the timely exchange of information on rulings in the form required by the transparency framework (ToR II.5).

It is not known whether Jamaica can legally issue any types of ruling within the scope of the transparency framework, or whether in practice Jamaica issued any such rulings.

As no exchanges of information on rulings were conducted, no peer input was received in respect of the exchanges of information on rulings received from Jamaica.

Introduction

663. This peer review covers Jamaica's implementation of the BEPS Action 5 transparency framework for the year 2017. The report has four parts, each relating to a key part of the Terms of Reference (ToR). Each part is discussed in turn. A summary of recommendations is included at the end of this report.

A. The information gathering process

664. Jamaica was not yet able to complete the peer review questionnaire. It is not known whether Jamaica has implemented the transparency framework.

Conclusion on section A

665. Jamaica is recommended to ensure that it has put in place an effective information gathering process to identify all relevant past and future rulings and all potential exchange jurisdictions and to implement a review and supervision mechanism, as soon as possible (ToR I.4).

B. The exchange of information

Legal basis for spontaneous exchange of information (ToR II.5.1, II.5.2)

666. It is not known whether Jamaica has the necessary domestic legal basis to exchange information on rulings spontaneously. Jamaica is recommended to put in place a domestic legal framework allowing spontaneous exchange of information on rulings if needed (ToR II.5.1).

667. Jamaica is a party to international agreements permitting spontaneous exchange of information, including (i) the *Multilateral Convention on Mutual Administrative Assistance in Tax Matters: Amended by the 2010 Protocol* (OECD/Council of Europe, 2011) ("the Convention"), and (ii) double tax agreements and tax information exchange agreements in force with 27 jurisdictions.[1]

Completion and exchange of templates (ToR II.5.3, II.5.4, II.5.5, II.5.6, II.5.7)

668. It is not known whether Jamaica has put in place a process to exchange information on rulings in accordance with the form and timelines required by the transparency framework. Jamaica is recommended to ensure the timely exchange of information on rulings in the form required by the transparency framework.

Conclusion on section B

669. Jamaica is recommended to put in place a domestic legal framework allowing spontaneous exchange of information on rulings if needed and to ensure the timely exchange of information on rulings in the form required by the transparency framework (ToR II.5).

C. Statistics (ToR IV)

670. As no information on rulings was exchanged for the year in review, no statistical data can be reported.

D. Matters related to intellectual property regimes (ToR I.4.1.3)

671. Jamaica does not offer an intellectual property regime for which transparency requirements under the Action 5 Report (OECD, 2015) were imposed.

Summary of recommendations on implementation of the transparency framework

Aspect of implementation of the transparency framework that should be improved	Recommendation for improvement
It is not known whether Jamaica has an information gathering process in place.	Jamaica is recommended to ensure that it has put in place an effective information gathering process to identify all relevant past and future rulings and all potential exchange jurisdictions and to implement a review and supervision mechanism, as soon as possible.
It is not known whether Jamaica has a domestic legal framework allowing spontaneous exchange of information on rulings and has in place a process for completion of templates and exchange of information on rulings.	Jamaica is recommended to put in place a domestic legal framework allowing spontaneous exchange of information on rulings if needed and to ensure the timely exchange of information on rulings in the form required by the transparency framework

Note

[1] Antigua and Barbuda, Barbados, Belize, Canada, China (People's Republic of), Denmark, Dominica, Faroe Islands, Finland, France, Germany, Greenland, Grenada, Guyana, Iceland, Israel, Norway, Saint Kitts and Nevis, Saint Lucia, Saint Vincent and the Grenadines, South Africa, Spain, Sweden, Switzerland, Trinidad and Tobago, United Kingdom and United States.

References

OECD (2017), *BEPS Action 5 on Harmful Tax Practices – Terms of Reference and Methodology for the Conduct of the Peer Reviews of the Action 5 Transparency Framework*, OECD/G20 Base Erosion and Profit Shifting Project, OECD, Paris. www.oecd.org/tax/beps/beps-action-5-harmful-tax-practices-peer-review-transparencyframework.pdf.

OECD (2015), *Countering Harmful Tax Practices More Effectively, Taking into Account Transparency and Substance, Action 5 - 2015 Final Report*, OECD/G20 Base Erosion and Profit Shifting Project, OECD Publishing, Paris. https://doi.org/10.1787/9789264241190-en.

OECD/Council of Europe (2011), *The Multilateral Convention on Mutual Administrative Assistance in Tax Matters: Amended by the 2010 Protocol*, OECD Publishing, Paris. http://dx.doi.org/10.1787/9789264115606-en.

Japan

Japan has met all aspects of the terms of reference (ToR) for the calendar year 2017 (year in review) and no recommendations are made.

Japan can legally issue three types of rulings within the scope of the transparency framework.

In practice, Japan has issued 51 past rulings; for the period 1 April 2016 - 31 December 2016, Japan issued 12 future rulings; and for the year in review, Japan issued 14 future rulings within the scope of the transparency framework.

Peer input was received from one jurisdiction in respect of the exchanges of information on rulings received from Japan. It was positive, noting that information was complete, in the correct format, received in a timely manner, and that the summary provided a good overview of the ruling.

Introduction

672. This peer review covers Japan's implementation of the BEPS Action 5 transparency framework for the year 2017. The report has four parts, each relating to a key part of the ToR. Each part is discussed in turn. A summary of recommendations is included at the end of this report.

A. The information gathering process

673. Japan can legally issue the three following types of rulings within the scope of the transparency framework: (i) cross-border unilateral advance pricing arrangements (APAs) and any other cross-border unilateral tax rulings (such as an advance tax ruling) covering transfer pricing or the application of transfer pricing principles; (ii) permanent establishment rulings; and (iii) related party conduit rulings. In Japan, the Rulings and Legal Affairs Divisions and APA Division in each of the 12 Regional Taxation Bureau of the National Tax Agency ("NTA") are authorised to issue rulings.

Past rulings (ToR I.4.1.1, I.4.1.2, I.4.2.1, I.4.2.2)

674. For Japan, past rulings are any tax rulings within scope that are issued either: (i) on or after 1 January 2014 but before 1 April 2016; or (ii) on or after 1 January 2010 but before 1 January 2014, provided they were still in effect as at 1 January 2014.

675. In the prior year peer review report, it was determined that the NTA's undertakings to identify past rulings and all potential exchange jurisdictions were sufficient to meet the minimum standard. The NTA's implementation in this regard remains unchanged, and therefore continues to meet the minimum standard.

Future rulings (ToR I.4.1.1, I.4.1.2, I.4.2.1)

676. For Japan, future rulings are any tax rulings within scope that are issued on or after 1 April 2016.

677. In the prior year peer review report, it was determined that the NTA's implementation of a new system to identify future rulings and all potential exchange jurisdictions was sufficient to meet the minimum standard. The NTA's implementation in this regard remains unchanged, and therefore continues to meet the minimum standard.

Review and supervision mechanism (ToR I.4.3)

678. In the prior year peer review report, it was determined that the NTA's review and supervision mechanism was sufficient to meet the minimum standard. The NTA's implementation in this regard remains unchanged, and therefore continues to meet the minimum standard.

Conclusion on section A

679. Japan has met all of the ToR for the information gathering process and no recommendations are made.

B. The exchange of information

Legal basis for spontaneous exchange of information (ToR II.5.1, II.5.2)

680. Japan has the necessary domestic legal basis to exchange information spontaneously. Japan notes that there are no legal or practical impediments that prevent the spontaneous exchange of information on rulings as contemplated in the Action 5 minimum standard.

681. Japan is a party to international agreements permitting spontaneous exchange of information, including (i) the *Multilateral Convention on Mutual Administrative Assistance in Tax Matters: Amended by the 2010 Protocol* (OECD/Council of Europe, 2011) ("the Convention") and (ii) double tax agreements in force with 68 jurisdictions.[1]

Completion and exchange of templates (ToR II.5.3, II.5.4, II.5.5, II.5.6, II.5.7)

682. In the prior year peer review report, it was determined that the NTA's completion and exchange of templates were sufficient to meet the minimum standard. The NTA's implementation in this regard remains unchanged, and therefore continues to meet the minimum standard. With respect to the completion of the summary section of the template, Japan confirms that it uses written guidance which provides instruction, including Japanese translation of the Annex C template and its instruction sheet, to complete each section of the template.

683. For the year in review, the timeliness of exchanges is as follows:

Past rulings in the scope of the transparency framework	Number of exchanges transmitted by 31 December 2017	Delayed exchanges		
		Number of exchanges not transmitted by 31 December 2017	Reasons for the delays	Any other comments
	11	0	N/A	These relate to the past rulings that needed to be exchanged with new members of the IF that joined in 2017
Future rulings in the scope of the transparency framework	Number of exchanges transmitted within three months of the information becoming available to the competent authority or immediately after legal impediments have been lifted	Delayed exchanges		
		Number of exchanges transmitted later than three months of the information on rulings becoming available to the competent authority	Reasons for the delays	Any other comments
	26	0	N/A	
Total	37	0		

Follow up requests received for exchange of the ruling	Number	Average time to provide response	Number of requests not answered
	5	70	N/A

Conclusion on section B

684. Japan has the necessary legal basis for spontaneous exchange of information, a process for completing the templates in a timely way and has completed all exchanges on

time. Japan has met all of the ToR for the exchange of information process and no recommendations are made.

C. Statistics (ToR IV)

685. The statistics for the year in review are as follows:

Category of ruling	Number of exchanges	Jurisdictions exchanged with
Rulings related to preferential regimes	N/A	N/A
Cross-border unilateral advance pricing arrangement (APAs) and any other cross-border unilateral tax rulings (such as an advance tax ruling) covering transfer pricing or the application of transfer pricing principles	37	Austria, China, Germany, Hong Kong (China), Netherlands, Philippines, Malaysia, Malta, Singapore, Sweden, Thailand, United States
Cross-border rulings providing for a unilateral downward adjustment to the taxpayer's taxable profits that is not directly reflected in the taxpayer's financial / commercial accounts	N/A	N/A
Permanent establishment rulings	0	N/A
Related party conduit rulings	0	N/A
De minimis rule	N/A	N/A
IP regimes: total exchanges on taxpayers benefitting from the third category of IP assets, new entrants benefitting from grandfathered IP regimes; and taxpayers making use of the option to treat the nexus ratio as a rebuttable presumption	N/A	N/A
Total	37	

D. Matters related to intellectual property regimes (ToR I.4.1.3)

686. Japan does not offer an intellectual property regime for which transparency requirements under the Action 5 Report (OECD, 2015) were imposed.

Summary of recommendations on implementation of the transparency framework

Aspect of implementation of the transparency framework that should be improved	Recommendation for improvement
	No recommendations are made.

Note

1 Parties to the Convention are available here: www.oecd.org/tax/exchange-of-tax-information/convention-on-mutual-administrative-assistance-in-tax-matters.htm. Japan also has bilateral agreements in force with Armenia, Bangladesh, Belarus, Brunei Darussalam, Egypt, Fiji, Hong Kong (China), Kuwait, Kyrgyzstan, Oman, Philippines, Qatar, Sri Lanka, Chinese Taipei, Tajikistan, Thailand, Turkey, Turkmenistan, United States, Uzbekistan, Viet Nam and Zambia.

References

OECD (2017), *BEPS Action 5 on Harmful Tax Practices – Terms of Reference and Methodology for the Conduct of the Peer Reviews of the Action 5 Transparency Framework*, OECD/G20 Base Erosion and Profit Shifting Project, OECD, Paris. www.oecd.org/tax/beps/beps-action-5-harmful-tax-practices-peer-review-transparencyframework.pdf.

OECD (2015), *Countering Harmful Tax Practices More Effectively, Taking into Account Transparency and Substance, Action 5 - 2015 Final Report*, OECD/G20 Base Erosion and Profit Shifting Project, OECD Publishing, Paris. https://doi.org/10.1787/9789264241190-en.

OECD/Council of Europe (2011), *The Multilateral Convention on Mutual Administrative Assistance in Tax Matters: Amended by the 2010 Protocol*, OECD Publishing, Paris. http://dx.doi.org/10.1787/9789264115606-en.

Jersey

Jersey has met the all aspects of the terms of reference (ToR) for the calendar year 2017 (year in review) and no recommendations are made.

Jersey can legally issue four types of rulings within the scope of the transparency framework.

In practice, Jersey has issued 16 past rulings; and for the year in review, Jersey issued one future ruling within the scope of the transparency framework.

No peer input was received in respect of the exchanges of information on rulings received from Jersey.

Introduction

687. This peer review covers Jersey's implementation of the BEPS Action 5 transparency framework for the year 2017. The report has four parts, each relating to a key part of the ToR. Each part is discussed in turn. A summary of recommendations is included at the end of this report.

A. The information gathering process

688. Jersey can legally issue the four following types of rulings within the scope of the transparency framework: (i) cross-border unilateral advance pricing arrangements (APAs) and any other cross-border unilateral tax rulings (such as an advance tax ruling) covering transfer pricing or the application of transfer pricing principles; (ii) cross-border rulings giving a unilateral downward adjustment to the taxpayer's taxable profits in the country giving the ruling; (iii) permanent establishment rulings; and (iv) related party conduit rulings. Rulings are generally issued by the Comptroller or Assistant Comptroller of Taxes.

Past rulings (ToR I.4.1.1, I.4.1.2, I.4.2.1, I.4.2.2)

689. For Jersey, past rulings are any tax rulings within scope that are issued either: (i) on or after 1 January 2015 but before 1 April 2017; or (ii) on or after 1 January 2012 but before 1 January 2015, provided they were still in effect as at 1 January 2015.

690. The process for identifying past rulings was conducted as follows: The Jersey Taxes Office (JTO) performed a multi-staged process in order to identify past rulings. Firstly, searches were performed for relevant words that related to rulings, in the description or name of all documents held in the JTO's database in order to identify potential rulings in scope, followed by a manual review of the files of each taxpayer identified in this way. Secondly, the files of all companies which were taxed at a rate other than 0% at any time in the previous five years were manually reviewed, as it was considered that companies taxed at the 0% rate were unlikely to have requested a ruling given that Jersey's standard rate of taxation is 0. This was considered necessary as the JTO's document storage systems do not permit electronic searches within the documents, in order to address the risk that rulings may have been filed in the database without using these words.

691. All files pertaining to taxpayers with a positive rate of taxation were manually reviewed by the JTO, as it was considered that these taxpayers were most likely to have requested rulings in order to clarify their Jersey tax liability. As a further precaution, both manual and electronic searches of all folders containing correspondence by all three Comptrollers of Taxes and the sole Assistant Comptroller of Taxes during the relevant period from 2012 were undertaken, as these officers were the ones who almost exclusively issued rulings in the period. An instruction was issued to all staff to review any files in-progress for assessment or audit at the time, to identify any paper or electronic rulings associated with the files. A central record of rulings has been maintained from 2015 and this was consulted in addition to the checks above for rulings from 2015 onwards.

692. The potential cases were manually reviewed by a small group of experienced staff members within the JTO. These staff members were instructed to identify whether anything in the files indicated a ruling with an international context may have been

issued. The instructions contained a broad and extensive definition for the international context of a ruling. Cases identified to be in scope of Action 5 were escalated to the final review panel which comprised of three senior officers: the Deputy Comptroller (Policy and International), the Assistant Comptroller, and the Director (International Taxes). The officers split the cases to be reviewed, summarised each file and made a recommendation as to whether the ruling was in scope of the transparency framework. This review panel then met to jointly review these summaries and recommendations, and come to a final decision as whether the past ruling was in scope for exchange.

693. In order to identify the potential exchange jurisdictions, the JTO used the "best efforts approach". This involved reviewing the available information in the taxpayer's files and those of any known associates, as well as accessing publicly available information regarding a taxpayer's ownership, activities, and immediate and ultimate parent entities. Jersey was able to identify all potential exchange jurisdictions in all cases.

Future rulings (ToR I.4.1.1, I.4.1.2, I.4.2.1)

694. For Jersey, future rulings are any tax rulings within scope that are issued on or after 1 April 2017.

695. The JTO suspended the issuance of rulings made on or after 1 April 2017, until the new policy on the treatment of requests for rulings was finalised. This new policy[1] was published on 26 May 2017, setting out new procedures for the request of rulings from the JTO, including a list of information which must accompany the request. Requests for rulings which do not meet the requirements are not processed until the specified information is provided, which includes a list of potentially relevant exchange jurisdictions for the types of rulings issued by Jersey. A panel of at least two senior officers is convened on a monthly basis to identify any requests for rulings that have been issued in the past month that may be relevant for the transparency framework. The new policy therefore requires all information necessary to identify the rulings as being in the scope of the transparency framework and information on all potential exchange jurisdictions.

Review and supervision mechanism (ToR I.4.3)

696. Jersey has a single centralised tax administration of approximately 104 staff. All JTO staff members were trained in the new policy on the treatment of requests for rulings in 2017, and they are periodically reminded of these new procedures. Managers undertaking quality assurance reviews of junior staff members are also required to check that rulings have not been inadvertently granted in the course of normal assessments and audits. Finally, a panel of senior officers is convened on a monthly basis for the review of future rulings granted.

Conclusion on section A

697. Jersey has met all of the ToR for the information gathering process and no recommendations are made.

B. The exchange of information

Legal basis for spontaneous exchange of information (ToR II.5.1, II.5.2)

698. Jersey has the necessary domestic legal basis to exchange information spontaneously. Jersey notes that there are no legal or practical impediments that prevent the spontaneous exchange of information on rulings as contemplated in the Action 5 minimum standard.

699. Jersey is a party to international agreements permitting spontaneous exchange of information, including (i) the *Multilateral Convention on Mutual Administrative Assistance in Tax Matters: Amended by the 2010 Protocol* (OECD/Council of Europe, 2011) ("the Convention") and (ii) arrangements in force with 14 jurisdictions which allow for spontaneous exchange of information.[2]

Completion and exchange of templates (ToR II.5.3, II.5.4, II.5.5, II.5.6, II.5.7)

700. In order to share the required information with other jurisdictions, Jersey developed a template based on Annex C of the 2015 Action 5 Report (OECD, 2015). Jersey has confirmed that their approach to the completion of the summary section in section 7 of Annex C of the 2015 Action 5 Report conforms with the prescribed instructions to the section. Where relevant, Jersey also utilises the internal FHTP suggested guidance.

701. For past rulings, templates were completed by the Assistant Comptroller of Taxes and submitted to the Competent Authority in December 2017. With respect to future rulings, a senior panel is convened on a monthly basis to review rulings, two members of which are the delegated Competent Authorities for Jersey. When it is determined that an exchange is required to occur under the transparency framework, the relevant template is completed by the Assistant Comptroller of Taxes and passed to any of Jersey's Competent Authorities. The Competent Authority then reviews the template, and when satisfied, arranges for the template to be exchanged.

702. For the year in review, the timeliness of exchanges is as follows:

Past rulings in the scope of the transparency framework	Number of exchanges transmitted by 31 December 2017	Delayed exchanges		
		Number of exchanges not transmitted by 31 December 2017	Reasons for the delays	Any other comments
	16	2	A minor error occurred in the identification of immediate and parent companies in the case of PE rulings.	This error was identified and further exchanges completed on 2 March 2018. This issue has been rectified and therefore not expected to recur.
Future rulings in the scope of the transparency framework	Number of exchanges transmitted within three months of the information becoming available to the competent authority or immediately after legal impediments have been lifted	Delayed exchanges		
		Number of exchanges transmitted later than three months of the information on rulings becoming available to the competent authority	Reasons for the delays	Any other comments
	1	0		
Total	17	2		

Follow up requests received for exchange of the ruling	Number	Average time to provide response	Number of requests not answered
	0	N/A	N/A

Conclusion on section B

703. Jersey has the necessary legal framework and administrative process in place for exchanging information on rulings. Jersey has timely exchanged the information on rulings within scope of the transparency framework, with a small number of delays which were swiftly remedied. Jersey has met all of the ToR for the exchange of information process and no recommendations are made.

C. Statistics (ToR IV)

704. The statistics for the year in review are as follows:

Category of ruling	Number of exchanges	Jurisdictions exchanged with
Rulings related to preferential regimes	N/A	N/A
Cross-border unilateral advance pricing arrangements (APAs) and any other cross-border unilateral tax rulings (such as an advance tax ruling) covering transfer pricing or the application of transfer pricing principles	7	Guernsey, Switzerland, United Kingdom
Cross-border rulings providing for a unilateral downward adjustment to the taxpayer's taxable profits that is not directly reflected in the taxpayer's financial / commercial accounts	Included in *de minimis*	N/A
Permanent establishment rulings	7	France, Guernsey, Isle of Man, Netherlands, United Kingdom
Related party conduit rulings	0	0
De minimis rule	3	N/A
IP regimes: total exchanges on taxpayers benefitting from the third category of IP assets, new entrants benefitting from grandfathered IP regimes; and taxpayers making use of the option to treat the nexus ratio as a rebuttable presumption	N/A	N/A
Total	17	

D. Matters related to intellectual property regimes (ToR I.4.1.3)

705. Jersey does not offer an intellectual property regime for which transparency requirements under the Action 5 Report (OECD, 2015) were imposed.

Summary of recommendations on implementation of the transparency framework

Aspect of implementation of the transparency framework that should be improved	Recommendation for improvement
No recommendations are made.	

Notes

[1] "Taxes Office's policy on tax rulings", www.gov.je/SiteCollectionDocuments (accessed 19 November 2018).

[2] Cyprus, Estonia, Guernsey, Hong Kong, Isle of Man, Luxembourg, Malta, Qatar, Rwanda, Seychelles, Singapore, United Arab Emirates, United Kingdom, United States.

Note by Turkey: The information in this document with reference to "Cyprus" relates to the southern part of the Island. There is no single authority representing both Turkish and Greek Cypriot people on the Island. Turkey recognises the Turkish Republic of Northern Cyprus (TRNC). Until a lasting and equitable solution is found within the context of the United Nations, Turkey shall preserve its position concerning the "Cyprus issue".

Note by all the European Union Member States of the OECD and the European Union. The Republic of Cyprus is recognised by all members of the United Nations with the exception of Turkey. The information in this document relates to the area under the effective control of the Government of the Republic of Cyprus.

References

OECD (2017), *BEPS Action 5 on Harmful Tax Practices – Terms of Reference and Methodology for the Conduct of the Peer Reviews of the Action 5 Transparency Framework*, OECD/G20 Base Erosion and Profit Shifting Project, OECD, Paris. www.oecd.org/tax/beps/beps-action-5-harmful-tax-practices-peer-review-transparencyframework.pdf.

OECD (2015), *Countering Harmful Tax Practices More Effectively, Taking into Account Transparency and Substance, Action 5 - 2015 Final Report*, OECD/G20 Base Erosion and Profit Shifting Project, OECD Publishing, Paris. https://doi.org/10.1787/9789264241190-en.

OECD/Council of Europe (2011), *The Multilateral Convention on Mutual Administrative Assistance in Tax Matters: Amended by the 2010 Protocol*, OECD Publishing, Paris. http://dx.doi.org/10.1787/9789264115606-en.

Jordan

Jordan has met all aspects of the terms of reference (ToR) for the calendar year 2017 (year in review) that can be met in the absence of rulings being issued.

Jordan indicates that it cannot legally issue any type of rulings within the scope of the transparency framework. Jordan issues "circulars" and "opinion statements" which give a general clarification with respect the interpretation and application of the tax legislation per specific taxpayer. Since these documents are very general and not legally binding on the tax administration, these tax opinions are not rulings as defined in the Action 5 report (OECD, 2015).

As no rulings were issued, no exchange of information was required under the transparency framework. No peer input was received in respect of the exchanges of information on rulings received from Jordan.

Introduction

706. This peer review covers Jordan's implementation of the BEPS Action 5 transparency framework for the year 2017. The report has four parts, each relating to a key part of the ToR. Each part is discussed in turn. A summary of recommendations is included at the end of this report.

A. The information gathering process

707. As no rulings are issued, this section is not assessed.

B. The exchange of information

708. As no rulings are issued, this section is not assessed.

C. Statistics (ToR IV)

709. As no rulings are issued, no statistical data can be reported.

D. Matters related to intellectual property regimes (ToR I.4.1.3)

710. Jordan offers one preferential regime, which also offers benefits to income from intellectual property ("IP regime").[1] However no transparency requirements under the Action 5 Report (OECD, 2015) were relevant, as follows:

- ***New entrants benefitting from the grandfathered IP regime***: not applicable for the year in review, because Jordan is currently in the process of amending/abolishing the Development zones regime and has not taken a decision yet on whether it will provide grandfathering to existing taxpayers. Should Jordan provide grandfathering to taxpayers for which IP income benefits and that entered the regimes after the publication of the 2017 Progress Report (OECD, 2017), which occurred on 16 October 2017, transparency requirements will apply and this will be taken into account during the subsequent peer review.
- ***Third category of IP assets***: not applicable to this regime, which in 2017 was in the process of being amended.
- ***Taxpayers making use of the option to treat the nexus ratio as a rebuttable presumption***: not applicable to this regime, which in 2017 was in the process of being amended.

Summary of recommendations on implementation of the transparency framework

Aspect of implementation of the transparency framework that should be improved	Recommendation for improvement
	No recommendations are made.

Note

[1] This regime is the Development zones.

References

OECD (2017), *BEPS Action 5 on Harmful Tax Practices – Terms of Reference and Methodology for the Conduct of the Peer Reviews of the Action 5 Transparency Framework*, OECD/G20 Base Erosion and Profit Shifting Project, OECD, Paris. www.oecd.org/tax/beps/beps-action-5-harmful-tax-practices-peer-review-transparencyframework.pdf.

OECD (2015), *Countering Harmful Tax Practices More Effectively, Taking into Account Transparency and Substance, Action 5 - 2015 Final Report*, OECD/G20 Base Erosion and Profit Shifting Project, OECD Publishing, Paris. https://doi.org/10.1787/9789264241190-en.

Korea

Korea has met all of the terms of reference (ToR) for the calendar year 2017 (year in review) and no recommendations are made. In the prior year report, Korea had received two recommendations. Korea has resolved these issues and therefore none of the prior year recommendations remain.

Korea can legally issue one type of rulings within the scope of the transparency framework.

In practice, Korea issued 45 past rulings; for the period 1 April 2016 - 31 December 2016, Korea issued one future ruling; and for the year in review, Korea issued four future rulings within the scope of the transparency framework.

Korea did not have the necessary domestic legal basis for spontaneous exchange of information on rulings for the year in review. As such, no exchanges on rulings were permitted to occur.[1] As no exchanges on rulings could be undertaken under Korea's domestic legal framework, no peer input was received in respect of the exchanges of information on rulings received from Korea.

Introduction

711. This peer review covers Korea's implementation of the BEPS Action 5 transparency framework for the year 2017. The report has four parts, each relating to a key part of the ToR. Each part is discussed in turn. A summary of recommendations is included at the end of this report.

A. The information gathering process

712. Korea can legally issue the following type of rulings within the scope of the transparency framework: cross-border unilateral APAs and any other cross-border unilateral tax rulings (such as an advance tax ruling) covering transfer pricing or the application of transfer pricing principles.[2] Rulings on APAs are issued by the International Taxation Bureau at the Central Office of the National Tax Service ("NTS").

Past rulings (ToR I.4.1.1, I.4.1.2, I.4.2.1, I.4.2.2)

713. For Korea, past rulings are any tax rulings within scope that are issued either: (i) on or after 1 January 2014 but before 1 April 2016; or (ii) on or after 1 January 2010 but before 1 January 2014, provided they were still in effect as at 1 January 2014.

714. In the prior year peer review report, it was determined that Korea's undertakings to identify past rulings and all potential exchange jurisdictions were sufficient to meet the minimum standard. Korea's implementation in this regard remains unchanged, and therefore continues to meet the minimum standard.

Future rulings (ToR I.4.1.1, I.4.1.2, I.4.2.1)

715. For Korea, future rulings are any tax rulings within scope that are issued on or after 1 April 2016.

716. In the prior year peer review report, it was determined that Korea's implementation of a new system to identify future rulings and all potential exchange jurisdictions was sufficient to meet the minimum standard. Korea's implementation in this regard remains unchanged, and therefore continues to meet the minimum standard.

Review and supervision mechanism (ToR I.4.3)

717. In the prior year peer review report, it was determined that Korea's review and supervision mechanism was sufficient to meet the minimum standard. Korea's implementation in this regard remains unchanged, and therefore continues to meet the minimum standard.

Conclusion on section A

718. Korea has met all of the ToR for the information gathering process and no recommendations are made.

B. The exchange of information

Legal basis for spontaneous exchange of information (ToR II.5.1, II.5.2)

719. For the year in review, Korea did not have the necessary domestic legal basis to spontaneously exchange information on unilateral APAs. This was because domestic

regulation specifically restricted the tax administration's use of data that is submitted in an application of an APA to (1) review of the APA and (2) follow-up procedures related to the APA.

720. As of 13 February 2018, a legislative amendment in Article 9(5) of the Enforcement Decree of the Adjustment of International Taxes Act was enacted, and Korea now has the necessary domestic legal basis to spontaneously exchange information on unilateral APAs.

721. Korea has international agreements permitting spontaneous exchange of information, including being a party to the (i) *Multilateral Convention on Mutual Administrative Assistance in Tax Matters: Amended by the 2010 Protocol* (OECD/Council of Europe, 2011) ("the Convention") and (ii) double tax agreements in force with 94 jurisdictions.[3]

Completion and exchange of templates (ToR II.5.3, II.5.4, II.5.5, II.5.6, II.5.7)

722. During 2017, tax officials in charge of the MAP division of the NTS completed the templates in the form of Annex C of the 2015 Action 5 Report (OECD, 2015), in anticipation of being able to quickly exchange after the domestic legal basis entered into effect. The templates were reviewed by a designated tax officer who has been put in charge of the exchange of unilateral APAs. With respect to future rulings, Korea has educated its tax officers to ensure that the completed templates on rulings are submitted to the Competent Authority on a quarterly basis and to ensure that the overall time by which the exchange of information is completed is within three months of the ruling being issued. The summary section of the template is completed in accordance with the internal FHTP suggested guidance. For the spontaneous exchange of information on unilateral APAs, the tax official will use the OECD XML Schema (OECD, 2017b).

723. The timeliness of exchanges is as follows:

Past rulings in the scope of the transparency framework	Number of exchanges transmitted by 31 December 2017	Delayed exchanges		
		Number of exchanges not transmitted by 31 December 2017	Reasons for the delays	Any other comments
	0	139	No domestic legal basis for the exchange of information.	
Future rulings in the scope of the transparency framework	Number of exchanges transmitted within three months of the information becoming available to the competent authority or immediately after legal impediments have been lifted	Delayed exchanges		
		Number of exchanges transmitted later than three months of the information on rulings becoming available to the competent authority	Reasons for the delays	Any other comments
	0	12	As above.	
Total	0	151		

Follow up requests received for exchange of the ruling	Number	Average time to provide response	Number of requests not answered
	0	N/A	N/A

724. The NTS finished the enhancement of its internal information transmission system, the "Automatic Exchange and Analysis of Foreign Financial Information System" (AXIS) to make it available for the exchange on information on rulings. The AXIS is connected to the OECD Common Transmission System. The NTS is testing whether the enhanced system works properly for each jurisdiction. When the results of these tests are positive, the NTS will use the enhanced AXIS system for the exchange of information on rulings. In advance of the finalisation of this system, a paper based format for the exchange of information on the 50 rulings was used. The first exchanges were sent by electronic and postal mail in March 2018 and additional exchanges were carried out in July 2018.

Conclusion on section B

725. For the year under review, Korea did not have the necessary legal framework in place for exchanging information on rulings. It is noted that Korea has now put in place the domestic legal basis, and commenced exchanges in the month following the entry into force of the new legal basis. Korea has met all of the ToR for the exchange of information process that can be met in the absence of the domestic legal framework and no recommendations are made.

C. Statistics (ToR IV)

726. As there was no legal basis for exchange in the year of review, no statistical data can be reported.

D. Matters related to intellectual property regimes (ToR I.4.1.3)

727. Korea offers an intellectual property regime ("IP regime") that is subject to transparency requirements under the Action 5 Report (OECD, 2015) (Special taxation for transfer, acquisition, etc. of technology). It states that the identification of the benefitting taxpayers will occur as follows:

- ***New entrants benefitting from the grandfathered IP regime***: as this is a new regime, grandfathering is not relevant.
- ***Third category of assets***: such assets are required to be registered and managed with the Korea Institute for Advancement of Technology. Information on the third category of assets is collected via the corporate tax returns. A new appendix table, attached to the tax return, under the Ordinance of Ministry of Strategy and Finance has been created to collect information on how many taxpayers enjoy benefits from the third category IP asset and the total amount of income generated from such assets. As the new IP regime came into effect as of 1 January 2017, the corporate tax returns will be filed within 3 months after the end of the tax year. Therefore, this data was not available for the year in review and the transparency requirements will be reviewed in the subsequent peer review. Korea notes that it will exchange the information received from the tax returns within three months after receiving the filed returns.

- ***Taxpayers making use of the option to treat the nexus ratio as a rebuttable presumption***: not applicable as the regime does not allow the nexus ratio to be treated as a rebuttable presumption.

Summary of recommendations on implementation of the transparency framework

Aspect of implementation of the transparency framework that should be improved	Recommendation for improvement
	No recommendations are made.

Notes

[1] The Action 5 Report notes that jurisdictions which do not currently have the necessary legal framework in place for spontaneous exchange of information on rulings will need to put in place such a framework in order to comply with the obligations under Action 5, but that in such cases the timelines are subject to a country's legal framework.

[2] Korea notes that although it has an advance rulings program, binding administrative guidance prevents a taxpayer from requesting, or the authority from granting, advance rulings which would depend on, or involve a determination of, the facts and circumstances (such as a permanent establishment or conduit arrangement). The issuance of these rulings is governed by the binding administrative guidance published by the NTS.

[3] Parties to the Convention are available here: www.oecd.org/tax/exchange-of-tax-information/convention-on-mutual-administrative-assistance-in-tax-matters.htm. Korea also has Double Tax Agreements with Albania, Algeria, Australia, Austria, Azerbaijan, Bahrain, Bangladesh, Belarus, Belgium, Brazil, Brunei Darussalam, Bulgaria, Canada, Chile, China (People's Republic of), Colombia, Croatia, Czech Republic, Democratic People's Republic of Korea, Denmark, Ecuador, Egypt, Estonia, Ethiopia, Fiji, Finland, France, Gabon, Georgia, Germany, Greece, Hong Kong (China), Hungary, Iceland, India, Indonesia, Iran, Ireland, Israel, Italy, Japan, Jordan, Kazakhstan, Kenya, Kuwait, Kyrgyzstan, Laos, Latvia, Lithuania, Luxembourg, Malaysia, Malta, Mexico, Mongolia, Morocco, Myanmar, Nepal, Netherlands, New Zealand, Norway, Oman, Pakistan, Panama, Papua New Guinea, Peru, Philippines, Poland, Portugal, Qatar, Romania, Russia, Saudi Arabia, Serbia, Singapore, Slovak Republic, Slovenia, South Africa, Spain, Sri Lanka, Sweden, Switzerland, Tajikistan, Thailand, Tunisia, Turkey, Turkmenistan, Ukraine, United Arab Emirates, United Kingdom, United States, Uruguay, Uzbekistan, Venezuela and Viet Nam.

References

OECD (2017), *BEPS Action 5 on Harmful Tax Practices – Terms of Reference and Methodology for the Conduct of the Peer Reviews of the Action 5 Transparency Framework*, OECD/G20 Base Erosion and Profit Shifting Project, OECD, Paris. www.oecd.org/tax/beps/beps-action-5-harmful-tax-practices-peer-review-transparencyframework.pdf.

OECD (2015), *Countering Harmful Tax Practices More Effectively, Taking into Account Transparency and Substance, Action 5 - 2015 Final Report*, OECD/G20 Base Erosion and Profit Shifting Project, OECD Publishing, Paris. https://doi.org/10.1787/9789264241190-en.

OECD/Council of Europe (2011), *The Multilateral Convention on Mutual Administrative Assistance in Tax Matters: Amended by the 2010 Protocol*, OECD Publishing, Paris. http://dx.doi.org/10.1787/9789264115606-en.

Latvia

Latvia has met all aspects of the terms of reference (ToR) for the calendar year 2017 (year in review) except for having in place necessary regulatory framework to exchange information on rulings with countries other than EU Member States (ToR II.5.1) and the timelines by which information on rulings is provided to the Competent Authority for exchange of information (ToR II.5.5). Latvia is recommended to finalise the amendments to their regulatory framework to allow exchange of information on rulings with non-EU Member States under the transparency framework as soon as possible and to reduce the timelines for providing the information to the Competent Authority.

Latvia can legally issue three types of rulings within the scope of the transparency framework.

In practice, Latvia has issued one past ruling;[1] for the period 1 April 2016 - 31 December 2016, Latvia issued one future ruling; and for the year in review, Latvia issued two future rulings within the scope of the transparency framework.

No peer input was received in respect of the exchanges of information on rulings received from Latvia.

Introduction

728. This peer review covers Latvia's implementation of the BEPS Action 5 transparency framework for the year 2017. The report has four parts, each relating to a key part of the ToR. Each part is discussed in turn. A summary of recommendations is included at the end of this report.

A. The information gathering process

729. Latvia can legally issue the following three types of rulings within the scope of the transparency framework: (i) rulings related to preferential regimes;[2] (ii) cross-border unilateral APAs and any other cross-border unilateral tax ruling (such as an ATR) covering transfer pricing or the application of transfer pricing principles; and (iii) permanent establishment rulings. In Latvia, rulings within the transparency framework are issued by the tax control department of the International Transactions Control, Analysis and Methodology Division of the State Revenue Service (the "SRS"). The summaries of these rulings are published in an anonymised way.[3]

730. In the prior year peer review report, the information gathering process with respect to past rulings was not assessed as Latvia had indicated that it did not have the necessary legal framework in place for exchanging information on rulings. However, Latvia re-evaluated its legal framework, and has now confirmed that its legal framework does in fact allow for spontaneous exchange of information, and as such the information gathering process has now been reviewed.

Past rulings (ToR I.4.1.1, I.4.1.2, I.4.2.1, I.4.2.2)

731. For Latvia, past rulings are any tax rulings within scope that are issued either: (i) on or after 1 January 2014 but before 1 April 2016; or (ii) on or after 1 January 2010 but before 1 January 2014, provided they were still in effect as at 1 January 2014.

732. The SRS has in place a centralised system in which all rulings are registered and monitored in the Latvian Tax Identification system. Given the limited number of rulings issued by the SRS, all tax rulings in scope of the transparency framework were identified manually by the personnel of the SRS, who issue the tax rulings. This involved reading each ruling to determine whether it was within one of the relevant categories, and whether it was issued within the period of validity defined as past rulings.

733. In order to identify potential exchange jurisdictions with respect to the past rulings, the tax officials responsible for issuing rulings manually reviewed the rulings and the ruling application. The law governing rulings had already required that information on related parties (including immediate and ultimate parent companies) and concerned jurisdictions be included in the ruling application.[4] The completeness of this information is verified by the corresponding division's manager and assigned to a tax inspector who manually analyses the information to ensure that the information is sufficient before issuing the tax ruling. The inspector can also revert back to the taxpayer to request additional information if needed. As such, Latvia was able to identify all potential exchange jurisdictions in all cases without using the best efforts approach.

Future rulings (ToR I.4.1.1, I.4.1.2, I.4.2.1)

734. For Latvia, future rulings are any tax rulings within scope that are issued on or after 1 April 2016.

735. In order to identify future rulings, the tax officials who issued the rulings also manually reviewed all rulings in the relevant period to identify if they were in scope of Action 5 and also to identify the potential exchange jurisdictions based on the information provided by the Latvian taxpayer when applying for the ruling, as required by Latvian legislation. The identification of future rulings is done at the point of issuance of the ruling.

Review and supervision mechanism (ToR I.4.3)

736. Supervisors were instructed to review the work of the tax officials that identified the rulings for the purposes of the transparency framework. The rulings process is carefully documented at every step and Latvia also explains that given the small number of rulings issued, the risk of inaccuracies was reduced because it was able to manually review every ruling issued.

Conclusion on section A

737. Latvia has met all of the ToR for the information gathering process and no recommendations are made.

B. The exchange of information

Legal basis for spontaneous exchange of information (ToR II.5.1, II.5.2)

738. Latvia has the necessary domestic legal basis to exchange information spontaneously. Following Latvia's evaluation of its legal framework, Latvia explains that the Latvian legislation[5] does in fact provide a legal basis for spontaneous exchange under the transparency framework, although the existing internal regulations of the tax administration do not permit exchange with jurisdictions other than the EU Member States. Latvia indicates that it is in the process of amending the internal regulations to allow exchange of information with all relevant jurisdictions under the transparency framework, including non-EU jurisdictions. This is expected to be completed by the end of 2018.

739. Latvia is a party to international agreements permitting spontaneous exchange of information, including (i) the *Multilateral Convention on Mutual Administrative Assistance in Tax Matters: Amended by the 2010 Protocol* (OECD/Council of Europe, 2011) ("the Convention"), (ii) the Directive 2011/16/EU with all other European Union Member States and (iii) double tax agreements in force with 61 jurisdictions. [6]

Completion and exchange of templates (ToR II.5.3, II.5.4, II.5.5, II.5.6, II.5.7)

740. The SRS has developed a separate Microsoft Word template for internal use, which is completed by the tax officials responsible for issuing rulings. After the template is completed, it is forwarded to the division responsible for the exchange of information. The person responsible for the exchange of information on rulings checks that all required information has been provided, translates the information into English and generates an XML file using European Commission's (EC) Central Directory. In the future, the SRS plans to use the EC Central Directory's in-built functionality to prepare XML files to be exchanged with non-EU Member States.

741. Latvia indicates that so far all exchanges have been made using the EC Central Directory which contains the information in Annex C of the 2015 Action 5 Report

(OECD, 2015). In order to complete the summary section. Latvia indicates that they provide all relevant information to assist the receiving tax administration to obtain a general overview of the particular ruling and to risk-assess the potential risks posed by the ruling. When completing the summary section in relation to rulings, the following elements were included: the type of transaction regarding which the agreement is concluded, taxpayer's type of economic activity, the determined comparable unrelated enterprises' operating profit's margin interquartile range, criteria used for the determination of the transfer pricing or the transfer price and other important information depending on the specifics of each particular ruling.

742. For the year in review, the timeliness of exchanges is as follows:

Past rulings in the scope of the transparency framework	Number of exchanges transmitted by 31 December 2017	Delayed exchanges		
		Number of exchanges not transmitted by 31 December 2017	Reasons for the delays	Any other comments
	1	0		The exchange covered only EU Member States and was transferred via European Commission's Central Directory.
Future rulings in the scope of the transparency framework	Number of exchanges transmitted within three months of the information becoming available to the competent authority or immediately after legal impediments have been lifted	Delayed exchanges		
		Number of exchanges transmitted later than three months of the information on rulings becoming available to the competent authority	Reasons for the delays	Any other comments
	0	6	Taking into account that the rulings covered only EU Member States, the information was transferred in accordance with Directive 2016/11/EU deadlines.	See below
Total	1	6		

Follow up requests received for exchange of the ruling	Number	Average time to provide response	Number of requests not answered
	0	N/A	N/A

743. Latvia explains that the delays in transmitting the information on the past ruling and the future rulings result from the issue of interpretation of the legislation. The exchange of past rulings was completed in 2017 once the legal basis was clarified, as per the below.

744. The timelines for the process of completing templates and exchanging information on rulings are stipulated in the tax administration's internal regulations, which are in the process of being amended to comply with the requirements of the

transparency framework. Latvia exchanged information on rulings with the EU jurisdictions in accordance with the EU Directive timelines. This means that the information on future rulings issued within the first semester of 2017 would have been exchanged by September 2017, which is later than otherwise would be required under the transparency framework.

745. Latvia also indicates that information on rulings concerning non-EU Member States will be transmitted immediately after amendments to Latvian tax administration's internal regulations come into force. This affects two future rulings which will be exchanged with non-EU jurisdictions by the end of 2018.

Conclusion on section B

746. Latvia has met the ToR for the exchange of information process except having the necessary regulatory framework for exchange with non-EU Member States (ToR II.5.1), and it is applying the timelines under the EU Directive (ToR II.5.5). Latvia is recommended to finalise its amendments to the internal regulations as soon as possible to allow exchange of information on rulings including non-EU Member States and to reduce the timelines for providing the information on future rulings to the Competent Authority.

C. Statistics (ToR IV)

747. The statistics for the year in review are as follows:

Category of ruling	Number of exchanges	Jurisdictions exchanged with
Rulings related to preferential regimes	0	N/A
Cross-border unilateral advance pricing arrangements (APAs) and any other cross-border unilateral tax rulings (such as an advance tax ruling) covering transfer pricing or the application of transfer pricing principles	7	Germany, Italy, Netherlands, Poland, Spain, Sweden
Cross-border rulings providing for a unilateral downward adjustment to the taxpayer's taxable profits that is not directly reflected in the taxpayer's financial / commercial accounts	N/A	N/A
Permanent establishment rulings	0	N/A
Related party conduit rulings	N/A	N/A
De minimis rule	N/A	N/A
IP regimes: total exchanges on taxpayers benefitting from the third category of IP assets, new entrants benefitting from grandfathered IP regimes; and taxpayers making use of the option to treat the nexus ratio as a rebuttable presumption	N/A	N/A
Total	7	

D. Matters related to intellectual property regimes (ToR I.4.1.3)

748. Latvia does not offer an intellectual property regime for which transparency requirements under the Action 5 Report (OECD, 2015) were imposed.

Summary of recommendations on implementation of the transparency framework

Aspect of implementation of the transparency framework that should be improved	Recommendation for improvement
The tax administration's internal regulations do not permit spontaneous exchange of information with non-EU countries.	Latvia is recommended to finalise the amendments to the tax administration's internal regulations to permit exchange of information on rulings with non-EU Member States.
Latvia transmits information on future rulings to EU Member States to the Competent Authority at six monthly intervals each year, to align with the EU Directive deadlines, which is longer than necessary.	Latvia is recommended to reduce the timelines for providing the information on future rulings to the Competent Authority.

Notes

[1] There are 59 past rulings reported by Latvia in the prior year peer review report, however, all 59 past rulings were related to a preferential regime and concerned only Latvian enterprises, i.e. no foreign jurisdictions were involved.

[2] With respect to the following preferential regimes: (1) Shipping tax regime and (2) Special economic zones (regime related with the taxpayers investments in special economic zones and free ports)

[3] Available at: www.vid.gov.lv (accessed 20 November 2018).

[4] The Cabinet of Ministers Regulations and Administrative Procedure Law.

[5] Section V of the Cabinet Regulations No 1245 dated 5 November 2013.

[6] Parties to the Convention are available here: www.oecd.org/tax/exchange-of-tax-information/convention-on-mutual-administrative-assistance-in-tax-matters.htm. Latvia also has bilateral agreements with Albania, Armenia, Austria, Azerbaijan, Belarus, Belgium, Bulgaria, Canada, China (People's Republic of), Croatia, Cyprus, Czech Republic, Denmark, Estonia, Finland, Former Yugoslav Republic of Macedonia, France, Georgia, Germany, Greece, Hong Kong, Hungary, Iceland, India, Ireland, Israel, Italy, Japan, Kazakhstan, Korea, Kuwait, Kyrgyzstan, Lithuania, Luxembourg, Malta, Mexico, Moldova, Morocco, Netherlands, Norway, Poland, Portugal, Qatar, Romania, Russia, Montenegro, Serbia, Singapore, Slovenia, Slovak Republic, Spain, Sweden, Switzerland, Tajikistan, Turkey, Turkmenistan, Ukraine, United Arab Emirates, United Kingdom, United States and Uzbekistan.

Note by Turkey: The information in this document with reference to "Cyprus" relates to the southern part of the Island. There is no single authority representing both Turkish and Greek Cypriot people on the Island. Turkey recognises the Turkish Republic of Northern Cyprus (TRNC). Until a lasting and equitable solution is found within the context of the United Nations, Turkey shall preserve its position concerning the "Cyprus issue".

Note by all the European Union Member States of the OECD and the European Union. The Republic of Cyprus is recognised by all members of the United Nations with the exception of Turkey. The information in this document relates to the area under the effective control of the Government of the Republic of Cyprus.

References

OECD (2017), *BEPS Action 5 on Harmful Tax Practices – Terms of Reference and Methodology for the Conduct of the Peer Reviews of the Action 5 Transparency Framework*, OECD/G20 Base Erosion and Profit Shifting Project, OECD, Paris. www.oecd.org/tax/beps/beps-action-5-harmful-tax-practices-peer-review-transparencyframework.pdf.

OECD (2015), *Countering Harmful Tax Practices More Effectively, Taking into Account Transparency and Substance, Action 5 - 2015 Final Report*, OECD/G20 Base Erosion and Profit Shifting Project, OECD Publishing, Paris. https://doi.org/10.1787/9789264241190-en.

OECD/Council of Europe (2011), *The Multilateral Convention on Mutual Administrative Assistance in Tax Matters: Amended by the 2010 Protocol*, OECD Publishing, Paris. http://dx.doi.org/10.1787/9789264115606-en.

Liberia

Liberia has met all aspects of the terms of reference (ToR) for the calendar year 2017 (year in review) that can be met in the absence of rulings being issued.

Liberia does not issue any type of rulings within the scope of the transparency framework. Theoretically, there is no impediment for Liberia to issue rulings, but in practice Liberia does not issue any rulings. In the event that Liberia put in place the administrative process or develop the administrative capacity to issue rulings, Liberia notes that it would implement the transparency framework obligations.

As no rulings were issued, no exchange of information was required under the transparency framework. No peer input was received in respect of the exchanges of information on rulings received from Liberia.

Introduction

749. This peer review covers Liberia's implementation of the BEPS Action 5 transparency framework for the year 2017. The report has four parts, each relating to a key part of the ToR. Each part is discussed in turn. A summary of recommendations is included at the end of this report.

A. The information gathering process

750. As no rulings are issued, this section is not assessed.

B. The exchange of information

751. As no rulings are issued, this section is not assessed.

C. Statistics (ToR IV)

752. As no rulings are issued, no statistical data can be reported.

D. Matters related to intellectual property regimes (ToR I.4.1.3)

753. Liberia does not offer an intellectual property regime for which transparency requirements under the Action 5 Report (OECD, 2015) were imposed.

Summary of recommendations on implementation of the transparency framework

Aspect of implementation of the transparency framework that should be improved	Recommendation for improvement
No recommendations are made.	

References

OECD (2017), *BEPS Action 5 on Harmful Tax Practices – Terms of Reference and Methodology for the Conduct of the Peer Reviews of the Action 5 Transparency Framework*, OECD/G20 Base Erosion and Profit Shifting Project, OECD, Paris. www.oecd.org/tax/beps/beps-action-5-harmful-tax-practices-peer-review-transparencyframework.pdf.

OECD (2015), *Countering Harmful Tax Practices More Effectively, Taking into Account Transparency and Substance, Action 5 - 2015 Final Report*, OECD/G20 Base Erosion and Profit Shifting Project, OECD Publishing, Paris. https://doi.org/10.1787/9789264241190-en.

Liechtenstein

Liechtenstein has met all aspects of the terms of reference (ToR) for the calendar year 2017 (year in review) that can be met in the absence of exchange of information being permitted and no recommendations are made.

Liechtenstein can legally issue five types of rulings within the scope of the transparency framework.

In practice, Liechtenstein has issued 18 past rulings;[1] and for the year in review, Liechtenstein issued six future rulings within the scope of the transparency framework.

Liechtenstein did not have the necessary domestic legal basis for spontaneous exchange of information on rulings for the year of review. As such, no exchanges on rulings were permitted to occur.[2] As no exchanges on rulings could be undertaken under Liechtenstein's domestic legal framework, no peer input was received in respect of the exchanges of information on rulings received from Liechtenstein.

Introduction

754. This peer review covers Liechtenstein's implementation of the BEPS Action 5 transparency framework for the year 2017. The report has four parts, each relating to a key part of the ToR. Each part is discussed in turn. A summary of recommendations is included at the end of this report.

A. The information gathering process

755. Liechtenstein can legally issue five types of rulings within the scope of the transparency framework: (i) rulings related to preferential regimes; (ii) cross-border unilateral advance pricing arrangements (APAs) and any other cross-border unilateral tax rulings (such as an advance tax ruling) covering transfer pricing or the application of transfer pricing principles; (iii) unilateral downward adjustment, (iv) permanent establishment rulings, and (v) related party conduit rulings. In Liechtenstein, rulings are issued by the Head of the Fiscal Authority (FA) in collaboration with the Legal Department of the FA and the Head of the respective technical department.

756. For the year in review, Liechtenstein has commenced the information gathering process in advance of the legal basis for spontaneously exchanging information on rulings being finalised.

Past rulings (ToR I.4.1.1, I.4.1.2, I.4.2.1, I.4.2.2)

757. For Liechtenstein, past rulings are any tax rulings within scope that are issued on or after 1 January 2012 until 1 April 2017, provided they were still in effect as at 1 January 2017 (see paragraph 12).

758. The process for identifying past rulings was conducted as follows: Since 2012 the Legal Department of the FA has maintained a central list in form of an XLS Schema of all rulings and was responsible for updating this list every time a ruling was issued. The Head of the FA, the Legal Department and the Head of the respective technical department, who are also responsible for the issuance of the rulings, searched the database manually to identify rulings issued in the period defined as past rulings. Each ruling was read to filter rulings in scope.

759. In order to identify potential exchange jurisdictions with respect to the past rulings, the taxpayers' files were manually reviewed. The files usually contained all information necessary to identify the potential exchange jurisdictions. In two cases the taxpayer was consulted directly to identify the potential exchange jurisdictions. As such, all potential exchange jurisdictions were identified for all past rulings.

Future rulings (ToR I.4.1.1, I.4.1.2, I.4.2.1)

760. For Liechtenstein, future rulings are any tax rulings within scope that are issued on or after 1 April 2017.

761. Future rulings in scope are being identified by the Head of FA, the Legal Department and the Head of the respective technical department at the point at which the rulings are issued. The Legal Department compiles all rulings in the centralised database and marks the relevant rulings as being in scope of Action 5. The Legal Department reviews the database regularly and informs the EOI-unit, which is also located within the FA of new rulings issued.

762. With effect as of 1 January 2017 Liechtenstein introduced a new mandatory request form for future rulings in scope, which gathers information on the relevant parties and jurisdictions. Since the introduction of the new application form for rulings, all information on potential exchange jurisdictions are contained in the ruling itself.

Review and supervision mechanism (ToR I.4.3)

763. As rulings are issued by the Head of the FA in collaboration with the Legal Department of the FA and the Head of the respective technical department, this means that each ruling is reviewed at least by two officials checking whether the ruling is in scope. In addition all staff involved in the issuing process has received professional training through internal workshops and the participation in international working groups.

Conclusion on section A

764. Liechtenstein has met all of the ToR for the information gathering process and no recommendations are made.

B. The exchange of information

Legal basis for spontaneous exchange of information (ToR II.5.1, II.5.2)

765. Liechtenstein did previously not have the necessary domestic legal basis to exchange information spontaneously for rulings. This has been introduced and entered into force on 10 November 2017 (Law on International Administrative Assistance in Tax Matters, LIAATM). The LIAATM came into effect as of 1 January 2018 and allows Liechtenstein to exchange information on rulings issued as of 1 January 2012, provided they were still in effect on 1 January 2017. Liechtenstein explained that the limitation of the possibility to exchange information on past rulings was necessary as Liechtenstein's constitution does not foresee the possibility of introducing legislation with retrospective effect. Due to this limitation, information on two past rulings could not be exchanged as they were not in effect as of 1 January 2017, and the exchanges can only take place as from 1 January 2018.[3]

766. Liechtenstein notes that apart from the restriction to exchange information on certain past rulings there are no legal or practical impediments that prevent the spontaneous exchange of information on rulings as contemplated in the Action 5 minimum standard.

767. Liechtenstein is a party to international agreements permitting spontaneous exchange of information, including (i) the *Multilateral Convention on Mutual Administrative Assistance in Tax Matters: Amended by the 2010 Protocol* (OECD/Council of Europe, 2011) ("the Convention") and (ii) double tax agreements in force with 5 jurisdictions, all of which allow for spontaneous exchange of information.[4]

Completion and exchange of templates (ToR II.5.3, II.5.4, II.5.5, II.5.6, II.5.7)

768. Although there was no domestic legal basis to permit exchange of information to occur in the year in review, Liechtenstein had put in place the process for the completion and exchange of templates, as follows: In order to exchange information with other jurisdictions, Liechtenstein would use the template in Annex C of the 2015 Action 5 Report (OECD, 2015) in the form of a Word document. For past rulings, the Head of the Division for Corporates of the Fiscal Authority would fill in the templates and the Head

of the FA and the Head of the Legal Department would review them. The templates would then be forwarded to the EOI-unit for exchange as soon as the approval of the taxpayer was received.

769. For future rulings, before a ruling in scope is issued, the taxpayer is requested to fill out the template based on the OECD guidelines. Liechtenstein confirms that they would complete the summary section in the Annex C as prescribed in the instruction to the section in the Action 5 Report (OECD, 2015). The Legal Department updates the centralised databank with the information on each ruling and would forward the templates on a monthly basis to the EOI-unit. The ruling itself would only be sent to the EOI-unit if the exchange jurisdiction has further requests. The EOI-unit would manually review the templates, to ensure that the template is complete.

770. For the year in review, as the domestic legal basis was not yet in effect, no exchange of information could take place.

Conclusion on section B

771. Liechtenstein has introduced the necessary legal basis for spontaneous exchange of information on rulings, which took effect from 1 January 2018. It is noted that Liechtenstein has already started putting in place the administrative practices for the completion and exchange of templates on rulings, and in practice Liechtenstein reports that all exchanges took place by the end of March 2018. Liechtenstein has met all of the ToR for the exchange of information process, and no recommendations are made.

C. Statistics (ToR IV)

772. As there were no rulings exchanged by Liechtenstein for the year in review, no statistics can be reported.

D. Matters related to intellectual property regimes (ToR I.4.1.3)

773. Liechtenstein offered an intellectual property regime ("IP regime") which was abolished with effect as of 1 January 2017, providing grandfathering for existing taxpayers and existing IP assets until 31 December 2020. Since transparency requirements for new Inclusive Framework members regarding grandfathered entrants only apply to those taxpayers that entered the regime after 16 October 2017, this does not apply to Liechtenstein. Therefore, Liechtenstein is not subject to transparency requirements under the Action 5 report (OECD, 2015).

Summary of recommendations on implementation of the transparency framework

Aspect of implementation of the transparency framework that should be improved	Recommendation for improvement
No recommendations are made.	

Notes

1 Including four that fell into more than one category under the BEPS Action 5 report.

2 The Action 5 Report notes that jurisdictions which do not currently have the necessary legal framework in place for spontaneous exchange of information on rulings will need to put in place such a framework in order to comply with the obligations under Action 5, but that in such cases the timelines are subject to a country's legal framework.

3 The Action 5 Report (OECD, 2015) notes that jurisdictions which do not currently have the necessary legal framework in place for spontaneous exchange of information on rulings will need to put in place such a framework in order to comply with the obligations under the transparency framework, but that in such cases the timelines are subject to a country's legal framework.

4 Parties to the Convention are available here: www.oecd.org/tax/exchange-of-tax-information/convention-on-mutual-administrative-assistance-in-tax-matters.htm. Liechtenstein also has bilateral agreements with Czech Republic, Germany, Hungary, San Marino and United Kingdom.

References

OECD (2017), *BEPS Action 5 on Harmful Tax Practices – Terms of Reference and Methodology for the Conduct of the Peer Reviews of the Action 5 Transparency Framework*, OECD/G20 Base Erosion and Profit Shifting Project, OECD, Paris. www.oecd.org/tax/beps/beps-action-5-harmful-tax-practices-peer-review-transparencyframework.pdf.

OECD (2015), *Countering Harmful Tax Practices More Effectively, Taking into Account Transparency and Substance, Action 5 - 2015 Final Report*, OECD/G20 Base Erosion and Profit Shifting Project, OECD Publishing, Paris. https://doi.org/10.1787/9789264241190-en.

OECD/Council of Europe (2011), *The Multilateral Convention on Mutual Administrative Assistance in Tax Matters: Amended by the 2010 Protocol*, OECD Publishing, Paris. http://dx.doi.org/10.1787/9789264115606-en.

Lithuania

Lithuania has met all of the terms of reference (ToR) for the calendar year 2017 (year in review) and no recommendations are made.

Lithuania can legally issue four types of rulings within the scope of the transparency framework.

In practice, Lithuania issued five past rulings; and for the year in review, Lithuania issued six future rulings within the scope of the transparency framework.

Peer input was received from one jurisdiction in respect of the exchanges of information on rulings received from Lithuania. It was positive, noting that information was complete, in the correct format and received in a timely manner.

Introduction

774. This peer review covers Lithuania's implementation of the BEPS Action 5 transparency framework for the year 2017. The report has four parts, each relating to a key part of the ToR. Each part is discussed in turn. A summary of recommendations is included at the end of this report.

A. The information gathering process

775. Lithuania can legally issue the following four types of rulings within the scope of the transparency framework: (i) rulings related to preferential regimes;[1] (ii) cross-border unilateral APAs and any other cross-border unilateral tax rulings (such as an advance tax ruling) covering transfer pricing or the application of transfer pricing principles; (iii) unilateral downward adjustments; and (iv) permanent establishment rulings. With respect to the issuing of rulings, Lithuania distinguishes two categories: APAs and binding tax rulings (other than transfer pricing). The APAs are issued by the APA working group, consisting of five-seven officers (transfer pricing specialists, lawyers and experts) from various departments (control department, law department and tax information department) of the State Tax Inspectorate under the Ministry of Finance ("STI"). The binding tax rulings are issued by the binding tax rulings working group, consisting of 11 officials from various departments (law department, control department, large taxpayer monitoring and controlling department, tax information department and excise duty administration department) of the STI.

Past rulings (ToR I.4.1.1, I.4.1.2, I.4.2.1, I.4.2.2)

776. For Lithuania, past rulings are any tax rulings within scope that are issued either: (i) on or after 1 January 2015 but before 1 April 2017; or (ii) on or after 1 January 2012 but before 1 January 2015, provided they were still in effect as at 1 January 2015.

777. The process for identifying past APAs was conducted as follows: All APAs are issued by the APA working group and are available in a central registration system. Two members of the APA working group were responsible for the identification of the APAs. Only the members of the working group had access to the APA data. The officials selected the APAs involving a transaction with at least one related party in a jurisdiction outside Lithuania that fell into the period of validity for past rulings.

778. The APAs generally contain information on the relevant related parties, as the legislation obliges the taxpayer to provide this information when the taxpayer requesting an APA.[2] In addition, officers of the APA working group carry out verification methods using information from the public Amadeus database and checking internal reports of the STI comprising information on controlling entities for tax purposes declared by Lithuanian taxpayers. Lithuania confirms that in all cases, all potential exchange jurisdictions were able to be identified.

779. The process for identifying past rulings other than APAs was conducted as follows: All rulings are registered in one central registration system. Five members of the binding tax rulings working group were responsible for the identification of other past rulings. These members identified all past rulings by a systematic review of all rulings. Once the past rulings were identified, a review of the content of each ruling was undertaken to identify whether they are within categories as defined in the transparency framework and whether they fell into the period of validity for past rulings.

780. In order to identify the potential exchange jurisdictions for the other binding tax rulings, the "best efforts approach" was used. This included a manual search within the existing information available within the STI as well as consulting publicly available information, including the Amadeus database. Lithuania confirms that in all cases, all potential exchange jurisdictions were able to be identified.

Future rulings (ToR I.4.1.1, I.4.1.2, I.4.2.1)

781. For Lithuania, future rulings are any tax rulings within scope that are issued on or after 1 April 2017.

782. The APA working group remains responsible for the identification of future APAs. Since all APAs are issued by the APA working group, the APAs are identified within the APA database at the point of issuing. The process of identifying the potential exchange jurisdictions is the same for future and for past rulings (see paragraph 8).

783. In March 2018, Lithuania made amendments to the legislation with respect to the responsibility of the members of the APA working group. The amendments codify the practical process for identifying APAs and potential exchange jurisdictions and therefore the current approach does not practically change.

784. With respect to binding tax rulings, for the period 1 April 2017 - 24 July 2017, the same information gathering process as for past rulings was used, using the central registry. The potential exchange jurisdictions were able to be identified in all cases.

785. As of 24 July 2017, the binding tax rulings working group is responsible for determining for every ruling request, at receipt, if the ruling falls within one of the categories for the transparency framework. In order to identify the potential exchange jurisdictions, the taxpayer is obliged to submit all relevant information when applying for a binding tax ruling, including the relevant exchange jurisdictions. If any relevant information is missing, the STI shall have the right to approach the taxpayer to collect this information. Officers of the binding tax rulings working group verify this information. This includes a manual search within the existing information available within the STI as well as consulting publicly available information, including the Amadeus database.

Review and supervision mechanism (ToR I.4.3)

786. The supervision of the process for identifying binding rulings was delegated to three members of the binding tax rulings working group who reviewed all the decisions and selected those which had the content of a cross-border element. In addition, internal guidance has been provided to the staff issuing tax rulings.

787. The collection of relevant information for APAs is done by the officer preparing the decision. As the APA working group makes the decisions on APAs collectively, the accuracy of the relevant information will be assured through the revision performed by every member of the group providing its opinion on the information to be exchanged.

Conclusion on section A

788. Lithuania has met all of the ToR for the information gathering process and no recommendations are made.

B. The exchange of information

Legal basis for spontaneous exchange of information (ToR II.5.1, II.5.2)

789. Lithuania has the necessary domestic legal basis to exchange information spontaneously. Lithuania notes that there are no legal or practical impediments that prevent the spontaneous exchange of information on rulings as contemplated in the Action 5 minimum standard.

790. Lithuania has international agreements permitting spontaneous exchange of information, including being a party to (i) the *Multilateral Convention on Mutual Administrative Assistance in Tax Matters: Amended by the 2010 Protocol* (OECD/Council of Europe, 2011) ("the Convention"), (ii) the Directive 2011/16/EU with all other European Union Member States and (iii) double tax agreements in force with 54 jurisdictions.[3]

Completion and exchange of templates (ToR II.5.3, II.5.4, II.5.5, II.5.6, II.5.7)

791. Lithuania started exchanging information on rulings as of 1 September 2017. The past rulings and the future rulings that have been issued before this date were reviewed by members of the APA working group and binding tax ruling group who were also responsible for filling out the templates (in the form of Annex C of the 2015 Action 5 Report (OECD, 2015)). The templates were provided to the STI Department of the International Cooperation ("Competent Authority") before 1 September 2017. For rulings, the summary section of the template is completed by describing the transaction or other activities covered by the ruling. Regarding APAs, the summary section provided information indicating the main business activities, the functional analysis, the entities involved in the transaction, the type of the relevant controlled transaction and the transfer pricing methodology. Lithuania will incorporate the internal FHTP suggested guidance in its processes.

792. As of 1 September 2017, each member of the APA working group and the binding tax ruling group is obliged to complete the template for the exchange of information on each specific case which is assigned to him or her within 30 days after the issuance of the decision and then provide the template to the Competent Authority. The Competent Authority should then exchange the information with the relevant jurisdictions within 10 days. The Competent Authority uses the Central Directory developed by the EU Commission (for exchanges with EU Member States) for the production of the XML file which conforms to the OECD XML schema, or the XML file is loaded onto the Common Transmission System (CTS) portal (for exchanges with non-EU Member States). If a non-EU jurisdiction has no access to the CTS, then the information on the ruling will be sent in hard copy. The Competent Authority maintains a database recording the information about sent and received rulings.

793. For the year in review, the timeliness of exchanges is as follows:

Past rulings in the scope of the transparency framework	Number of exchanges transmitted by 31 December 2017	Delayed exchanges		
		Number of exchanges not transmitted by 31 December 2017	Reasons for the delays	Any other comments
	11	0	N/A	N/A
Future rulings in the scope of the transparency framework	Number of exchanges transmitted within three months of the information becoming available to the competent authority or immediately after legal impediments have been lifted	Delayed exchanges		
		Number of exchanges transmitted later than three months of the information on rulings becoming available to the competent authority	Reasons for the delays	Any other comments
	4	0	N/A	N/A
Total	15	0		

Follow up requests received for exchange of the ruling	Number	Average time to provide response	Number of requests not answered
	0	N/A	N/A

794. Two future rulings were issued in April and May 2017 and exchanged on 1 September 2017. As this delay was attributable to the implementation of Lithuania's new process on exchange of information on rulings, no recommendations are made in this regard as it is not anticipated to be a recurring issue.

Conclusion on section B

795. Lithuania has the necessary legal framework and administrative process in place for exchanging information on rulings. Lithuania has timely exchanged the rulings within scope of the transparency framework. Lithuania has met all of the ToR for the exchange of information process and no recommendations are made.

C. Statistics (ToR IV)

796. The statistics for the year in review are as follows:

Category of ruling	Number of exchanges	Jurisdictions exchanged with
Rulings related to preferential regimes	7	Bulgaria, Latvia, Luxembourg, United States
Cross-border unilateral advance pricing arrangements (APAs) and any other cross-border unilateral tax rulings (such as an advance tax ruling) covering transfer pricing or the application of transfer pricing principles	5	Finland, Hungary, Singapore, Sweden
Cross-border rulings providing for a unilateral downward adjustment to the taxpayer's taxable profits that is not directly reflected in the taxpayer's financial / commercial accounts	Included in *de minimis*	N/A
Permanent establishment rulings	Included in *de minimis*	N/A
Related party conduit rulings	N/A	N/A
De minimis rule	3	N/A
IP regimes: total exchanges on taxpayers benefitting from the third category of IP assets, new entrants benefitting from grandfathered IP regimes; and taxpayers making use of the option to treat the nexus ratio as a rebuttable presumption	N/A	N/A
Total	15	

D. Matters related to intellectual property regimes (ToR I.4.1.3)

797. Lithuania offers an intellectual property regime ("IP regime") which came into effect from 1 January 2018. Although this is after the year in review, it is noted that this regime is not subject to transparency requirements under the Action 5 report (OECD, 2015), because:

- ***New entrants benefitting from the grandfathered IP regime***: as this is a new IP regime rather than a grandfathered IP regime, transparency on new entrants was not relevant.
- ***Third category of IP assets***: not applicable as the regime does not allow the third category of IP assets to qualify for the benefits.
- ***Taxpayers making use of the option to treat the nexus ratio as a rebuttable presumption***: not applicable as the regime does not allow the nexus ratio to be treated as a rebuttable presumption.

Summary of recommendations on implementation of the transparency framework

Aspect of implementation of the transparency framework that should be improved	Recommendation for improvement
No recommendations are made.	

Notes

1 With respect to the following regimes: 1) Free economic zone taxation regime, 2) Tonnage tax regime and 3) IP regime.

2 This is established in The Rules for the Submission of a Taxpayer's Request to Consent to the Principles of Pricing of a Future Controlled Transaction, Adoption and Amendment of the Decision Obligating the STI (adopted by the Order No. VA-106 of Head of STI dated 21 October 2011).

3 Parties to the Convention are available here: www.oecd.org/tax/exchange-of-tax-information/convention-on-mutual-administrative-assistance-in-tax-matters.htm. Lithuania also has Double Tax Agreements with Armenia, Austria, Azerbaijan, Belarus, Belgium, Bulgaria, Canada, China (People's Republic of), Croatia, Czech Republic, Denmark, Estonia, Finland, Former Yugoslav Republic of Macedonia, France, Georgia, Germany, Greece, Hungary, Iceland, India, Ireland, Israel, Italy, Kazakhstan, Korea, Kuwait, Kyrgyzstan, Latvia, Luxembourg, Malta, Mexico, Moldova, Netherlands, Norway, Poland, Portugal, Romania, Russia, Serbia, Slovak Republic, Slovenia, Spain, Sweden, Switzerland, Turkey, Turkmenistan, United Arab Emirates, United Kingdom, United States and Uzbekistan.

References

OECD (2017), *BEPS Action 5 on Harmful Tax Practices – Terms of Reference and Methodology for the Conduct of the Peer Reviews of the Action 5 Transparency Framework*, OECD/G20 Base Erosion and Profit Shifting Project, OECD, Paris. www.oecd.org/tax/beps/beps-action-5-harmful-tax-practices-peer-review-transparencyframework.pdf.

OECD (2015), *Countering Harmful Tax Practices More Effectively, Taking into Account Transparency and Substance, Action 5 - 2015 Final Report*, OECD/G20 Base Erosion and Profit Shifting Project, OECD Publishing, Paris. https://doi.org/10.1787/9789264241190-en.

OECD/Council of Europe (2011), *The Multilateral Convention on Mutual Administrative Assistance in Tax Matters: Amended by the 2010 Protocol*, OECD Publishing, Paris. http://dx.doi.org/10.1787/9789264115606-en.

Luxembourg

Luxembourg has met all aspects of the terms of reference (ToR) for the calendar year 2017 (year in review) and no recommendations are made. In the prior year report, Luxembourg had received three recommendations. Luxembourg has resolved these issues and therefore none of the prior year recommendations remain.

Luxembourg can legally issue four types of rulings within the scope of the transparency framework.

In practice, Luxembourg issued 1 922 past rulings; for the period 1 April 2016 - 31 December 2016, Luxembourg issued 73 future rulings; and for the year in review, Luxembourg issued 18 future rulings within the scope of the transparency framework.[1] These rulings are published in a summarised and anonymised form in the annual report of the tax administration.

Peer input was received from four jurisdictions in respect of the exchanges of information on rulings received from Luxembourg. The input was generally positive, noting that information was complete, in a correct format and almost all received in a timely manner.

Introduction

798. This peer review covers Luxembourg's implementation of the BEPS Action 5 transparency framework for the year 2017. The report has four parts, each relating to a key part of the ToR. Each part is discussed in turn. A summary of recommendations is included at the end of this report.

A. The information gathering process

799. Luxembourg can legally issue the following four types of rulings within the scope of the transparency framework: (i) rulings related to preferential regimes; [2] (ii) cross-border unilateral APAs and any other cross-border unilateral tax rulings (such as an advance tax ruling) covering transfer pricing or the application of transfer pricing principles; (iii) unilateral downward adjustments; and (iv) permanent establishment rulings. To the extent that conduit rulings are provided, they are already covered under the second category. Competent tax offices are able to issue rulings, based on the opinion of the tax ruling commission.

Past rulings (ToR I.4.1.1, I.4.1.2, I.4.2.1, I.4.2.2)

800. For Luxembourg, past rulings are any tax rulings within scope that are issued either: (i) on or after 1 January 2014 but before 1 April 2016; or (ii) on or after 1 January 2010 but before 1 January 2014, provided they were still in effect as at 1 January 2014.

801. In the prior year peer review report, it was determined that Luxemburg's undertakings to identify past rulings and all potential exchange jurisdictions have met all the ToR, except for identifying all past rulings in the relevant categories (ToR 1.4.1.1 and I.4.1.1.2). Therefore, Luxembourg was recommended to continue its work to complete its information-gathering process on past rulings as soon as possible.

802. During the year in review, Luxembourg increased the number of officers in the team responsible for the information gathering process. This team has been able to identify all past rulings by 31 December 2017. It is therefore determined that Luxemburg's undertakings to identify past rulings meet the minimum standard.

Future rulings (ToR I.4.1.1, I.4.1.2, I.4.2.1)

803. For Luxembourg, future rulings are any tax rulings within scope that are issued on or after 1 April 2016.

804. In the prior year peer review report, it was determined that Luxembourg's implementation of a new system to identify future rulings and all potential exchange jurisdictions was sufficient to meet the minimum standard. Luxembourg's implementation in this regard remains unchanged, and therefore continues to meet the minimum standard.

Review and supervision (ToR I.4.3)

805. In the prior year peer review report, it was determined that Luxembourg's review and supervision mechanism was sufficient to meet the minimum standard. Luxembourg's implementation in this regard remains unchanged, and therefore continues to meet the minimum standard.

Conclusion on section A

806. Luxembourg has met all of the ToR for the information gathering process and no recommendations are made.

B. The exchange of information

Legal basis for spontaneous exchange of information (ToR II.5.1, II.5.2)

807. Luxembourg has the necessary domestic legal basis to exchange information spontaneously. Luxembourg notes that there are no legal or practical impediments that prevent the spontaneous exchange of information on rulings as contemplated in the Action 5 minimum standard.

808. Luxembourg has international agreements permitting spontaneous exchange of information, including being a party to the (i) *Multilateral Convention on Mutual Administrative Assistance in Tax Matters: Amended by the 2010 Protocol* (OECD/Council of Europe, 2011) ("the Convention"), (ii) the Directive 2011/16/EU with all other European Union Member States and (iii) double tax agreements in force with 75 jurisdictions.[3]

Completion and exchange of templates (ToR II.5.3, II.5.4, II.5.5, II.5.6, II.5.7)

809. In the prior year peer review report, Luxembourg's process for the completion and exchange of templates was described. Luxembourg experienced significant delays in exchanging past rulings mostly due to the administrative burden which stems from the issuance of a large number of rulings within the scope of the transparency framework. The process met the ToR, except that Luxembourg was not able to timely exchange information on past rulings and therefore it was recommended to continue to ensure that all information on past rulings is exchanged as soon as possible, and to complete the exchange process by the end of 2017. Luxembourg exchanged all information on past rulings by 31 December 2017.

810. The summary section of the template has to be completed in line with the internal FHTP suggested guidance. In order to clarify what information has to be provided, Luxembourg issued an internal guide which was shared with the advisory community in order to follow a standardised approach.

811. For the year in review, the timeliness of exchanges is as follows:

Past rulings in the scope of the transparency framework	Number of exchanges transmitted by 31 December 2017	Delayed exchanges		
		Number of exchanges not transmitted by 31 December 2017	Reasons for the delays	Any other comments
	3 775	0	N/A	Exchange process for past rulings was completed by 31 December 2017. This includes exchanges with Inclusive Framework members that joined in 2017.
Future rulings in the scope of the transparency framework	Number of exchanges transmitted within three months of the information becoming available to the competent authority or immediately after legal impediments have been lifted	Delayed exchanges		
		Number of exchanges transmitted later than three months of the information on rulings becoming available to the competent authority	Reasons for the delays	Any other comments
	74	0	N/A	N/A
Total	3 849[4]	0		

Follow up requests received for exchange of the ruling	Number	Average time to provide response	Number of requests not answered
	35	1.5 months	0

Conclusion on section B

812. Luxembourg has the necessary legal basis for spontaneous exchange of information, a process for completing the templates in a timely way and has completed all exchanges. Luxembourg has met all of the ToR for the exchange of information process and no recommendations are made.

C. Statistics (ToR IV)

Category of ruling	Number of exchanges	Jurisdictions exchanged with
Rulings related to preferential regimes	66	Belgium, Canada, China (People's Republic of), Cyprus, Czech Republic, France, Germany, Hungary, Ireland, Israel, Italy, Korea, Malta, Netherlands, Poland, Russia, Singapore, Slovak Republic, South Africa, Spain, Switzerland, United Kingdom, United States
Cross-border unilateral advance pricing agreements (APAs) and any other cross-border unilateral tax rulings (such as an advance tax ruling) covering transfer pricing or the application of transfer pricing principles	2 975	Austria, Azerbaijan, Barbados, Belgium, Brazil, Bulgaria, Canada, China (People's Republic of), Croatia, Cyprus, Czech Republic, Denmark, Estonia, Finland, France, Germany, Greece, Guernsey, Hungary, Iceland, India, Indonesia, Ireland, Israel, Italy, Japan, Jersey, Korea, Latvia, Liechtenstein, Lithuania, Malaysia, Malta, Mauritius, Mexico, Monaco, Morocco, Netherlands, Norway, Panama, Poland, Portugal, Qatar, Romania, Russia, Singapore, Slovak Republic, Slovenia, South Africa, Spain, Sweden, Switzerland, Thailand, Turkey, United Arab Emirates, United Kingdom, United States, Viet Nam
Cross-border rulings providing for a unilateral downward adjustment to the taxpayer's taxable profits that is not directly reflected in the taxpayer's financial / commercial accounts	205	Austria, Belgium, Brazil, Canada, China (People's Republic of), Cyprus, Denmark, Finland, France, Germany, Greece, Iceland, Ireland, Italy, Japan, Latvia, Malta, Mauritius, Monaco, Netherlands, Norway, Poland, Portugal, Romania, Singapore, South Africa, Spain, Sweden, Switzerland, United Arab Emirates, United Kingdom, United States
Permanent establishment rulings	603	Austria, Barbados, Belgium, Brazil, Bulgaria, Canada, China (People's Republic of), Cyprus, Denmark, Finland, France, Germany, Hungary, Iceland, India, Ireland, Italy, Japan, Korea, Liechtenstein, Lithuania, Malaysia, Malta, Mexico, Netherlands, Norway, Panama, Poland, Singapore, Slovak Republic, Slovenia, South Africa, Spain, Sweden, Switzerland, United Arab Emirates, United Kingdom, United States
Related party conduit rulings	N/A	N/A
De minimis rule	N/A	N/A
IP regimes: total exchanges on taxpayers benefitting from the third category of IP assets, new entrants benefitting from grandfathered IP regimes; and taxpayers making use of the option to treat the nexus ratio as a rebuttable presumption	24	Belgium, Brazil, France, Hungary, Italy, Mauritius, Norway, Spain, Switzerland, United Kingdom, United States
Total	3 873[5]	

813. The statistics for the year in review are as follows:

D. Matters related to intellectual property regimes (ToR I.4.1.3)

814. Luxembourg offered an intellectual property regime (IP regime)[6] that was abolished as of 1 July 2016 and is subject to transparency requirements under the Action 5 Report (OECD, 2015). It states that the identification of the benefitting taxpayers will occur as follows:

- ***New entrants benefitting from the grandfathered IP regime***: in order to assist the heads of the corporate tax offices in accelerating the information gathering process, an IT research was launched with the aim to identify all the taxpayers who requested the application of the IP regime in their tax return. These lists were sent to the competent corporate tax offices which were asked to gather the necessary information and to transmit them to the Competent Authority for exchange of information without delay. The exchanges covered both information with respect to new taxpayers and new IP assets from existing taxpayers.
- ***Third category of IP assets***: not applicable as the IP regime has been abolished.
- ***Taxpayers making use of the option to treat the nexus ratio as a rebuttable presumption***: not applicable as the IP regime has been abolished.

815. In addition, Luxembourg introduced a new IP regime which came into effect from 1 January 2018. Although this is after the year in review, it is noted that this regime is not subject to transparency requirements under the Action 5 report (OECD, 2015), because:

- ***New entrants benefitting from the grandfathered IP regime***: as this is a new IP regime rather than a grandfathered IP regime, transparency on new entrants is not relevant.
- ***Third category of IP assets***: not applicable as the regime does not allow the third category of IP assets to qualify for the benefits.
- ***Taxpayers making use of the option to treat the nexus ratio as a rebuttable presumption***: not applicable as the regime does not allow the nexus ratio to be treated as a rebuttable presumption.

Summary of recommendations on implementation of the transparency framework

Aspect of implementation of the transparency framework that should be improved	Recommendation for improvement
No recommendations are made.	

Notes

[1] In addition to the rulings in the scope of the transparency framework Luxembourg issued 3 310 relating to "other types of rulings".

These "other types of rulings" cover an additional category of rulings that Luxembourg identified, related to intragroup financing activities which in the absence of transparency may cause BEPS concerns. These rulings are not otherwise covered by one of the five categories within the scope of the transparency framework and are therefore defined as "other type of rulings". Luxembourg exchanged these rulings with the relevant IF members using the transparency framework.

[2] With respect to the following preferential regimes: 1) Private asset management company, 2) Investment company in risk capital, 3) Provision for fluctuations in reinsurance companies, and 4) Informal capital and partial exemption for income/gains derived from certain IP rights.

[3] Parties to the Convention are available here: www.oecd.org/tax/exchange-of-tax-information/convention-on-mutual-administrative-assistance-in-tax-matters.htm. Luxembourg also has Double Tax Agreements with Andorra, Armenia, Austria, Azerbaijan, Bahrain, Bailiwick of Guernsey, Barbados, Belgium, Brazil, Bulgaria, Canada, China (People's Republic of), Cook Islands, Croatia, Czech Republic, Denmark, Estonia, Finland, Former Yugoslav Republic of Macedonia, France, Georgia, Germany, Greece, Hungary, Iceland, India, Indonesia, Ireland, Isle of Man, Israel, Italy, Japan, Jersey, Kazakhstan, Korea, Lao People's Democratic Republic, Latvia, Liechtenstein, Lithuania, Malaysia, Malta, Mauritius, Mexico, Moldova, Monaco, Morocco, Netherlands, Norway, Panama, Poland, Portugal, Qatar, Romania, Russia, San Marino, Saudi Arabia, Serbia, Seychelles, Singapore, Slovak Republic, Slovenia, South Africa, Spain, Sri Lanka, Sweden, Switzerland, Chinese Taipei, Tajikistan, Thailand, Trinidad and Tobago, Tunisia, Turkey, United Arab Emirates, United Kingdom, United States, Uzbekistan and Viet Nam.

[4] In addition to the rulings in the scope of the transparency framework Luxembourg transmitted 5 606 exchanges relating to "other types of rulings" during the year in review.

[5] Additional 5 606 exchanges of "other types of rulings" were transmitted by 31 December 2017 inter alia to the following countries: Australia, Austria, Bahrain, Belgium, Brazil, Canada, China (People's Republic of), Cyprus, Czech Republic, Denmark, Finland, France, Germany, Guernsey, Hungary, Iceland, India, Ireland, Isle of Man, Israel, Italy, Japan, Jersey, Korea, Lithuania, Malaysia, Malta, Mauritius, Mexico, Netherlands, Norway, Panama, Poland, Portugal, Qatar, Russia, Singapore, Slovak Republic, South Africa, Spain, Sweden, United Arab Emirates, United Kingdom, United States.

Note by Turkey: The information in this document with reference to "Cyprus" relates to the southern part of the Island. There is no single authority representing both Turkish and Greek Cypriot people on the Island. Turkey recognises the Turkish Republic of Northern Cyprus (TRNC). Until a lasting and equitable solution is found within the context of the United Nations, Turkey shall preserve its position concerning the "Cyprus issue".

Note by all the European Union Member States of the OECD and the European Union. The Republic of Cyprus is recognised by all members of the United Nations with the exception of Turkey. The information in this document relates to the area under the effective control of the Government of the Republic of Cyprus.

[6] This regime is the Partial exemption for income/gains derived from certain IP rights.

References

OECD (2017), *BEPS Action 5 on Harmful Tax Practices – Terms of Reference and Methodology for the Conduct of the Peer Reviews of the Action 5 Transparency Framework*, OECD/G20 Base Erosion and Profit Shifting Project, OECD, Paris. www.oecd.org/tax/beps/beps-action-5-harmful-tax-practices-peer-review-transparencyframework.pdf.

OECD (2015), *Countering Harmful Tax Practices More Effectively, Taking into Account Transparency and Substance, Action 5 - 2015 Final Report*, OECD/G20 Base Erosion and Profit Shifting Project, OECD Publishing, Paris. https://doi.org/10.1787/9789264241190-en.

OECD/Council of Europe (2011), *The Multilateral Convention on Mutual Administrative Assistance in Tax Matters: Amended by the 2010 Protocol*, OECD Publishing, Paris. http://dx.doi.org/10.1787/9789264115606-en.

Macau (China)

Macau (China) (hereafter "Macau") has met all aspects of the terms of reference (ToR) for the calendar year 2017 (year in review) that can be met given in the absence of rulings being issued.

Macau cannot legally issue any type of rulings within the scope of the transparency framework.

As no rulings were issued, no exchange of information is required under the transparency framework. No peer input was received in respect of the exchanges of information on rulings received from Macau.

Introduction

816. This peer review covers Macau's implementation of the BEPS Action 5 transparency framework for the year 2017. The report has four parts, each relating to a key part of the ToR. Each part is discussed in turn. A summary of recommendations is included at the end of this report.

A. The information gathering process

817. As no rulings are issued, this section is not assessed.

B. The exchange of information

818. As no rulings are issued, this section is not assessed.

C. Statistics (ToR IV)

819. As no rulings are issued, no statistical data can be reported.

D. Matters related to intellectual property regimes (ToR I.4.1.3)

820. Macau offers a preferential regime, the Macau offshore institution, which also offers benefits to income from intellectual property ("IP regime"). However no transparency requirements under the Action 5 Report (OECD, 2015) were relevant, as follows:

- ***New entrants benefitting from the grandfathered IP regime***: not applicable for the year in review, because Macau is currently in the process of abolishing the Macau offshore institution regime and application of the non-finance offshore license has been suspended since 31 January 2018. Macau reports that there have been no new entrants in the regime after the publication of the 2017 Progress Report (OECD, 2017b) (which occurred on 16 October 2017). Therefore, the enhanced transparency requirements will not apply.
- ***Third category of IP assets***: not applicable to this regime, which in 2017 was in the process of being amended.
- ***Taxpayers making the use of the option to treat the nexus ratio as a rebuttable presumption***: not applicable to this regime, which in 2017 was in the process of being amended..

Summary of recommendations on implementation of the transparency framework

Aspect of implementation of the transparency framework that should be improved	Recommendation for improvement
	No recommendations are made.

References

OECD (2017a), *BEPS Action 5 on Harmful Tax Practices – Terms of Reference and Methodology for the Conduct of the Peer Reviews of the Action 5 Transparency Framework*, OECD/G20 Base Erosion and Profit Shifting Project, OECD, Paris. www.oecd.org/tax/beps/beps-action-5-harmful-tax-practices-peer-review-transparencyframework.pdf.

OECD (2017b), *Harmful Tax Practices - 2017 Progress Report on Preferential Regimes: Inclusive Framework on BEPS: Action 5*, OECD/G20 Base Erosion and Profit Shifting Project, OECD Publishing, Paris. http://dx.doi.org/10.1787/9789264283954-en.

OECD (2015), *Countering Harmful Tax Practices More Effectively, Taking into Account Transparency and Substance, Action 5 - 2015 Final Report*, OECD/G20 Base Erosion and Profit Shifting Project, OECD Publishing, Paris. https://doi.org/10.1787/9789264241190-en.

Malaysia

Malaysia's implementation of the transparency framework is still in the early stages of development. Malaysia is recommended to finalise its information gathering process for identifying all past and future rulings and potential exchange jurisdictions, with a review and supervision mechanism, as soon as possible (ToR I.4). Malaysia is recommended to continue its efforts to complete the templates for all relevant rulings and to ensure that the exchanges of information on rulings occur as soon as possible (ToR II.5).

Malaysia can legally issue five types of rulings within the scope of the transparency framework.

In practice, Malaysia has issued 1836 past rulings, and for the year in review, Malaysia issued 173 future rulings within the scope of the transparency framework.

As no exchanges of information on rulings were conducted during the year in review, no peer input was received in respect of the exchanges of information on rulings received from Malaysia.

Introduction

821. This peer review covers Malaysia's implementation of the BEPS Action 5 transparency framework for the year 2017. The report has four parts, each relating to a key part of the ToR. Each part is discussed in turn. A summary of recommendations is included at the end of this report.

A. The information gathering process

822. Malaysia can legally issue the five following types of rulings within the scope of the transparency framework: (i) rulings related to preferential regimes;[1] (ii) cross-border unilateral advance pricing arrangements (APAs) and any other cross-border unilateral tax rulings (such as an advance tax ruling) covering transfer pricing or the application of transfer pricing principles; (iii) rulings providing for a downward adjustments of taxable profits; (iv) permanent establishment rulings and (v) related party conduit rulings.

823. Rulings related to preferential regimes are granted by the Investment Promotional Agency via the issuance of letters of award relating to the preferential regime. These letters are subsequently transmitted to and processed by the Tax Incentive Advisory Division under the Tax Policy Department of Inland Revenue Board Malaysia (IRBM) for the purposes of the exchange of information on rulings under the transparency framework. Rulings in relation to APAs or permanent establishments are issued by the Mutual Agreement Procedure and Transfer Pricing Policy Division under the Department of International Taxation in IRBM and processed for the exchange of information on rulings under the transparency framework.

824. During the year in review, Malaysia identified one past ruling in scope of the transparency framework, and conducted one exchange on this ruling. This was due to it being the first year of implementation of the transparency framework for Malaysia, and a misunderstanding as to the types of rulings in scope of the transparency framework. Since clarification of the scope of the transparency framework with the Secretariat, Malaysia has been working closely with the Secretariat throughout the 2018 peer review process to ensure that the processes are in place in Malaysia to implement the transparency framework going forward. Over 2 000 rulings were subsequently identified in 2018.

Past rulings (ToR I.4.1.1, I.4.1.2, I.4.2.1, I.4.2.2)

825. For Malaysia, past rulings are any tax rulings within scope that are issued either: (i) on or after 1 January 2015 but before 1 September 2017; or (ii) on or after 1 January 2012 but before 1 January 2015, provided they were still in effect as at 1 January 2015.

826. Malaysia acknowledges that it did not correctly implement the information gathering process during the year in review, due to a misunderstanding of the types of rulings in scope of the transparency framework. As a result, only one past ruling was identified for the year in review.

827. However, Malaysia has implemented new processes to identify past rulings in 2018. The International Affairs and Exchange of Information Division is overseeing the process for the identification of past rulings in the Tax Incentive Advisory Division and Mutual Agreement Procedure and Transfer Pricing Policy Division. For rulings related to preferential regimes, the relevant promotional agency will identify the potential exchange jurisdictions by reviewing the internal database for the name and structure of the MNE group, and other group financial information if available. Malaysia has also utilised the

"best efforts approach" where relevant, in addition to seeking the relevant information from the taxpayer where relevant.

Future rulings (ToR I.4.1.1, I.4.1.2, I.4.2.1)

828. For Malaysia, future rulings are any tax rulings within scope that are issued on or after 1 September 2017.

829. Malaysia acknowledges that it did not correctly implement the information gathering process during the year in review, due to a misunderstanding of the types of rulings in scope of the transparency framework. As a result, no future rulings were identified for the year in review.

830. Since 2018, Malaysia's information gathering process for future rulings is identical to the process for past rulings.

Review and supervision mechanism (ToR I.4.3)

831. Malaysia did not yet have an appropriate information gathering process under the transparency framework for the year in review. Since 2018, one manager from the Tax Advisory Incentive Division, one manager from the Transfer Pricing Policy Division, one manager from the International Affairs and Exchange of Information Division and six managers from the respective promotional agencies now supervise the information gathering process. Malaysia will conduct regular meetings among the agencies to verify information under the transparency framework. The designated officers in the promotional agencies identifying rulings in scope are informed and guided by the Ministry of Finance (MoF) and IRBM.

Conclusion on section A

832. Malaysia is recommended to finalise its information gathering process for identifying all past and future rulings and potential exchange jurisdictions, with a review and supervision mechanism, as soon as possible (ToR I.4). It is recognised that Malaysia has made efforts to rectify their information gathering process in 2018, and Malaysia's implementation of the information gathering process during 2018 will be assessed in the next annual peer review.

B. The exchange of information

Legal basis for spontaneous exchange of information (ToR II.5.1, II.5.2)

833. Malaysia has the necessary domestic legal basis to exchange information spontaneously. Malaysia notes that there are no legal or practical impediments that prevent the spontaneous exchange of information on rulings as contemplated in the Action 5 minimum standard.

834. Malaysia is a party to international agreements permitting spontaneous exchange of information, including (i) the *Multilateral Convention on Mutual Administrative Assistance in Tax Matters: Amended by the 2010 Protocol* (OECD/Council of Europe, 2011) ("the Convention") and (ii) double tax agreements in force with 74 jurisdictions.[2]

Completion and exchange of templates (ToR II.5.3, II.5.4, II.5.5, II.5.6, II.5.7)

835. For the year in review, Malaysia identified one past ruling in scope of the transparency framework, and conducted one delayed exchange on this ruling.

836. Since 2018, Malaysia has been finalising a process to complete the templates on relevant rulings, to make them available to the Competent Authority for exchange of information and to exchange them with relevant jurisdictions.

837. For the year in review, the timeliness of exchanges is as follows:

Past rulings in the scope of the transparency framework	Number of exchanges transmitted by 31 December 2017	Delayed exchanges		
		Number of exchanges not transmitted by 31 December 2017	Reasons for the delays	Any other comments
	0	1	The delay in exchanging the APA was due to the delay in receiving the relevant information from the taxpayer	As this was the first year of implementation of the transparency framework for Malaysia, processes were still being developed and staff members being familiarised with the framework.
Future rulings in the scope of the transparency framework	Number of exchanges transmitted within three months of the information becoming available to the competent authority or immediately after legal impediments have been lifted	Delayed exchanges		
		Number of exchanges transmitted later than three months of the information on rulings becoming available to the competent authority	Reasons for the delays	Any other comments
	0	0	N/A	N/A
Total	0	1		

Follow up requests received for exchange of the ruling	Number	Average time to provide response	Number of requests not answered
	0	N/A	N/A

Conclusion on section B

838. Malaysia has the necessary legal basis to undertake spontaneous exchange of information. Malaysia is recommended to continue its efforts to complete the templates for all relevant rulings and to ensure that the exchanges of information on rulings occur as soon as possible (ToR II.5).

C. Statistics (ToR IV)

839. As no information on rulings was exchanged for the year in review, no statistical data can be reported.

D. Matters related to intellectual property regimes (ToR I.4.1.3)

840. Malaysia offers four preferential regimes, which also offer benefits to income from intellectual property ("IP regime").[3] However for the year in review no transparency requirements under the Action 5 Report (OECD, 2015) were relevant, as follows:

- ***New entrants benefitting from the grandfathered IP regime***: not applicable for the year in review, because Malaysia is currently in the process of amending the two regimes and has not taken a decision yet on whether it will provide grandfathering to existing taxpayers. Should Malaysia provide grandfathering to taxpayers for which IP income benefits and that entered the regimes after the publication of the 2017 Progress Report (OECD, 2017) which occurred on 16 October 2017, transparency requirements will apply and this will be taken into account during the 2018 peer review.
- ***Third category of IP assets***: not applicable to these regimes, which in 2017 were in the process of being amended.
- ***Taxpayers making the use of the option to treat the nexus ratio as a rebuttable presumption***: not applicable to these regimes, which in 2017 were in the process of being amended.

Summary of recommendations on implementation of the transparency framework

Aspect of implementation of the transparency framework that should be improved	Recommendation for improvement
Malaysia did not accurately complete the information gathering process during the year in review.	Malaysia is recommended to finalise its information gathering process for identifying all past and future rulings and potential exchange jurisdictions, with a review and supervision mechanism, as soon as possible.
Malaysia did not undertake spontaneous exchange of information on all tax rulings within scope of the transparency framework during the year in review.	Malaysia is recommended to continue its efforts to complete the templates for all relevant rulings and to ensure that the exchanges of information on rulings occur as soon as possible.

Notes

1 Pioneer status – high technology and contract R&D; Principal hub; Green technology services; Bionexus status; MSC status; Special economic regions – Iskandar Malaysia, East Coast Economic Region, and Sabah Development Corridor

2 Albania, Argentina, Australia, Austria, Bahrain, Bangladesh, Belgium, Bosnia and Herzegovina, Brunei, Canada, Chile, China (People's Republic of), Croatia, Czech Republic, Denmark, Egypt, Fiji, Finland, France, Germany, Hong Kong, Hungary, India, Indonesia, Iran, Ireland, Italy, Japan, Jordan, Kazakhstan, Korea, Kuwait, Kyrgyzstan, Laos, Lebanon, Luxembourg, Malta, Mauritius, Mongolia, Morocco, Myanmar, Namibia, Netherlands, New Zealand, Norway, Pakistan, Papua New Guinea, Philippines, Poland, Qatar, Romania, Russia, San Marino, Saudi Arabia, Seychelles, Singapore, South Africa, Spain, Slovak Republic, Sri Lanka, Sudan, Sweden, Switzerland, Syria, Thailand, Turkey, Turkmenistan, United Arab Emirates, United Kingdom, United States, Uzbekistan, Venezuela, Viet Nam and Zimbabwe.

3 These regimes are: 1) Principal hub, 2) MSC Malaysia, 3) Pioneer Status, and 4) Biotechnology industry.

References

OECD (2017), *BEPS Action 5 on Harmful Tax Practices – Terms of Reference and Methodology for the Conduct of the Peer Reviews of the Action 5 Transparency Framework*, OECD/G20 Base Erosion and Profit Shifting Project, OECD, Paris. www.oecd.org/tax/beps/beps-action-5-harmful-tax-practices-peer-review-transparencyframework.pdf.

OECD (2015), *Countering Harmful Tax Practices More Effectively, Taking into Account Transparency and Substance, Action 5 - 2015 Final Report*, OECD/G20 Base Erosion and Profit Shifting Project, OECD Publishing, Paris. https://doi.org/10.1787/9789264241190-en.

OECD/Council of Europe (2011), *The Multilateral Convention on Mutual Administrative Assistance in Tax Matters: Amended by the 2010 Protocol*, OECD Publishing, Paris. http://dx.doi.org/10.1787/9789264115606-en.

Malta

Malta has met all aspects of the terms of reference (ToR) for the calendar year 2017 (year in review) and no recommendations are made.

Malta can legally issue four types of rulings within the scope of the transparency framework.

In practice, Malta has issued seven past rulings; and for the year in review, Malta issued four future rulings within the scope of the transparency framework.

No peer input was received in respect of the exchanges of information on rulings received from Malta.

Introduction

841. This peer review covers Malta's implementation of the BEPS Action 5 transparency framework for the year 2017. The report has four parts, each relating to a key part of the ToR. Each part is discussed in turn. A summary of recommendations is included at the end of this report.

A. The information gathering process

842. Malta can legally issue the four following types of rulings within the scope of the transparency framework: (i) cross-border unilateral APAs and any other unilateral tax ruling (such as an ATR) covering transfer pricing or the application of transfer pricing principles; (ii) cross-border giving a unilateral downward adjustment to the taxpayer's taxable profits in the country giving the ruling; (iii) permanent establishment rulings; and (iv) related party conduit rulings. In Malta, the Commissioner for Inland Revenue is responsible for issuing tax rulings.

Past rulings (ToR I.4.1.1, I.4.1.2, I.4.2.1, I.4.2.2)

843. For Malta, past rulings are any tax rulings within scope that are issued either: (i) on or after 1 January 2015 but before 1 April 2017; or (ii) on or after 1 January 2012 but before 1 January 2015, provided they were still in effect as at 1 January 2015.

844. Malta has a centralised system and all tax rulings issued are recorded in an electronic database. In order to identify rulings for the "past ruling" period as defined under transparency framework, filters were used to determine the date of issue and validity of the rulings. After applying the filter, a manual review was undertaken by the Exchange of Information ("EOI") team to verify the dates and whether the rulings were within scope of the transparency framework.

845. In order to identify potential exchange jurisdictions for past rulings, Malta manually examined each ruling to obtain the relevant information, as rulings were already required to contain information on all potential exchange jurisdictions. As such, the "best efforts approach" was not required to be used.

Future rulings (ToR I.4.1.1, I.4.1.2, I.4.2.1)

846. For Malta, future rulings are any tax rulings within scope that are issued on or after 1 April 2017.

847. Malta indicates that as part of the rulings process in place, future rulings as defined under Action 5 are flagged as such as soon as they are entered into the electronic database of rulings. In addition, a manual review of the identified future rulings by the EOI team is carried out to ensure that they fall within scope.

848. Information contained in the ruling is used to identify the potential exchange jurisdictions for those that are flagged as being within scope of Action 5 as soon as the rulings are entered into the database.

Review and supervision mechanism (ToR I.4.3)

849. Malta notes that personnel who issue the tax rulings will forward the rulings which are in scope to personnel within the EOI team. The EOI staff then reviews the content of these rulings and verifies that the relevant information for the past and future

rulings were captured through the filtering of the electronic database. The personnel issuing rulings and the EOI team reviewing the information were required to familiarise themselves with the transparency framework and were also involved in the negotiation and implementation of the EU Council Directive 2015/2376/EU ("EU Directive").

Conclusion on section A

850. Malta has met all of the ToR for the information gathering process and no recommendations are made.

B. The exchange of information

Legal basis for spontaneous exchange of information (ToR II.5.1, II.5.2)

851. Malta has the necessary domestic legal basis to exchange information spontaneously. Malta notes that there are no legal or practical impediments that prevent the spontaneous exchange of information on rulings as contemplated in the Action 5 minimum standard.

852. Malta is a party to international agreements permitting spontaneous exchange of information, including (i) the *Multilateral Convention on Mutual Administrative Assistance in Tax Matters: Amended by the 2010 Protocol* (OECD/Council of Europe, 2011) ("the Convention") and (ii) double tax agreements in force with 73 jurisdictions.[1]

Completion and exchange of templates (ToR II.5.3, II.5.4, II.5.5, II.5.6, II.5.7)

853. Malta notes that the team responsible for issuing tax rulings (both past and future rulings) is also responsible for identifying those rulings which are to be exchanged under Action 5. The team fills in the template as contained in Annex C of the 2015 Action 5 Report (OECD, 2015) in PDF format for those rulings which are in scope for Action 5. The EOI team in the same office is then responsible for the manual review of the template against the ruling itself to ensure that the template captures all required information and is accurate.

854. In order to complete the summary section of the template under Annex C, Malta explains that the core details of the ruling have to be included in the summary and this is verified during the manual review step.

855. Malta also indicates that the process for making the information available to the Competent Authority is shortened by the fact that the same office that issues rulings is also responsible for exchanging the information on the rulings. The templates on past rulings that were within scope were all submitted at once, close to the exchange deadline of 31 December 2017. Information on future rulings is to be exchanged within three months after a particular ruling is issued, and in practice this is usually within a week after the future ruling is issued.

856. For the year in review, the timeliness of exchanges is as follows:

Past rulings in the scope of the transparency framework	Number of exchanges transmitted by 31 December 2017	Delayed exchanges		
		Number of exchanges not transmitted by 31 December 2017	Reasons for the delays	Any other comments
	8	4	See below	N/A
Future rulings in the scope of the transparency framework	**Number of exchanges transmitted within three months of the information becoming available to the competent authority or immediately after legal impediments have been lifted**	**Delayed exchanges**		
		Number of exchanges transmitted later than three months of the information on rulings becoming available to the competent authority	Reasons for the delays	Any other comments
	0	6	See below	N/A
Total	8	10		

Follow up requests received for exchange of the ruling	Number	Average time to provide response	Number of requests not answered
	0	N/A	N/A

857. Malta provided the following explanation for the transmission delay regarding past and future rulings during 2017. Malta experienced some technical issues in the implementation of the EU Directive for exchange of information on rulings within the EU, which was also required to be completed during the year in review, and was focused on this process. As such, information under the transparency framework which was also relevant under the EU Directive was exchanged as a priority. In addition, Malta indicated that steps were taken to exchange all outstanding information on rulings for the relevant period with the non-EU jurisdictions by April 2018.

Conclusion on section B

858. Malta has the necessary legal basis for spontaneous exchange of information and process for completing the templates for exchange. There were some delays for exchanging past and future rulings, however as this is not a recurring issue and was resolved within a short period of the deadline, no recommendation is made. Malta has met all of the ToR for the exchange of information process and no recommendations are made.

C. Statistics (ToR IV)

859. The statistics for the year in review are as follows:

Category of ruling	Number of exchanges	Jurisdictions exchanged with
Rulings related to preferential regimes	N/A	N/A
Cross-border unilateral advance pricing arrangements (APAs) and any other cross-border unilateral tax rulings (such as an advance tax ruling) covering transfer pricing or the application of transfer pricing principles	0	N/A
Cross-border rulings providing for a unilateral downward adjustment to the taxpayer's taxable profits that is not directly reflected in the taxpayer's financial / commercial accounts	0	N/A
Permanent establishment rulings	Included in *de minimis*	N/A
Related party conduit rulings	11	Belgium, Germany, Hungary, Ireland, Jersey, Luxembourg, Netherlands, Panama, Portugal, Singapore, Switzerland, United Kingdom
De minimis rule	3	N/A
IP regimes: total exchanges on taxpayers benefitting from the third category of IP assets, new entrants benefitting from grandfathered IP regimes; and taxpayers making use of the option to treat the nexus ratio as a rebuttable presumption	N/A	N/A
Total	14	

D. Matters related to intellectual property regimes (ToR I.4.1.3)

860. Malta does not offer an intellectual property regime for which transparency requirements under the Action 5 Report (OECD, 2015) were imposed.

Summary of recommendations on implementation of the transparency framework

Aspect of implementation of the transparency framework that should be improved	Recommendation for improvement
	No recommendations are made.

Notes

1 Parties to the Convention are available here: www.oecd.org/tax/exchange-of-tax-information/convention-on-mutual-administrative-assistance-in-tax-matters.htm. Malta also has bilateral agreements in force with Albania, Andorra, Australia, Austria, Azerbaijan, Bahrain, Barbados, Belgium, Bulgaria, Canada, China (People's Republic of), Cyprus, Czech Republic, Denmark, Egypt, Estonia, Finland, France, Georgia, Germany, Greece, Guernsey, Hungary, Iceland, India, Ireland, Isle of Man, Israel, Italy, Jersey, Jordan, Korea), Kuwait, Latvia, Lebanon, Libya, Liechtenstein, Lithuania, Luxembourg, Malaysia, Mauritius, Mexico, Moldova, Montenegro, Morocco, Netherlands, Norway, Pakistan, Poland, Portugal, Qatar, Romania, Russia, San Marino, Saudi Arabia, Serbia, Singapore, Slovakia, Slovenia, South Africa, Spain, Sweden, Switzerland, Syria, Tunisia, Turkey, United Arab Emirates, United Kingdom, United States, Uruguay and Viet Nam.

Note by Turkey: The information in this document with reference to "Cyprus" relates to the southern part of the Island. There is no single authority representing both Turkish and Greek Cypriot people on the Island. Turkey recognises the Turkish Republic of Northern Cyprus (TRNC). Until a lasting and equitable solution is found within the context of the United Nations, Turkey shall preserve its position concerning the "Cyprus issue".

Note by all the European Union Member States of the OECD and the European Union. The Republic of Cyprus is recognised by all members of the United Nations with the exception of Turkey. The information in this document relates to the area under the effective control of the Government of the Republic of Cyprus.

References

OECD (2017), *BEPS Action 5 on Harmful Tax Practices – Terms of Reference and Methodology for the Conduct of the Peer Reviews of the Action 5 Transparency Framework*, OECD/G20 Base Erosion and Profit Shifting Project, OECD, Paris. www.oecd.org/tax/beps/beps-action-5-harmful-tax-practices-peer-review-transparencyframework.pdf.

OECD (2015), *Countering Harmful Tax Practices More Effectively, Taking into Account Transparency and Substance, Action 5 - 2015 Final Report*, OECD/G20 Base Erosion and Profit Shifting Project, OECD Publishing, Paris. https://doi.org/10.1787/9789264241190-en.

OECD/Council of Europe (2011), *The Multilateral Convention on Mutual Administrative Assistance in Tax Matters: Amended by the 2010 Protocol*, OECD Publishing, Paris. http://dx.doi.org/10.1787/9789264115606-en.

Mauritius

Mauritius has met all aspects of the terms of reference (ToR) for the calendar year 2017 (year in review) and no recommendations are made.

Mauritius can legally issue three types of rulings within the scope of the transparency framework.

In practice, Mauritius has issued 20 past rulings; [1] and for the year in review, Mauritius issued no future rulings within the scope of the transparency framework.

No peer input was received in respect of the exchanges of information on rulings received from Mauritius.

Introduction

861. This peer review covers Mauritius's implementation of the BEPS Action 5 transparency framework for the year 2017. The report has four parts, each relating to a key part of the ToR. Each part is discussed in turn. A summary of recommendations is included at the end of this report.

A. The information gathering process

862. Mauritius can legally issue the three following types of rulings within the scope of the transparency framework: (i) rulings related to preferential regimes;[2] (ii) Cross-border unilateral APAs and any other unilateral tax ruling (such as an advance tax ruling) covering transfer pricing or the application of transfer pricing principles; and (iii) permanent establishment rulings. Rulings are issued by the Mauritius Revenue Authority ("MRA"). Mauritius publishes taxpayer specific rulings in redacted form.[3]

Past rulings (ToR I.4.1.1, I.4.1.2, I.4.2.1, I.4.2.2)

863. For Mauritius, past rulings are any tax rulings within scope that are issued either: (i) on or after 1 January 2015 but before 1 September 2017; or (ii) on or after 1 January 2012 but before 1 January 2015, provided they were still in effect as at 1 January 2015.

864. Mauritius has a centralised system and all tax rulings issued by the MRA are stored in the taxpayer specific files at the Medium and Small Taxpayers Department ("MSTD") and maintained by the Secretary of the Tax Ruling Committee (the "Secretary"). The records of the name of the applicant, the date of issuance of the ruling and the date it was gazetted and the reference of the ruling are maintained in an excel spreadsheet. The Secretary is also responsible for uploading the ruling on the MRA website once it is gazetted.

865. A team comprising the Section Head, a Team Leader, four officers and a support officer in the International Taxation Section ("ITS") of Large Taxpayers Department ("LTD") is involved in the implementation of the transparency framework. To identify past rulings, the Secretary filtered the excel spreadsheet for the period defined as "past rulings" and transmitted the list of rulings identified to the Team Leader and Section Head of the ITS.

866. The Team Leader of ITS allocated past rulings to four officers to identify those rulings that are within the scope of the transparency framework. The officers read and analysed each ruling within a prescribed deadline and the outcome was reported to the Team Leader, Section Head and ultimately the Director of LTD.

867. In order to identify the potential exchange jurisdictions, all rulings which are in scope were read and analysed by the officers. The information on potential exchange jurisdictions was either available in the ruling itself or where necessary was gathered by using the "best efforts approach". This involved checking information in the taxpayer specific files. In a few cases where additional information was needed, the MRA requested the information by directly contacting the management company who applied for the ruling on behalf of the taxpayer. Mauritius indicates that this process was done in a co-operative and timely manner. The jurisdictions thus identified were verified by the Team Leader and Section Head of the ITS and then approved by the Director.

Future rulings (ToR I.4.1.1, I.4.1.2, I.4.2.1)

868. For Mauritius, future rulings are any tax rulings within scope that are issued on or after 1 September 2017.

869. Mauritius indicates when a future ruling is issued, the Secretary immediately submits the list to the Team Leader and the Section Head of the ITS along with a copy of the selected ruling. The Team Leader then allocates the future ruling to an officer who reads the ruling to identify whether it is in scope of Action 5.

870. The Team Leader notes the date of allocation and monitors the timeline for future rulings. The support officer is responsible for inputting the details of the ruling which is in scope in the excel file and also provides regular updates to the Team Leader on the approaching deadlines.

871. In order to identify the potential exchange jurisdictions in the future rulings issued, each officer would read the ruling itself or the taxpayer specific file kept at the MSTD.

872. In addition, the Director of the LTD has appointed the Secretary to collect all required information on potential exchange jurisdictions when the application for the ruling is being processed and has explained this updated process to all members of the Tax Ruling Committee.

Review and supervision mechanism (ToR I.4.3)

873. Mauritius notes that the LTD Directorate, which is also the Competent Authority, is in charge of supervising the entire process of identifying relevant rulings and the timely exchange of the information on rulings under the transparency framework. The LTD Director and the MSTD Director agreed on the process for identifying and exchanging past and future rulings in a timely manner.

874. In addition, the Director of the LTD gave a presentation to the members of the Tax Ruling Committee to brief them on the transparency framework and the information required. Training was also provided to the staff of ITS and the officers in charge of identifying relevant rulings which are in scope of Action 5.

Conclusion on section A

875. Mauritius has met all of the ToR for the information gathering process and no recommendations are made.

B. The exchange of information

Legal basis for spontaneous exchange of information (ToR II.5.1, II.5.2)

876. Mauritius has the necessary domestic legal basis to exchange information spontaneously. Mauritius notes that there are no legal or practical impediments that prevent the spontaneous exchange of information on rulings as contemplated in the Action 5 minimum standard.

877. Mauritius is a party to international agreements permitting spontaneous exchange of information, including (i) the *Multilateral Convention on Mutual Administrative Assistance in Tax Matters: Amended by the 2010 Protocol* (OECD/Council of Europe,

2011) ("the Convention"), (ii) double tax agreements in force with 43 jurisdictions and (iii) ten tax information exchange agreements.[4]

Completion and exchange of templates (ToR II.5.3, II.5.4, II.5.5, II.5.6, II.5.7)

878. Mauritius notes that the officer in charge of identifying whether the ruling is in scope of Action 5 also completes the template under Annex C of the 2015 Action 5 Report (OECD, 2015) which is then reviewed by the Team Leader and Section Head of the ITS to ensure completeness and accuracy. The template is then vetted by the Director of LTD (who is also the Competent Authority) before being exchanged.

879. Mauritius also notes that the FHTP internal suggested guide has been utilised during the process to complete the summary section of the template contained in Annex C of the 2015 Action 5 Report.

880. To ensure the timely exchange of all past rulings within scope by 31 December 2017, the process involved a regular review by the Team Leader of the pending rulings to be exchanged as prepared by the support officer. The Team Leader also regularly updated the status of the excel workbook which was reviewed by the Section Head.

881. The same process applies to future rulings. The monitoring process ensures that information on all future rulings is exchanged within three months of the date of issue of the ruling.

882. For the year in review, the timeliness of exchanges is as follows:

Past rulings in the scope of the transparency framework	Number of exchanges transmitted by 31 December 2017	Delayed exchanges		
		Number of exchanges not transmitted by 31 December 2017	Reasons for the delays	Any other comments
	26	0	N/A	
Future rulings in the scope of the transparency framework	Number of exchanges transmitted within three months of the information becoming available to the competent authority or immediately after legal impediments have been lifted	Delayed exchanges		
		Number of exchanges transmitted later than three months of the information on rulings becoming available to the competent authority	Reasons for the delays	Any other comments
	0	0	N/A	
Total	26	0		

Follow up requests received for exchange of the ruling	Number	Average time to provide response	Number of requests not answered
	0	N/A	N/A

Conclusion on section B

883. Mauritius has the necessary legal basis for spontaneous exchange of information, a process for completing the templates in a timely way and has completed all exchanges on time. Mauritius has met all of the ToR for the exchange of information process and no recommendations are made.

C. Statistics (ToR IV)

884. The statistics for the year in review are as follows:

Category of ruling	Number of exchanges	Jurisdictions exchanged with
Rulings related to preferential regimes	20[5]	Bangladesh, Barbados, France, Germany, Ireland, Jersey, Malta, Mozambique, Qatar, Singapore, South Africa, Thailand, United Kingdom, Zimbabwe
Cross-border unilateral advance pricing arrangements (APAs) and any other cross-border unilateral tax rulings (such as an advance tax ruling) covering transfer pricing or the application of transfer pricing principles	Included in *de minimis*	N/A
Cross-border rulings providing for a unilateral downward adjustment to the taxpayer's taxable profits that is not directly reflected in the taxpayer's financial / commercial accounts	N/A	N/A
Permanent establishment rulings	Included in *de minimis*	N/A
Related party conduit rulings	N/A	N/A
De minimis rule	6	N/A
IP regimes: total exchanges on taxpayers benefitting from the third category of IP assets, new entrants benefitting from grandfathered IP regimes; and taxpayers making use of the option to treat the nexus ratio as a rebuttable presumption	N/A	N/A
Total	26	

D. Matters related to intellectual property regimes (ToR I.4.1.3)

885. Mauritius offers two preferential regimes, which also offer benefits to income from intellectual property ("IP regime").[6] However for the year in review no transparency requirements under the Action 5 Report (OECD, 2015) were relevant, as follows:

- ***New entrants benefitting from the grandfathered IP regime***: not applicable for the year in review, because Mauritius is currently in the process of amending the two regimes and has not taken a decision yet on whether it will provide grandfathering to existing taxpayers. Should Mauritius provide grandfathering to taxpayers for which IP income benefits and that entered the regimes after the publication of the 2017 Progress Report (OECD, 2017b), which occurred on 16 October 2017, transparency requirements will apply and this will be taken into account during the 2018 peer review.
- ***Third category of IP assets***: not applicable to these regimes, which in 2017 were in the process of being amended.
- ***Taxpayers making the use of the option to treat the nexus ratio as a rebuttable presumption***: not applicable to these regimes, which in 2017 were in the process of being amended.

Summary of recommendations on implementation of the transparency framework

Aspect of implementation of the transparency framework that should be improved	Recommendation for improvement
No recommendations are made.	

Notes

[1] Including one that fell into more than one category under the BEPS Action 5 Report.

[2] With respect to the following preferential regimes: 1) Global business license 1, 2) Global business license 2, 3) Global headquarters administration regime, 4) Global treasury activities, 5) Captive insurances, 6) Segment B banking, 7) Investment banking, 8) Freeport zone and 9) Shipping regime.

[3] Available at: www.mra.mu/index.php/media-centre/rulings/income-tax-rulings (accessed 19 November 2018).

[4] Parties to the Convention are available here: www.oecd.org/tax/exchange-of-tax-information/convention-on-mutual-administrative-assistance-in-tax-matters.htm. Mauritius also has bilateral agreements in force with Australia, Bangladesh, Barbados, Belgium, Botswana, China (People's Republic of), Congo, Croatia, Cyprus, France, Germany, Guernsey, India, Italy, Kuwait, Latvia, Lesotho, Luxembourg, Madagascar, Malaysia, Malta, Monaco, Mozambique, Namibia, Nepal, Oman, Pakistan, Qatar, Rwanda, Senegal, Seychelles, Singapore, South Africa, Sri Lanka, Swaziland, Sweden, Thailand, Tunisia, Uganda, United Arab Emirates, United Kingdom, Zambia, Zimbabwe and United States.

Note by Turkey: The information in this document with reference to "Cyprus" relates to the southern part of the Island. There is no single authority representing both Turkish and Greek Cypriot people on the Island. Turkey recognises the Turkish Republic of Northern Cyprus (TRNC). Until a lasting and equitable solution is found within the context of the United Nations, Turkey shall preserve its position concerning the "Cyprus issue".

Note by all the European Union Member States of the OECD and the European Union. The Republic of Cyprus is recognised by all members of the United Nations with the exception of Turkey. The information in this document relates to the area under the effective control of the Government of the Republic of Cyprus.

[5] One of the rulings related to preferential regimes also relates to APA.

[6] These regimes are: 1) Global Business Licence 1 and 2) Global Business Licence 2.

References

OECD (2017a), *BEPS Action 5 on Harmful Tax Practices – Terms of Reference and Methodology for the Conduct of the Peer Reviews of the Action 5 Transparency Framework*, OECD/G20 Base Erosion and Profit Shifting Project, OECD, Paris. www.oecd.org/tax/beps/beps-action-5-harmful-tax-practices-peer-review-transparencyframework.pdf.

OECD (2017b), *Harmful Tax Practices - 2017 Progress Report on Preferential Regimes: Inclusive Framework on BEPS: Action 5*, OECD/G20 Base Erosion and Profit Shifting Project, OECD Publishing, Paris. http://dx.doi.org/10.1787/9789264283954-en.

OECD (2015), *Countering Harmful Tax Practices More Effectively, Taking into Account Transparency and Substance, Action 5 - 2015 Final Report*, OECD/G20 Base Erosion and Profit Shifting Project, OECD Publishing, Paris. https://doi.org/10.1787/9789264241190-en.

OECD/Council of Europe (2011), *The Multilateral Convention on Mutual Administrative Assistance in Tax Matters: Amended by the 2010 Protocol*, OECD Publishing, Paris. http://dx.doi.org/10.1787/9789264115606-en.

Mexico

Mexico has met all aspects of the terms of reference (ToR) for the calendar year 2017 (year in review) except the timely exchange of information on future rulings (ToR II.5.6). Mexico experienced significant delays in exchanging information on future rulings. Mexico is recommended to ensure that all information on future rulings is exchanged as soon as possible.

Mexico can legally issue two types of rulings within the scope of the transparency framework.

In practice, Mexico has issued 13 past rulings; for the period 1 April 2016 - 31 December 2016, Mexico issued one future rulings; and for the year in review, Mexico issued 328 future rulings within the scope of the transparency framework.

Peer input was received from one jurisdiction in respect of the exchanges of information on rulings received from Mexico. It was positive, noting that information was complete in a correct format and received in a timely manner.

Introduction

886. This peer review covers Mexico's implementation of the BEPS Action 5 transparency framework for the year 2017. The report has four parts, each relating to a key part of the ToR. Each part is discussed in turn. A summary of recommendations is included at the end of this report.

A. The information gathering process

887. Mexico can legally issue the two following types of rulings within the scope of the transparency framework: (i) cross-border unilateral advance pricing arrangements (APAs) and any other cross-border unilateral tax rulings (such as an advance tax ruling) covering transfer pricing or the application of transfer pricing principles; and (ii) permanent establishment rulings. In Mexico, rulings are issued either by the Large Taxpayer's Legal Affairs and Transfer Pricing offices or by the Oil and Gas Legal Affairs office. Rulings (other than APAs) can be published in a redacted summarised form.

Past rulings (ToR I.4.1.1, I.4.1.2, I.4.2.1, I.4.2.2)

888. For Mexico, past rulings are any tax rulings within scope that are issued either: (i) on or after 1 January 2014 but before 1 April 2016; or (ii) on or after 1 January 2010 but before 1 January 2014, provided they were still in effect as at 1 January 2014.

889. In the prior year peer review report, it was determined that Mexico's undertakings to identify past rulings and all potential exchange jurisdictions were sufficient to meet the minimum standard. Mexico's implementation in this regard remains unchanged, and therefore continues to meet the minimum standard.

Future rulings (ToR I.4.1.1, I.4.1.2, I.4.2.1)

890. For Mexico, future rulings are any tax rulings within scope that are issued on or after 1 April 2016.

891. In the prior year peer review report, it was determined that Mexico's implementation of a system to identify future rulings and all potential exchange jurisdictions was sufficient to meet the minimum standard. Mexico's implementation in this regard remains unchanged, and therefore continues to meet the minimum standard.

Review and supervision mechanism (ToR I.4.3)

892. In the prior year peer review report, it was determined that Mexico's review and supervision mechanism was sufficient to meet the minimum standard. Mexico's implementation in this regard remains unchanged, and therefore continues to meet the minimum standard.

Conclusion on section A

893. Mexico has met all of the ToR for the information gathering process and no recommendations are made.

B. The exchange of information

Legal basis for spontaneous exchange of information (ToR II.5.1, II.5.2)

894. Mexico has the necessary domestic legal basis to exchange information spontaneously. Mexico notes that there are no legal or practical impediments that prevent the spontaneous exchange of information on rulings as contemplated in the Action 5 minimum standard.

895. Mexico is a party to international agreements permitting spontaneous exchange of information, including (i) the *Multilateral Convention on Mutual Administrative Assistance in Tax Matters: Amended by the 2010 Protocol* (OECD/Council of Europe, 2011) ("the Convention"), (ii) double tax agreements in force with seven jurisdictions, and (iii) tax information exchange agreements in force with three jurisdictions.[1]

Completion and exchange of templates (ToR II.5.3, II.5.4, II.5.5, II.5.6, II.5.7)

896. In the prior year peer review report, it was determined that Mexico's completion and exchange of templates were sufficient to meet the minimum standard. Mexico notes that internal guidelines have been issued in order to regulate the way to proceed when information within the scope of the transparency framework is exchanged.

897. During the year in review, Mexico experienced a significant increase on the number of rulings issued, after having reached an agreement with the United States on applying a standard transfer pricing methodology for certain similar types of cases and which allowed the decision-making on granting those types of rulings to be much faster. As a result of the increase in volume of rulings issued, Mexico experienced delays in exchanging information on future rulings. However, it is noted that the United States was already aware of the methodology used to solve these cases, as well as of the taxpayers in Mexico and in the United States that qualified for these kind of agreements. Mexico is in the process of finding the most efficient way to exchange this information in order to meet the exchange timelines. Mexico is recommended to complete all outstanding exchanges of information as soon as possible.

898. Mexico notes that the summary section is completed by tax administration officials according to information provided by taxpayers when filling in APA's and ruling requests. It is noted that guidelines may be modified to make them consistent with FHTP's internal suggested guide in the near future.

899. For the year in review, the timeliness of exchanges is as follows:

Past rulings in the scope of the transparency framework	Number of exchanges transmitted by 31 December 2017	Delayed exchanges		
		Number of exchanges not transmitted by 31 December 2017	Reasons for the delays	Any other comments
	N/A	0	N/A	
Future rulings in the scope of the transparency framework	**Number of exchanges transmitted within three months of the information becoming available to the competent authority or immediately after legal impediments have been lifted**	**Delayed exchanges**		
		Number of exchanges transmitted later than three months of the information on rulings becoming available to the competent authority	Reasons for the delays	Any other comments
	0	328[2]		
Total	0	0		

Follow up requests received for exchange of the ruling	Number	Average time to provide response	Number of requests not answered
	1	30 days	N/A

Conclusion on section B

900. Mexico has the necessary legal framework and administrative process in place for exchanging information on rulings. Mexico has met all of the ToR for the exchange of information process except the timely exchange of information on future rulings (ToR II.5.6). Mexico is recommended to ensure that all information on future rulings is exchanged as soon as possible.

C. Statistics (ToR IV)

901. As no information on rulings was exchanged for the year in review, no statistical data can be reported.

D. Matters related to intellectual property regimes (ToR I.4.1.3)

902. Mexico does not offer an intellectual property regime for which transparency requirements under the Action 5 Report (OECD, 2015) were imposed.

Summary of recommendations on implementation of the transparency framework

Aspect of implementation of the transparency framework that should be improved	Recommendation for improvement
Mexico experienced significant delays in exchanging information on future rulings.	Mexico is recommended to ensure that all information on future rulings is exchanged as soon as possible.

Notes

[1] Parties to the Convention are available here: www.oecd.org/tax/exchange-of-tax-information/convention-on-mutual-administrative-assistance-in-tax-matters.htm . Mexico also has bilateral agreements in force with Austria, Canada, Hong Kong (China), Russia, South Africa, Ukraine and the United States. In addition, Mexico has Tax Information Exchange Agreements permitting spontaneous exchange of information with Aruba, Canada and the United States.

[2] This number represents the number of future rulings on which exchanges would be required. Once the exchanges have been completed, the statistics on the number of exchanges, which may be different from the number of rulings, will be updated.

References

OECD (2017), *BEPS Action 5 on Harmful Tax Practices – Terms of Reference and Methodology for the Conduct of the Peer Reviews of the Action 5 Transparency Framework*, OECD/G20 Base Erosion and Profit Shifting Project, OECD, Paris. www.oecd.org/tax/beps/beps-action-5-harmful-tax-practices-peer-review-transparencyframework.pdf.

OECD (2015), *Countering Harmful Tax Practices More Effectively, Taking into Account Transparency and Substance, Action 5 - 2015 Final Report*, OECD/G20 Base Erosion and Profit Shifting Project, OECD Publishing, Paris. https://doi.org/10.1787/9789264241190-en.

OECD/Council of Europe (2011), *The Multilateral Convention on Mutual Administrative Assistance in Tax Matters: Amended by the 2010 Protocol*, OECD Publishing, Paris. http://dx.doi.org/10.1787/9789264115606-en.

Monaco

Monaco has met the terms of reference (ToR) for the calendar year 2017 (year in review) that can be met in the absence of rulings being issued and no recommendation is made.

Monaco does not issue any type of ruling within the scope of the transparency framework. Therefore, Monaco has not issued any specific decision to a taxpayer within the scope of the five types of rulings subject to this framework. In the event that Monaco puts in place the administrative process to issue rulings within the scope of the transparency framework, Monaco notes that it would implement the transparency framework obligations.

As no rulings were issued, no exchange of information was required. Therefore, no peer input was received in respect of exchanges of information on rulings received from Monaco.

Introduction

903. This peer review covers Monaco's implementation of the BEPS Action 5 transparency framework for the year 2017. The report has four parts, each relating to a key part of the ToR. Each part is discussed in turn. A summary of recommendations is included at the end of this report.

A. The information gathering process

904. As no rulings are issued, this section is not assessed.

B. The exchange of information

905. As no rulings are issued, this section is not assessed.

C. Statistics (ToR IV)

906. As no rulings are issued, no statistical data can be reported.

D. Matters related to intellectual property regimes (ToR I.4.1.3)

907. Monaco does not offer an intellectual property regime for which transparency requirements under the Action 5 Report (OECD, 2015) were imposed.

Summary of recommendations on implementation of the transparency framework

Aspect of implementation of the transparency framework that should be improved	Recommendation for improvement
No recommendations are made.	

Reference

OECD (2015), *Countering Harmful Tax Practices More Effectively, Taking into Account Transparency and Substance, Action 5 - 2015 Final Report*, OECD/G20 Base Erosion and Profit Shifting Project, OECD Publishing, Paris. https://doi.org/10.1787/9789264241190-en.

Montserrat

Montserrat has met all aspects of the terms of reference (ToR) for the calendar year 2017 (year in review) that can be met in the absence of rulings being issued.

Montserrat indicates that it cannot legally issue any type of rulings within the scope of the transparency framework.

As no rulings were issued, no exchange of information was required. No peer input was received in respect of the exchanges of information on rulings received from Montserrat.

Introduction

908. This peer review covers Montserrat's implementation of the BEPS Action 5 transparency framework for the year 2017. The report has four parts, each relating to a key part of the ToR. Each part is discussed in turn. A summary of recommendations is included at the end of this report.

A. The information gathering process

909. As no rulings are issued, this section is not assessed.

B. The exchange of information

910. As no rulings are issued, this section is not assessed.

C. Statistics (ToR IV)

911. As no rulings are issued, no statistical data can be reported.

D. Matters related to intellectual property regimes (ToR I.4.1.3)

912. Montserrat does not offer an intellectual property regime for which transparency requirements under the Action 5 Report (OECD, 2015) were imposed.

Summary of recommendations on implementation of the transparency framework

Aspect of implementation of the transparency framework that should be improved	Recommendation for improvement
	No recommendations are made.

References

OECD (2017), *BEPS Action 5 on Harmful Tax Practices – Terms of Reference and Methodology for the Conduct of the Peer Reviews of the Action 5 Transparency Framework*, OECD/G20 Base Erosion and Profit Shifting Project, OECD, Paris. www.oecd.org/tax/beps/beps-action-5-harmful-tax-practices-peer-review-transparencyframework.pdf.

OECD (2015), *Countering Harmful Tax Practices More Effectively, Taking into Account Transparency and Substance, Action 5 - 2015 Final Report*, OECD/G20 Base Erosion and Profit Shifting Project, OECD Publishing, Paris. https://doi.org/10.1787/9789264241190-en.

The Netherlands

The Netherlands has met all aspects of the terms of reference (ToR) for the calendar year 2017 (year in review) except identifying and exchanging information on all taxpayers benefitting from the third category of assets in the IP regime if they have not requested a ruling. (ToR I.4.1.3). The Netherlands has addressed all three of the recommendations that were made in the prior year peer review report with regard to the completion of the information gathering process on past rulings, the swift exchange of information on past and future rulings and the swift exchange of information on new entrants of the grandfathered IP regime and these recommendations are removed. The Netherlands is recommended to continue its efforts to identify and exchange information on taxpayers benefitting from the third category of IP assets as soon as possible.

The Netherlands can legally issue four types of rulings within the scope of the transparency framework.

In practice, the Netherlands has issued 2 198 past rulings; for the period 1 April 2016 – 31 December 2016, the Netherlands issued 297 future rulings; and for the year in review, the Netherlands issued 213 future rulings within the scope of the transparency framework.

Peer input was received from six jurisdictions in respect of the exchanges of information on rulings received from the Netherlands. In general the input was positive, noting that information received was complete and in the correct format.

Introduction

913. This peer review covers the Netherlands' implementation of the BEPS Action 5 transparency framework for the year 2017. The report has four parts, each relating to a key part of the ToR. Each part is discussed in turn. A summary of recommendations is included at the end of this report.

A. The information gathering process

914. The Netherlands can legally issue the four following types of rulings within the scope of the transparency framework: (i) preferential regimes;[1] (ii) cross-border unilateral advance pricing agreements (APAs) and any other cross-border unilateral tax rulings (such as an advance tax ruling) covering transfer pricing or the application of transfer pricing principles; (iii) downward adjustments; and (iv) permanent establishment rulings. To the extent that conduit rulings are provided, in the Netherlands they are already covered under the second category. APAs and advance tax rulings are co-issued by a specialised team based in Rotterdam and the competent local tax inspector. Rulings on preferential regimes are mostly co-issued by specialised teams within the Dutch tax administration and the competent local tax inspector. Certain forms of PE rulings (as well as some rulings that would fall into the APA category) are issued by local tax inspectors throughout the country. Rulings are not published. However, the Netherlands are publishing a description of the most frequent types of rulings and provide one or more example for each type.[2] Additionally the APA/ATR-Team publishes a report which discloses the number of centrally issued rulings, i.e. APAs and ATRs, which is accessible on the internet.[3]

Past rulings (ToR I.4.1.1, I.4.1.2, I.4.2.1, I.4.2.2)

915. For the Netherlands, past rulings are any tax rulings within scope that are issued either: (i) on or after 1 January 2014 but before 1 April 2016; or (ii) on or after 1 January 2010 but before 1 January 2014, provided they were still in effect as at 1 January 2014.

916. In the prior year peer review report, it was determined that the Dutch tax administration's undertakings to identify past rulings and all potential exchange jurisdictions met all the ToR except for identifying all past rulings (ToR I.4.1.1) as the process of identifying past rulings was not completed in time. The Netherlands were recommended to complete its information-gathering process on past rulings as soon as possible.

917. The Dutch tax administration committed in last year's review to have the information-gathering process on past rulings completed in 2017. It has confirmed that the identification process was completed by 31 December 2017. A total of 1 901 additional past rulings were identified during the year of review. The Dutch tax administration's procedures to identify past rulings therefore meet the minimum standard and no recommendations are made.

Future rulings (ToR I.4.1.1, I.4.1.2, I.4.2.1)

918. For the Netherlands, future rulings are any tax rulings within scope that are issued on or after 1 April 2016.

919. In the prior year peer review report, it was determined that the Dutch tax administration's implementation of a new system to identify future rulings and all

potential exchange jurisdictions was sufficient to meet the minimum standard. In the year in review. The Dutch tax administration amended the procedure to enhance the timeliness of the processes in place. With effect from 9 May 2017 all taxpayers applying for a cross-border ruling are obliged by a new Decree on Administrative Law in Tax Matters to fill out the template containing all the information to identify the category of ruling and the potential exchange jurisdictions. The respective tax inspectors remain responsible for ensuring that the template is completed correctly, and that rulings, which have not been identified by the taxpayer as being cross-border are nonetheless identified as being in scope of the transparency framework. Furthermore, all rulings on which information needs to be exchanged are registered in a centralised database since September 2017. The Netherland's implementation continues to meet the minimum standard.

Review and supervision mechanism (ToR I.4.3)

920. In the prior year peer review report, it was determined that the Dutch tax administration's review and supervisions mechanisms were sufficient to meet the minimum standard. The Dutch tax administration's implementation in this regard remains unchanged, and therefore continues to meet the minimum standard.

Conclusion on section A

921. The Netherlands has met all of the ToR for the information gathering process and no recommendations are made.

B. The exchange of information

Legal basis for spontaneous exchange of information (ToR II.5.1, II.5.2)

922. The Netherlands have the necessary domestic legal basis to exchange information spontaneously. The Netherlands note that there are no legal or practical impediments that prevent the spontaneous exchange of information on rulings as contemplated in the Action 5 minimum standard.

923. The Netherlands is a party to international agreements permitting spontaneous exchange of information, including (i) the *Multilateral Convention on Mutual Administrative Assistance in Tax Matters: Amended by the 2010 Protocol* (OECD/Council of Europe, 2011) ("the Convention"), (ii) the Directive 2011/16/EU with all other European Union Member States and (iii) double tax agreements in force with 142 jurisdictions.[4]

Completion and exchange of templates (ToR II.5.3, II.5.4, II.5.5, II.5.6, II.5.7)

924. In the prior year peer review report, it was determined that the Netherlands' process for the completion and exchange of templates was sufficient to meet the minimum standard, except that information on past rulings was exchanged with considerable delay due to the large number of past rulings that had to be exchanged. The Netherlands was recommended to continue to ensure that all information on past rulings was exchanged as soon as possible and to fulfil its commitment to compete the exchange of information on past rulings by no later than 31 December 2017. The Netherlands met its commitment and completed the exchange of information on past rulings by 31 December 2017. Furthermore, the Netherlands met the timelines for exchanging information on future rulings and is in addition expected to reduce the time of transmitting information on future rulings to the Competent Authority as they issued a

Decree in May 2017, which obliges taxpayers to provide all necessary information to be filled in the template before a ruling is issued.

925. Regarding the completion of the summary section of the template, the Netherlands has introduced "standard" paragraphs for each type of ruling, which are completed with the specifics of the individual ruling and if needed, are adapted to the case at hand. Those standard paragraphs include the names of the involved parties and where they are based, the value of the transaction and as applicable the activities of the applicants, the nature of the transactions and/or the transfer pricing methods used.

926. The timeliness of exchanges is as follows.

Past rulings in the scope of the transparency framework	Number of exchanges transmitted by 31 December 2017	Delayed exchanges		
		Number of exchanges not transmitted by 31 December 2017	Reasons for the delays	Any other comments
	4 436	0	N/A	This reflects the exchanges on the 1 901 past rulings identified during 2017 and includes exchanges with new Inclusive Framework members
Future rulings in the scope of the transparency framework	Number of exchanges transmitted within three months of the information becoming available to the competent authority or immediately after legal impediments have been lifted	Delayed exchanges		
		Number of exchanges transmitted later than three months of the information on rulings becoming available to the competent authority	Reasons for the delays	Any other comments
	1 238	0	N/A	
Total	5 674	0		

Follow up requests received for exchange of the ruling	Number	Average time to provide response	Number of requests not answered
	61	98 days	N/A

Conclusion on section B

927. The Netherlands has the necessary legal basis for spontaneous exchange of information, a process for completing the templates in a timely way and has completed all exchanges on time. The Netherlands has met all of the ToR for the exchange of information process and no recommendations are made.

C. Statistics (ToR IV)

928. The statistics for the year in review are as follows:

Category of ruling	Number of exchanges	Jurisdictions exchanged with
Rulings related to preferential regimes	2 446	Argentina, Armenia, Aruba, Australia, Austria, Azerbaijan, Belarus, Belgium, Bosnia and Herzegovina, Brazil, Bulgaria, Canada, Chile, China (People's Republic of), Colombia, Croatia, Curaçao, Cyprus,[5] Czech Republic, Denmark, Egypt, Estonia, Finland, Former Yugoslav Republic of Macedonia France, Georgia, Germany, Ghana, Greece, Hong Kong (China), Hungary, Iceland, India, Indonesia, Ireland, Israel, Italy, Japan, Jordan, Kazakhstan, Korea, Latvia, Lithuania, Luxembourg, Malaysia, Malta, Mauritius, Mexico, Morocco, New Zealand, Nigeria, Norway, Oman, Pakistan, Panama, Philippines, Poland, Portugal, Qatar, Romania, Russia, Saint Eustatius, Saudi Arabia, Serbia, Singapore, Slovak Republic, Slovenia, South Africa, Spain, Sri Lanka, Sweden, Switzerland, Chinese Taipei, Thailand, Tunisia, Turkey, Ukraine, United Arab Emirates, United Kingdom, United States, Uruguay, Uzbekistan, Viet Nam
Cross-border unilateral advance pricing agreements (APAs) and any other cross-border unilateral tax rulings (such as an advance tax ruling) covering transfer pricing or the application of transfer pricing principles	2 851	Argentina, Armenia, Aruba, Australia, Austria, Barbados, Belarus, Belgium, Belize, Bosnia and Herzegovina, Brazil, Bulgaria, Cameroon, Canada, Chile, China (People's Republic of), Colombia, Costa Rica, Croatia, Curaçao, Cyprus, Czech Republic, Denmark, Egypt, Estonia, Finland, France, Georgia, Germany, Ghana, Gibraltar, Greece, Guernsey, Hong Kong (China), Hungary, Iceland, India, Indonesia, Ireland, Isle of Man, Israel, Italy, Japan, Jersey, Jordan, Kazakhstan, Korea, Kuwait, Latvia, Liechtenstein, Lithuania, Luxembourg, Malaysia, Malta, Mexico, Moldavia, Morocco, New Zealand, Nigeria, Norway, Oman, Pakistan, Panama, Philippines, Poland, Portugal, Qatar, Romania, Russia, Saint Eustatius, Samoa, Saudi Arabia, Senegal, Serbia, Singapore, Sint Maarten, Slovak Republic, Slovenia, South Africa, Spain, Sri Lanka, Suriname, Sweden, Switzerland, Chinese Taipei, Thailand, Tunisia, Turkey, Ukraine, United Arab Emirates, United Kingdom, United States, Uruguay, Venezuela, Viet Nam, Zimbabwe

Category of ruling	Number of exchanges	Jurisdictions exchanged with
Cross-border rulings providing for a unilateral downward adjustment to the taxpayer's taxable profits that is not directly reflected in the taxpayer's financial / commercial accounts	107	Armenia, Australia, Austria, Belgium, Brazil, Bulgaria, Canada, China (People's Republic of), Curaçao, Cyprus, Denmark, Finland, France, Germany, Hong Kong (China), Hungary, Italy, Japan, Jersey, Luxembourg, Malta, Mexico, New Zealand, Poland, Qatar, Romania, Russia, Spain, Sweden, Switzerland, Chinese Taipei, Thailand, Turkey, Ukraine, United Kingdom, United States, Uruguay
Permanent establishment rulings	270	Aruba, Australia, Austria, Belgium, Brazil, Canada, China (People's Republic of), Colombia, Curaçao, Czech Republic, Denmark, Finland, France, Germany, Hong Kong (China), Hungary, Ireland, Italy, Japan, Jersey, Liechtenstein, Luxembourg, Mexico, Norway, Poland, Portugal, Romania, Russia, Saint Eustatius, Serbia, Sint Maarten, Slovak Republic, Spain, Sweden, Switzerland, Turkey, United Arab Emirates, United Kingdom, United States
Related party conduit rulings	N/A	N/A
De minimis rule	N/A	N/A
IP regimes: total exchanges on taxpayers benefitting from the third category of IP assets, new entrants benefitting from grandfathered IP regimes; and taxpayers making use of the option to treat the nexus ratio as a rebuttable presumption	If they have a ruling, the number is included in the rulings related to preferential regimes.[6]	N/A
Total	5 674	

D. Matters related to intellectual property regimes (ToR I.4.1.3)

929. In the prior year peer review report, it was determined that the Netherlands' implementation regarding matters related to intellectual property regimes was sufficient to meet the minimum standard except for the exchange of information on new entrants benefitting from the grandfathered IP regime.

- ***New entrants benefitting from the grandfathered IP regime:*** as the Dutch IP regime was in nearly all cases offered by way of ruling, new entrants (both new taxpayers and new assets of existing taxpayers) benefitting from the grandfathered IP regime were identified using the approach described above for past rulings on preferential regimes. Therefore, the completion of the exchanges was also subject to some delays. It was recommended that the Netherlands continue to ensure that all information on past rulings, including rulings on new entrants to the IP regime, is exchanged as soon as possible. The Netherlands completed the exchange on those rulings by 31 December 2017.

  New entrants (both new taxpayers and new assets of existing taxpayers) who did not apply for a ruling can be identified once they have filed their corporate income tax returns. The tax return form was amended and now includes a question as to whether the taxpayer applied the provisions of the innovation box. If the taxpayer indicated this, the tax return will be flagged for the tax inspector. If the taxpayer has requested a ruling, the information was already exchanged. If a tax inspector comes across information that still needs to be exchanged, he will make sure a template is filled out and exchange the information accordingly.

- ***Third category of IP assets:*** there is no requirement to apply for a ruling in order to benefit from the new innovation box, but the Netherlands notes that in practice most taxpayers do apply for a ruling. If this is the case, information on that ruling is exchanged within the applicable timelines for future rulings. To the extent that a taxpayer does not apply for a ruling in order to obtain the benefit from the third category of assets, his tax return is treated the same way as described above with respect to new entrants, meaning that the Netherlands would exchange information on all taxpayers that applied the provisions of the innovation box who fall into the definition of small and medium enterprises regardless whether they have applied for a ruling or not. The Netherlands is currently evaluating ways to collect information and reporting information to the FHTP as part of the ongoing monitoring requirements set out in the Action 5 Report (OECD, 2015).
- ***Taxpayers making use of the option to treat the nexus ratio as a rebuttable presumption***: not applicable as the regime does not allow the nexus ratio to be treated as a rebuttable presumption.

930. As nearly all taxpayers apply for a ruling to benefit from the grandfathered regime or from the third category of IP assets under the new innovation box, the information is exchanged in the same manner as past rulings (regarding new entrants to the grandfathered regime) and future rulings (regarding taxpayers benefitting from the third category of IP assets). However, it is possible that there could be a number of taxpayers who did not apply for a ruling. With respect to the new entrants to the grandfathered regime, these will be identified by the tax return and exchanged upon in due course. With respect to taxpayers benefitting from the third category of assets, the Netherlands is recommended to continue its efforts to identify and exchange information on taxpayers benefitting from the third category of IP assets as soon as possible.

Summary of recommendations on implementation of the transparency framework

Aspect of implementation of the transparency framework that should be improved	Recommendation for improvement
Although most taxpayers benefitting from the third category of assets in the new IP regime obtain a ruling and are identified and exchanged upon in accordance with the process used for all other rulings, the Netherlands is not yet able to identify taxpayers benefitting from the third category of assets in the IP regime to the extent they do not obtain a ruling.	The Netherlands is recommended to continue its efforts to identify and exchange information on taxpayers benefitting from the third category of IP assets as soon as possible.

Notes

[1] With respect to the following preferential regimes: 1) Innovation box and 2) International shipping.

[2] www.rijksoverheid.nl/ministeries/ministerie-van-financien/documenten/kamerstukken/2018/02/18/bijlage-v-jaarverslag-apa-atr (accessed 20 November 2018).

[3] www.rijksoverheid.nl/documenten/kamerstukken/2017/05/23/beschrijving-apa-atr-praktijk (accessed 20 November 2018).

[4] Parties to the Convention are available here: www.oecd.org/tax/exchange-of-tax-information/convention-on-mutual-administrative-assistance-in-tax-matters.htm. the Netherlands also has bilateral agreements with Albania, Argentina, Armenia, Australia, Austria, Azerbaijan, Bahrain, Bangladesh, Barbados, Belarus, Belgium, Bermuda, Bosnia and Herzegovina, Brazil, Bulgaria, Canada, China (People's Republic of), Croatia, Curacao, Czech Republic, Denmark, Egypt, Estonia, Ethiopia, Finland, Former Yugoslav Republic of Macedonia, France, Georgia, Germany, Ghana, Greece, Hong Kong (China), Hungary, Iceland, India, Indonesia, Ireland, Israel, Italy, Japan, Jordan, Kazakhstan, Kenya, Korea, Kuwait, Latvia, Lithuania, Luxembourg, Malawi, Malaysia, Malta, Mexico, Moldova, Montenegro, Morocco, New Zealand, Nigeria, Norway, Oman, Pakistan, Panama, Philippines, Poland, Portugal, Qatar, Romania, Russia, Saint Martin, Saudi Arabia, Serbia, Singapore, Slovak Republic, Slovenia, South Africa, Spain, Sri Lanka, Suriname, Sweden, Switzerland, Chinese Taipei, Tajikistan, Thailand, Tunisia, Turkey, Uganda, Ukraine, United Arab Emirates, United Kingdom, United States, Uzbekistan, Venezuela, Viet Nam, Zambia and Zimbabwe.

[5] Note by Turkey: The information in this document with reference to "Cyprus" relates to the southern part of the Island. There is no single authority representing both Turkish and Greek Cypriot people on the Island. Turkey recognises the Turkish Republic of Northern Cyprus (TRNC). Until a lasting and equitable solution is found within the context of the United Nations, Turkey shall preserve its position concerning the "Cyprus issue".

Note by all the European Union Member States of the OECD and the European Union. The Republic of Cyprus is recognised by all members of the United Nations with the exception of Turkey. The information in this document relates to the area under the effective control of the Government of the Republic of Cyprus.

[6] It is noted that the Netherlands is using the same code to exchange information on new entrants of the grandfathered IP regime, entrants of the new innovation box, entrants of the new innovation box benefitting from the third category of assets, and beneficiaries of the shipping regime. Therefore exact figures of new entrants benefitting from the grandfathered regime and from the third category of assets as required for statistical purposes cannot yet be provided.

References

OECD (2017), *BEPS Action 5 on Harmful Tax Practices – Terms of Reference and Methodology for the Conduct of the Peer Reviews of the Action 5 Transparency Framework*, OECD/G20 Base Erosion and Profit Shifting Project, OECD, Paris. www.oecd.org/tax/beps/beps-action-5-harmful-tax-practices-peer-review-transparencyframework.pdf.

OECD (2015), *Countering Harmful Tax Practices More Effectively, Taking into Account Transparency and Substance, Action 5 - 2015 Final Report*, OECD/G20 Base Erosion and Profit Shifting Project, OECD Publishing, Paris. https://doi.org/10.1787/9789264241190-en.

OECD/Council of Europe (2011), *The Multilateral Convention on Mutual Administrative Assistance in Tax Matters: Amended by the 2010 Protocol*, OECD Publishing, Paris. http://dx.doi.org/10.1787/9789264115606-en.

New Zealand

New Zealand has met all aspects of the terms of reference (ToR) for the calendar year 2017 (year in review) and no recommendations are made.

New Zealand can legally issue five types of rulings within the scope of the transparency framework.

In practice, New Zealand has issued 69 past rulings; for the period 1 April 2016 - 31 December 2016, New Zealand issued 14 future rulings; and for the year in review, New Zealand issued 15 future rulings within the scope of the transparency framework.

Peer input was received from three jurisdictions in respect of the exchanges of information on rulings received from New Zealand. It was positive, noting that information was complete, in the correct format, and received in a timely manner with the summary provided a good overview of the ruling.

Introduction

931. This peer review covers New Zealand's implementation of the BEPS Action 5 transparency framework for the year 2017. The report has four parts, each relating to a key part of the ToR. Each part is discussed in turn. A summary of recommendations is included at the end of this report.

A. The information gathering process

932. New Zealand can legally issue the five following types of rulings within the scope of the transparency framework: (i) rulings related to preferential regimes; (ii) cross-border unilateral advance pricing arrangements (APAs) and any other cross-border unilateral tax rulings (such as an advance tax ruling) covering transfer pricing or the application of transfer pricing principles; (iii) cross-border rulings giving a unilateral downward adjustment to the taxpayer's taxable profits in the country giving the ruling; (iv) permanent establishment rulings; and (v) related party conduit rulings. In New Zealand, senior officers in the three areas (namely Taxpayer Rulings Unit, Specialist Advice and Investigations) in the New Zealand Inland Revenue Department ("IRD") are authorised to issue opinions.

Past rulings (ToR I.4.1.1, I.4.1.2, I.4.2.1, I.4.2.2)

933. For New Zealand, past rulings are any tax rulings within scope that are issued either: (i) on or after 1 January 2014 but before 1 April 2016; or (ii) on or after 1 January 2010 but before 1 January 2014, provided they were still in effect as at 1 January 2014.

934. In the prior year peer review report, it was determined that the IRD's undertakings to identify past rulings and all potential exchange jurisdictions were sufficient to meet the minimum standard. The IRD's implementation continues to meet the minimum standard.

Future rulings (ToR I.4.1.1, I.4.1.2, I.4.2.1)

935. For New Zealand, future rulings are any tax rulings within scope that are issued on or after 1 April 2016.

936. In the prior year peer review report, it was determined that the IRD's implementation of a new system to identify future rulings and all potential exchange jurisdictions was sufficient to meet the minimum standard. For the year in review, New Zealand has made a relatively minor change to the process of identifying all relevant jurisdictions in relation to its unilateral APAs. This involves the transfer pricing principal advisor summarising the ruling after issuing the APA. Thereafter, a copy of the summary and the ruling is submitted to the Senior Advisor for exchange. This ensures an additional check on the accuracy of the identification of all relevant jurisdictions for which the tax ruling would be relevant and therefore continues to meet the minimum standard.

Review and supervision mechanism (ToR I.4.3)

937. In the prior year peer review report, it was determined that the IRD's review and supervision mechanism was sufficient to meet the minimum standard. The IRD's implementation in this regard remains unchanged, and therefore continues to meet the minimum standard.

Conclusion on section A

938. New Zealand has met all of the ToR for the information gathering process and no recommendations are made.

B. The exchange of information

Legal basis for spontaneous exchange of information (ToR II.5.1, II.5.2)

939. New Zealand has the necessary domestic legal basis to exchange information spontaneously. New Zealand notes that there are no legal or practical impediments that prevent the spontaneous exchange of information on rulings as contemplated in the Action 5 minimum standard.

940. New Zealand is a party to international agreements permitting spontaneous exchange of information, including (i) the *Multilateral Convention on Mutual Administrative Assistance in Tax Matters: Amended by the 2010 Protocol* (OECD/Council of Europe, 2011) ("the Convention") and (ii) double tax agreements in force with 39 jurisdictions.[1]

Completion and exchange of templates (ToR II.5.3, II.5.4, II.5.5, II.5.6, II.5.7)

941. In the prior year peer review report, it was determined that the IRD's completion and exchange of templates were sufficient to meet the minimum standard. The IRD's implementation in this regard remains unchanged, and therefore continues to meet the minimum standard.

942. For the year in review, the timeliness of exchanges is as follows:

Past rulings in the scope of the transparency framework	Number of exchanges transmitted by 31 December 2017	Delayed exchanges		
		Number of exchanges not transmitted by 31 December 2017	Reasons for the delays	Any other comments
	0	0	N/A	See below
Future rulings in the scope of the transparency framework	Number of exchanges transmitted within three months of the information becoming available to the competent authority or immediately after legal impediments have been lifted	Delayed exchanges		
		Number of exchanges transmitted later than three months of the information on rulings becoming available to the competent authority	Reasons for the delays	Any other comments
	38	0	N/A	
Total	38	0		

Follow up requests received for exchange of the ruling	Number	Average time to provide response	Number of requests not answered
	0	N/A	N/A

943. For the year in review, no past rulings had to be exchanged with new members of the Inclusive Framework that joined in 2017 and as such no additional exchanges on past rulings were required.

Conclusion on section B

944. New Zealand has the necessary legal basis for spontaneous exchange of information, a process for completing the templates in a timely way and has completed all exchanges on time. New Zealand has met all of the ToR for the exchange of information process and no recommendations are made.

C. Statistics (ToR IV)

945. The statistics for the year in review are as follows:

Category of ruling	Number of exchanges	Jurisdictions exchanged with
Rulings related to preferential regimes	0	N/A
Cross-border unilateral advance pricing arrangement (APAs) and any other cross-border unilateral tax rulings (such as an advance tax ruling) covering transfer pricing or the application of transfer pricing principles	35	Australia, Barbados, China (People's Republic of), France, Japan, Malaysia, Mexico, Netherlands, Romania, Singapore, Spain, United Kingdom, United States
Cross-border rulings providing for a unilateral downward adjustment to the taxpayer's taxable profits that is not directly reflected in the taxpayer's financial / commercial accounts	Included in *de minimis*	N/A
Permanent establishment rulings	0	N/A
Related party conduit rulings	Included in *de minimis*	N/A
De minimis rule	3	N/A
IP regimes: total exchanges on taxpayers benefitting from the third category of IP assets, new entrants benefitting from grandfathered IP regimes; and taxpayers making use of the option to treat the nexus ratio as a rebuttable presumption	N/A	N/A
Total	38	

D. Matters related to intellectual property regimes (ToR I.4.1.3)

946. New Zealand does not offer an intellectual property regime for which transparency requirements under the Action 5 Report (OECD, 2015) were imposed.

Summary of recommendations on implementation of the transparency framework

Aspect of implementation of the transparency framework that should be improved	Recommendation for improvement
No recommendations are made.	

Note

1 Parties to the Convention are available here: www.oecd.org/tax/exchange-of-tax-information/convention-on-mutual-administrative-assistance-in-tax-matters.htm. New Zealand also has bilateral agreements in force with Fiji, Papua New Guinea, Philippines, Chinese Taipei, Thailand, Turkey, United Arab Emirates, United States and Viet Nam.

References

OECD (2017), *BEPS Action 5 on Harmful Tax Practices – Terms of Reference and Methodology for the Conduct of the Peer Reviews of the Action 5 Transparency Framework*, OECD/G20 Base Erosion and Profit Shifting Project, OECD, Paris. www.oecd.org/tax/beps/beps-action-5-harmful-tax-practices-peer-review-transparencyframework.pdf.

OECD (2015), *Countering Harmful Tax Practices More Effectively, Taking into Account Transparency and Substance, Action 5 - 2015 Final Report*, OECD/G20 Base Erosion and Profit Shifting Project, OECD Publishing, Paris. https://doi.org/10.1787/9789264241190-en.

OECD/Council of Europe (2011), *The Multilateral Convention on Mutual Administrative Assistance in Tax Matters: Amended by the 2010 Protocol*, OECD Publishing, Paris. http://dx.doi.org/10.1787/9789264115606-en.

Nigeria

Nigeria has met the terms of reference (ToR) for the calendar year 2017 (year in review) that can be met in the absence of rulings being issued.

Nigeria does not issue any type of ruling within the scope of the transparency framework. Nigeria issues rulings on the tax consequences of a transaction which are binding for the tax authorities. However, the rulings issued by Nigeria do not relate to a preferential tax regime, determine or decide on the existence or the absence of a permanent establishment or provide for how much profit will be attributed to a permanent establishment, advance pricing arrangements, downward adjustment or a conduit ruling and are therefore not considered rulings as defined in the Action 5 report (OECD, 2015). In the event that Nigeria puts in place the administrative process to issue rulings within the scope of the transparency framework, Nigeria notes that it would implement the transparency framework obligations.

As there were no rulings issued, no exchange of information was required. Therefore, no peer input was received in respect of exchanges of information on rulings received from Nigeria.

Introduction

947. This peer review covers Nigeria's implementation of the BEPS Action 5 transparency framework for the year 2017. The report has four parts, each relating to a key part of the ToR. Each part is discussed in turn. A summary of recommendations is included at the end of this report.

A. The information gathering process

948. As no rulings are issued, this section is not assessed.

B. The exchange of information

949. As no rulings are issued, this section is not assessed.

C. Statistics (ToR IV)

950. As no rulings are issued, no statistical data can be reported.

D. Matters related to intellectual property regimes (ToR I.4.1.3)

951. Nigeria does not offer an intellectual property regime for which transparency requirements under the Action 5 Report (OECD, 2015) were imposed.

Summary of recommendations on implementation of the transparency framework

Aspect of implementation of the transparency framework that should be improved	Recommendation for improvement
	No recommendations are made.

References

OECD (2017), *BEPS Action 5 on Harmful Tax Practices – Terms of Reference and Methodology for the Conduct of the Peer Reviews of the Action 5 Transparency Framework*, OECD/G20 Base Erosion and Profit Shifting Project, OECD, Paris. www.oecd.org/tax/beps/beps-action-5-harmful-tax-practices-peer-review-transparencyframework.pdf.

OECD (2015), *Countering Harmful Tax Practices More Effectively, Taking into Account Transparency and Substance, Action 5 - 2015 Final Report*, OECD/G20 Base Erosion and Profit Shifting Project, OECD Publishing, Paris. https://doi.org/10.1787/9789264241190-en.

Norway

Norway has met all aspects of the terms of reference (ToR) for the calendar year 2017 (year in review) and no recommendations are made.

Norway can legally issue three types of rulings within the scope of the transparency framework.

In practice, Norway has issued one past ruling; for the period 1 April 2016 - 31 December 2016; and for the year in review, Norway issued no future rulings within the scope of the transparency framework.

No peer input was received in respect of the exchanges of information on rulings received from Norway.

Introduction

952. This peer review covers Norway's implementation of the BEPS Action 5 transparency framework for the year 2017. The report has four parts, each relating to a key part of the ToR. Each part is discussed in turn. A summary of recommendations is included at the end of this report.

A. The information gathering process

953. Norway can legally issue the three following types of rulings within the scope of the transparency framework: (i) rulings related to preferential regimes[1]; (ii) cross-border unilateral advance pricing arrangements (APAs) covering transfer pricing or the application of transfer pricing principles in relation to realisation of natural gas for companies liable to tax under the Petroleum Tax Act; and (iii) related party conduit rulings. In Norway, the Central Tax Office for Large Enterprise issues rulings on the preferential regime and unilateral APAs in relation to petroleum tax are issued by the Petroleum Taxation Office. The Norwegian Directorate of Taxes can also issue rulings involving complex tax questions, tax matters of interest to the broader public and principle tax matters.

Past rulings (ToR I.4.1.1, I.4.1.2, I.4.2.1, I.4.2.2)

954. For Norway, past rulings are any tax rulings within scope that are issued either: (i) on or after 1 January 2014 but before 1 April 2016; or (ii) on or after 1 January 2010 but before 1 January 2014, provided they were still in effect as at 1 January 2014.

955. In the prior year peer review report, it was determined that the Norwegian tax administration's undertakings to identify past rulings and all potential exchange jurisdictions were sufficient to meet the minimum standard. The Norwegian tax administration's implementation in this regard remains unchanged, and therefore continues to meet the minimum standard.

Future rulings (ToR I.4.1.1, I.4.1.2, I.4.2.1)

956. For Norway, future rulings are any tax rulings within scope that are issued on or after 1 April 2016.

957. In the prior year peer review report, it was determined that the Norwegian tax administration's implementation of a new system to identify future rulings and all potential exchange jurisdictions was sufficient to meet the minimum standard. The Norwegian tax administration's implementation in this regard remains unchanged, and therefore continues to meet the minimum standard.

Review and supervision mechanism (ToR I.4.3)

958. In the prior year peer review report, it was determined that the Norwegian tax administration's review and supervision mechanism was sufficient to meet the minimum standard. The Norwegian tax administration's implementation in this regard remains unchanged, and therefore continues to meet the minimum standard.

Conclusion on section A

959. Norway has met all of the ToR for the information gathering process and no recommendations are made.

B. The exchange of information

Legal basis for spontaneous exchange of information (ToR II.5.1, II.5.2)

960. Norway has the necessary domestic legal basis to exchange information spontaneously. Norway notes that there are no legal or practical impediments that prevent the spontaneous exchange of information on rulings as contemplated in the Action 5 minimum standard.

961. Norway is a party to international agreements permitting spontaneous exchange of information, including (i) the *Multilateral Convention on Mutual Administrative Assistance in Tax Matters: Amended by the 2010 Protocol* (OECD/Council of Europe, 2011) ("the Convention"), (ii) the Nordic Convention on Assistance in Tax Matters and (iii) double tax agreements in force with 84 jurisdictions.[2]

Completion and exchange of templates (ToR II.5.3, II.5.4, II.5.5, II.5.6, II.5.7)

962. In the prior year peer review report, it was determined that the Norwegian tax administration's completion and exchange of templates were sufficient to meet the minimum standard. The Norwegian tax administration's implementation in this regard remains unchanged, and therefore continues to meet the minimum standard.

963. With respect to the completion of the summary section of the template, Norway confirms that it uses the suggested FHTP internal guidance.

964. For the year in review, no past rulings had to be exchanged with new members of the Inclusive Framework that joined in 2017 and as such no additional exchanges on past rulings were required. In addition, no rulings within the scope of the transparency framework have been issued in the year of review. Therefore, Norway was not required to complete any exchanges of information and there is no data to report on the timeliness of exchanges

Conclusion on section B

965. Norway has the necessary legal basis for spontaneous exchange of information, a process for completing the templates in a timely way and has completed all exchanges on time. Norway has met all of the ToR for the exchange of information process and no recommendations are made.

C. Statistics (ToR IV)

966. As there were no rulings required to be exchanged by Norway for the year in review, no statistics can be reported.

D. Matters related to intellectual property regimes (ToR I.4.1.3)

967. Norway does not offer an intellectual property regime for which transparency requirements under the Action 5 Report (OECD, 2015) were imposed.

Summary of recommendations on implementation of the transparency framework

Aspect of implementation of the transparency framework that should be improved	Recommendation for improvement
No recommendations are made.	

Notes

1 With respect to the following preferential regimes: 1) International shipping regime.

2 Parties to the Convention are available here: www.oecd.org/tax/exchange-of-tax-information/convention-on-mutual-administrative-assistance-in-tax-matters.htm. Parties to the Nordic Convention on Assistance in Tax Matters are Denmark, Faroe Islands, Finland, Greenland, Iceland, Sweden and Norway. Norway also has bilateral agreements in force with Albania, Argentina, Australia, Austria, Azerbaijan, Bangladesh, Barbados, Belgium, Benin, Bonaire, Bosnia and Herzegovina, Brazil, Bulgaria, Canada, Chile, China (People's Republic of), Croatia, Curacao, Cyprus, Czech Republic, Egypt, Estonia, France, Gambia, Georgia, Germany, Greece, Hungary, India, Indonesia, Ireland, Israel, Italy, Ivory Coast, Jamaica, Japan, Kazakhstan, Kenya, Latvia, Lithuania, Luxembourg, Macedonia, Malawi, Malaysia, Malta, Mexico, Montenegro, Morocco, Nepal, Netherlands, New Zealand, Pakistan, Philippines, Poland, Portugal, Qatar, Romania, Russia, Saba, Senegal, Serbia, Sierra Leone, Singapore, Saint. Eustatius, Sint Maarten, Slovak Republic, Slovenia, South Africa, South Korea, Spain, Sri Lanka, Switzerland, Tanzania, Thailand, Tunisia, Turkey, Uganda, Ukraine, United Kingdom, United States, Venezuela, Viet Nam, Zambia and Zimbabwe.

Note by Turkey: The information in this document with reference to "Cyprus" relates to the southern part of the Island. There is no single authority representing both Turkish and Greek Cypriot people on the Island. Turkey recognises the Turkish Republic of Northern Cyprus (TRNC). Until a lasting and equitable solution is found within the context of the United Nations, Turkey shall preserve its position concerning the "Cyprus issue".

Note by all the European Union Member States of the OECD and the European Union. The Republic of Cyprus is recognised by all members of the United Nations with the exception of Turkey. The information in this document relates to the area under the effective control of the Government of the Republic of Cyprus.

References

OECD (2017), *BEPS Action 5 on Harmful Tax Practices – Terms of Reference and Methodology for the Conduct of the Peer Reviews of the Action 5 Transparency Framework*, OECD/G20 Base Erosion and Profit Shifting Project, OECD, Paris. www.oecd.org/tax/beps/beps-action-5-harmful-tax-practices-peer-review-transparencyframework.pdf.

OECD (2015), *Countering Harmful Tax Practices More Effectively, Taking into Account Transparency and Substance, Action 5 - 2015 Final Report*, OECD/G20 Base Erosion and Profit Shifting Project, OECD Publishing, Paris. https://doi.org/10.1787/9789264241190-en.

OECD/Council of Europe (2011), *The Multilateral Convention on Mutual Administrative Assistance in Tax Matters: Amended by the 2010 Protocol*, OECD Publishing, Paris. http://dx.doi.org/10.1787/9789264115606-en.

Pakistan

Pakistan has met all aspects of the terms of reference (ToR) for the calendar year 2017 (year in review) that can be met in the absence of rulings in scope being issued and no recommendations are made.

Pakistan does not issue any type of rulings within the scope of the transparency framework.

As no rulings were issued, no exchange of information was required. No peer input was received in respect of the exchanges of information on rulings received from Pakistan.

Introduction

968. This peer review covers Pakistan's implementation of the BEPS Action 5 transparency framework for the year 2017. The report has four parts, each relating to a key part of the ToR. Each part is discussed in turn. A summary of recommendations is included at the end of this report.

A. The information gathering process

969. Pakistan does not issue any type of rulings within the scope of the transparency framework. Pakistan only issues advanced tax rulings to non-resident taxpayers setting out the tax consequences to a transaction proposed or entered into by the taxpayer, regardless whether income is generated through a permanent establishment or not. The tax rulings, once issued, are binding for the tax authorities. However, the rulings issued by Pakistan do not determine or decide on the existence or the absence of a permanent establishment or provide for how much profit will be attributed to a permanent establishment and are therefore not considered rulings as defined in the Action 5 report (OECD, 2015). As no rulings are issued, this section is not assessed.

B. The exchange of information

970. As no rulings are issued, this section is not assessed.

C. Statistics (ToR IV)

971. As no rulings are issued, no statistical data can be reported.

D. Matters related to intellectual property regimes (ToR I.4.1.3)

972. Pakistan does not offer an intellectual property regime for which transparency requirements under the Action 5 Report (OECD, 2015) were imposed.

Summary of recommendations on implementation of the transparency framework

Aspect of implementation of the transparency framework that should be improved	Recommendation for improvement
	No recommendations are made.

References

OECD (2017), *BEPS Action 5 on Harmful Tax Practices – Terms of Reference and Methodology for the Conduct of the Peer Reviews of the Action 5 Transparency Framework*, OECD/G20 Base Erosion and Profit Shifting Project, OECD, Paris. www.oecd.org/tax/beps/beps-action-5-harmful-tax-practices-peer-review-transparencyframework.pdf.

OECD (2015), *Countering Harmful Tax Practices More Effectively, Taking into Account Transparency and Substance, Action 5 - 2015 Final Report*, OECD/G20 Base Erosion and Profit Shifting Project, OECD Publishing, Paris. https://doi.org/10.1787/9789264241190-en.

Panama

Panama has met the terms of reference (ToR) for the calendar year 2017 (year in review).

Panama can legally issue one type of ruling within the scope of the transparency framework.

In practice, Panama has issued one past ruling; and for the year in review, Panama issued no future rulings within the scope of the transparency framework.

As no exchange of information was undertaken by Panama, no peer input was received in respect of the exchanges of information on rulings received from Panama.

Introduction

973. This peer review covers Panama's implementation of the BEPS Action 5 transparency framework for the year 2017. The report has four parts, each relating to a key part of the ToR. Each part is discussed in turn. A summary of recommendations is included at the end of this report.

A. The information gathering process

974. Panama can legally issue one type of ruling within the scope of the transparency framework: rulings related to preferential regime,[1] which are known as "fiscal agreements". A company that holds a MHQ/SEM license can negotiate fiscal agreements with the Ministry of Economy and Finance. The request shall be address to the Director General of Revenue of the Ministry of Economy and Finance. Once the agreement is settled and signed by the Minister of Economy and Finance, the company will present a copy of the fiscal agreement to the Technical Secretariat of the Ministry of Commerce and Industries (i.e. the office of the Director of Multinational Headquarters).

Past rulings (ToR I.4.1.1, I.4.1.2, I.4.2.1, I.4.2.2)

975. For Panama, past rulings are any tax rulings within scope that are issued either: (i) on or after 1 January 2015 but before 1 April 2017; or (ii) on or after 1 January 2012 but before 1 January 2015, provided they were still in effect as at 1 January 2015.

976. The process for identifying past rulings was conducted as follows. Each unit and relevant department within the tax administration manually reviewed all of the files related to all existing fiscal agreements to identify those fiscal agreements that could qualify as "rulings" under the transparency framework. Those files are stored in the tax analysis office at the Ministry of Economy and Finance which is responsible for documenting and collecting statistics on rulings. An analyst is in charge of gathering the relevant information and passing it to the head of the unit, who verifies their accuracy. This search resulted in the identification of only one ruling within scope of Action 5.

977. In order to identify potential exchange jurisdictions this information was found in the ruling itself and as such Panama did not need to use the "best efforts approach".

Future rulings (ToR I.4.1.1, I.4.1.2, I.4.2.1)

978. For Panama, future rulings are any tax rulings within scope that are issued on or after 1 April 2017.

979. The process used to identify future rulings was the same as adopted for past rulings. Each unit and relevant department within the tax administration manually reviewed the fiscal agreement files stored in the tax analysis office at the Ministry of Economy and Finance, and confirmed that no future rulings in scope of the transparency framework had been issued. The review of future rulings is carried out on a rolling basis. Every time a ruling is negotiated, the tax analysis office would receive the relevant documents signed by the Minister of Economy and Finance. However, Panama notes that article 25 of Law 41 of 2007, which allows for the negotiation of fiscal agreements, is being abolished and this will be confirmed in the subsequent peer review.

980. As no future rulings were issued, it was not relevant for Panama to identify the potential exchange jurisdictions for the year in review. If a future ruling is issued in the

following year, Panama would be able to identify the information from the ruling itself as was the case for past rulings.

Review and supervision mechanism (ToR I.4.3)

981. Each unit and relevant department is in charge of the review and supervision mechanism.

982. Officials in charge of complying with the transparency framework have received internal and external guidance and training about the transparency framework requirements. Two senior officers within the tax analysis office (i.e. a BEPS analyst, responsible for compliance with the transparency framework and the head of the office coordinating the implementation of the BEPS Project) are in charge of providing oversight on the process to ensure that the relevant information is captured accurately.

Conclusion on section A

983. Panama has met all of the ToR for the information gathering process and no recommendations are made.

B. The exchange of information

Legal basis for spontaneous exchange of information (ToR II.5.1, II.5.2)

984. For the year in review, Panama did not have the necessary domestic legal basis to exchange information spontaneously. However, domestic legislation implementing the *Multilateral Convention on Mutual Administrative Assistance in Tax Matters: Amended by the 2010 Protocol* (OECD/Council of Europe, 2011) ("the Convention") was introduced in 2017 and permits spontaneous exchange of information under the Convention for taxable periods beginning on or after 1 January 2018.

985. Panama is a party to international agreements permitting spontaneous exchange of information, including the Convention. The Convention was ratified through Law no. 5 of 21 February 2017 and entered into force as of 1 July 2017. Since the Convention will have effect for administrative assistance related to taxable periods beginning on or after 1 January 2018, no exchanges could occur under the Convention for the year in review. Panama also has double tax agreements in force with 17 jurisdictions, however spontaneous exchange of information under these agreements is not authorised by Panama's domestic law as noted above.[2]

Completion and exchange of templates (ToR II.5.3, II.5.4, II.5.5, II.5.6, II.5.7)

986. Two dedicated officials within the tax analysis office (i.e. a BEPS analyst, responsible for compliance with the transparency framework and the head of the office coordinating the implementation of the BEPS Project) were in charge of completing the template contained in Annex C of the 2015 Action 5 Report (OECD, 2015). In respect of the one past ruling in scope of the transparency framework, the template was completed according to the instructions in the Action 5 Report, and the summary was drafted including the relevant details of the fiscal agreement. The template was then compared with the ruling itself and reviewed by two officers, one of which is a senior officer. The completed template was sent to the exchange of information office within the Dirección General de Ingresos ("DGI' or tax administration). Before transmitting the file to the

relevant jurisdictions, the exchange of information office reviews the technical and legal aspects of the exchanges.

987. The template on the past ruling was submitted to the exchange of information office in December 2017. If a future ruling was to be issued, it would be submitted to tax analysis office immediately after it had been issued. The tax analysis office shall complete the template and submit it to the exchange of information office for the actual exchange with relevant jurisdictions.

988. For the year in review, the timeliness of exchanges is as follows:

Past rulings in the scope of the transparency framework	Number of exchanges transmitted by 31 December 2017	Delayed exchanges		
		Number of exchanges not transmitted by 31 December 2017	Reasons for the delays	Any other comments
	0	1	See below	N/A
Future rulings in the scope of the transparency framework	Number of exchanges transmitted within three months of the information becoming available to the competent authority or immediately after legal impediments have been lifted	Delayed exchanges		
		Number of exchanges transmitted later than three months of the information on rulings becoming available to the competent authority	Reasons for the delays	Any other comments
	N/A	N/A	N/A	N/A
Total	0	1		

Follow up requests received for exchange of the ruling	Number	Average time to provide response	Number of requests not answered
	N/A	N/A	N/A

989. Information on the one ruling was not able to be exchanged as there was no legal basis permitting spontaneous exchange of information for the year in review. Panama will undertake the exchange of information in 2018 to the extent covered by the Convention.

Conclusion on section B

990. For the year under review, Panama was not required to undertake exchanges as it did not have the necessary legal framework in place for spontaneously exchanging information on rulings. Panama has implemented the legal framework and will conduct exchanges of information pursuant to that legal framework in 2018. Panama has met all of the ToR for the exchange of information.

C. Statistics (ToR IV)

991. As no information on rulings was exchanged for the year in review, no statistical data can be reported.

D. Matters related to intellectual property regimes (ToR I.4.1.3)

992. Panama offers an intellectual property regime ("IP regime").[3] However for the year in review no transparency requirements under the Action 5 report (OECD, 2015) were relevant, as follows:

- ***New entrants benefitting from the grandfathered IP regime***: not applicable for the year in review, because Panama is currently in the process of amending/abolishing the regime and has not yet decided whether it will allow grandfathering for new entrants. Should Panama provide grandfathering to taxpayers for which IP income benefits and that entered the regimes after the publication of the 2017 Progress Report (OECD, 2017), which occurred on 16 October 2017, transparency requirements will apply and this will be taken into account during the subsequent peer review.
- ***Third category of IP assets***: not applicable to this regimes, which in 2017 was in the process of being amended.
- ***Taxpayers making use of the option to treat the nexus ratio as a rebuttable presumption***: not applicable to this regimes, which in 2017 was in the process of being amended.

Summary of recommendations on implementation of the transparency framework

Aspect of implementation of the transparency framework that should be improved	Recommendation for improvement
	No recommendations are made.

Notes

[1] With respect to the following preferential regime: Multinational Companies Headquarters' regime (i.e. MHQ/SEM).

[2] Barbados, Czech Republic, France, Ireland, Israel, Italy, Korea, Luxembourg, Mexico, Netherlands, Portugal, Qatar, Singapore, Spain, United Arab Emirates, United Kingdom and Viet Nam.

[3] This regime is the City of knowledge technical zone.

References

OECD (2017), *BEPS Action 5 on Harmful Tax Practices – Terms of Reference and Methodology for the Conduct of the Peer Reviews of the Action 5 Transparency Framework*, OECD/G20 Base Erosion and Profit Shifting Project, OECD, Paris. www.oecd.org/tax/beps/beps-action-5-harmful-tax-practices-peer-review-transparencyframework.pdf.

OECD (2015), *Countering Harmful Tax Practices More Effectively, Taking into Account Transparency and Substance, Action 5 - 2015 Final Report*, OECD/G20 Base Erosion and Profit Shifting Project, OECD Publishing, Paris. https://doi.org/10.1787/9789264241190-en.

OECD/Council of Europe (2011), *The Multilateral Convention on Mutual Administrative Assistance in Tax Matters: Amended by the 2010 Protocol*, OECD Publishing, Paris. http://dx.doi.org/10.1787/9789264115606-en.

Papua New Guinea

Papua New Guinea has met all aspects of the terms of reference (ToR) for the calendar year 2017 (year in review) that can be met in the absence of rulings being issued.

Papua New Guinea cannot legally issue any type of rulings within the scope of the transparency framework.

As no rulings were issued, no exchange of information was required. Therefore no peer input was received in respect of the exchanges of information on rulings received from Papua New Guinea.

Introduction

993. This peer review covers Papua New Guinea's implementation of the BEPS Action 5 transparency framework for the year 2017. The report has four parts, each relating to a key part of the ToR. Each part is discussed in turn. A summary of recommendations is included at the end of this report.

A. The information gathering process

994. As no rulings are issued, this section is not assessed.

B. The exchange of information

995. As no rulings are issued, this section is not assessed.

C. Statistics (ToR IV)

996. As no rulings are issued, no statistical data can be reported.

D. Matters related to intellectual property regimes (ToR I.4.1.3)

997. Papua New Guinea does not offer an intellectual property regime for which transparency requirements under the Action 5 Report (OECD, 2015) were imposed.

Summary of recommendations on implementation of the transparency framework

Aspect of implementation of the transparency framework that should be improved	Recommendation for improvement
No recommendations are made.	

References

OECD (2017), *BEPS Action 5 on Harmful Tax Practices – Terms of Reference and Methodology for the Conduct of the Peer Reviews of the Action 5 Transparency Framework*, OECD/G20 Base Erosion and Profit Shifting Project, OECD, Paris. www.oecd.org/tax/beps/beps-action-5-harmful-tax-practices-peer-review-transparencyframework.pdf.

OECD (2015), *Countering Harmful Tax Practices More Effectively, Taking into Account Transparency and Substance, Action 5 - 2015 Final Report*, OECD/G20 Base Erosion and Profit Shifting Project, OECD Publishing, Paris. https://doi.org/10.1787/9789264241190-en.

Paraguay

Paraguay is taking steps to implement the legal basis for the transparency framework and to commence administrative preparations to ensure that information on rulings will be exchanged in a timely manner. Paraguay is recommended to finalise its information gathering process for identifying all past and future rulings and potential exchange jurisdictions, with a review and supervision mechanism, as soon as possible (ToR I.4). Paraguay is recommended to continue to put in place a domestic legal framework allowing spontaneous exchange of information on rulings and to continue its efforts to complete the templates for all relevant rulings and to ensure that the exchanges of information on rulings occur as soon as possible (ToR II.5).

Paraguay can legally issue one type of rulings within the scope of the transparency framework.

In practice, Paraguay has issued two past rulings; and for the calendar year 2017 (year in review), Paraguay issued no future rulings within the scope of the transparency framework.

As no exchanges of information on rulings were conducted, no peer input was received in respect of the exchanges of information on rulings received from Paraguay.

Introduction

998. This peer review covers Paraguay's implementation of the BEPS Action 5 transparency framework for the year 2017. The report has four parts, each relating to a key part of the ToR. Each part is discussed in turn. A summary of recommendations is included at the end of this report.

A. The information gathering process

999. Paraguay can legally issue one type of rulings within the scope of the transparency framework: rulings related to preferential regimes.[1] Rulings are issued by the drafting and interpretation department, part of the technical tax directorate of the secretary of state for taxation. This secretary is part of the Ministry of Finance. Rulings are published in the Paraguayan tax administration website in a redacted form.[2]

Past rulings (ToR I.4.1.1, I.4.1.2, I.4.2.1, I.4.2.2)

1000. For Paraguay, past rulings are any tax rulings within scope that are issued either: (i) on or after 1 January 2015 but before 1 April 2017; or (ii) on or after 1 January 2012 but before 1 January 2015, provided they were still in effect as at 1 January 2015.

1001. In Paraguay, taxpayers applying for a ruling submit the appropriate form along with other requested documentation and the ruling is drafted by a case officer and reviewed by the head of department, legal coordinator, Director of technical tax directorate, before it is signed by the tax vice minister and entered into a database. A team of seven people were responsible for the verification process whether a ruling it is in scope.

1002. Paraguay's tax administration checked the date of issue of each ruling in the database to determine whether it qualified as a past ruling. Once selected as a past ruling, it was then checked against the category of rulings to determine if it is within scope of Action 5. This was done by manually reading the ruling.

1003. In order to identify potential exchange jurisdictions, Paraguay made use of the "best efforts approach," which involved searching information in the general database of the tax administration. In most of the cases, Paraguay was able to identify all potential exchange jurisdictions.

Future rulings (ToR I.4.1.1, I.4.1.2, I.4.2.1)

1004. For Paraguay, future rulings are any tax rulings within scope that are issued on or after 1 April 2017.

1005. Paraguay's tax administration acknowledges that it is not yet recording information on tax rulings issued with the necessary level of detail to timely identify any new rulings. However, if a future ruling was issued, Paraguay acknowledges it can request this information from the taxpayers or it could access it in the tax administration database. As such, it is expected that Paraguay could obtain information on all potential exchange jurisdictions in most of the cases. It is noted that Paraguay intends to implement guidelines and practices to make sure the necessary information to meet the requirements of the transparency framework is required in all cases.

Review and supervision mechanism (ToR I.4.3)

1006. Paraguay did not yet have a review and supervision mechanism for past or future rulings under the transparency framework for the year in review. Paraguay is discussing the implementation of a revision and supervision mechanism for future rulings.

Conclusion on section A

1007. Paraguay is recommended to finalise its information gathering process for identifying all past and future rulings and potential exchange jurisdictions, with a review and supervision mechanism, as soon as possible (ToR I.4).

B. The exchange of information

Legal basis for spontaneous exchange of information (ToR II.5.1, II.5.2)

1008. Paraguay does not have the necessary domestic legal basis to exchange information on rulings spontaneously. This is because a domestic regulations on bank, professional and commercial secrecy, confidentiality and data protection specifically restrict the tax administration's use of the taxpayer's data. Paraguay is in the process of drafting legislation to address this legal impediment. Under Paraguay's legal system, treaty provisions enabling administrative power such as exchange of information can automatically override the legal provision regarding the restrictions on use of rulings information. However, Paraguay does not have yet any international agreements that provide for spontaneous exchange of information.

1009. Paraguay has signed the *Multilateral Convention on Mutual Administrative Assistance in Tax Matters: Amended by the 2010 Protocol* (OECD/Council of Europe, 2011) (the "Convention") which is currently in undergoing internal process before being sent to the Paraguayan Senate for ratification. Paraguay is encouraged to continue its efforts to expand its international exchange of information instruments to be able to exchange rulings with all members of the Inclusive Framework.

Completion and exchange of templates (ToR II.5.3, II.5.4, II.5.5, II.5.6, II.5.7)

1010. Paraguay is still developing a process to complete the templates on relevant rulings, to make them available to the Competent Authority for exchange of information, and to exchange them with relevant jurisdictions.

1011. With respect to the two past rulings identified within the scope of the transparency framework, it is noted that there was no obligation to exchange these rulings as there is no exchange of information agreement in place with the relevant jurisdictions.

Conclusion on section B

1012. Paraguay is recommended to continue to put in place a domestic legal framework allowing spontaneous exchange of information on rulings and to continue its efforts to complete the templates for all relevant rulings and to ensure that the exchanges of information on rulings occur as soon as possible (ToR II.5).

C. Statistics (ToR IV)

1013. As there was no legal basis for exchange in the year of review, no statistical data can be reported.

E. Matters related to intellectual property regimes (ToR I.4.1.3)

1014. Paraguay does not offer an intellectual property regime for which transparency requirements under the Action 5 Report (OECD, 2015) were imposed.

Summary of recommendations on implementation of the transparency framework

Aspect of implementation of the transparency framework that should be improved	Recommendation for improvement
Paraguay does not yet have in place a process to identify all information on potential exchange jurisdictions.	Paraguay is recommended to finalise its information gathering process for identifying all past and future rulings and potential exchange jurisdictions, with a review and supervision mechanism, as soon as possible.
Paraguay does not yet have in place a process for completion of templates and exchange of information on rulings.	Paraguay is recommended to continue to put in place a domestic legal framework allowing spontaneous exchange of information on rulings and to continue its efforts to complete the templates for all relevant rulings and to ensure that the exchanges of information on rulings occur as soon as possible.

Notes

[1] With respect to the following preferential regimes: Tax incentive for national and foreign origin investments regime.

[2] Available at: www.set.gov.py/portal/PARAGUAY-SET/Home/Normativas (accessed 20 November 2018).

References

OECD (2017), *BEPS Action 5 on Harmful Tax Practices – Terms of Reference and Methodology for the Conduct of the Peer Reviews of the Action 5 Transparency Framework*, OECD/G20 Base Erosion and Profit Shifting Project, OECD, Paris. www.oecd.org/tax/beps/beps-action-5-harmful-tax-practices-peer-review-transparencyframework.pdf.

OECD (2015), *Countering Harmful Tax Practices More Effectively, Taking into Account Transparency and Substance, Action 5 - 2015 Final Report*, OECD/G20 Base Erosion and Profit Shifting Project, OECD Publishing, Paris. https://doi.org/10.1787/9789264241190-en.

OECD/Council of Europe (2011), *The Multilateral Convention on Mutual Administrative Assistance in Tax Matters: Amended by the 2010 Protocol*, OECD Publishing, Paris. http://dx.doi.org/10.1787/9789264115606-en.

Peru

Peru has met the terms of reference (ToR) for the calendar year 2017 (year in review).

Peru can legally issue five types of rulings within the scope of the transparency framework.

In practice, Peru issued no rulings within in the scope of the transparency framework.

As no rulings were issued, no exchange of information was required. Therefore no peer input was received in respect of exchanges of information on rulings received from Peru.

Introduction

1015. This peer review covers Peru's implementation of the BEPS Action 5 transparency framework for the year 2017. The report has four parts, each relating to a key part of the ToR. Each part is discussed in turn. A summary of recommendations is included at the end of this report.

A. The information gathering process

1016. Peru can legally issue the five following types of rulings within the scope of the transparency framework: (i) rulings relating to a preferential regime;[1] (ii) cross-border unilateral advance pricing arrangements (APAs) and any other cross-border unilateral tax rulings (such as an advance tax ruling) covering transfer pricing or the application of transfer pricing principles; (iii) cross-border rulings providing for a downward adjustment of taxable profits; (iv) permanent establishment (PE) rulings; and (v) related party conduit rulings. Rulings other than APAs are known in Peru as "particular consultations." In Peru, the Central Office of Large National Taxpayers (*Intendencia de Principales Contribuyentes Nacionales - IPCN*), which is an operational area of SUNAT, is in charge of issuing both the particular consultations and the APAs.

Past rulings (ToR I.4.1.1, I.4.1.2, I.4.2.1, I.4.2.2)

1017. For Peru, past rulings are any tax rulings within scope that are issued either: (i) on or after 1 January 2015 but before 1 September 2017; or (ii) on or after 1 January 2012 but before 1 January 2015, provided still in effect as at 1 January 2015.

1018. The process for identifying past rulings was conducted as follows. The SUNAT Central Legal Area (*Intendencia Nacional Jurídica Tributaria- INJT*) was in charge of identifying all possible documents that could qualify as rulings under the transparency framework. As a result of the evaluation carried out, INJT concluded that particular consultations and the APAs could be in scope of the transparency framework because they are binding on the tax administration and apply to specific taxpayer circumstances.

1019. The IPCN office works independently but under the control of the Strategy and Risk Unit (*Intendencia Nacional de Estrategias y Riesgos – INER*). IPCN is compelled to report to INER on the issuance of particular consultations and APAs on a rolling basis. An internal database is maintained by the IPCN office for particular consultations, but not yet for APA rulings since the IPCN office has not issued any APAs. If and when APA rulings will be issued, a dedicated database will be maintained by the IPCN office. INER reviewed the report sent by the IPCN office, which is based on the internal database, and read each particular consultation issued by that unit in order to determine if it was in the scope of the transparency framework, and if it was within the period of validity defined as past rulings. INER confirmed that no relevant rulings had been issued.

1020. As there were no relevant rulings issued, it was not relevant to identify any potential exchange jurisdictions.

Future rulings (ToR I.4.1.1, I.4.1.2, I.4.2.1)

1021. For Peru, future rulings are any tax rulings within scope that are issued on or after 1 September 2017.

1022. Based on the same procedure adopted for past rulings, the INER established that no future rulings in the scope of the transparency framework had been issued. INER reviewed the reports sent, on a rolling basis, by the IPCN office, which is based on the internal database (available for particular consultations but not for APA rulings since the IPCN office has not issued any APA yet) and read each particular consultation issued by that unit in order to determine if it was in the scope of the transparency framework, and if it was within the period of validity defined as future rulings. A dedicated team within INER will be appointed to analyse the issuance of rulings on a monthly basis and to keep information updated and report statistics to all interested stakeholders.

1023. As no future rulings were issued, it was not relevant for Peru to identify the potential exchange jurisdictions for the year in review. If a relevant ruling was issued in the future, Peru notes its intention to put in place a procedure by the end of 2019 for identifying the relevant exchange jurisdictions. Peru notes that if a ruling was issued before the establishment of the new procedure, then INER would review information contained in the ruling itself, and if necessary additional information could be obtained by consulting the taxpayer´s internal file or asking the taxpayer directly.

Review and supervision mechanism (ToR I.4.3)

1024. Officers at the INER have been trained on the requirements of the transparency framework. A "Strategic Office Manager" is currently in charge of supervising the process. Peru notes that by the end of 2019, it will put in place a more formal procedure on this subject.

Conclusion on section A

1025. Peru has met all of the ToR for the information gathering process and no recommendations are made.

B. The exchange of information

Legal basis for spontaneous exchange of information (ToR II.5.1, II.5.2)

1026. Peru has the necessary domestic legal basis to exchange information spontaneously. Peru notes that there are no legal or practical impediments that prevent the spontaneous exchange of information on rulings as contemplated in the Action 5 minimum standard.

1027. Peru is a party to international agreements permitting spontaneous exchange of information, including (i) the *Multilateral Convention on Mutual Administrative Assistance in Tax Matters: Amended by the 2010 Protocol* (OECD/Council of Europe, 2011) ("the Convention")[2] and (ii) international tax agreements in force with ten jurisdictions.[3]

Completion and exchange of templates (ToR II.5.3, II.5.4, II.5.5, II.5.6, II.5.7)

1028. Peru will put in place a formal procedure for the completion and exchange of templates by the end of 2019. Peru notes that if a ruling was issued before the establishment of the new procedure, then the process would be the following. The Strategic Office Manager at INER will be in charge of the evaluation of the particular consultations and APA rulings with respect to the identification of the jurisdictions affected by cross-border rulings and will be responsible for the preparation of the templates. The templates, including reference to the internal FHTP suggested guidance on the summary section, will then be delivered to the Peruvian Competent Authority through an internal procedure currently used for the exchange of information on request. The Peruvian Competent Authority will forward the templates to the Competent Authorities of the relevant jurisdictions without undue delay and according to the timelines in the transparency framework.

1029. As Peru did not issue any past or future rulings in scope of the transparency framework in the relevant periods, Peru was not required to exchange any information on rulings in the year in review and no data on the timeliness of exchanges can be reported.

Conclusion on section B

1030. Peru has the necessary legal framework and administrative process in place for exchanging information on rulings. Peru has met all of the ToR for the exchange of information process that can be met in the absence of rulings being issued and exchanged in practice and no recommendations are made.

C. Statistics (ToR IV)

1031. As there were no rulings required to be exchanged by Peru for the year in review, no statistics can be reported.

D. Matters related to intellectual property regimes (ToR I.4.1.3)

1032. Peru does not offer an intellectual property regime for which transparency requirements under the Action 5 Report (OECD, 2015) were imposed.

Summary of recommendations on implementation of the transparency framework

Aspect of implementation of the transparency framework that should be improved	Recommendation for improvement
	No recommendations are made.

Notes

[1] With respect to the following preferential regimes: Special economic zone 1 (Ceticos) and/or Special economic zone 2 (Zofratacna).

[2] The Convention was signed on 25 October 2017 and ratified by Supreme Decree N° 012-2018-RE, published on 24 May 2018.

[3] Peru has bilateral agreements in force with Argentina, Brazil, Canada, Chile, Ecuador, Korea, Mexico, Portugal, Switzerland and United States.

References

OECD (2017), *BEPS Action 5 on Harmful Tax Practices – Terms of Reference and Methodology for the Conduct of the Peer Reviews of the Action 5 Transparency Framework*, OECD/G20 Base Erosion and Profit Shifting Project, OECD, Paris. www.oecd.org/tax/beps/beps-action-5-harmful-tax-practices-peer-review-transparencyframework.pdf.

OECD (2015), *Countering Harmful Tax Practices More Effectively, Taking into Account Transparency and Substance, Action 5 - 2015 Final Report*, OECD/G20 Base Erosion and Profit Shifting Project, OECD Publishing, Paris. https://doi.org/10.1787/9789264241190-en.

OECD/Council of Europe (2011), *The Multilateral Convention on Mutual Administrative Assistance in Tax Matters: Amended by the 2010 Protocol*, OECD Publishing, Paris. http://dx.doi.org/10.1787/9789264115606-en.

Philippines

The Philippines is taking steps to implement the legal basis for the transparency framework and to commence administrative preparations to ensure that information on rulings will be exchanged once the new legal basis is in place. The Philippines has met all of the terms of reference (ToR) for the calendar year 2017 (year in review) except for identifying all potential exchange jurisdictions for both past and future rulings (ToR I.4.2.1 and ToR I.4.2.2) and having in place a review and supervision mechanism (ToR I.4.3), having in place a domestic legal framework allowing spontaneous exchange of information on rulings by ensuring the timely exchange of information on rulings in the form required by the transparency framework (ToR II.5). The Philippines is recommended to apply the "best efforts approach" to identify potential exchange jurisdictions for all past rulings, to ensure that all potential exchange jurisdictions are identified swiftly for future rulings and to have in place a review and supervision mechanism to ensure that all relevant information is captured adequately, and to continue its efforts to put in place a domestic legal framework allowing spontaneous exchange of information on rulings and to ensure the timely exchange of information on rulings in the form required by the transparency framework.

The Philippines can legally issue one type of rulings within the scope of the transparency framework.

In practice, the Philippines has issued 78 past rulings; and for the period 1 September 2017 - 31 December 2017, the Philippines issued four future rulings within the scope of the transparency framework.

As the Philippines did not have the necessary domestic legal framework for spontaneous exchange of information for the year in review, no exchanges were permitted to occur.[1] As such, no peer input was received in respect of the exchanges of information on rulings received from the Philippines.

Introduction

1033. This peer review covers the Philippines's implementation of the BEPS Action 5 transparency framework for the year 2017. The report has four parts, each relating to a key part of the ToR. Each part is discussed in turn. A summary of recommendations is included at the end of this report.

A. The information gathering process

1034. The Philippnes can legally issue the following type of rulings within the scope of the transparency framework: permanent establishment rulings.[2] Rulings are issued by the International Affairs Division ("ITAD") of the Bureau of Internal Revenue ("BIR"). The Philippines published taxpayer specific rulings in redacted form until 2015.[3]

1035. The Philippines has commenced the information gathering process in advance of the legal basis for spontaneously exchanging information on rulings being finalised.

Past rulings (ToR I.4.1.1, I.4.1.2, I.4.2.1, I.4.2.2)

1036. For the Philippines, past rulings are any tax rulings within scope that are issued either: (i) on or after 1 January 2015 but before 1 September 2017; or (ii) on or after 1 January 2012 but before 1 January 2015, provided they were still in effect as at 1 January 2015.

1037. All rulings issued by BIR had been recorded in a database. In order to determine the period of validity for past rulings, the BIR checked the date of issue of each ruling in the database. Once selected as a past ruling, each ruling was then read and checked against the category of rulings to determine whether it was within scope of the Action 5 Report.

1038. In order to identify potential exchange jurisdictions, the BIR checked each ruling manually. With respect to PE rulings, the rulings contain information identifying the residence country of the head office or of the PE and the immediate parent company as this information has to be provided by the taxpayer in the form of audited financial statements and/or other corporate documents when applying for the ruling. It is noted however, that for the PE rulings (including tax treaty relief rulings), information on the ultimate parent company is not provided by the taxpayer. As such, the Philippines is recommended to apply the "best efforts approach" to identify potential exchange jurisdictions for all past rulings.

Future rulings (ToR I.4.1.1, I.4.1.2, I.4.2.1)

1039. For the Philippines, future rulings are any tax rulings within scope that are issued on or after 1 September 2017.

1040. The BIR checked the date of issue of each ruling in the database to determine whether it qualified as a future ruling. Once selected as a future ruling, it was then checked against the category of rulings to determine if it is within scope of Action 5.

1041. The BIR also indicated that it is in the process of updating the rulings process with respect to future rulings in order to flag future rulings in the database that are in scope of Action 5 at the point at which they are issued.

1042. In order to identify the potential exchange jurisdictions, the BIR would read the ruling itself, which, as is the case for past rulings, would contain information on all potential exchange jurisdictions, except the ultimate parent company. As such, the Philippines is recommended to ensure that all potential exchange jurisdictions are identified swiftly for future rulings.

Review and supervision mechanism (ToR I.4.3)

1043. The Philippines has a review and supervision process governing the issuance and recording of rulings, which facilitates the identification of past and future rulings. However, it is not clear that the Philippines has a process for reviewing and supervising the implementation of the transparency framework to ensure that all relevant information on the identification of rulings and potential exchange jurisdictions is captured adequately. Therefore, the Philippines is recommended to have in place a review and supervision mechanism to ensure that all relevant information is captured adequately.

Conclusion on section A

1044. The Philippines has met all of the ToR for the information gathering process, except for applying the "best efforts approach" for past rulings (ToR I.4.2.2), identifying all potential exchange jurisdictions for future rulings (ToR I.4.2.1) and having in place a review and supervision mechanism (ToR I.4.3). The Philippines is recommended to apply the "best efforts approach" for past rulings with respect to identifying the ultimate parent company, to ensure that all potential exchange jurisdictions are identified swiftly for future rulings and to have in place a review and supervision mechanism to ensure that all relevant information is captured adequately.

B. The exchange of information

Legal basis for spontaneous exchange of information (ToR II.5.1, II.5.2)

1045. The Philippines does not have the necessary domestic legal basis to exchange information on rulings spontaneously. This is because the Philippines is legally prohibited from sharing information on, or copies of, rulings other than to the applicant taxpayer. The Philippines is currently in the process of amending the Tax Code to allow spontaneous exchange of ruling information through a comprehensive tax reform programme currently underway.

1046. The Philippines is a party to international agreements permitting spontaneous exchange of information, including double tax agreements with 43 jurisdictions.[4] The Philippines has signed the *Multilateral Convention on Mutual Administrative Assistance in Tax Matters: Amended by the 2010 Protocol* (OECD/Council of Europe, 2011) ("the Convention") which is currently with the Philippines Senate for concurrence. Once the Convention enters into force, the spontaneous exchange of information could also be done with all jurisdictions that are covered by the Convention.

Completion and exchange of templates (ToR II.5.3, II.5.4, II.5.5, II.5.6, II.5.7)

1047. As the Philippines does not yet have the legal basis for exchanges, the process for the completion and exchange of templates has not been put in place.

1048. For the year in review, as there is no domestic legal basis for exchange, no data on the timeliness of exchanges can be reported.

Conclusion on section B

1049. The Philippines is recommended to continue its efforts to put in place a domestic legal framework allowing spontaneous exchange of information on rulings and to ensure the timely exchange of information on rulings in the form required by the transparency framework (ToR II.5).

C. Statistics (ToR IV)

1050. As there was no legal basis for exchange in the year of review, no statistical data can be reported.

D. Matters related to intellectual property regimes (ToR I.4.1.3)

1051. The Philippines does not offer an intellectual property regime for which transparency requirements under the Action 5 Report (OECD, 2015) were imposed.

Summary of recommendations on implementation of the transparency framework

Aspect of implementation of the transparency framework that should be improved	Recommendation for improvement
The Philippines does not currently collect information on all potential exchange jurisdictions, particularly the ultimate parent company for past rulings.	The Philippines is recommended to apply the "best efforts approach" to identify potential exchange jurisdictions for all past rulings.
The Philippines does not currently collect information on all potential exchange jurisdictions, particularly the ultimate parent company for future rulings.	The Philippines is recommended to ensure that all potential exchange jurisdictions are identified swiftly for future rulings.
The Philippines does not have a review and supervision mechanism in place to ensure that all relevant information on the identification of rulings and potential exchange jurisdictions is captured adequately.	The Philippines is recommended to have in place a review and supervision mechanism to ensure that all relevant information is captured adequately.
The Philippines does not yet have the necessary domestic legal framework in place for exchanging information on rulings and a process in place to ensure the timely exchange of information on rulings in the form required by the transparency framework.	The Philippines is recommended to continue to put in place a domestic legal framework allowing spontaneous exchange of information on rulings and to ensure the timely exchange of information on rulings in the form required by the transparency framework.

Notes

[1] The Action 5 Report notes that jurisdictions which do not currently have the necessary legal framework in place for spontaneous exchange of information on rulings will need to put in place such a framework in order to comply with the obligations under Action 5, but that in such cases the timelines are subject to a country's legal framework.

[2] The Philippines is currently in the process of implementing international standards on transfer pricing and therefore not yet able to issue rulings which involve transfer pricing.

[3] Available at: www.bir.gov.ph/index.php/rulings-and-legal-matters/rulings.html (accessed 20 November 2018).

[4] The Philippines has bilateral agreements in force with Australia, Austria, Bahrain, Bangladesh, Belgium, Brazil, Canada, China (People's Republic), Czech Republic, Denmark, Finland, France, Germany, Hungary, India, Indonesia, Israel, Italy, Japan, Korea, Kuwait, Malaysia, Mexico, Netherlands, New Zealand, Nigeria, Norway, Pakistan, Poland, Qatar, Romania, Russia, Singapore, Spain, Sri Lanka, Sweden, Switzerland, Thailand, Turkey, United Arab Emirates, United Kingdom, United States and Viet Nam.

References

OECD (2017), *BEPS Action 5 on Harmful Tax Practices – Terms of Reference and Methodology for the Conduct of the Peer Reviews of the Action 5 Transparency Framework*, OECD/G20 Base Erosion and Profit Shifting Project, OECD, Paris. www.oecd.org/tax/beps/beps-action-5-harmful-tax-practices-peer-review-transparencyframework.pdf.

OECD (2015), *Countering Harmful Tax Practices More Effectively, Taking into Account Transparency and Substance, Action 5 - 2015 Final Report*, OECD/G20 Base Erosion and Profit Shifting Project, OECD Publishing, Paris. https://doi.org/10.1787/9789264241190-en.

OECD/Council of Europe (2011), *The Multilateral Convention on Mutual Administrative Assistance in Tax Matters: Amended by the 2010 Protocol*, OECD Publishing, Paris. http://dx.doi.org/10.1787/9789264115606-en.

Poland

Poland has met all aspects of the terms of reference (ToR) for the calendar year 2017 (year in review) except for identifying all potential exchange jurisdictions for future rulings other than APAs (ToR I.4.2.1). Poland is recommended to ensure all potential exchange jurisdictions are swiftly identified for all future rulings other than APAs.

Poland can legally issue four types of rulings within the scope of the transparency framework.

In practice, Poland has issued 84 past rulings; for the period 1 April 2016 - 31 December 2016, Poland issued six future rulings; and for the year in review, Poland issued 20 future rulings within the scope of the transparency framework.

Peer input was received from two jurisdictions in respect of the exchanges of information on rulings from Poland. The input was positive, noting that the information was complete, in the correct format and received in a timely manner.

Introduction

1052. This peer review covers Poland's implementation of the BEPS Action 5 transparency framework for the year 2017. The report has four parts, each relating to a key part of the ToR. Each part is discussed in turn. A summary of recommendations is included at the end of this report.

A. The information gathering process

1053. Poland can legally issue the four following types of rulings within the scope of the transparency framework: (i) cross-border unilateral advance pricing arrangements (APAs) and any other cross-border unilateral tax ruling (such as an advance tax ruling) covering transfer pricing or the application of transfer pricing principles; (ii) unilateral downward adjustments; (iii) permanent establishment rulings and (iv) related party conduit rulings. In Poland, rulings within the transparency framework (except for APAs) were before 1 March 2017 issued by the authorised directors of Tax Chambers of the National Revenue Administration in five local offices in Bydgoszcz, Katowice, Lodz, Poznan and Warsaw ("NRA"). As of 1 March 2017 rulings are issued by the Director of National Fiscal Information. APAs are issued by a separate unit in the Ministry of Finance. Rulings other than APAs are published in anonymised form.

Past rulings (ToR I.4.1.1, I.4.1.2, I.4.2.1, I.4.2.2)

1054. For Poland, past rulings are any tax rulings within scope that are issued either: (i) on or after 1 January 2014 but before 1 April 2016; or (ii) on or after 1 January 2010 but before 1 January 2014, provided they were still in effect as at 1 January 2014.

1055. In the prior year peer review report, it was determined that Poland's undertakings to identify past rulings were sufficient to meet the minimum standard. However, Poland only started the identification process of past rulings other than APAs in May 2017. Poland identified an additional 65 past rulings which were not identified in the prior year. As this is a non-recurring issue, and Poland completed the identification of these past rulings within the year of review, no recommendation is made.

1056. Further, in the prior year peer review report Poland was recommended to complete the process for identifying the potential exchange jurisdictions for past rulings other than APAs by using the "best efforts approach". Poland has used the "best efforts approach" which involved verifying the rulings applications and searching through internal databases to identify the potential exchange jurisdictions for all past rulings other than APAs. Poland confirms that in all cases, all potential exchange jurisdictions were able to be identified. It is therefore determined that Poland's undertakings to identify the potential exchange jurisdictions with respect to past rulings meet the minimum standard.

Future rulings (ToR I.4.1.1, I.4.1.2, I.4.2.1)

1057. For Poland, future rulings are any tax rulings within scope that are issued on or after 1 April 2016.

1058. In the prior year peer review report, it was determined that Poland's undertakings to identify future rulings were sufficient to meet the minimum standard. However, it was recommended that Poland amend its rulings practices for all future rulings (APAs and other rulings) to capture information on all potential exchange jurisdictions in the course of issuing the rulings.

1059. With respect to APAs, in May 2017 Poland changed the process for issuing APAs, to include a requirement that the taxpayer provides details of all foreign entities related to the taxpayer, and therefore including all potential exchange jurisdictions. Prior to the adoption of this new procedure, in any cases where the information was not provided by the taxpayer, the Orbis database was searched to identify all potential exchange jurisdictions. The information on all potential exchange jurisdictions is verified during the exchange of information process.

1060. With respect to rulings other than APAs, it is noted that there were some delays in identifying all potential exchange jurisdictions during the year in review, meaning that not all potential exchange jurisdictions for these future rulings issued in 2017 were able to be identified (and therefore could not be exchanged). This was due to staff shortages, organisational changes and administrative constraints, which Poland has taken steps to address. As such, Poland is recommended to continue its efforts to ensure that all potential exchange jurisdictions are identified swiftly for future rulings other than APAs. Poland notes that in order to address this issue it has started legislative work to introduce a new section in the ruling request form obliging taxpayers to indicate all potential jurisdictions affected by other rulings. Poland foresees that this form will be used as from 1 January 2019.

Review and supervision mechanism (ToR I.4.3)

1061. In the prior year peer review report, it was determined that the Poland's review and supervision mechanism was sufficient to meet the minimum standard.

Conclusion on section A

1062. Poland has met all of the ToR for the information gathering process, except for identifying all potential exchange jurisdictions for future rulings other than APAs (ToR I.4.2.1). As such, Poland is recommended to ensure that all potential exchange jurisdictions are identified swiftly for future rulings other than APAs.

B. The exchange of information

Legal basis for spontaneous exchange of information (ToR II.5.1, II.5.2)

1063. Poland has the necessary domestic legal basis to exchange information spontaneously. Poland notes that there are no legal or practical impediments that prevent the spontaneous exchange of information on rulings as contemplated in the Action 5 minimum standard.

1064. Poland is a party to international agreements permitting spontaneous exchange of information, including (i) the *Multilateral Convention on Mutual Administrative Assistance in Tax Matters: Amended by the 2010 Protocol* (OECD/Council of Europe, 2011) ("the Convention"), (ii) the Directive 2011/16/EU with all other European Union Member States and (iii) double tax agreements in force with 85 jurisdictions.[1]

Completion and exchange of templates (ToR II.5.3, II.5.4, II.5.5, II.5.6, II.5.7)

1065. In the prior year peer review report, it was recommended that Poland put in place the necessary process to prepare the information and exchange all information on rulings with the relevant jurisdictions as soon as possible.

1066. In May 2017, Poland put in place a process for exchanging information on rulings under the transparency framework. An internal APA unit was developed and the exchange information responsibility was assigned to a dedicated employee within the APA unit. The information template was prepared by the designated employee using the OECD XML template and the European Commission's central directory, which ensured that all necessary fields in the form are completed. A final check is undertaken outside APA unit. Poland has put in place a similar process for rulings other than APAs, with the exception that the information is sent to Central Liaison Office by an employee of the National Fiscal Administration (being the office in charge of issuing other rulings), instead of an employee of the Ministry of Finance.

1067. Poland used the suggested FHTP internal guidance to complete the summary section (section 7) of the template contained in Annex C of the Action 5 Report (OECD, 2015). Poland also indicates that the process for completing the template has been updated as of 1 January 2018 and this will be assessed in the next annual peer review.

1068. In Poland, information on rulings to be exchanged under the transparency framework is sent to the Head of the NRA Information Centre, who is the Competent Authority, no later than by the end of the month following the month in which the tax ruling was issued, amended or renewed, as prescribed by the NRA's internal regulations.

1069. For the year in review, the timeliness of exchanges is as follows:

Past rulings in the scope of the transparency framework	Number of exchanges transmitted by 31 December 2017	Delayed exchanges		
		Number of exchanges not transmitted by 31 December 2017	Reasons for the delays	Any other comments
	96	9	See below	The nine outstanding exchanges were completed by February 2018.
Future rulings in the scope of the transparency framework	Number of exchanges transmitted within three months of the information becoming available to the competent authority or immediately after legal impediments have been lifted	Delayed exchanges		
		Number of exchanges transmitted later than three months of the information on rulings becoming available to the competent authority	Reasons for the delays	Any other comments
	22	2	See below	The two outstanding exchanges were completed by February 2018.
Total	118	11		

Follow up requests received for exchange of the ruling	Number	Average time to provide response	Number of requests not answered
	0	N/A	N/A

1070. Poland explains that the delays in transmitting the information on APA rulings result from staff shortages within the APA unit, with only one employee being in charge of the completion process for templates in the APA unit in 2017. In addition, in Poland, internal law also requires APA proceedings to be held in Polish and as a result of very strict limitation on access to data, the translation from Polish to English of all the APAs had to be done by a single person, thus exacerbating the delays. As a result of organisational changes within the Polish tax administration, there were also delays in exchanging other rulings. Poland indicates that it has taken steps in late 2017 and beginning of 2018 to ensure that the problems are addressed and to ensure that the remaining exchanges on rulings were completed by February 2018.

Conclusion on section B

1071. In the year in review, Poland has put in place procedures and processes to complete the templates and exchange the information with other jurisdictions. However, it is noted that there were delays for a number of exchanges for past and future rulings. Poland has exchanged all information on past and future rulings by February 2018. It is determined that the delays will not be a recurring issue and that Poland has met all of the ToR for the exchange of information process and no recommendations are made.

C. Statistics (ToR IV)

1072. The statistics for the year in review are as follows:

Category of ruling	Number of exchanges	Jurisdictions exchanged with
Rulings related to preferential regimes	N/A	N/A
Cross-border unilateral advance pricing agreements (APAs) and any other cross-border unilateral tax rulings (such as an advance tax ruling) covering transfer pricing or the application of transfer pricing principles	18	Austria, Belgium, France, Germany, Italy, Luxembourg, Netherlands, Portugal, Spain, Sweden, United Kingdom
Cross-border rulings providing for a unilateral downward adjustment to the taxpayer's taxable profits that is not directly reflected in the taxpayer's financial / commercial accounts	14	Australia, Germany, Norway, Switzerland, United States
Permanent establishment rulings	30	Belgium, Cyprus, Denmark, France, Germany, Ireland, Iceland, Liechtenstein, Lithuania, Netherlands, Sweden, Switzerland, United States
Related party conduit rulings	56	Canada, Cyprus, Denmark, France, Germany, Ireland, Korea, Luxembourg, Netherlands, Portugal, Sweden, Switzerland, United States
De minimis rule	N/A	N/A
IP regimes: total exchanges on taxpayers benefitting from the third category of IP assets, new entrants benefitting from grandfathered IP regimes; and taxpayers making use of the option to treat the nexus ratio as a rebuttable presumption	N/A	N/A
Total	118	

D. Matters related to intellectual property regimes (ToR I.4.1.3)

1073. Poland does not offer an intellectual property regime for which transparency requirements under the Action 5 Report (OECD, 2015) were imposed.

Summary of recommendations on implementation of the transparency framework

Aspect of implementation of the transparency framework that should be improved	Recommendation for improvement
Poland encountered delays in identifying all potential exchange jurisdictions for future rulings other than APAs. This is a continuing recommendation from the prior year peer review.	Poland is recommended to ensure that all potential exchange jurisdictions are identified swiftly for future rulings other than APAs.
A number of the exchanges on information on rulings were not sent to all potential exchange jurisdictions.	No recommendation is made because Poland completed the exchanges of information on all past and future rulings by February 2018 and steps have been taken to ensure that this does not recur.

Note

1 Parties to the Convention are available here: www.oecd.org/tax/exchange-of-tax-information/convention-on-mutual-administrative-assistance-in-tax-matters.htm. Poland also has bilateral agreements with Albania, Armenia, Australia, Austria, Azerbaijan, Bangladesh, Belarus, Belgium, Bosnia and Herzegovina, Bulgaria, Canada, Chile, China (People's Republic of), Croatia, Cyprus, Czech Republic, Denmark, Egypt, Estonia, Finland, Former Yugoslav Republic of Macedonia, France, Georgia, Germany, Greece, Guernsey, Hungary, Iceland, India, Indonesia, Iran, Ireland, Isle of Man, Israel, Italy, Japan, Jersey, Jordan, Kazakhstan, Korea, Kuwait, Kyrgyzstan, Latvia, Lebanon, Lithuania, Luxembourg, Malaysia, Malta, Mexico, Moldova, Mongolia, Montenegro, Morocco, Netherlands, New Zealand, Norway, Pakistan, Philippines, Portugal, Qatar, Romania, Russia, Saudi Arabia, Serbia, Singapore, Slovak Republic, Slovenia, South Africa, Spain, Sri Lanka, Sweden, Switzerland, Syria, Chinese Taipei, Tajikistan, Thailand, Tunisia, Turkey, Ukraine, United Arab Emirates, United Kingdom, United States, Uzbekistan, Viet Nam and Zimbabwe.

Note by Turkey: The information in this document with reference to "Cyprus" relates to the southern part of the Island. There is no single authority representing both Turkish and Greek Cypriot people on the Island. Turkey recognises the Turkish Republic of Northern Cyprus (TRNC). Until a lasting and equitable solution is found within the context of the United Nations, Turkey shall preserve its position concerning the "Cyprus issue".

Note by all the European Union Member States of the OECD and the European Union. The Republic of Cyprus is recognised by all members of the United Nations with the exception of Turkey. The information in this document relates to the area under the effective control of the Government of the Republic of Cyprus.

References

OECD (2017), *BEPS Action 5 on Harmful Tax Practices – Terms of Reference and Methodology for the Conduct of the Peer Reviews of the Action 5 Transparency Framework*, OECD/G20 Base Erosion and Profit Shifting Project, OECD, Paris. www.oecd.org/tax/beps/beps-action-5-harmful-tax-practices-peer-review-transparencyframework.pdf.

OECD (2015), *Countering Harmful Tax Practices More Effectively, Taking into Account Transparency and Substance, Action 5 - 2015 Final Report*, OECD/G20 Base Erosion and Profit Shifting Project, OECD Publishing, Paris. https://doi.org/10.1787/9789264241190-en.

OECD/Council of Europe (2011), *The Multilateral Convention on Mutual Administrative Assistance in Tax Matters: Amended by the 2010 Protocol*, OECD Publishing, Paris. http://dx.doi.org/10.1787/9789264115606-en.

Portugal

Portugal has met all of the terms of reference (ToR) for the calendar year 2017 (year in review) other than the timely exchange of information on future rulings (ToR II.5.6). Portugal is recommended to ensure that all information on future rulings is exchanged as soon as possible. This recommendation was also included in the prior year peer review report.

Portugal can legally issue two types of rulings within the scope of the transparency framework.

In practice, Portugal issued 24 past rulings; for the period 1 April 2016 - 31 December 2016, Portugal issued two future rulings; and for the year in review, Portugal issued 11 future rulings within the scope of the transparency framework.

Peer input was received from three jurisdictions in respect of the exchanges of information on rulings received from Portugal. This input was largely positive, noting that information was complete, in the correct format, and mostly received in a timely manner. One jurisdiction noted exchange delays in relation to future rulings.

Introduction

1074. This peer review covers Portugal's implementation of the BEPS Action 5 transparency framework for the year 2017. The report has four parts, each relating to a key part of the ToR. Each part is discussed in turn. A summary of recommendations is included at the end of this report.

A. The information gathering process

1075. Portugal can legally issue the following two types of rulings within the scope of the transparency framework: (i) cross-border unilateral APAs and any other cross-border unilateral tax ruling (such as an ATR) covering transfer pricing or the application of transfer pricing principles; and (ii) permanent establishment rulings. In Portugal, the Large Taxpayers Office is responsible for issuing APAs and the Corporate Income Tax Office (IRC Directorate) is responsible for issuing the other categories of rulings.

Past rulings (ToR I.4.1.1, I.4.1.2, I.4.2.1, I.4.2.2)

1076. For Portugal, past rulings are any tax rulings within scope that are issued either: (i) on or after 1 January 2014 but before 1 April 2016; or (ii) on or after 1 January 2010 but before 1 January 2014, provided they were still in effect as at 1 January 2014.

1077. In the prior year peer review report, it was determined that the Portuguese tax administration's undertakings to identify past rulings and all potential exchange jurisdictions were sufficient to meet the minimum standard. The Portuguese tax administration's implementation in this regard remains unchanged, and therefore continues to meet the minimum standard.

Future rulings (ToR I.4.1.1, I.4.1.2, I.4.2.1)

1078. For Portugal, future rulings are any tax rulings within scope that are issued on or after 1 April 2016.

1079. In the prior year peer review report, it was determined that the Portuguese tax administration's implementation of a new system to identify future rulings and all potential exchange jurisdictions was sufficient to meet the minimum standard. The Portuguese tax administration's implementation in this regard remains unchanged, and therefore continues to meet the minimum standard.

Review and supervision mechanism (ToR I.4.3)

1080. In the prior year peer review report, it was determined that the Portuguese tax administration's review and supervision mechanism was sufficient to meet the minimum standard. The Portuguese tax administration's implementation in this regard remains unchanged, and therefore continues to meet the minimum standard.

Conclusion on section A

1081. Portugal has met all of the ToR for the information gathering process and no recommendations are made.

B. The exchange of information

Legal basis for spontaneous exchange of information (ToR II.5.1, II.5.2)

1082. Portugal has the necessary domestic legal basis to exchange information spontaneously. Portugal notes that there are no legal or practical impediments that prevent the spontaneous exchange of information on rulings as contemplated in the Action 5 minimum standard.

1083. Portugal is a party to international agreements permitting spontaneous exchange of information, including (i) the *Multilateral Convention on Mutual Administrative Assistance in Tax Matters: Amended by the 2010 Protocol* (OECD/Council of Europe, 2011) (the Convention), (ii) the Directive 2011/16/EU with all other European Union Member States and (iii) double tax agreements in force with 76 jurisdictions.[1]

Completion and exchange of templates (ToR II.5.3, II.5.4, II.5.5, II.5.6, II.5.7)

1084. In the prior year peer review report, it was determined that the Portuguese tax administration's completion and exchange of templates was sufficient to meet the minimum standard, except for the timely exchange of information on past and future rulings (ToR II.5.6). Portugal received a recommendation to ensure the speedy exchange of all past and future rulings. Portugal has now completed the exchange of all past rulings that were delayed from the prior year peer review report, and most of the future rulings delayed from the prior year peer review report.

1085. Portugal uses both Annex C of the Action 5 Report (OECD, 2015) and the OECD XML Schema. Before sending the information to the competent authority, its accuracy and completeness is guaranteed by the Director of the Corporate Income Tax Directorate or of the Large Taxpayers Office who does the final review.

1086. For the year in review, the timeliness of exchanges is as follows:

Past rulings in the scope of the transparency framework	Number of exchanges transmitted by 31 December 2017	Delayed exchanges		
		Number of exchanges not transmitted by 31 December 2017	Reasons for the delays	Any other comments
	17	0	N/A	These relate to the delayed exchanges reported in the prior year peer review report and were exchanged in 2017
Future rulings in the scope of the transparency framework	Number of exchanges transmitted within three months of the information becoming available to the competent authority or immediately after legal impediments have been lifted	Delayed exchanges		
		Number of exchanges transmitted later than three months of the information on rulings becoming available to the competent authority	Reasons for the delays	Any other comments
	6	6	N/A	
Total	23	6		

Follow up requests received for exchange of the ruling	Number	Average time to provide response	Number of requests not answered
	0	N/A	N/A

1087. Portugal explains that the exchange delays on future rulings occurred for multiple reasons. The delay in exchanges for two rulings related to exchange with other EU Member States, and Portugal's uncertainty regarding the appropriate alignment with EU Directive timelines. A minor delay for one APA was due to issues in completing the template, and this issue was resolved quickly. Portugal reports that all delayed exchanges were completed in the same year of the ruling's issuance. Portugal has remedied the issues that were the cause of delays during the year in review, and therefore does not believe such delays will be a recurring issue. Furthermore, Portugal notes that an IT application with an automatic signalling and alert mechanism will be introduced in 2018. Portugal anticipates that this new system will resolve any remaining issues, and allow the immediate identification of rulings in scope for exchange. The information on the application will be shared with the Competent Authority, and facilitate an automated and speedier process for the identification and exchange of relevant rulings. However, as there were delays encountered in the year in review, the recommendation is retained for Portugal to ensure that all information on future rulings is exchanged as soon as possible.

Conclusion on section B

1088. Portugal has the necessary legal framework and administrative processes in place for exchanging information on rulings. Portugal encountered some delays in the exchange of future rulings, but anticipates that these delays will be remedied with the introduction of a new IT application in 2018. Portugal has met all of the ToR for the exchange of information process except for the timely exchange of information on future rulings (ToR II.5.6) and Portugal is recommended to ensure that all information on future rulings is exchanged as soon as possible.

C. Statistics (ToR IV)

1089. The statistics for the year in review are as follows:

Category of ruling	Number of exchanges	Jurisdictions exchanged with
Rulings related to preferential regimes	N/A	N/A
Cross-border unilateral advance pricing arrangements (APAs) and any other cross-border unilateral tax rulings (such as an advance tax ruling) covering transfer pricing or the application of transfer pricing principles	10	Brazil, China (People's Republic of), France, Germany, Hong Kong (China), Mauritius, United Kingdom, United States
Cross-border rulings providing for a unilateral downward adjustment to the taxpayer's taxable profits that is not directly reflected in the taxpayer's financial / commercial accounts	N/A	N/A
Permanent establishment rulings	18	France, Germany, Ireland, Italy, Luxembourg, Spain, Sweden, Switzerland, United States
Related party conduit rulings	N/A	N/A
De minimis rule	N/A	N/A
IP regimes: total exchanges on taxpayers benefitting from the third category of IP assets, new entrants benefitting from grandfathered IP regimes; and taxpayers making use of the option to treat the nexus ratio as a rebuttable presumption	0	N/A
Total	29	

D. Matters related to intellectual property regimes (ToR I.4.1.3)

1090. Portugal offers an intellectual property regime that is subject to transparency requirements under the Action 5 Report (OECD, 2015) (Partial exemption for income from patents and other industrial property rights). It states that the identification of the benefitting taxpayers will occur as follows:

- ***New entrants benefitting from the grandfathered IP regime***: Portugal did not identify any new entrants benefitting from the grandfathered IP regime that should be subject to spontaneous exchange of information with other jurisdictions.
- ***Third category of assets***: not applicable, as this option has not been incorporated in the Portuguese IP regime.
- ***Taxpayers making use of the option to treat the nexus ratio as a rebuttable presumption***: not applicable, as this option has not been incorporated in the Portuguese IP regime.

Summary of recommendations on implementation of the transparency framework

Aspect of implementation of the transparency framework that should be improved	Recommendation for improvement
Portugal encountered some minor delays in the exchange of information on rulings within scope of the transparency framework. This is a continuing recommendation from the prior year peer review.	Portugal is recommended to ensure that all information on future rulings is exchanged as soon as possible.

Notes

[1] Algeria, Andorra, Austria, Bahrain, Belgium, Brazil, Bulgaria, Cabo Verde, Canada, Chile, China (People's Republic of), Colombia, Côte d'Ivoire, Croatia, Cuba, Cyprus, Czech Republic, Denmark, Estonia, Ethiopia, Finland, France, Georgia, Germany, Greece, Guinea-Bissau, Hong Kong (China), Hungary, Iceland, India, Indonesia, Ireland, Israel, Italy, Japan, Korea, Kuwait, Latvia, Lithuania, Luxembourg, Macau (China), Malta, Mexico, Moldova, Morocco, Mozambique, Netherlands, Norway, Oman, Pakistan, Panama, Peru, Poland, Qatar, Romania, Russia, San Marino, Sao Tome and Principe, Saudi Arabia, Senegal, Singapore, Slovak Republic, Slovenia, South Africa, Spain, Sweden, Switzerland, Tunisia, Turkey, Ukraine, United Arab Emirates, United Kingdom, United States, Uruguay, Venezuela and Viet Nam.

Note by Turkey: The information in this document with reference to "Cyprus" relates to the southern part of the Island. There is no single authority representing both Turkish and Greek Cypriot people on the Island. Turkey recognises the Turkish Republic of Northern Cyprus (TRNC). Until a lasting and equitable solution is found within the context of the United Nations, Turkey shall preserve its position concerning the "Cyprus issue".

Note by all the European Union Member States of the OECD and the European Union. The Republic of Cyprus is recognised by all members of the United Nations with the exception of Turkey. The information in this document relates to the area under the effective control of the Government of the Republic of Cyprus.

References

OECD (2017), *BEPS Action 5 on Harmful Tax Practices – Terms of Reference and Methodology for the Conduct of the Peer Reviews of the Action 5 Transparency Framework*, OECD/G20 Base Erosion and Profit Shifting Project, OECD, Paris. www.oecd.org/tax/beps/beps-action-5-harmful-tax-practices-peer-review-transparencyframework.pdf.

OECD (2015), *Countering Harmful Tax Practices More Effectively, Taking into Account Transparency and Substance, Action 5 - 2015 Final Report*, OECD/G20 Base Erosion and Profit Shifting Project, OECD Publishing, Paris. https://doi.org/10.1787/9789264241190-en.

OECD/Council of Europe (2011), *The Multilateral Convention on Mutual Administrative Assistance in Tax Matters: Amended by the 2010 Protocol*, OECD Publishing, Paris. http://dx.doi.org/10.1787/9789264115606-en.

Romania

Romania is taking steps to commence administrative preparations to ensure that information on rulings will be exchanged in a timely manner. Romania is recommended to implement a review and supervision mechanism (ToR I.4.3) and to continue its efforts to complete the templates for all relevant rulings and to ensure that the exchanges of information on rulings occur as soon as possible (ToR II.5).

Romania can legally issue two types of rulings within the scope of the transparency framework.

In practice, Romania has issued 12 past rulings; and for the year in review, Romania issued five future rulings within the scope of the transparency framework.

As no exchange of information on rulings was conducted, no peer input was received in respect of the exchanges of information on rulings received from Romania.

Introduction

1091. This peer review covers Romania's implementation of the BEPS Action 5 transparency framework for the calendar year 2017 (year in review). The report has four parts, each relating to a key part of the ToR. Each part is discussed in turn. A summary of recommendations is included at the end of this report.

A. The information gathering process

1092. Romania can legally issue the following two types of ruling within the scope of the transparency framework: (i) cross-border unilateral advance pricing arrangements (APAs) and any other cross-border unilateral tax rulings (such as an advance tax ruling) covering transfer pricing or the application of transfer pricing principles and (ii) permanent establishment rulings. Rulings are issued by the Directorate for Transfer Pricing and Tax Rulings. This directorate is part of the National Agency for Fiscal Administration (NAFA). These rulings are not published.

1093. Tax rulings are drafted by the Advanced Individual Tax Rulings Unit, endorsed by three stages of supervision: the Director of Directorate for Transfer Pricing and Tax Rulings, the General Director of Tax Audit Coordination General Directorate and the Vice-President of the NAFA. The rulings are then formally issued by NAFA's President.

Past rulings (ToR I.4.1.1, I.4.1.2, I.4.2.1, I.4.2.2)

1094. For Romania, past rulings are any tax rulings within scope that are issued either: (i) on or after 1 January 2015 but before 1 April 2017; or (ii) on or after 1 January 2012 but before 1 January 2015, provided they were still in effect as at 1 January 2015.

1095. In Romania, taxpayers applying for a ruling submit the appropriate form along with other requested documentation.

1096. Romania's tax administration has a database including all the rulings issued according to the issuance date. The rulings were recorded in an electronic database, as well as physically archived at the taxpayers' file and in the archives of the Advanced Individual Tax Rulings Unit. Access is restricted to staff that has access to the tax rulings module. The date of issuance of each ruling was checked to determine whether it qualified as a past ruling. Once selected as a past ruling, it was then checked against the category of rulings to determine if it is within scope of Action 5 by manually reading the ruling and to identify potential exchange jurisdictions. Romania confirms that in all cases, all potential exchange jurisdictions were able to be identified. It is therefore determined that Romania's undertakings to identify the potential exchange jurisdictions with respect to past rulings meet the minimum standard.

Future rulings (ToR I.4.1.1, I.4.1.2, I.4.2.1)

1097. For Romania, future rulings are any tax rulings within scope that are issued on or after 1 April 2017.

1098. The process for issuing and storing rulings in the database was maintained for future rulings in the same way as for past rulings. Romania is currently checking all the rulings issued since 1 April 2017. In order to identify all potential exchange jurisdictions, Romania's legislation requires the taxpayer to identify these jurisdictions (including for the immediate parent company and ultimate parent company) and to include this information in its ruling request.

Review and supervision mechanism (ToR I.4.3)

1099. Romania did not yet have a review and supervision mechanism for past or future rulings under the transparency framework for the year in review. Romania is discussing the implementation of a revision and supervision mechanism for future rulings.

Conclusion on section A

1100. Romania has met all of the ToR for the information gathering process except for having a review and supervision mechanism for the year in review (ToR I.4.3). Romania is recommended to implement a review and supervision mechanism.

B. The exchange of information

Legal basis for spontaneous exchange of information (ToR II.5.1, II.5.2)

1101. Romania has the necessary domestic legal basis to exchange information spontaneously. Romania notes that there are no legal or practical impediments that prevent the spontaneous exchange of information on rulings as contemplated in the Action 5 minimum standard.

1102. Romania is a party to international agreements permitting spontaneous exchange of information, including (i) the *Multilateral Convention on Mutual Administrative Assistance in Tax Matters: Amended by the 2010 Protocol* (OECD/Council of Europe, 2011) ("the Convention"), (ii) the Directive 2011/16/EU with all other European Union Member States and (iii) double tax agreements in force with 88 jurisdictions.[1]

Completion and exchange of templates (ToR II.5.3, II.5.4, II.5.5, II.5.6, II.5.7)

1103. Romania noted that it will exchange past and future rulings as soon as all the potential exchange jurisdictions of the rulings issued are identified.

1104. With respect to future rulings, Romania did not have a process in place regarding the completion and exchange of templates for the year in review. It is noted that Romania is elaborating a written procedure in line with the transparency framework to educate its tax officers to ensure that spontaneous exchange of information is implemented effectively, including maintaining a platform with the information to be exchanged.

1105. As there were no exchanges for the year in review, no data on the timeliness of exchanges can be reported.

Conclusion on section B

1106. Romania has the necessary legal basis to undertake spontaneous exchange of information. However, Romania did not undertake spontaneous exchange of information on tax rulings within scope of the transparency framework during the year in review. Romania is recommended to continue its efforts to complete the templates for all relevant rulings and to ensure that the exchanges of information on rulings occur as soon as possible (ToR II.5).

C. Statistics (ToR IV)

1107. As no information on rulings was exchanged for the year in review, no statistical data can be reported.

D. Matters related to intellectual property regimes (ToR I.4.1.3)

1108. Romania does not offer an intellectual property regime for which transparency requirements under the Action 5 Report (OECD, 2015) were imposed.

Summary of recommendations on implementation of the transparency framework

Aspect of implementation of the transparency framework that should be improved	Recommendation for improvement
Romania does not have a review and supervision mechanism in place to ensure that all relevant information on the identification of rulings and potential exchange jurisdictions is captured adequately.	Romania is recommended to have in place a review and supervision mechanism to ensure that all relevant information is captured adequately.
In the year in review, Romania did not have in place a process for completion of templates and exchange of information on rulings.	Romania is recommended to continue its efforts to complete the templates for all relevant rulings and to ensure that the exchanges of information on rulings occur as soon as possible

Note

[1] Parties to the Convention are available here: Romania also has bilateral agreements in force with Albania, Algeria, Armenia, Australia, Austria, Azerbaijan, Bangladesh, Belarus, Belgium, Bosnia and Herzegovina, Bulgaria, Canada, China (People's Republic of), Croatia, Cyprus, Czech Republic, Denmark, Ecuador, Egypt, Estonia, Ethiopia, Finland, France, Georgia, Germany, Greece, Hong Kong, Hungary, Iceland, India, Indonesia, Iran, Ireland, Israel, Italy, Japan, Jordan, Kazakhstan, Korea (Democratic People's Rep.), Korea (Rep.), Kuwait, Latvia, Lebanon, Lithuania, Luxembourg, Macedonia (FYR), Malaysia, Malta, Mexico, Moldova, Montenegro, Morocco, Namibia, Netherlands, Nigeria, Norway, Pakistan, Philippines, Poland, Portugal, Qatar, Russia, San Marino, Saudi Arabia, Serbia, Montenegro, Singapore, Slovenia, Slovak Republic, South Africa, Spain, Sri Lanka, Sudan, Sweden, Switzerland, Syrian Arab Republic, Tajikistan, Thailand, Tunisia, Turkey, Turkmenistan, Ukraine, United Arab Emirates, United Kingdom, United States, Uruguay, Uzbekistan, Viet Nam and Zambia.

References

OECD (2017), *BEPS Action 5 on Harmful Tax Practices – Terms of Reference and Methodology for the Conduct of the Peer Reviews of the Action 5 Transparency Framework*, OECD/G20 Base Erosion and Profit Shifting Project, OECD, Paris. www.oecd.org/tax/beps/beps-action-5-harmful-tax-practices-peer-review-transparencyframework.pdf.

OECD (2015), *Countering Harmful Tax Practices More Effectively, Taking into Account Transparency and Substance, Action 5 - 2015 Final Report*, OECD/G20 Base Erosion and Profit Shifting Project, OECD Publishing, Paris. https://doi.org/10.1787/9789264241190-en.

OECD/Council of Europe (2011), *The Multilateral Convention on Mutual Administrative Assistance in Tax Matters: Amended by the 2010 Protocol*, OECD Publishing, Paris. http://dx.doi.org/10.1787/9789264115606-en.

Russian Federation

Russia has met all aspects of the terms of reference (ToR) for the calendar year 2017 (year in review) and no recommendations are made. In the prior year peer review report, Russia was recommended to complete all outstanding exchanges of information as soon as possible and put in place a process to meet the exchange timelines on a going forward basis. Russia has now put in place the process and exchanged all information on past rulings by 31 December 2017 and the recommendation is removed.

Russia can legally issue five types of rulings within the scope of the transparency framework.

In practice, Russia has issued one past ruling; and for the period 1 April 2016 to the year in review, Russia issued no future rulings within the scope of the transparency framework.

No peer input was received in respect of the exchanges of information on rulings received from Russia.

Introduction

1109. This peer review covers Russia's implementation of the BEPS Action 5 transparency framework for the year 2017. The report has four parts, each relating to a key part of the ToR. Each part is discussed in turn. A summary of recommendations is included at the end of this report.

A. The information gathering process

1110. Russia can legally issue the five following types of rulings within the scope of the transparency framework: (i) rulings related to preferential regimes (special economic/industry zones); (ii) cross-border unilateral advance pricing agreements (APAs) and any other cross-border unilateral tax rulings (such as an advance tax ruling) covering transfer pricing or the application of transfer pricing principles; (iii) cross-border rulings giving a unilateral downward adjustment to the taxpayer's taxable profits in the country giving the ruling; (iv) permanent establishment rulings; and (v) related party conduit rulings. Rulings other than APAs are known as a "motivated opinions." Motivated opinions were introduced on 1 May 2016, and therefore are only relevant as future rulings. APAs are issued by the Transfer Pricing Directorate of the Central Office of the Federal Tax Service of Russia ("FTS") and motivated opinions are drafted by the nine large taxpayers' offices and for the year in review would be considered and finalised by the Directorate for Desk Audits at the Central Office.

Past rulings (ToR I.4.1.1, I.4.1.2, I.4.2.1, I.4.2.2)

1111. For Russia, past rulings are any tax rulings within scope that are issued either: (i) on or after 1 January 2014 but before 1 April 2016; or (ii) on or after 1 January 2010 but before 1 January 2014, provided they were still in effect as at 1 January 2014.

1112. In the prior year peer review report, it was determined that Russia's undertakings to identify past rulings and all potential exchange jurisdictions were sufficient to meet the minimum standard. Russia noted that one of the two past rulings reported last year was found to have expired in 2012 during a double check which was performed in the year of review. As such, it was not within the period of validity which applies for past rulings. Russia confirms that the other past ruling issued was in the scope of transparency framework. As this correction in applying the definition of past rulings has been remedied and is not a recurring issue, Russia has met all of the ToR for the information-gathering process and no recommendation is made on this point.

Future rulings (ToR I.4.1.1, I.4.1.2, I.4.2.1)

1113. For Russia, future rulings are any tax rulings within scope that are issued on or after 1 April 2016.

1114. In the prior year peer review report, it was determined that Russian Tax Administration's implementation of a new system to identify future rulings and all potential exchange jurisdictions was sufficient to meet the minimum standard. The Russian Tax Administration's implementation in this regard remains unchanged, and therefore continues to meet the minimum standard.

Review and supervision mechanism (ToR I.4.3)

1115. In the prior year peer review report, it was determined that the Russian Tax Administration's review and supervision mechanism was sufficient to meet the minimum standard. The Russian Tax Administration's implementation in this regard remains unchanged, and therefore continues to meet the minimum standard.

Conclusion on section A

1116. Russia has met all of the ToR for the information gathering process and no recommendations are made.

B. The exchange of information

Legal basis for spontaneous exchange of information (ToR II.5.1, II.5.2)

1117. Russia has the necessary domestic legal basis to exchange information spontaneously. Russia notes that there are no legal or practical impediments that prevent the spontaneous exchange of information on rulings as contemplated in the Action 5 minimum standard.

1118. Russia is a party to international agreements permitting spontaneous exchange of information, including (i) the *Multilateral Convention on Mutual Administrative Assistance in Tax Matters: Amended by the 2010 Protocol* (OECD/Council of Europe, 2011) ("the Convention"), (ii) the Directive 2011/16/EU with all other European Union Member States and (iii) double tax agreements in force with 83 jurisdictions.[1]

Completion and exchange of templates (ToR II.5.3, II.5.4, II.5.5, II.5.6, II.5.7)

1119. In the prior year peer review report, Russia's process for the completion and exchange of templates was described. It was noted that no exchanges of information took place as of 1 February 2017. In the prior year peer review report, Russia was recommended to complete all outstanding exchanges of information as soon as possible and put in place a process to meet the exchange timelines on a going forward basis. In the year in review, Russia notes that a process has been put in place to ensure that the required information should be completed in the form of the template contained in Annex C of the 2015 Action 5 Report (OECD, 2015). Russia has exchanged all information on the one past ruling by 31 December 2017.

1120. Russia notes that it is not currently relevant to introduce any specific guide for collecting information to complete the summary section, but that it has instructed its officials to ensure that the summary section is duly completed, including details of the facts and the decision made in the ruling. Russia notes that the FHTP suggested internal guide will be consulted and considered if in the future there is a need to organise and manage more elements to collect the information to be reported.

1121. For the year in review, the timeliness of exchanges is as follows:

Past rulings in the scope of the transparency framework	Number of exchanges transmitted by 31 December 2017	Delayed exchanges		
		Number of exchanges not transmitted by 31 December 2017	Reasons for the delays	Any other comments
	1	0	N/A	This exchange relates to the delayed exchanges reported in the prior year peer review report.
Future rulings in the scope of the transparency framework	Number of exchanges transmitted within three months of the information becoming available to the competent authority or immediately after legal impediments have been lifted	Delayed exchanges		
		Number of exchanges transmitted later than three months of the information on rulings becoming available to the competent authority	Reasons for the delays	Any other comments
	0	0	N/A	N/A
Total	1	0		

Follow up requests received for exchange of the ruling	Number	Average time to provide response	Number of requests not answered
	0	N/A	N/A

Conclusion on section B

1122. Russia has the necessary legal basis for spontaneous exchange of information, and a process for completing the templates in a timely way and has completed all exchanges. Russia has met all of the ToR for the exchange of information process and no recommendations are made.

C. Statistics (ToR IV)

1123. The statistics for the year in review are as follows:

Category of ruling	Number of exchanges	Jurisdictions exchanged with
Rulings related to preferential regimes	0	N/A
Cross-border unilateral advance pricing arrangements (APAs) and any other cross-border unilateral tax rulings (such as an advance tax ruling) covering transfer pricing or the application of transfer pricing principles	Included in *de minimis*	N/A
Cross-border rulings providing for a unilateral downward adjustment to the taxpayer's taxable profits that is not directly reflected in the taxpayer's financial / commercial accounts	0	N/A
Permanent establishment rulings	0	N/A
Related party conduit rulings	0	N/A
De minimis rule	1	N/A
IP regimes: total exchanges on taxpayers benefitting from the third category of IP assets, new entrants benefitting from grandfathered IP regimes; and taxpayers making use of the option to treat the nexus ratio as a rebuttable presumption	N/A	N/A
Total	1	

D. Matters related to intellectual property regimes (ToR I.4.1.3)

1124. Russia does not offer an intellectual property regime for which transparency requirements under the Action 5 Report (OECD, 2015) were imposed.

Summary of recommendations on implementation of the transparency framework

Aspect of implementation of the transparency framework that should be improved	Recommendation for improvement
No recommendations are made.	

Notes

[1] Parties to the Convention are available here: www.oecd.org/tax/exchange-of-tax-information/convention-on-mutual-administrative-assistance-in-tax-matters.htm. Russia has bilateral agreements in force with: Albania, Algeria, Argentina, Armenia, Australia, Austria, Azerbaijan, Belarus, Belgium, Botswana, Bulgaria, Canada, Chile, China (People's Republic of), Croatia, Cuba, Cyprus, Czech Republic, Democratic People's Republic of Korea, Denmark, Egypt, Finland, Former Yugoslav Republic of Macedonia, France, Georgia, Germany, Greece, Hungary, Iceland, India, Indonesia, Iran, Ireland, Israel, Italy, Japan, Kazakhstan, Korea, Kuwait, Kyrgyzstan, Latvia, Lebanon, Lithuania, Luxembourg, Malaysia, Mali, Malta, Morocco, Mexico, Moldova, Mongolia, Montenegro, Namibia, Netherlands, New Zealand, Nigeria, Norway, Philippines, Poland, Portugal, Qatar, Romania, Saudi Arabia, Serbia, Singapore, Slovak Republic, Slovenia, South Africa, Spain, Sri Lanka, Sweden, Syria, Tajikistan, Thailand, Turkey, Turkmenia, Ukraine, United Arab Emirates, United Kingdom, United States, Uzbekistan, Venezuela and Viet Nam.

Note by Turkey: The information in this document with reference to "Cyprus" relates to the southern part of the Island. There is no single authority representing both Turkish and Greek Cypriot people on the Island. Turkey recognises the Turkish Republic of Northern Cyprus (TRNC). Until a lasting and equitable solution is found within the context of the United Nations, Turkey shall preserve its position concerning the "Cyprus issue".

Note by all the European Union Member States of the OECD and the European Union. The Republic of Cyprus is recognised by all members of the United Nations with the exception of Turkey. The information in this document relates to the area under the effective control of the Government of the Republic of Cyprus.

References

OECD (2017), *BEPS Action 5 on Harmful Tax Practices – Terms of Reference and Methodology for the Conduct of the Peer Reviews of the Action 5 Transparency Framework*, OECD/G20 Base Erosion and Profit Shifting Project, OECD, Paris. www.oecd.org/tax/beps/beps-action-5-harmful-tax-practices-peer-review-transparencyframework.pdf.

OECD (2015), *Countering Harmful Tax Practices More Effectively, Taking into Account Transparency and Substance, Action 5 - 2015 Final Report*, OECD/G20 Base Erosion and Profit Shifting Project, OECD Publishing, Paris. https://doi.org/10.1787/9789264241190-en.

OECD/Council of Europe (2011), *The Multilateral Convention on Mutual Administrative Assistance in Tax Matters: Amended by the 2010 Protocol*, OECD Publishing, Paris. http://dx.doi.org/10.1787/9789264115606-en.

San Marino

San Marino has met all aspects of the terms of reference (ToR) for the calendar year 2017 (year in review) and no recommendations are made.

San Marino cannot legally issue any type of rulings within the scope of the transparency framework.

As no rulings were issued, no exchange of information was required. No peer input was received in respect of the exchanges of information on rulings received from San Marino.

Introduction

1125. This peer review covers San Marino's implementation of the BEPS Action 5 transparency framework for the year 2017. The report has four parts, each relating to a key part of the ToR. Each part is discussed in turn. A summary of recommendations is included at the end of this report.

A. The information gathering process

1126. As no rulings are issued, this section is not assessed.

B. The exchange of information

1127. As no rulings are issued, this section is not assessed.

C. Statistics (ToR IV)

1128. As no rulings are issued, no statistical data can be reported.

D. Matters related to intellectual property regimes (ToR I.4.1.3)

1129. San Marino offers two intellectual property regimes ("IP regime").[1] However for the year in review no transparency requirements were relevant, as follows:

- ***New entrants benefitting from the grandfathered IP regime***: not applicable for the year in review, because (i) San Marino is currently amending the New companies regime and has not taken a decision yet on whether it will provide grandfathering to existing taxpayers. Should San Marino provide grandfathering to taxpayers that entered the regime after the publication of the 2017 Progress Report (OECD, 2017b), which occurred on 16 October 2017, then the enhanced transparency requirements will apply and this will be taken into account during the subsequent peer review. (ii) San Marino is currently amending the Regime for high-tech, however there are no entrants in the regime, due to absence of administrative guidelines by San Marino which would operationalise the regime, and therefore the enhanced transparency requirements do not apply.
- ***Third category of IP assets***: not applicable to this regimes, which in 2017 was in the process of being amended.
- ***Taxpayers making the use of the option to treat the nexus ratio as a rebuttable presumption***: not applicable to this regimes, which in 2017 was in the process of being amended.

Summary of recommendations on implementation of the transparency framework

Aspect of implementation of the transparency framework that should be improved	Recommendation for improvement
	No recommendations are made.

Note

[1] These regimes are: 1) New companies regime provided by art. 73, law no. 166/2013 ("New companies regime") and 2) Regime for high-tech start-up companies under law no. 71/2013 and delegated decree no. 116/2014 ("Regime for high-tech").

References

OECD (2017a), *BEPS Action 5 on Harmful Tax Practices – Terms of Reference and Methodology for the Conduct of the Peer Reviews of the Action 5 Transparency Framework*, OECD/G20 Base Erosion and Profit Shifting Project, OECD, Paris. www.oecd.org/tax/beps/beps-action-5-harmful-tax-practices-peer-review-transparencyframework.pdf.

OECD (2017b), *Harmful Tax Practices - 2017 Progress Report on Preferential Regimes: Inclusive Framework on BEPS: Action 5*, OECD/G20 Base Erosion and Profit Shifting Project, OECD Publishing, Paris. http://dx.doi.org/10.1787/9789264283954-en.

Saudi Arabia

Saudi Arabia has met all aspects of the terms of reference (ToR) for the calendar year 2017 (year in review) that can be met in the absence of rulings being issued.

Saudi Arabia cannot legally issue any type of rulings within the scope of the transparency framework.

As no rulings were issued, no exchange of information was required. No peer input was received in respect of the exchanges of information on rulings received from Saudi Arabia.

Introduction

1130. This peer review covers Saudi Arabia's implementation of the BEPS Action 5 transparency framework for the year 2017. The report has four parts, each relating to a key part of the ToR. Each part is discussed in turn. A summary of recommendations is included at the end of this report.

A. The information gathering process

1131. As no rulings are issued, this section is not assessed.

B. The exchange of information

1132. As no rulings are issued, this section is not assessed.

C. Statistics (ToR IV)

1133. As no rulings are issued, no statistical data can be reported.

D. Matters related to intellectual property regimes (ToR I.4.1.3)

1134. Saudi Arabia does not offer an intellectual property regime for which transparency requirements under the Action 5 Report (OECD, 2015) were imposed.

Summary of recommendations on implementation of the transparency framework

Aspect of implementation of the transparency framework that should be improved	Recommendation for improvement
	No recommendations are made.

References

OECD (2017), *BEPS Action 5 on Harmful Tax Practices – Terms of Reference and Methodology for the Conduct of the Peer Reviews of the Action 5 Transparency Framework*, OECD/G20 Base Erosion and Profit Shifting Project, OECD, Paris. www.oecd.org/tax/beps/beps-action-5-harmful-tax-practices-peer-review-transparencyframework.pdf.

OECD (2015), *Countering Harmful Tax Practices More Effectively, Taking into Account Transparency and Substance, Action 5 - 2015 Final Report*, OECD/G20 Base Erosion and Profit Shifting Project, OECD Publishing, Paris. https://doi.org/10.1787/9789264241190-en.

Seychelles

Seychelles has met all aspects of the terms of reference (ToR) for the calendar year 2017 (year in review) and no recommendations are made.

Seychelles can legally issue five types of rulings within the scope of the transparency framework.

In practice, Seychelles issued no rulings within the scope of the transparency framework.

As no rulings were issued, no exchange of information was required. No peer input was received in respect of the exchanges of information on rulings received from Seychelles.

Introduction

1135. This peer review covers Seychelles' implementation of the BEPS Action 5 transparency framework for the year 2017. The report has four parts, each relating to a key part of the ToR. Each part is discussed in turn. A summary of recommendations is included at the end of this report.

A. The information gathering process

1136. Seychelles can legally issue the five following types of rulings within the scope of the transparency framework: (i) rulings related to preferential regimes;[1] (ii) cross-border unilateral APAs and any other unilateral tax ruling (such as an advance tax ruling) covering transfer pricing or the application of transfer pricing principles; (iii) cross-border rulings giving a unilateral downward adjustment to the taxpayer's taxable profits in the country giving the ruling; (iv) permanent establishment rulings; and (v) related party conduit rulings. Private rulings are issued by the legal unit of the Seychelles Revenue Commission ("SRC"). Seychelles can legally publish taxpayer specific rulings in redacted form subject to the consent of the taxpayer. Seychelles can legally publish taxpayer specific rulings in redacted form subject to the consent of the taxpayer.

Past rulings (ToR I.4.1.1, I.4.1.2, I.4.2.1, I.4.2.2)

1137. For Seychelles, past rulings are any tax rulings within scope that are issued either: (i) on or after 1 January 2015 but before 1 April 2017; or (ii) on or after 1 January 2012 but before 1 January 2015, provided they were still in effect as at 1 January 2015.

1138. Tax payers requesting a private ruling in the Seychelles have to submit a form available on the SRC website to the Revenue Commissioner, which is forwarded to the legal unit of the SRC for processing and issuing the ruling. The legal unit records the taxpayer details, date of request of the ruling, the type of ruling requested, the period it refers to and the date of issuance of the ruling in a central database in the form of a spreadsheet. In order to identify rulings in scope of Action 5 for the "past ruling" period, the legal unit of the SRC searched through the database and then manually reviewed the taxpayer files to ensure whether any rulings in scope of Action 5 had been issued in the relevant period.

1139. As there were no rulings issued, it was not relevant to identify any potential exchange jurisdictions.

Future rulings (ToR I.4.1.1, I.4.1.2, I.4.2.1)

1140. For Seychelles, future rulings are any tax rulings within scope that are issued on or after 1 September 2017.

1141. Seychelles used the same filtering process and manual review for identifying future rulings as for past rulings and found no future ruling issued in the relevant period. In the event that Seychelles may issue private rulings in the future, the SRC is in the process of amending the rulings application form to capture more specific information to determine whether there are cross-border elements such that the ruling is possibly in the scope of Action 5.

1142. In order to identify potential exchange jurisdictions in the future, the SRC also intends to request information on the new form of any related parties in or outside

Seychelles, and the jurisdiction of residence of the (i) related parties, (ii) ultimate parent company and (iii) immediate parent company, as applicable. Seychelles expects the new form to be finalised by 1 September 2018.

1143. If any future rulings are issued before the new form is finalised, Seychelles indicates that it will use its gathering power to obtain information that is missing under the Revenue Administration Act. Although these new processes were not in place as from 1 April 2017, as no rulings were issued for the year in review, this had no impact in practice.

Review and supervision mechanism (ToR I.4.3)

1144. Seychelles notes that the legal unit of the SRC is responsible for issuing tax rulings and obtaining all necessary information from the taxpayer to ensure that the ruling issued is within scope of Action 5.The legal officer is supervised by the director of the legal unit. In addition, formal training will be provided to the legal officers within the SRC on the requirements to collect the information under the transparency framework.

Conclusion on section A

1145. Seychelles has met all of the ToR for the information gathering process and no recommendations are made.

B. The exchange of information

Legal basis for spontaneous exchange of information (ToR II.5.1, II.5.2)

1146. Seychelles has the necessary domestic legal basis to exchange information spontaneously. Seychelles notes that there are no legal or practical impediments that prevent the spontaneous exchange of information on rulings as contemplated in the Action 5 minimum standard.

1147. Seychelles is a party to international agreements permitting spontaneous exchange of information, including (i) the *Multilateral Convention on Mutual Administrative Assistance in Tax Matters: Amended by the 2010 Protocol* (OECD/Council of Europe, 2011) ("the Convention")and (ii) double tax agreements in force with 28 jurisdictions and one tax information exchange agreement.[2]

Completion and exchange of templates (ToR II.5.3, II.5.4, II.5.5, II.5.6, II.5.7)

1148. Seychelles notes that the same legal officer in the SRC in charge of issuing the ruling and identifying whether the ruling is in scope of Action 5 will also complete the template under Annex C of the 2015 Action 5 Report (OECD, 2015) based on the different steps listed in the FHTP's internal suggested guide as these are in accordance with the legal and administrative practices in place in Seychelles. The template would then be reviewed by the director of the legal department who would ensure accuracy by verifying that the information in the template is line with the information contained in the excel database and the taxpayer file. The SRC explained also that it is in consultation with the IT department to discuss the feasibility of a validation tool similar to that used for the Common Reporting Standard.

1149. To ensure the timely exchange of future rulings within scope, a reminder email will be sent to the director of legal department within 15 days of a ruling being issued, who will send the template along with the ruling to the Commissioner General for approval and exchange of the template. Seychelles indicates it also intends to issue an internal manual to ensure that officers in charge will know the procedures and the timelines within which they have to operate to ensure the rulings are complete and sent on time.

1150. As Seychelles did not issue any past or future rulings in scope of Action 5 in the relevant periods, Seychelles did not exchange any information on rulings in the year in review and no data on the timeliness of exchanges can be reported.

Conclusion on section B

1151. Seychelles has the necessary legal basis for spontaneous exchange of information. Seychelles has met all of the ToR for the exchange of information process and no recommendations are made.

C. Statistics (ToR IV)

1152. As there were no rulings required to be exchanged by Seychelles for the year in review, no statistics can be reported.

D. Matters related to intellectual property regimes (ToR I.4.1.3)

1153. Seychelles offers three preferential regimes, which also offer benefits to income from intellectual property ("IP regime").[3] However for the year in review no transparency requirements were relevant, as follows:

- ***New entrants benefitting from the grandfathered IP regime***: Seychelles is currently in the process of amending all three regimes and it indicates that it will not allow grandfathering for any new entrants into the regimes as of 16 October 2017, the date of publication of 2017 Progress Report (OECD, 2017b). As such, the transparency requirements will not apply.
- ***Third category of IP assets***: not applicable to this regimes, which in 2017 was in the process of being amended.
- ***Taxpayers making the use of the option to treat the nexus ratio as a rebuttable presumption***: not applicable to this regimes, which in 2017 was in the process of being amended.

Summary of recommendations on implementation of the transparency framework

Aspect of implementation of the transparency framework that should be improved	Recommendation for improvement
	No recommendations are made.

Notes

[1] With respect to the following preferential regimes: 1) International business companies, 2) Companies special license, 3)International trade zone licensees, 4) Offshore banking, 5) Non-domestic insurance business, 6) Fund administration business, 7) Securities business under the securities act and 8) Reinsurance business.

[2] Parties to the Convention are available here: www.oecd.org/tax/exchange-of-tax-information/convention-on-mutual-administrative-assistance-in-tax-matters.htm. Seychelles also has bilateral agreements in force with Bahrain, Barbados, Belgium, Bermuda, Botswana, China (People's Republic of), Cyprus, Ethiopia, Guernsey, Indonesia, Isle of Man, Jersey, Kenya, Luxembourg, Malaysia, Mauritius, Monaco, Oman, Qatar, San Marino, Singapore, South Africa, Sri Lanka, Swaziland, Thailand, United Arab Emirates, Viet Nam and Zambia.

Note by Turkey: The information in this document with reference to "Cyprus" relates to the southern part of the Island. There is no single authority representing both Turkish and Greek Cypriot people on the Island. Turkey recognises the Turkish Republic of Northern Cyprus (TRNC). Until a lasting and equitable solution is found within the context of the United Nations, Turkey shall preserve its position concerning the "Cyprus issue".

Note by all the European Union Member States of the OECD and the European Union. The Republic of Cyprus is recognised by all members of the United Nations with the exception of Turkey. The information in this document relates to the area under the effective control of the Government of the Republic of Cyprus.

[3] These regimes are: 1) International business companies, 2) Companies special license and 3) International trade zone licensees.

References

OECD (2017a), *BEPS Action 5 on Harmful Tax Practices – Terms of Reference and Methodology for the Conduct of the Peer Reviews of the Action 5 Transparency Framework*, OECD/G20 Base Erosion and Profit Shifting Project, OECD, Paris. www.oecd.org/tax/beps/beps-action-5-harmful-tax-practices-peer-review-transparencyframework.pdf.

OECD (2017b), *Harmful Tax Practices - 2017 Progress Report on Preferential Regimes: Inclusive Framework on BEPS: Action 5*, OECD/G20 Base Erosion and Profit Shifting Project, OECD Publishing, Paris. http://dx.doi.org/10.1787/9789264283954-en.

Sierra Leone

Sierra Leone has met all aspects of the terms of reference (ToR) for the calendar year 2017 (year in review) that can be met in the absence of rulings being issued.

Sierra Leone indicates that it cannot legally issue any type of rulings within the scope of the transparency framework.

As no rulings were issued, no exchange of information was required. No peer input was received in respect of the exchanges of information on rulings received from Sierra Leone.

Introduction

1154. This peer review covers Sierra Leone's implementation of the BEPS Action 5 transparency framework for the year 2017. The report has four parts, each relating to a key part of the ToR. Each part is discussed in turn. A summary of recommendations is included at the end of this report.

A. The information gathering process

1155. As no rulings are issued, this section is not assessed.

B. The exchange of information

1156. As no rulings are issued, this section is not assessed.

C. Statistics (ToR IV)

1157. As no rulings are issued, no statistical data can be reported.

D. Matters related to intellectual property regimes (ToR I.4.1.3)

1158. Sierra Leone does not offer an intellectual property regime for which transparency requirements under the Action 5 Report (OECD, 2015) were imposed.

Summary of recommendations on implementation of the transparency framework

Aspect of implementation of the transparency framework that should be improved	Recommendation for improvement
	No recommendations are made.

References

OECD (2017), *BEPS Action 5 on Harmful Tax Practices – Terms of Reference and Methodology for the Conduct of the Peer Reviews of the Action 5 Transparency Framework*, OECD/G20 Base Erosion and Profit Shifting Project, OECD, Paris. www.oecd.org/tax/beps/beps-action-5-harmful-tax-practices-peer-review-transparencyframework.pdf.

OECD (2015), *Countering Harmful Tax Practices More Effectively, Taking into Account Transparency and Substance, Action 5 - 2015 Final Report*, OECD/G20 Base Erosion and Profit Shifting Project, OECD Publishing, Paris. https://doi.org/10.1787/9789264241190-en.

Singapore

Singapore has met all aspects of the terms of reference (ToR) for the calendar year 2017 (year in review) and no recommendations are made.

Singapore can legally issue five types of rulings within the scope of the transparency framework.

In practice, Singapore has issued 1 008 past rulings;[1] and for the year in review, Singapore issued 85 future rulings within the scope of the transparency framework.

Peer input was received from five jurisdictions in respect of exchanges of information received from Singapore. The input was in general positive, noting that information was complete, in the correct format and received mostly in a timely manner. One peer noted that some of the past rulings were received after 31 December 2017.

Introduction

1159. This peer review covers Singapore's implementation of the BEPS Action 5 transparency framework for the year 2017. The report has four parts, each relating to a key part of the ToR. Each part is discussed in turn. A summary of recommendations is included at the end of this report.

A. The information gathering process

1160. Singapore can legally issue the five following types of rulings within the scope of the transparency framework: (i) rulings related to preferential regimes[2]; (ii) cross-border unilateral advance pricing arrangements ("APAs") and any other cross-border unilateral tax rulings (such as an advance tax ruling) covering transfer pricing or the application of transfer pricing principles; (iii) rulings providing for a downward adjustment of taxable profits, (iv) permanent establishment ("PE") rulings, and (v) related party conduit rulings. Rulings are issued by two specialised teams within the Inland Revenue Authority of Singapore (Singaporean tax administration, hereafter "IRAS"): the International Tax Branch ("ITB") is responsible for the issuing of transfer pricing rulings such as cross-border unilateral APAs; the Advance Ruling ("AR") team is responsible for rulings that are not transfer pricing related such as rulings on permanent establishments. Singapore notes that rulings related to preferential regimes refer to the letters of awards ("LoAs") relating to preferential regimes administered by economic agencies, which Singapore has committed to exchange within the transparency framework.[3]

Past rulings (ToR I.4.1.1, I.4.1.2, I.4.2.1, I.4.2.2)

1161. For Singapore, past rulings are any tax rulings within scope that are issued either: (i) on or after 1 January 2015 but before 1 April 2017; or (ii) on or after 1 January 2012 but before 1 January 2015, provided they were still in effect as at 1 January 2015.

1162. The IRAS set up a specialised team, the Spontaneous Exchange of Information (SEOI) team, responsible for the processes regarding the transparency framework, and the work processes for the compilation of the data required to be exchanged. The following steps have been taken to identify the past rulings.

1163. Regarding APAs and PE rulings, the ITB and the AR teams maintain records of all of the issued rulings in a database, which were used to identify the past rulings for the purpose of the transparency framework. The ITB and the AR teams searched their records to identify the rulings issued that fall within the scope of past rulings, filtering all rulings by conducting a search for keywords and the issuing dates. The content of the filtered rulings was then manually reviewed.

1164. Regarding the LoAs, designated officers from the economic agencies administering the respective incentive schemes searched their records, which are kept centrally, to identify LoAs within the scope of past rulings. The search process involved filtering the database by keywords and dates, and then manually reviewing the filtered LoAs. The economic agencies then transmitted the necessary information for the completion of the SEOI templates, such as name of the preferential regime, details of the company, issuing date and period covered by the LoA, to the IRAS, where the SEOI team then checked the information received. In order to identify the potential exchange jurisdictions, the applications for the rulings/LoAs were reviewed by the ITB/AR team, or the economic agency that had issued the rulings/LoAs. In cases where the applications did not provide the relevant information, the "best efforts approach" was used which included checking taxpayers' financial statements, searching the website of the Accounting and Corporate Regulatory Authority of Singapore for company details and searching the internet. Singapore was able to identify most potential exchange jurisdictions using the "best efforts approach".

Future rulings (ToR I.4.1.1, I.4.1.2, I.4.2.1)

1165. For Singapore, future rulings are any tax rulings within scope that are issued on or after 1 April 2017.

1166. In order to identify all potential exchange jurisdictions, the IRAS and economic agencies amended the application process for future rulings and LoAs. The relevant information under the transparency framework is obtained as part of the application process. The process set up within the IRAS to gather and transmit information on future rulings issued is similar to the process introduced for past rulings. Regarding rulings, the ITB and the AR teams identify rulings in scope when they issue the ruling and complete the SEOI templates. Regarding the LoAs, the relevant economic agency identifies LoAs in scope and transmits the necessary information to the IRAS within fifteen days from the end of each quarter.

Review and supervision mechanism (ToR I.4.3)

1167. The SEOI team organised the processes and briefed the ITB and AR teams, and the designated officers from the economic agencies on identifying past and future rulings in scope. The designated officers from the economic agencies include senior personnel who supervise and approve the work of the economic agencies. The review process led to the identification of 37 additional LoAs after the year of review, which were not identified in the first search.

1168. The SEOI team also provides ongoing assistance to the ITB and AR teams, and the economic agencies. The SEOI team is supervised by a manager within the IRAS.

Conclusion on section A

1169. Singapore has met all of the ToR for the information gathering process and no recommendations are made.

B. The exchange of information

Legal basis for spontaneous exchange of information (ToR II.5.1, II.5.2)

1170. Singapore has the necessary domestic legal basis to exchange information spontaneously. Singapore notes that there are no legal or practical impediments that prevent the spontaneous exchange of information on rulings as contemplated in the Action 5 minimum standard.

1171. Singapore is a party to international agreements permitting spontaneous exchange of information, including (i) the *Multilateral Convention on Mutual Administrative Assistance in Tax Matters: Amended by the 2010 Protocol* (OECD/Council of Europe, 2011) ("the Convention") and (ii) double tax agreements in force with 79 jurisdictions, which allow for spontaneous exchange of information with 79 jurisdictions.[4]

Completion and exchange of templates (ToR II.5.3, II.5.4, II.5.5, II.5.6, II.5.7)

1172. In order to share the required information with other jurisdictions, Singapore developed a template (SEOI template) which includes all the relevant fields contained in the template in Annex C of the 2015 Action 5 Report (OECD, 2015). It is completed by the ITB or the AR team when a past ruling was identified, or when a future ruling is issued, and is completed by the SEOI team for LoAs after the relevant information is received from the respective economic agencies. Singapore confirmed that the FHTP's suggested guide is taken into account when completing the summary section of the SEOI template. This would usually include a summary of the transaction or activity covered by the ruling/LoA, a reference to the particular preferential regime involved, the key conclusions reached in issuing the ruling, and the agreed arm's length rate, where applicable.

1173. After the SEOI template is checked by a supervisor, the template is uploaded to a central location and an internal spreadsheet with details of each SEOI template is updated. To ensure that the information on rulings is made available to the EOI team in a timely way, the SEOI team set out timelines for all teams and agencies involved in the process. These are as follows:

1174. Information on past APAs and PE rulings were provided by the ITB and the AR teams to the EOI team by December 2017, whilst the economic agencies provided information on LoAs to the SEOI team from July 2017 onwards. Regarding future rulings, the economic agencies are required to provide the relevant information on the LoAs to the SEOI team within 15 days of the end of each quarter in which the LoAs have been issued and accepted by the taxpayer. Once the information is provided to the SEOI team, they are to be exchanged with the relevant exchange jurisdictions within three months. During this period, the SEOI template is completed by the SEOI team, reviewed by the supervisor, uploaded to the central location and retrieved by the EOI team for exchange. The timelines are monitored and reminders are sent to the economic agencies to ensure that the economic agencies provide the information to the SEOI team in time. The EOI team generally retrieves the SEOI templates from the central location on a monthly basis, transmits the information to the relevant exchange jurisdictions and updates the internal tracking spreadsheet. This means that in practice most SEOI templates relating to the LoAs would be exchanged before the three months from when the relevant information is received by the SEOI team.

1175. With respect to the other future rulings, they are to be exchanged within three months after they have been issued by the ITB or the AR team. This overall timeline includes the completion of the SEOI templates by the respective teams, the approval of the SEOI templates by the supervisor, and their upload to the central location for retrieval by the EOI team. The EOI team generally retrieves the SEOI templates from the central location on a monthly basis, transmits the information to the relevant exchange jurisdictions and updates the internal tracking spreadsheet.

1176. For the year in review, the timeliness of exchanges is as follows:

Past rulings in the scope of the transparency framework	Number of exchanges transmitted by 31 December 2017	Delayed exchanges		
		Number of exchanges not transmitted by 31 December 2017	Reasons for the delays	Any other comments
	1 406	269	Delays occurred due to the time needed to implement the necessary processes and because 37 past LoAs were not identified in the first search. They are not expected to be a recurring issue.	The delayed exchanges were complete by May 2018, and the recently identified LoAs will be exchanged by August 2018.
Future rulings in the scope of the transparency framework	**Number of exchanges transmitted within three months of the information becoming available to the competent authority or immediately after legal impediments have been lifted**	**Delayed exchanges**		
		Number of exchanges transmitted later than three months of the information on rulings becoming available to the competent authority	Reasons for the delays	Any other comments
	5	18	Delays occurred due to the time needed to implement the necessary processes and are not expected to be a recurring issue.	The delayed exchanges on future rulings were exchanged within 10 days from the due date.
Total	1 411	287		

Follow up requests received for exchange of the ruling	Number	Average time to provide response	Number of requests not answered
	0	N/A	N/A

1177. Singapore notes that the delay in the exchange of rulings were a result of the implementation of the new processes and the large number of past rulings that had to be exchanged in 2017. Singapore also states that information on future rulings was exchanged within ten days from the due date, and that such delays are not expected in the future as the various teams involved in the process were able to familiarise themselves with the processes.

Conclusion on section B

1178. Singapore has the necessary legal basis for spontaneous exchange of information, a process for completing the templates in a timely way and has completed most exchanges on time. As the delays occurred due to the time needed by the IRAS and the economic agencies to implement the new process, Singapore notes that they do not expect further delays in the exchange of information. With respect to the delays on future rulings, these were exchanged within a very short period of time from the three-month deadline. It is therefore determined that the delays will not be a recurring issue and that Singapore has met all of the ToR for the exchange of information process and no recommendations are made.

C. Statistics (ToR IV)

1179. The statistics for the year in review are as follows:

Category of ruling	Number of exchanges	Jurisdictions exchanged with
Ruling/letters of awards related to a preferential regime	1 401	Australia, Belgium, Canada, China (People's Republic of), Denmark, Finland, France, Germany, Guernsey, Hungary, India, Ireland, Italy, Japan, Jersey, Korea, Latvia, Lithuania, Luxembourg, Malaysia, Malta, Mauritius, Mexico, Netherlands, New Zealand, Norway, Poland, Portugal, Russia, Saudi Arabia, South Africa, Spain, United Kingdom
Cross-border unilateral advance pricing arrangements (APAs) and any other cross-border unilateral tax rulings (such as an advance tax ruling) covering transfer pricing or the application of transfer pricing principles	27[5]	Australia, China (People's Republic of), India, Ireland, Japan, Korea, Malaysia, Netherlands, New Zealand, United Kingdom
Cross-border rulings providing for a unilateral downward adjustment to the taxpayer's taxable profits that is not directly reflected in the taxpayer's financial / commercial accounts	N/A	N/A
Permanent establishment rulings	Included in *de minimis*	N/A
Related party conduit rulings	N/A	N/A
De minimis rule	1	N/A
IP regimes: total exchanges on taxpayers benefitting from the third category of IP assets, new entrants benefitting from grandfathered IP regimes; and taxpayers making use of the option to treat the nexus ratio as a rebuttable presumption	0	N/A
Total	1 429	

D. Matters related to intellectual property regimes (ToR I.4.1.3)

1180. Singapore offers two preferential regimes, which also offer benefits to income from intellectual property ("IP regime").[6] Both IP parts of the regimes are abolished as of 30 June 2018. Grandfathering will be provided and therefore both regimes are subject to transparency requirements under the Action 5 Report (OECD, 2015). It states that the identification of the benefitting taxpayers will occur as follows:

- ***New entrants benefitting from grandfathered regimes*:** new entrants include both (i) new taxpayers not previously benefitting from the regimes and (ii) new IP assets owned by taxpayers already benefitting from the regimes. Singapore has to exchange information on new entrants, which entered the (grandfathered) regimes from 17 October 2017[7] onwards. As Singapore's IP regimes are offered by way of issuing a LoA, new entrants of the first category will be identified using the approach described above for identifying future rulings issued by the economic agency. In order to identify new IP assets of taxpayers already benefitting from the regimes, Singapore introduced a new process requiring all existing taxpayers under the grandfathered IP regimes to provide information on new IP assets to the administering economic agency. The economic agency will transmit the information provided by the taxpayers to the SEOI team for exchange, under the same process for exchanging information on future rulings as described above.

- ***Third category of IP assets***: not applicable to these regimes, which are abolished as of 30 June 2018.
- ***Taxpayers making use of the option to treat the nexus ratio as a rebuttable presumption***: not applicable to these regimes, which are abolished as of 30 June 2018.

1181. In addition, Singapore introduced a new IP regime which, subject to legislature's approval by late 2018, would come into effect from 1 July 2018.[8] Although this is after the year in review, it is noted that this regime is not subject to transparency requirements under the Action 5 report (OECD, 2015), because:

- ***New entrants benefitting from the grandfathered IP regime***: as this is a new IP regime rather than a grandfathered IP regime, transparency on new entrants is not relevant.
- ***Third category of IP assets***: not applicable as the regime does not allow the third category of IP assets to qualify for the benefits.
- ***Taxpayers making use of the option to treat the nexus ratio as a rebuttable presumption***: not applicable as the regime does not allow the nexus ratio to be treated as a rebuttable presumption.

Summary of recommendations on implementation of the transparency framework

Aspect of implementation of the transparency framework that should be improved	Recommendation for improvement
Singapore identified additional 37 past rulings only in 2018 during a review process.	No recommendation is made because Singapore has addressed the issue and it is not expected to recur.
Singapore experienced some delays in exchanging information on past and future rulings.	No recommendation is made because Singapore completed the exchange of all past rulings by May 2018 (except the recently identified LoAs which will be exchanged by August 2018) and this is not a recurring issue. The future rulings were exchanged within a very short period of the deadline and steps have been taken to ensure that this does not recur.

Notes

[1] Including two that fell into more than one category under the BEPS Action 5 report

[2] With respect to the following preferential regimes: 1) Development and Expansion Incentive - Services, 2) Pioneer Service Company, 3) Aircraft Leasing Scheme, 4) Finance and Treasury Centre, 5) Insurance Business Development, 6) Financial Sector Incentive, 7) Global Trader Programme, 8) DEI-Legal Services (abolished), 9) International Growth Scheme (abolished).

[3] The Singapore Economic Development Board administers the following regimes: 1) Development and Expansion Incentive – Services, 2) Pioneer Service Company, 3) Aircraft Leasing Scheme, 4) Finance and Treasury Centre, and 5) DEI-Legal Services. The Monetary Authority of Singapore administers the Insurance Business Development, and the Financial Sector Incentive. The Enterprise Singapore (previously known as the "International Enterprise Singapore") administers the Global Trader Programme and the International Growth Scheme.

[4] Singapore has DTAs allowing for SEOI with Albania, Australia, Bahrain, Bangladesh, Barbados, Belarus, Belgium Darussalam, Brunei, Bulgaria, Cambodia, Canada, China (People's Republic of), Cyprus, Czech Republic, Denmark, Ecuador, Egypt, Estonia, Ethiopia, Fiji, Finland, France, Georgia, Germany, Guernsey, Hungary, India, Indonesia, Ireland, Isle of Man, Israel, Italy, Japan, Jersey, Kazakhstan, Korea, Kuwait, Lao People's Democratic Republic, Latvia, Libya, Lithuania, Luxembourg, Malaysia, Malta, Mauritius, Mexico, Mongolia, Morocco, Myanmar, Netherlands, New Zealand, Norway, Oman, Pakistan, Papua New Guinea, Philippines, Poland, Portugal, Qatar, Romania, Russia, Rwanda, San Marino, Saudi Arabia, Seychelles, Slovak Republic, Slovenia, South Africa, Spain, Sri Lanka, Sweden, Thailand, Turkey, Ukraine, United Arab Emirates, United Kingdom, Uruguay, Uzbekistan and Vietnam.

Note by Turkey: The information in this document with reference to "Cyprus" relates to the southern part of the Island. There is no single authority representing both Turkish and Greek Cypriot people on the Island. Turkey recognises the Turkish Republic of Northern Cyprus (TRNC). Until a lasting and equitable solution is found within the context of the United Nations, Turkey shall preserve its position concerning the "Cyprus issue".

Note by all the European Union Member States of the OECD and the European Union. The Republic of Cyprus is recognised by all members of the United Nations with the exception of Turkey. The information in this document relates to the area under the effective control of the Government of the Republic of Cyprus.

[5] Two of the APAs also qualified as PE rulings, but have only been reflected here.

[6] These regimes are: 1) Pioneer service company and 2) Development and expansion incentive – services.

[7] After the publication date of the 2017 Progress Report (OECD, 2017b), which was 16 October 2017.

[8] This regime is the IP development incentive.

References

OECD (2017a), *BEPS Action 5 on Harmful Tax Practices – Terms of Reference and Methodology for the Conduct of the Peer Reviews of the Action 5 Transparency Framework*, OECD/G20 Base Erosion and Profit Shifting Project, OECD, Paris. www.oecd.org/tax/beps/beps-action-5-harmful-tax-practices-peer-review-transparencyframework.pdf.

OECD (2017b), *Harmful Tax Practices - 2017 Progress Report on Preferential Regimes: Inclusive Framework on BEPS: Action 5*, OECD/G20 Base Erosion and Profit Shifting Project, OECD Publishing, Paris. http://dx.doi.org/10.1787/9789264283954-en.

OECD (2015), *Countering Harmful Tax Practices More Effectively, Taking into Account Transparency and Substance, Action 5 - 2015 Final Report*, OECD/G20 Base Erosion and Profit Shifting Project, OECD Publishing, Paris. https://doi.org/10.1787/9789264241190-en.

OECD/Council of Europe (2011), *The Multilateral Convention on Mutual Administrative Assistance in Tax Matters: Amended by the 2010 Protocol*, OECD Publishing, Paris. http://dx.doi.org/10.1787/9789264115606-en.

Slovak Republic

The Slovak Republic has met all aspects of the terms of reference (ToR) for the calendar year 2017 (year in review) and no recommendations are made.

The Slovak Republic can legally issue two types of rulings within the scope of the transparency framework.

In practice, the Slovak Republic has issued one past ruling; for the period 1 April 2016 - 31 December 2016, the Slovak Republic issued two future rulings; and for the year in review, the Slovak Republic issued five future rulings within the scope of the transparency framework.

No peer input was received in respect of the exchanges of information on rulings received from the Slovak Republic.

Introduction

1182. This peer review covers the Slovak Republic's implementation of the BEPS Action 5 transparency framework for the year 2017. The report has four parts, each relating to a key part of the ToR. Each part is discussed in turn. A summary of recommendations is included at the end of this report.

A. The information gathering process

1183. The Slovak Republic can legally issue the two following types of rulings within the scope of the transparency framework: (i) cross-border unilateral APAs and any other cross-border unilateral tax ruling (such as an ATR) covering transfer pricing or the application of transfer pricing principles; and (ii) permanent establishment rulings. As of 2017, in the Slovak Republic, rulings are issued by the Tax Office for selected taxpayers.

Past rulings (ToR I.4.1.1, I.4.1.2, I.4.2.1, I.4.2.2)

1184. For the Slovak Republic, past rulings are any tax rulings within scope that are issued either: (i) on or after 1 January 2014 but before 1 April 2016; or (ii) on or after 1 January 2010 but before 1 January 2014, provided they were still in effect as at 1 January 2014.

1185. In the prior year peer review report, it was determined that the Slovak Republic's undertakings to identify past rulings and all potential exchange jurisdictions were sufficient to meet the minimum standard. The Slovak Republic's implementation in this regard remains unchanged, and therefore continues to meet the minimum standard.

Future rulings (ToR I.4.1.1, I.4.1.2, I.4.2.1)

1186. For the Slovak Republic, future rulings are any tax rulings within scope that are issued on or after 1 April 2016.

1187. In the prior year peer review report, it was determined that the Slovak Republic's undertakings to identify future rulings and all potential exchange jurisdictions were sufficient to meet the minimum standard. The Slovak Republic's implementation in this regard remains unchanged, and therefore continues to meet the minimum standard.

Review and supervision mechanism (ToR I.4.3)

1188. In the prior year peer review report, it was determined that the Slovak Republic Tax Administration's review and supervision mechanisms were sufficient to meet the minimum standard. The Slovak Republic Tax Office's implementation in this regard remains unchanged, and therefore continues to meet the minimum standard.

Conclusion on section A

1189. The Slovak Republic has met all of the ToR for the information gathering process and no recommendations are made.

B. The exchange of information

Legal basis for spontaneous exchange of information (ToR II.5.1, II.5.2)

1190. The Slovak Republic has the necessary domestic legal basis to exchange information spontaneously. Slovak Republic notes that there are no legal or practical impediments that prevent the spontaneous exchange of information on rulings as contemplated in the Action 5 minimum standard.

1191. The Slovak Republic is a party to international agreements permitting spontaneous exchange of information, including (i) the *Multilateral Convention on Mutual Administrative Assistance in Tax Matters: Amended by the 2010 Protocol* (OECD/Council of Europe, 2011) ("the Convention"), (ii) the Directive 2011/16/EU with all other European Union Member States and (iii) double tax agreements in force with 68 jurisdictions.[1]

Completion and exchange of templates (ToR II.5.3, II.5.4, II.5.5, II.5.6, II.5.7)

1192. In the prior year peer review report, it was determined that the Slovak Republic's completion and exchange of templates were sufficient to meet the minimum standard. The Slovak Republic's implementation in this regard remains unchanged, and therefore continues to meet the minimum standard.

1193. In order to complete the summary section, the Slovak Republic explains that the AEOI unit responsible for the exchange of rulings provided instructions on how to complete the summary section of the ruling template to the tax officers who prepare the template and the tax specialist who reviews the information in the template, which included describing the transaction/activity and providing key relevant facts about the ruling. In most cases the Slovak tax officers described the partners of the transaction, the transaction itself, the outcome of their investigation as well as the calculation of interquartile range and commented on the method used.

1194. For the year in review, the timeliness of exchanges is as follows:

Past rulings in the scope of the transparency framework	Number of exchanges transmitted by 31 December 2017	Delayed exchanges		
		Number of exchanges not transmitted by 31 December 2017	Reasons for the delays	Any other comments
	1	0	N/A	See below
Future rulings in the scope of the transparency framework	**Number of exchanges transmitted within three months of the information becoming available to the competent authority or immediately after legal impediments have been lifted**	**Delayed exchanges**		
		Number of exchanges transmitted later than three months of the information on rulings becoming available to the competent authority	**Reasons for the delays**	**Any other comments**
	6	0	N/A	N/A
Total	7	0		

Follow up requests received for exchange of the ruling	Number	Average time to provide response	Number of requests not answered
	0	N/A	N/A

1195. The Slovak Republic indicates that the exchange of information on the past ruling in 2017 was with a jurisdiction that is an Inclusive Framework member and as such the exchange was not required until 2017. The exchanges on future rulings includes one exchange which relates to a future ruling which was issued in late 2016 but exchanged in March 2017, within the three month deadline under the transparency framework.

Conclusion on section B

1196. The Slovak Republic has met all of the ToR for the exchange of information process and no recommendations are made.

C. Statistics (ToR IV)

1197. The statistics for the year in review are as follows:

Category of ruling	Number of exchanges	Jurisdictions exchanged with
Rulings related to preferential regimes	N/A	N/A
Cross-border unilateral advance pricing arrangements (APAs) and any other cross-border unilateral tax rulings (such as an advance tax ruling) covering transfer pricing or the application of transfer pricing principles	5	Czech Republic, Germany, Hungary, Sweden
Cross-border rulings providing for a unilateral downward adjustment to the taxpayer's taxable profits that is not directly reflected in the taxpayer's financial / commercial accounts	N/A	N/A
Permanent establishment rulings	Included in *de minimis*	N/A
Related party conduit rulings	N/A	N/A
De minimis rule	2	N/A
IP regimes: total exchanges on taxpayers benefitting from the third category of IP assets, new entrants benefitting from grandfathered IP regimes; and taxpayers making use of the option to treat the nexus ratio as a rebuttable presumption	N/A	N/A
Total	7	

D. Matters related to intellectual property regimes (ToR I.4.1.3)

1198. As of 1 January 2018, the Slovak Republic has introduced an IP regime which is nexus-compliant. Although this is after the year in review, it is noted that this regime is not subject to transparency requirements under the Action 5 report (OECD, 2015), because:

- ***New entrants benefitting from the grandfathered IP regime***: the regime is a new nexus-compliant regime and therefore there is no grandfathered IP regime for which enhanced transparency requirements will apply.
- ***Third category of IP assets***: not applicable as the regime does not allow the third category of IP assets to qualify for the benefits.

- ***Taxpayers making the use of the option to treat the nexus ratio as a rebuttable presumption***: not applicable the regime does not allow the nexus ratio to be treated as a rebuttable presumption.

Summary of recommendations on implementation of the transparency framework

Aspect of implementation of the transparency framework that should be improved	Recommendation for improvement
	No recommendations are made.

Note

1 Parties to the Convention are available here: www.oecd.org/tax/exchange-of-tax-information/convention-on-mutual-administrative-assistance-in-tax-matters.htm.
The Slovak Republic also has bilateral agreements with Armenia, Australia, Austria, Belarus, Belgium, Bosnia and Herzegovina, Brazil, Bulgaria, Canada, China (People's Republic of), , Croatia, Cyprus, Czech Republic, Denmark, Estonia, Finland, Former Yugoslav Republic of Macedonia, France, Georgia, Germany, Greece, Hungary, Iceland, India, Indonesia, Ireland, Israel, Italy, Japan, Kazakhstan, Korea, Kuwait, Latvia, Libya, Lithuania, Luxembourg, , Malaysia, Malta, Mexico, Moldova, Mongolia, Montenegro, Netherlands, Nigeria, Norway, Poland, Portugal, Romania, Russia, Serbia, Singapore, Slovenia, South Africa, Spain, Sri Lanka, Sweden, Switzerland, Syrian Arab Republic, Chinese Taipei, Tunisia, Turkey, Turkmenistan, Ukraine, United Arab Emirates, United Kingdom, United States, Uzbekistan and Viet Nam.

Note by Turkey: The information in this document with reference to "Cyprus" relates to the southern part of the Island. There is no single authority representing both Turkish and Greek Cypriot people on the Island. Turkey recognises the Turkish Republic of Northern Cyprus (TRNC). Until a lasting and equitable solution is found within the context of the United Nations, Turkey shall preserve its position concerning the "Cyprus issue".

Note by all the European Union Member States of the OECD and the European Union. The Republic of Cyprus is recognised by all members of the United Nations with the exception of Turkey. The information in this document relates to the area under the effective control of the Government of the Republic of Cyprus.

References

OECD (2017), *BEPS Action 5 on Harmful Tax Practices – Terms of Reference and Methodology for the Conduct of the Peer Reviews of the Action 5 Transparency Framework*, OECD/G20 Base Erosion and Profit Shifting Project, OECD, Paris. www.oecd.org/tax/beps/beps-action-5-harmful-tax-practices-peer-review-transparencyframework.pdf.

OECD (2015), *Countering Harmful Tax Practices More Effectively, Taking into Account Transparency and Substance, Action 5 - 2015 Final Report*, OECD/G20 Base Erosion and Profit Shifting Project, OECD Publishing, Paris. https://doi.org/10.1787/9789264241190-en.

OECD/Council of Europe (2011), *The Multilateral Convention on Mutual Administrative Assistance in Tax Matters: Amended by the 2010 Protocol*, OECD Publishing, Paris. http://dx.doi.org/10.1787/9789264115606-en.

Slovenia

Slovenia has met all aspects of the terms of reference (ToR) for the calendar year 2017 (year in review) and no recommendations are made.

Slovenia can legally issue three types of rulings within the scope of the transparency framework.

In practice, Slovenia has issued eight past rulings; for the period 1 April 2016 - 31 December 2016, Slovenia issued no future rulings; and for the year in review, Slovenia issued one future ruling within the scope of the transparency framework.

Peer input was received from one jurisdiction in respect of the exchanges of information on rulings received from Slovenia. It was positive, noting that information was complete, in the correct format and indicating that co-operation with Slovenia had been positive.

Introduction

1199. This peer review covers Slovenia's implementation of the BEPS Action 5 transparency framework for the year 2017. The report has four parts, each relating to a key part of the ToR. Each part is discussed in turn. A summary of recommendations is included at the end of this report.

A. The information gathering process

1200. Slovenia can legally issue the following three types of rulings within the scope of the transparency framework: (i) cross-border unilateral advance pricing agreements (APAs) and any other cross-border unilateral tax rulings (such as an advance tax ruling) covering transfer pricing or the application of transfer pricing principles;[1] (ii) permanent establishment rulings; and (iii) related party conduit rulings. In Slovenia, rulings are issued by different financial offices, namely the General Financial Office, Special Financial Office and Regional Financial Offices, except for APAs that are issued only by the General Financial Office.

Past rulings (ToR I.4.1.1, I.4.1.2, I.4.2.1, I.4.2.2)

1201. For Slovenia, past rulings are any tax rulings within scope that are issued either: (i) on or after 1 January 2014 but before 1 April 2016; or (ii) on or after 1 January 2010 but before 1 January 2014, provided they were still in effect as at 1 January 2014.

1202. In the prior year peer review report, it was determined that Slovenia's undertakings to identify past rulings and all potential exchange jurisdictions were sufficient to meet the minimum standard. Slovenia's implementation in this regard remains unchanged, and therefore continues to meet the minimum standard.

Future rulings (ToR I.4.1.1, I.4.1.2, I.4.2.1)

1203. For Slovenia, future rulings are any tax rulings within scope that are issued on or after 1 April 2016.

1204. In the prior year peer review report, it was determined that Slovenia's undertakings to identify future rulings were sufficient to meet the minimum standards. The prior year peer review report noted that it was not clear that potential exchange jurisdictions were able to be identified in all cases, but noted that Slovenia's updated rulings process was in place as of 1 January 2017 which remedied this issue and no recommendations were made.

1205. Under the new process in place as of 1 January 2017, all rulings and APAs issued after 1 January 2017 are registered in the centralised documentation database of the Financial Administration and are attributed a special identification number (code). The code allows for the ruling or APA to be identified and tracked though the system. The Financial Administration also created a special template, similar to the Annex C in the 2015 Action 5 Report (OECD, 2015), to be completed for any ruling or APA being issued, that requests relevant information on the taxpayer and potential exchange jurisdictions. The template is available on the intranet site of the Financial Administration. In this way, Slovenia notes that it is ensured that information on all issued rulings/APAs is always obtained and thus ensures that information is collected on potential exchange jurisdictions.

Review and supervision mechanism (ToR I.4.3)

1206. In the prior year peer review report, it was determined that the General Financial Office's review and supervision mechanisms were sufficient to meet the minimum standard. In 2017, the General Financial Office issued instructions on the updated process for identification of future rulings and APAs issued as of 1 January 2017 and the creation of the special template to capture all information relevant under Action 5. In addition, a check is performed to ensure that all issued rulings have been reported to the General Financial Office. Slovenia also indicates training was provided for handling future rulings issued in 2017.

Conclusion on section A

1207. Slovenia has met all of the ToR for the information gathering process and no recommendations are made.

B. The exchange of information

Legal basis for spontaneous exchange of information (ToR II.5.1, II.5.2)

1208. Slovenia has the necessary domestic legal basis to exchange information spontaneously. Slovenia notes that there are no legal or practical impediments that prevent the spontaneous exchange of information on rulings as contemplated in the Action 5 minimum standard.

1209. Slovenia is a party to international agreements permitting spontaneous exchange of information, including (i) the *Multilateral Convention on Mutual Administrative Assistance in Tax Matters: Amended by the 2010 Protocol* (OECD/Council of Europe, 2011) ("the Convention"), (ii) the Directive 2011/16/EU with all other European Union Member States and (iii) double tax agreements in force with 59 jurisdictions.[2]

Completion and exchange of templates (ToR II.5.3, II.5.4, II.5.5, II.5.6, II.5.7)

1210. Slovenia uses the EU central directory deployed by the European Commission to exchange information on rulings and APAs among the EU Member States as well as non-EU Member States. The process for the completion and exchange of templates has been updated to incorporate the use of the central directory.

1211. The officials handling different aspects of the exchange of information process are attributed specific user profiles and access rights to the intranet application shared by the different financial offices. The same officer who issues a ruling is required to complete a template available on the intranet which contains all information on rulings as requested in Annex C of the Action 5 report (OECD, 2015). This information template is then reviewed by an official of the General Finance Office ("DAC3 ruling encoder") who checks whether the ruling is in scope of Action 5 and DAC3 and verifies that all conditions for exchange are met. For those rulings which are relevant to non-EU Member States, the Annex C template is prepared for exchange and it is also entered into the EU central directory by the DAC3 ruling encoder. The information is reviewed by another official of the General Finance Office ("DAC3 ruling reviewer"). Once reviewed, the information template is then sent to the Competent Authority to submit the information on the ruling or APA for exchange, in the OECD XML or Annex C format. The information on ruling or APA is exchanged in a week or two after the ruling or APA information is received by the personnel responsible for the exchange of information.

1212. Slovenia indicates that it has relied on the guidelines in the XML Schema and User Guide for the exchange of information on rulings for the year in review and the prior year by including a short summary of the ruling which includes relevant information that could help the receiving tax administration to assess potential base erosion and profit shifting risks. In the future, Slovenia intends to incorporate the FHTP internal suggested guide in its rulings processes.

1213. For the year in review, the timeliness of exchanges is as follows:

Past rulings in the scope of the transparency framework	Number of exchanges transmitted by 31 December 2017	Delayed exchanges		
		Number of exchanges not transmitted by 31 December 2017	Reasons for the delays	Any other comments
	N/A	N/A		No past rulings had to be exchanged with new members of the IF that joined in 2017 and as such no additional exchanges on past rulings were required.
Future rulings in the scope of the transparency framework	**Number of exchanges transmitted within three months of the information becoming available to the competent authority or immediately after legal impediments have been lifted**	**Delayed exchanges**		
		Number of exchanges transmitted later than three months of the information on rulings becoming available to the competent authority	**Reasons for the delays**	**Any other comments**
	1	0	N/A	
Total	1	0		

Follow up requests received for exchange of the ruling	Number	Average time to provide response	Number of requests not answered
	0	N/A	N/A

Conclusion on section B

1214. Slovenia has met all of the ToR for the exchange of information process and no recommendations are made.

C. Statistics (ToR IV)

1215. The statistics for the year in review are as follows:

Category of ruling	Number of exchanges	Jurisdictions exchanged with
Rulings related to preferential regimes	N/A	N/A
Cross-border unilateral advance pricing agreements (APAs) and any other cross-border unilateral tax rulings (such as an advance tax ruling) covering transfer pricing or the application of transfer pricing principles	0	N/A
Cross-border rulings providing for a unilateral downward adjustment to the taxpayer's taxable profits that is not directly reflected in the taxpayer's financial / commercial accounts	N/A	N/A
Permanent establishment rulings	Included in *de minimis*	N/A
Related party conduit rulings	0	N/A
De minimis rule	1	N/A
IP regimes: total exchanges on taxpayers benefitting from the third category of IP assets, new entrants benefitting from grandfathered IP regimes; and taxpayers making use of the option to treat the nexus ratio as a rebuttable presumption	N/A	N/A
Total	1	

D. Matters related to intellectual property regimes (ToR I.4.1.3)

1216. Slovenia does not offer an intellectual property regime for which transparency requirements under the Action 5 Report (OECD, 2015) were imposed.

Summary of recommendations on implementation of the transparency framework

Aspect of implementation of the transparency framework that should be improved	Recommendation for improvement
	No recommendations are made.

Notes

[1] Slovenia introduced an APA program starting on 1 January 2017 that involves all transfer pricing issues.

[2] Parties to the Convention are available here: www.oecd.org/tax/exchange-of-tax-information/convention-on-mutual-administrative-assistance-in-tax-matters.htm. Slovenia also has bilateral agreements with Albania, Armenia, Austria, Azerbaijan, Belgium, Belarus, Bosnia and Herzegovina, Bulgaria, Canada, China (People's Republic of), Croatia, Cyprus, Czech Republic, Denmark, Estonia, Finland, Former Yugoslav Republic of Macedonia, France, Georgia, Germany, Greece, Hungary, Iceland, India, Iran, Ireland, Isle Of Man, Israel, Italy, Kazakhstan, Korea, Kosovo, Kuwait, Latvia, Lithuania, Luxembourg, Malta, Moldova, Netherlands, Norway, Poland, Portugal, Qatar, Romania, Russia, Serbia, Montenegro, Singapore, Slovak Republic, Spain, Sweden, Switzerland, Thailand, Turkey, Ukraine, United Arab Emirates, United Kingdom, United States and Uzbekistan.

Note by Turkey: The information in this document with reference to "Cyprus" relates to the southern part of the Island. There is no single authority representing both Turkish and Greek Cypriot people on the Island. Turkey recognises the Turkish Republic of Northern Cyprus (TRNC). Until a lasting and equitable solution is found within the context of the United Nations, Turkey shall preserve its position concerning the "Cyprus issue".

Note by all the European Union Member States of the OECD and the European Union. The Republic of Cyprus is recognised by all members of the United Nations with the exception of Turkey. The information in this document relates to the area under the effective control of the Government of the Republic of Cyprus.

References

OECD (2017), *BEPS Action 5 on Harmful Tax Practices – Terms of Reference and Methodology for the Conduct of the Peer Reviews of the Action 5 Transparency Framework*, OECD/G20 Base Erosion and Profit Shifting Project, OECD, Paris. www.oecd.org/tax/beps/beps-action-5-harmful-tax-practices-peer-review-transparencyframework.pdf.

OECD (2015), *Countering Harmful Tax Practices More Effectively, Taking into Account Transparency and Substance, Action 5 - 2015 Final Report*, OECD/G20 Base Erosion and Profit Shifting Project, OECD Publishing, Paris. https://doi.org/10.1787/9789264241190-en.

OECD/Council of Europe (2011), *The Multilateral Convention on Mutual Administrative Assistance in Tax Matters: Amended by the 2010 Protocol*, OECD Publishing, Paris. http://dx.doi.org/10.1787/9789264115606-en.

South Africa

South Africa has met all aspects of the terms of reference (ToR) for the calendar year 2017 (year in review) and no recommendations are made.

South Africa can legally issue one type of rulings within the scope of the transparency framework.

In practice, South Africa has issued one past ruling; and for the period 1 April 2016 - 31 December 2016 and for the year in review, South Africa issued no future rulings within the scope of the transparency framework.

No peer input was received in respect of the exchanges of information on rulings received from South Africa.

Introduction

1217. This peer review covers South Africa's implementation of the BEPS Action 5 transparency framework for the year 2017. The report has four parts, each relating to a key part of the ToR. Each part is discussed in turn. A summary of recommendations is included at the end of this report.

A. The information gathering process

1218. South Africa can legally issue one type of rulings within the scope of the transparency framework: rulings related to preferential regimes.[1] In South Africa, rulings are issued by the rulings division, a centralised department within the legal advisory division of the South African Revenue Service ("SARS"). Anonymised copies of rulings are published on the South African Revenue Service website.[2]

Past rulings (ToR I.4.1.1, I.4.1.2, I.4.2.1, I.4.2.2)

1219. For South Africa, past rulings are any tax rulings within scope that are issued either: (i) on or after 1 January 2014 but before 1 April 2016; or (ii) on or after 1 January 2010 but before 1 January 2014, provided they were still in effect as at 1 January 2014.

1220. In the prior year peer review report, it was determined that South Africa's undertakings to identify past rulings and all potential exchange jurisdictions were sufficient to meet the minimum standard. South Africa's implementation in this regard remains unchanged, and therefore continues to meet the minimum standard.

Future rulings (ToR I.4.1.1, I.4.1.2, I.4.2.1)

1221. For South Africa, future rulings are any tax rulings within scope that are issued on or after 1 April 2016.

1222. In the prior year peer review report, it was determined that South Africa's undertakings to identify future rulings and all potential exchange jurisdictions were sufficient to meet the minimum standards. South Africa's implementation in this regard continues to meet the minimum standard.

Review and supervision mechanism (ToR I.4.3)

1223. In the prior year peer review report, it was determined that the South African Tax Administration's review and supervision mechanisms were sufficient to meet the minimum standard. The South African Tax Administration's implementation in this regard continues to meet the minimum standard.

Conclusion on section A

1224. South Africa has met all of the ToR for the information gathering process and no recommendations are made.

B. The exchange of information

Legal basis for spontaneous exchange of information (ToR II.5.1, II.5.2)

1225. South Africa has the necessary domestic legal basis to exchange information spontaneously. South Africa notes that there are no legal or practical impediments that prevent the spontaneous exchange of information on rulings as contemplated in the Action 5 minimum standard.

1226. South Africa is a party to international agreements permitting spontaneous exchange of information, including (i) the *Multilateral Convention on Mutual Administrative Assistance in Tax Matters: Amended by the 2010 Protocol* (OECD/Council of Europe, 2011) ("the Convention") and (ii) double tax agreements in force with 67 jurisdictions.[3]

Completion and exchange of templates (ToR II.5.3, II.5.4, II.5.5, II.5.6, II.5.7)

1227. In the prior year peer review report, it was determined that the South Africa's completion and exchange of templates were sufficient to meet the minimum standard. South Africa' implementation in this regard remains unchanged, and therefore continues to meet the minimum standard.

1228. South Africa indicates that the FHTP internal suggested guide will be utilised for completing the summary section of Annex C of the 2015 Action 5 Report (OECD, 2015) for information exchanged under the transparency framework and it will be incorporated into South Africa's processes in the future. In addition, focus will be placed on the facts of the transaction to ensure that it is adequately explained and the summary will also be reviewed by a group executive for quality purposes.

1229. For the year in review, the timeliness of exchanges is as follows:

Past rulings in the scope of the transparency framework	Number of exchanges transmitted by 31 December 2017	Delayed exchanges		
		Number of exchanges not transmitted by 31 December 2017	Reasons for the delays	Any other comments
	1	N/A	N/A	Exchange transmitted to country that is a new Inclusive Framework member.
Future rulings in the scope of the transparency framework	**Number of exchanges transmitted within three months of the information becoming available to the competent authority or immediately after legal impediments have been lifted**	**Delayed exchanges**		
		Number of exchanges transmitted later than three months of the information on rulings becoming available to the competent authority	**Reasons for the delays**	**Any other comments**
	N/A	N/A	N/A	
Total	1	N/A		

Follow up requests received for exchange of the ruling	Number	Average time to provide response	Number of requests not answered
	0	N/A	N/A

Conclusion on section B

1230. South Africa has met all of the ToR for the exchange of information process and no recommendations are made.

C. Statistics (ToR IV)

1231. The statistics for the year in review are as follows:

Category of ruling	Number of exchanges	Jurisdictions exchanged with
Rulings related to preferential regimes	Included in *de minimis*	N/A
Cross-border unilateral advance pricing agreements (APAs) and any other cross-border unilateral tax rulings (such as an advance tax ruling) covering transfer pricing or the application of transfer pricing principles	N/A	N/A
Cross-border rulings providing for a unilateral downward adjustment to the taxpayer's taxable profits that is not directly reflected in the taxpayer's financial / commercial accounts	N/A	N/A
Permanent establishment rulings	N/A	N/A
Related party conduit rulings	N/A	N/A
De minimis rule	1	N/A
IP regimes: total exchanges on taxpayers benefitting from the third category of IP assets, new entrants benefitting from grandfathered IP regimes; and taxpayers making use of the option to treat the nexus ratio as a rebuttable presumption	N/A	N/A
Total	1	

D. Matters related to intellectual property regimes (ToR I.4.1.3)

1232. South Africa does not offer an intellectual property regime for which transparency requirements under the Action 5 Report (OECD, 2015) were imposed.

Summary of recommendations on implementation of the transparency framework

Aspect of implementation of the transparency framework that should be improved	Recommendation for improvement
	No recommendations are made.

Notes

[1] With respect to the following preferential regimes: 1) Shipping regime and 2) Headquarters regime.

[2] Available at: www.sars.gov.za (accessed 20 November 2018).

[3] Parties to the Multilateral Convention are available here: www.oecd.org/tax/exchange-of-tax-information/convention-on-mutual-administrative-assistance-in-tax-matters.htm. South Africa also has bilateral agreements with Algeria, Australia, Austria, Belarus, Belgium, Botswana, Brazil, Bulgaria, Cameroon, Canada, Chile, China (People's Republic of), Croatia, Cyprus, Czech Republic, Democratic Republic of Congo, Denmark, Egypt, Ethiopia, Finland, France, Ghana, Greece, Hong Kong, Hungary, India, Indonesia, Iran, Ireland, Italy, Japan, Kenya, Korea, Lesotho, Luxembourg, Malaysia, Malta, Mauritius, Mexico, Mozambique, Namibia, Netherlands, New Zealand, Nigeria, Norway, Oman, Pakistan, Poland, Portugal, Qatar, Rwanda, Samoa, Saudi Arabia, Seychelles, Singapore, Slovak Republic, Spain, Swaziland, Sweden, Tanzania, Turkey, Uganda, Ukraine, United Arab Emirates, United Kingdom, United States and Zimbabwe.

Note by Turkey: The information in this document with reference to "Cyprus" relates to the southern part of the Island. There is no single authority representing both Turkish and Greek Cypriot people on the Island. Turkey recognises the Turkish Republic of Northern Cyprus (TRNC). Until a lasting and equitable solution is found within the context of the United Nations, Turkey shall preserve its position concerning the "Cyprus issue".

Note by all the European Union Member States of the OECD and the European Union. The Republic of Cyprus is recognised by all members of the United Nations with the exception of Turkey. The information in this document relates to the area under the effective control of the Government of the Republic of Cyprus.

References

OECD (2017), *BEPS Action 5 on Harmful Tax Practices – Terms of Reference and Methodology for the Conduct of the Peer Reviews of the Action 5 Transparency Framework*, OECD/G20 Base Erosion and Profit Shifting Project, OECD, Paris. www.oecd.org/tax/beps/beps-action-5-harmful-tax-practices-peer-review-transparencyframework.pdf.

OECD (2015), *Countering Harmful Tax Practices More Effectively, Taking into Account Transparency and Substance, Action 5 - 2015 Final Report*, OECD/G20 Base Erosion and Profit Shifting Project, OECD Publishing, Paris. https://doi.org/10.1787/9789264241190-en.

OECD/Council of Europe (2011), *The Multilateral Convention on Mutual Administrative Assistance in Tax Matters: Amended by the 2010 Protocol*, OECD Publishing, Paris. http://dx.doi.org/10.1787/9789264115606-en.

Spain

Spain has met all aspects of the terms of reference (ToR) for the calendar year 2017 (year in review), except for collecting and exchanging information on new assets of existing taxpayers benefitting from the grandfathered IP regime (ToR I.4.1.3). For the year in review, Spain is recommended to identify and exchange relevant information on new assets of existing taxpayers benefitting from the grandfathered IP regime.

Spain can legally issue three types of rulings within the scope of the transparency framework.

In practice, Spain has issued 146 past rulings; for the period 1 April 2016 - 31 December 2016, Spain issued 28 future rulings; and for the year in review, Spain issued 46 future rulings within the scope of the transparency framework.

Peer input was received from four jurisdictions in respect of the exchanges of information on rulings received from Spain. It was positive, noting that information was complete, in the correct format and received in a timely manner.

Introduction

1233. This peer review covers Spain's implementation of the BEPS Action 5 transparency framework for the year 2017. The report has four parts, each relating to a key part of the ToR. Each part is discussed in turn. A summary of recommendations is included at the end of this report.

A. The information gathering process

1234. Spain can legally issue the three following types of rulings within the scope of the transparency framework: (i) rulings related to preferential regimes;[1] (ii) cross-border unilateral (APAs) and any other cross-border unilateral tax rulings (such as an advance tax ruling) covering transfer pricing or the application of transfer pricing principles; and (iii) permanent establishment rulings. Depending on the type of ruling, such decisions are made and coordinated either by two national offices: the General Directorate for Taxation (Ministry of Finance) and the International Taxation Office (Spanish Tax Agency) or by one of four subnational offices in Basque Country and Navarra. Rulings excluding APAs are published in anonymised form.[2]

Past rulings (ToR I.4.1.1, I.4.1.2, I.4.2.1, I.4.2.2)

1235. For Spain, past rulings are any tax rulings within scope that are issued either: (i) on or after 1 January 2014 but before 1 April 2016; or (ii) on or after 1 January 2010 but before 1 January 2014, provided they were still in effect as at 1 January 2014.

1236. In the prior year peer review report, it was determined that Spain's undertakings to identify past rulings met the ToR, except that Spain was recommended to use the "best efforts approach" to identify the potential exchange jurisdictions for past rulings, which were preferential regimes or permanent establishment rulings (ToR I.4.2.2). Spain has used the "best efforts approach" by verifying the information already available within the tax administration, which is obtained through the General Directorate of Taxation database. Where necessary, publicly available information was used. Spain confirms that in all cases, all potential exchange jurisdictions were able to be identified. It is therefore determined that Spain's undertakings to identify the potential exchange jurisdictions with respect to past rulings meet the minimum standard.

Future rulings (ToR I.4.1.1, I.4.1.2, I.4.2.1)

1237. For Spain, future rulings are any tax rulings within scope that are issued on or after 1 April 2016.

1238. In the prior year peer review report, the process of issuing and identifying future ruling was described. This process met the ToR, except that Spain did not yet collect information on all potential exchange jurisdictions for future rulings which are preferential regimes or permanent establishment rulings (ToR I.4.2.1). Therefore, it was recommended that Spain continues with its proposal to amend its rulings practice for all future rulings to require taxpayers to provide information on all potential exchange jurisdictions as part of the ruling process.

1239. As of 29 December 2017, Spain modified the Royal Decree 1065/2007 of 27 July, to expand the information that the taxpayer must provide when asking for a ruling, including all the information required to identify potential exchange jurisdictions. For the period until 29 December 2017, Spain used the "best efforts approach" by using internal information to identify the potential exchange jurisdictions. Spain was able to obtain information on potential exchange jurisdictions and therefore it is determined that Spain's undertakings to identify the potential exchange jurisdictions with respect to future rulings before the amended Decree took effect meet the minimum standard.

Review and supervision mechanism (ToR I.4.3)

1240. In the prior year peer review report, it was determined that Spain's review and supervision mechanism was sufficient to meet the minimum standard. Spain's implementation in this regard remains unchanged, and therefore continues to meet the minimum standard.

Conclusion on section A

1241. Spain has met all the ToR for the information gathering process and no recommendations are made.

B. The exchange of information

Legal basis for spontaneous exchange of information (ToR II.5.1, II.5.2)

1242. Spain has the necessary domestic legal basis to exchange information spontaneously. Spain notes that there are no legal or practical impediments that prevent the spontaneous exchange of information on rulings as contemplated in the Action 5 minimum standard.

1243. Spain is a party to international agreements permitting spontaneous exchange of information, including (i) the *Multilateral Convention on Mutual Administrative Assistance in Tax Matters: Amended by the 2010 Protocol* (OECD/Council of Europe, 2011) ("the Convention"), (ii) the Directive 2011/16/EU with all other European Union Member States and (iii) double tax agreements in force with 12 jurisdictions and (iv) tax information exchange agreements with 92 jurisdictions.[3]

Completion and exchange of templates (ToR II.5.3, II.5.4, II.5.5, II.5.6, II.5.7)

1244. In the prior year peer review report, Spain's process for the completion and exchange of templates was sufficient to meet the minimum standard, except that Spain transmitted information on future rulings to the Competent Authority at six monthly intervals each year, to align with the EU Directive deadlines, which are longer than necessary. Therefore, Spain was recommended to reduce the timelines for providing the information on future rulings to the Competent Authority.

1245. In the year of review, Spain has set up a system to accelerate the time of sending the information to the Competent Authority. This system is based on an electronic template which is populated when an APA is signed and this makes the information available within two months to the Competent Authority for the exchange. For other types of rulings, the system is based on a template to be completed when the ruling is published (one month after it is signed) and the information is made available to the Competent Authority for the exchange of information within two months. After the template has been made available to the Competent Authority, the exchange with the relevant jurisdictions has to take place within three months.

1246. This process was implemented on 4 December 2017, which is relatively late in the year of review. However, the recommendation in the prior year peer review report acknowledged that the approach taken by Spain in 2016 reflected its understanding at the time that such timelines would be consistent with the ToR for the transparency framework, and this interpretation issue was resolved by the FHTP in October 2017, when most of the year in review had already passed. Spain has taken its best efforts to implement this new process as soon as possible after the issuance of the recommendation and therefore the prior year recommendation has been removed. The timeliness of the new process will be reviewed in the subsequent peer review.

1247. For completing the summary section of the template, tax officers are instructed to include a brief description of the subject and outcome of the issue contained in the rulings. In addition, with respect to APAs, the summary section includes a description of the relevant business activity or transactions or series of transactions and a summary of the functional analysis performed, and where appropriate, the functional profile of the entity. The summary section is completed in English and Spanish.

1248. For the year in review, the timeliness of exchanges is as follows:

Past rulings in the scope of the transparency framework	Number of exchanges transmitted by 31 December 2017	Delayed exchanges		
		Number of exchanges not transmitted by 31 December 2017	Reasons for the delays	Any other comments
	0	0	N/A	
Future rulings in the scope of the transparency framework	Number of exchanges transmitted within three months of the information becoming available to the competent authority or immediately after legal impediments have been lifted	Delayed exchanges		
		Number of exchanges transmitted later than three months of the information on rulings becoming available to the competent authority	Reasons for the delays	Any other comments
	124	0	N/A	
Total	124	0		

Follow up requests received for exchange of the ruling	Number	Average time to provide response	Number of requests not answered
	0	N/A	N/A

Conclusion on section B

1249. Spain has the necessary legal framework and administrative processes in place for exchanging information on rulings. Spain has met all of the ToR for the exchange of information process.

C. Statistics (ToR IV)

1250. The statistics for the year in review are as follows:

Category of ruling	Number of exchanges	Jurisdictions exchanged with
Rulings related to preferential regimes	Included in *de minimis*	N/A
Cross-border unilateral advance pricing agreements (APAs) and any other cross-border unilateral tax rulings (such as an advance tax ruling) covering transfer pricing or the application of transfer pricing principles	89	Argentina, Australia, Brazil, Canada, Czech Republic, Germany, France, Hungary, Ireland, Italy, Luxembourg, Mexico, Netherlands, Norway, Portugal, Romania, South Africa, United Kingdom, United States
Cross-border rulings providing for a unilateral downward adjustment to the taxpayer's taxable profits that is not directly reflected in the taxpayer's financial / commercial accounts	N/A	N/A
Permanent establishment rulings	25	Andorra, Austria, Finland, Germany, Latvia, Luxembourg, Netherlands, Norway, Portugal, Romania, United Kingdom
Related party conduit rulings	N/A	N/A
De minimis rule	2	N/A
IP regimes: total exchanges on taxpayers benefitting from the third category of IP assets, new entrants benefitting from grandfathered IP regimes; and taxpayers making use of the option to treat the nexus ratio as a rebuttable presumption	8	Argentina, Brazil, Italy, Mexico, Portugal
Total	124	

D. Matters related to intellectual property regimes (ToR I.4.1.3)

1251. Spain offers three intellectual property regimes ("IP regime") that are subject to transparency requirements under the Action 5 Report (OECD, 2015).[4] It states that the identification of the benefitting taxpayers will occur as follows:

- ***New entrants benefitting from the grandfathered IP regime***: specific provisions were included in the corporate income tax returns as of 2016 to identify new taxpayers, which apply starting with the 2015 tax period. Specific provisions for the subnational regimes were also included in their 2016 corporate income tax returns. The first tax returns were filed by 25 July 2016 for taxpayers on a calendar year. Spain completed eight exchanges of information on new entrants for the year 2015 in May 2017. Information from taxpayers which use a non-calendar year for tax purposes and file their return later will be exchanged in the next year. Spain plans to send information on new entrants on an annual basis. A new tax form was adopted in August 2017 in order to include, among other items, information about new entrants benefitting from the grandfathered IP regime. This tax return will be submitted by taxpayers using the calendar year by the end of November. Therefore, as soon as information on new entrants for tax year 2016 is reviewed by the Tax Agency, it will be sent on an annual basis. However, new IP assets cannot be identified in the absence of the relevant data in the tax returns. This information could be collected in the case of a formal investigation. It is noted that it would not be practicable for Spain to open a formal investigation solely to obtain this information. Spain is considering how best to collect this information. Therefore, Spain is recommended to identify and exchange relevant information on new assets of existing taxpayers benefitting from the grandfathered IP regime.

- ***Third category of IP assets***: not applicable to these IP regimes, which in 2017 were in the process of being amended. See below for recent updates.
- ***Taxpayers making use of the option to treat the nexus ratio as a rebuttable presumption***: not applicable to these IP regimes, which in 2017 were in the process of being amended. See below for recent updates.

Summary of recommendations on implementation of the transparency framework

Aspect of implementation of the transparency framework that should be improved	Recommendation for improvement
Spain has not exchanged information on new assets of existing taxpayers benefitting from the grandfathered regime as this information was not available during the year in review.	Spain is recommended to identify and exchange relevant information on new assets of existing taxpayers benefitting from the grandfathered IP regime.

Jurisdiction's response and recent developments

1252. With effect from 1 January 2018, Spain has amended its IP regimes. The federal IP regime is now concluded as "not harmful".[1] The third category of IP assets and the treatment of the nexus ratio as a rebuttable presumption are not included in the amended regimes and therefore no transparency requirements are relevant. In addition to this, Spain notes that these two options were also not included in the previous regimes.

[1] Spain's partial exemption for income from certain intangible assets was inconsistent with the nexus approach for IP assets acquired from related parties for the period from 1 January 2017 to 31 December 2017 and for new taxpayers entering the regime in the period from 1 July 2016 to 31 December 2017.

Notes

[1] With respect to the following preferential regimes: 1) Partial exemption for income from certain intangible assets and 2) Shipping regime.

[2] For rulings issued by the General Directorate of Taxation, available at http://petete.minhafp.gob.es/consultas/ (accessed 20 November 2018).

[3] Parties to the Convention are available here: www.oecd.org/tax/exchange-of-tax-information/convention-on-mutual-administrative-assistance-in-tax-matters.htm. Spain also has Double Tax Agreements with: Spain has Double Tax Agreements with Albania, Algeria, Andorra, Argentina, Armenia, Australia, Austria, Barbados, Belarus, Belgium, Bolivia, Bosnia and Herzegovina, Brazil, Bulgaria, Canada, Chile, China (People's Republic of), Colombia, Costa Rica, Croatia, Cuba, Cyprus, Czech Republic, Dominican Republic, Ecuador, Egypt, El Salvador, Estonia, Finland, Former Yugoslav Republic of Macedonia, France, Georgia, Germany, Greece, Hong Kong (China), Hungary, Iceland, India, Indonesia, Iran, Ireland, Israel, Italy, Jamaica, Japan, Kazakhstan, Korea, Kuwait, Kyrgyzstan, Latvia, Lithuania, Luxembourg, Malaysia, Malta, Mexico, Moldova, Morocco, Netherlands, New Zealand, Nigeria, Norway, Oman, Pakistan, Panama, Philippines, Poland, Portugal, Romania, Russia, Saudi Arabia, Senegal, Serbia, Singapore, Slovak Republic, Slovenia, South Africa, Sweden, Switzerland, Tajikistan, Thailand, Trinidad and Tobago, Tunisia, Turkey, Turkmenistan, Ukraine, United Arab Emirates, United Kingdom, United States, Uruguay, Uzbekistan, Venezuela and Viet Nam.

Note by Turkey: The information in this document with reference to "Cyprus" relates to the southern part of the Island. There is no single authority representing both Turkish and Greek Cypriot people on the Island. Turkey recognises the Turkish Republic of Northern Cyprus (TRNC). Until a lasting and equitable solution is found within the context of the United Nations, Turkey shall preserve its position concerning the "Cyprus issue".

Note by all the European Union Member States of the OECD and the European Union. The Republic of Cyprus is recognised by all members of the United Nations with the exception of Turkey. The information in this document relates to the area under the effective control of the Government of the Republic of Cyprus.

[4] These regimes are the partial exemptions for income from certain intangible assets for: 1) Federal regime, 2) Basque country and 3) Navarra.

References

OECD (2017), *BEPS Action 5 on Harmful Tax Practices – Terms of Reference and Methodology for the Conduct of the Peer Reviews of the Action 5 Transparency Framework*, OECD/G20 Base Erosion and Profit Shifting Project, OECD, Paris. www.oecd.org/tax/beps/beps-action-5-harmful-tax-practices-peer-review-transparencyframework.pdf.

OECD (2015), *Countering Harmful Tax Practices More Effectively, Taking into Account Transparency and Substance, Action 5 - 2015 Final Report*, OECD/G20 Base Erosion and Profit Shifting Project, OECD Publishing, Paris. https://doi.org/10.1787/9789264241190-en.

OECD/Council of Europe (2011), *The Multilateral Convention on Mutual Administrative Assistance in Tax Matters: Amended by the 2010 Protocol*, OECD Publishing, Paris. http://dx.doi.org/10.1787/9789264115606-en.

Sri Lanka

Sri Lanka was not yet able to complete the peer review questionnaire.[1] It is not known whether Sri Lanka has implemented the transparency framework. Sri Lanka is recommended to ensure that it has put in place an effective information gathering process to identify all relevant past and future rulings and all potential exchange jurisdictions and to implement a review and supervision mechanism, as soon as possible (ToR I.4.). Sri Lanka is recommended to put in place a domestic legal framework allowing spontaneous exchange of information on rulings if needed and to ensure the timely exchange of information on rulings in the form required by the transparency framework (ToR II.5).

It is not known whether Sri Lanka can legally issue any types of ruling within the scope of the transparency framework, or whether in practice Sri Lanka issued any such rulings.

No peer input was received in respect of the exchanges of information on rulings received from Sri Lanka.

Introduction

1253. This peer review covers Sri Lanka's implementation of the BEPS Action 5 transparency framework for the year 2017. The report has four parts, each relating to a key part of the ToR. Each part is discussed in turn. A summary of recommendations is included at the end of this report.

A. The information gathering process

1254. Sri Lanka was not yet able to complete the peer review questionnaire. It is not known whether Sri Lanka has implemented the transparency framework.

1255. Sri Lanka is recommended to ensure that it has put in place an effective information gathering process to identify all relevant past and future rulings and all potential exchange jurisdictions and to implement a review and supervision mechanism, as soon as possible (ToR I.4).

B. The exchange of information

Legal basis for spontaneous exchange of information (ToR II.5.1, II.5.2)

1256. It is not known whether Sri Lanka has the necessary domestic legal basis to exchange information spontaneously. Sri Lanka is recommended to put in place a domestic legal framework allowing spontaneous exchange of information on rulings if needed.

1257. Sri Lanka has 44 bilateral agreements in force which would allow for spontaneous exchange of information under the transparency framework.[2] Sri Lanka is not a party to the *Multilateral Convention on Mutual Administrative Assistance in Tax Matters: Amended by the 2010 Protocol* (OECD/Council of Europe, 2011) ("the Convention").

Completion and exchange of templates (ToR II.5.3, II.5.4, II.5.5, II.5.6, II.5.7)

1258. Sri Lanka is recommended to put in place a domestic legal framework allowing spontaneous exchange of information on rulings if needed and to ensure the timely exchange of information on rulings in the form required by the transparency framework (ToR II.5).

C. Statistics (ToR IV)

1259. Sri Lanka did not provide statistical data for the year in review. In the absence of this information, no statistics can be reported.

E. Matters related to intellectual property regimes (ToR I.4.1.3)

1260. Sri Lanka does not offer an intellectual property regime for which transparency requirements under the Action 5 Report (OECD, 2015) were imposed.

Summary of recommendations on implementation of the transparency framework

Aspect of implementation of the transparency framework that should be improved	Recommendation for improvement
It is not known whether Sri Lanka has an information gathering process in place	Sri Lanka is recommended to ensure that it has put in place an effective information gathering process to identify all relevant past and future rulings and all potential exchange jurisdictions and to implement a review and supervision mechanism, as soon as possible.
It is not known whether Sri Lanka has a domestic legal framework allowing spontaneous exchange of information on rulings and has a process in place to ensure the timely exchange of information on rulings in the form required by the transparency framework	Sri Lanka is recommended to put in place a domestic legal framework allowing spontaneous exchange of information on rulings if needed and to ensure the timely exchange of information on rulings in the form required by the transparency framework.

Notes

[1] Sri Lanka did not provide written comments on this peer review report.

[2] Sri Lanka has bilateral agreements in force with Australia, Bangladesh, Bahrain, Belarus, Belgium, Canada, China (People's Republic of), Czech Republic, Denmark, Finland, France, Germany, Hong Kong (China), India, Indonesia, Iran, Italy, Japan, Korea, Kuwait, Luxembourg, Malaysia, Mauritius, Nepal, Netherlands, Norway, Oman, Pakistan, Palestinian Authority, Philippines, Poland, Qatar, Romania, Russia, Saudi Arabia, Seychelles, Singapore, Sweden, Switzerland, Thailand, United Arab Emirates, United Kingdom, United States, and Viet Nam.

References

OECD (2017), *BEPS Action 5 on Harmful Tax Practices – Terms of Reference and Methodology for the Conduct of the Peer Reviews of the Action 5 Transparency Framework*, OECD/G20 Base Erosion and Profit Shifting Project, OECD, Paris. www.oecd.org/tax/beps/beps-action-5-harmful-tax-practices-peer-review-transparencyframework.pdf.

OECD (2015), *Countering Harmful Tax Practices More Effectively, Taking into Account Transparency and Substance, Action 5 - 2015 Final Report*, OECD/G20 Base Erosion and Profit Shifting Project, OECD Publishing, Paris. https://doi.org/10.1787/9789264241190-en.

OECD/Council of Europe (2011), *The Multilateral Convention on Mutual Administrative Assistance in Tax Matters: Amended by the 2010 Protocol*, OECD Publishing, Paris. http://dx.doi.org/10.1787/9789264115606-en.

Sweden

Sweden has met all aspects of the terms of reference (ToR) for the calendar year 2017 (year in review) except for identifying past rulings (ToR I.4.1.2) and for identifying all potential exchange jurisdictions for future rulings (ToR I.4.2.1). Sweden has reviewed its process for identifying both past and future rulings and given that the error in identifying additional past rulings in 2017 is not a recurring issue, no recommendation is made. However, the recommendation from the prior year peer review for Sweden to amend its rulings practice to require taxpayers to provide information on potential exchange jurisdictions as part of the ruling process remains in place.

Sweden can legally issue three types of rulings within the scope of the transparency framework.

In practice, Sweden has issued 28 past rulings; for the period 1 April 2016 - 31 December 2016, Sweden issued five future rulings; and for the year in review, Sweden issued three future rulings within the scope of the transparency framework.

No peer input was received in respect of the exchanges of information on rulings received from Sweden.

Introduction

1261. This peer review covers Sweden's implementation of the BEPS Action 5 transparency framework for the year 2017. The report has four parts, each relating to a key part of the ToR. Each part is discussed in turn. A summary of recommendations is included at the end of this report.

A. The information gathering process

1262. Sweden can legally issue the following three types of rulings within the scope of the transparency framework: (i) rulings related to preferential regimes;[1] (ii) PE rulings; and (iii) related party conduit rulings. In Sweden, rulings are issued both by the National Board of Advance Tax Rulings ("National Board")[2] and the Swedish Tax Agency ("STA"). Some of these rulings are published in anonymised form.[3]

Past rulings (ToR I.4.1.1, I.4.1.2, I.4.2.1, I.4.2.2)

1263. For Sweden, past rulings are any tax rulings within scope that are issued either: (i) on or after 1 January 2014 but before 1 April 2016; or (ii) on or after 1 January 2010 but before 1 January 2014, provided they were still in effect as at 1 January 2014.

1264. In the prior year peer review report, it was determined that Sweden's undertakings to identify past rulings were sufficient to meet the minimum standard. However, Sweden indicated that four additional past rulings were identified in February and June 2017 (three of which related to OECD/G20 countries and one related to a member joining the Inclusive Framework in 2016) in addition to the 24 past rulings reported in the prior year report. The STA explained that the past rulings, which were identified only during the year of review, had been issued by a separate department within the STA, which had not yet been introduced to the transparency framework and therefore had been erroneously left out of the calculation of the number of rulings within scope of Action 5. The STA notes that the issue has been addressed and that each department went through all the relevant rulings once more to ensure that all rulings in scope were correctly identified. Since this issue has been remedied and should not be a recurring issue, no recommendation is made.

Future rulings (ToR I.4.1.1, I.4.1.2, I.4.2.1)

1265. For Sweden, future rulings are any tax rulings within scope that are issued on or after 1 April 2016.

1266. In the prior year peer review report, it was determined that Sweden's ruling process did not necessarily contain information on all potential exchange jurisdictions and a recommendation was issued for Sweden to amend its rulings practice to require taxpayers to provide all information on potential exchange jurisdictions for future rulings.

1267. The STA has acknowledged that there is a need to amend the process for issuing rulings both within the STA and the National Board to obtain all information required under Action 5. The Ministry of Finance have also acknowledged the need for legislative amendments in order to collect information on potential exchange jurisdictions and the Ministry of Finance is looking into this process.

1268. In order to ensure that all future rulings are correctly identified, the STA has implemented several measures in its rulings process to ensure that all relevant rulings are captured which includes additional training being given to a number of experienced tax officers to support the other officers in the process of identifying tax rulings which may be in scope of Action 5. In addition, the STA has published a position paper which explains its interpretation of the transparency framework. Among other issues, the position paper covers the scope, definitions, timelines and potential exchange jurisdictions under Action 5. The STA has also reviewed the process for identifying future rulings in order to ensure that all rulings are identified in a timely manner, including with respect to the department within STA where the additional past rulings were more recently identified. The STA has furthermore informed the relevant heads for each relevant department of the updated process and information is also published on the intranet of the STA.

1269. In the year of review, there was no change from the prior year process adopted by the STA to identify the information on potential exchange jurisdictions for the relevant future rulings, which consisted in consulting the text of the ruling. As such, the recommendation issued to Sweden remains in place.

Review and supervision mechanism (ToR I.4.3)

1270. In the prior year peer review report, it was determined that the STA's review and supervision mechanisms were sufficient to meet the minimum standard. In addition, the STA has enhanced its review and supervision mechanism. The STA has provided training for its staff to ensure that the personnel working on the implementation of the transparency framework are well equipped to make decisions on questions arising in their work. The STA has also set out a process for dealing with practical and theoretical issues related to the exchange of rulings. In addition, the STA has published a position paper outlining the requirements under Action 5. Therefore the STA's implementation in this regard continues to meet the minimum standard.

Conclusion on section A

1271. Sweden has met all the ToR for the information gathering process, except for the identification of past rulings (ToR I.4.1.2) and the identification of all potential exchange jurisdictions for future rulings (ToR I.4.2.1). The STA has reviewed the process for identifying rulings in order to ensure that in the future, all rulings are identified in timely manner. Therefore, as this issue has already been remedied and should not be a recurring issue, no recommendation is issued with regards to the identification of rulings within scope of Action 5. With regard to identifying potential exchange jurisdictions, Sweden is taking steps to address the issue and is recommended to continue to work on the necessary legislative amendments for identifying all potential exchange jurisdictions for future rulings. As such, the recommendation remains in place.

B. The exchange of information

Legal basis for spontaneous exchange of information (ToR II.5.1, II.5.2)

1272. Sweden has the necessary domestic legal basis to exchange information spontaneously. Sweden notes that there are no legal or practical impediments that prevent the spontaneous exchange of information on rulings as contemplated in the Action 5 minimum standard.

1273. Sweden is a party to international agreements permitting spontaneous exchange of information, including (i) the *Multilateral Convention on Mutual Administrative*

Assistance in Tax Matters: Amended by the 2010 Protocol (OECD/Council of Europe, 2011) ("the Convention"), (ii) the Directive 2011/16/EU with all other European Union Member States, (iii) the Nordic Convention on Assistance in Tax Matters and (iv) double tax agreements in force with 62 jurisdictions.[4]

Completion and exchange of templates (ToR II.5.3, II.5.4, II.5.5, II.5.6, II.5.7)

1274. Sweden uses the EU Central Directory developed by the European Commission to exchange information on rulings and APAs among the EU Member States as well as non-EU countries. The process for the completion and exchange of templates has been updated to incorporate the use of the Central Directory.

1275. Sweden indicates that when the officer issuing a tax ruling determines that it is within scope of Action 5, the identified ruling is reported to one of the appointed encoders at the STA responsible for preparing an information template using the EU Central Directory database. The template is then sent to a reviewer for a quality check to ensure that the information template is accurate and compliant with the Action 5 requirements. It is then submitted by certain appointed tax officers ("the Competent Authority") to the relevant jurisdiction in a secure and timely manner. Each ruling is sent in two different file types: an XML file created by the Central Directory and a pdf file, which reflects the fields contained in the template in Annex C of the 2015 Action 5 Report (OECD, 2015).

1276. For completing the summary section of the template, the STA points out that the summary is written in English and provides the following information: (i) the category of transaction or activity covered by the ruling, (ii) a description of the relevant circumstances, (iii) the STA's decision including key conclusions and (iv) an explanation for the STA's view of the interpretation of the tax law, where relevant.

1277. For the year in review, the timeliness of exchanges is as follows:

Past rulings in the scope of the transparency framework	Number of exchanges transmitted by 31 December 2017	Delayed exchanges		
		Number of exchanges not transmitted by 31 December 2017	Reasons for the delays	Any other comments
	4	0		See below
Future rulings in the scope of the transparency framework	**Number of exchanges transmitted within three months of the information becoming available to the competent authority or immediately after legal impediments have been lifted**	**Delayed exchanges**		
		Number of exchanges transmitted later than three months of the information on rulings becoming available to the competent authority	Reasons for the delays	Any other comments
	3	0	N/A	
Total	7	0		

Follow up requests received for exchange of the ruling	Number	Average time to provide response	Number of requests not answered
	0	N/A	N/A

1278. Sweden notes that four past rulings were identified in 2017, three of which related to the OECD/G20 countries and should have been exchanged by 31 December 2016. The

STA explained that two of the rulings were exchanged in February 2017 and one was exchanged in June 2017.

Conclusion on section B

1279. Although information on three past rulings should have been exchanged in 2017, the issue was on account of an error in the identification process explained in Part A. Once the rulings were identified, the exchange process was completed swiftly. Sweden has met all of the ToR for the exchange of information process and no recommendations are made.

C. Statistics (ToR IV)

1280. The statistics for the year in review are as follows:

Category of ruling	Number of exchanges	Jurisdictions exchanged with
Rulings related to preferential regimes	Included in *de minimis*	N/A
Cross-border unilateral advance pricing agreements (APAs) and any other cross-border unilateral tax rulings (such as an advance tax ruling) covering transfer pricing or the application of transfer pricing principles	N/A	N/A
Cross-border rulings providing for a unilateral downward adjustment to the taxpayer's taxable profits that is not directly reflected in the taxpayer's financial / commercial accounts	N/A	N/A
Permanent establishment rulings	Included in *de minimis*	N/A
Related party conduit rulings	Included in *de minimis*	N/A
De minimis rule	7	N/A
IP regimes: total exchanges on taxpayers benefitting from the third category of IP assets, new entrants benefitting from grandfathered IP regimes; and taxpayers making use of the option to treat the nexus ratio as a rebuttable presumption	N/A	N/A
Total	7	

D. Matters related to intellectual property regimes (ToR I.4.1.3)

1281. Sweden does not offer an intellectual property regime for which transparency requirements under the Action 5 Report (OECD, 2015) were imposed.

Summary of recommendations on implementation of the transparency framework

Aspect of implementation of the transparency framework that should be improved	Recommendation for improvement
Sweden did not identify all past rulings.	No recommendation is made because Sweden identified additional past rulings in 2017 which it has exchanged by June 2017 and Sweden has reviewed its process for identifying past and future rulings to ensure that this is not a recurring issue.
Sweden did not identify all potential exchange jurisdictions for future rulings. This is a continuing recommendation from the prior year peer review.	Sweden is recommended to amend its rulings practice to require taxpayers to provide information on all potential exchange jurisdictions for future rulings as soon as possible.

Notes

[1] With respect to the Tonnage tax regime which takes effect as of the fiscal year starting 1 January 2017.

[2] In Swedish: "Skatterättsnämnden".

[3] Available at www.skatterattsnamnden.se (accessed 20 November 2018).

[4] Parties to the Convention are available here: www.oecd.org/tax/exchange-of-tax-information/convention-on-mutual-administrative-assistance-in-tax-matters.htm. Parties to the Nordic Convention on Assistance in Tax Matters are Denmark, Faroe Islands, Finland, Iceland and Sweden. Sweden also has bilateral agreements with Argentina, Australia, Austria, Barbados, Belgium, Botswana, Brazil, Bulgaria, Canada, Chile, China (People's Republic of), Croatia, Czech Republic, Egypt, Estonia, France, Georgia, Germany, Greece, Hungary, India, Indonesia, Ireland, Israel, Italy, Jamaica, Japan, Kazakhstan, Kenya, Korea, Latvia, Lithuania, Luxembourg, Malaysia, Malta, Mauritius, Mexico, Netherlands, New Zealand, Nigeria, Pakistan, Poland, Portugal, Romania, Russia, Saudi Arabia, Singapore, Slovak Republic, Slovenia, South Africa, Spain, Sri Lanka, Switzerland, Thailand, Trinidad and Tobago, Turkey, Ukraine, United Kingdom, United States, Viet Nam and Zambia.

References

OECD (2017), *BEPS Action 5 on Harmful Tax Practices – Terms of Reference and Methodology for the Conduct of the Peer Reviews of the Action 5 Transparency Framework*, OECD/G20 Base Erosion and Profit Shifting Project, OECD, Paris. www.oecd.org/tax/beps/beps-action-5-harmful-tax-practices-peer-review-transparencyframework.pdf.

OECD (2015), *Countering Harmful Tax Practices More Effectively, Taking into Account Transparency and Substance, Action 5 - 2015 Final Report*, OECD/G20 Base Erosion and Profit Shifting Project, OECD Publishing, Paris. https://doi.org/10.1787/9789264241190-en.

OECD/Council of Europe (2011), *The Multilateral Convention on Mutual Administrative Assistance in Tax Matters: Amended by the 2010 Protocol*, OECD Publishing, Paris. http://dx.doi.org/10.1787/9789264115606-en.

Switzerland

Switzerland has implemented a legal framework which permits spontaneous exchange on rulings from 2018 onwards. Switzerland has met all the terms of reference (ToR) that can be met in the absence of exchange of information being permitted for the year in review and no recommendations are made.

The Swiss tax authorities can legally issue four types of rulings within the scope of the transparency framework.

Switzerland did not have the necessary domestic and international legal framework for spontaneous exchange of information for the year of review.[1] As such, no exchanges were permitted to occur. The domestic legal framework for spontaneous exchange of information entered into force on 1 January 2017, together with the *Multilateral Convention on Mutual Administrative Assistance in Tax Matters: Amended by the 2010 Protocol* (OECD/Council of Europe, 2011), the international legal framework permitting spontaneous exchange of information.[2] In accordance with the legal framework, exchange of information on ruling commenced from 1 January 2018. This includes rulings issued since 1 January 2010, provided that they are in effect when the international legal framework becomes applicable on 1 January 2018. Switzerland has undertaken administrative and organisational preparations to be ready to exchange information pursuant to the new legal framework.

As Switzerland did not have the necessary domestic legal basis for spontaneous exchange of information on rulings for the year of review, no exchanges on rulings were permitted to occur. As no exchanges could be undertaken under Switzerland's legal framework, no peer input was received in respect of the exchanges of information on rulings received from Switzerland.

Introduction

1282. This peer review covers Switzerland's implementation of the BEPS Action 5 transparency framework for the year 2017. The report has four parts, each relating to a key part of the ToR. Each part is discussed in turn. A summary of recommendations is included at the end of this report.

A. The information gathering process

1283. The Swiss tax authorities can legally issue the following four types of rulings within the scope of the transparency framework: (i) rulings related to preferential regimes;[3] (ii) cross-border unilateral APAs and any other cross-border unilateral tax ruling (such as an ATR) covering transfer pricing or the application of transfer pricing principles; (iii) permanent establishment rulings and (iv) related party conduit rulings. In Switzerland, rulings are issued by the cantonal and federal tax authorities.

Past rulings (ToR I.4.1.1, I.4.1.2, I.4.2.1, I.4.2.2)

1284. For Switzerland, past rulings are any tax rulings within scope that are issued on or after 1 January 2010 until 31 December 2016, provided they were still in effect as at 1 January 2018 (see paragraph 9 f.).

1285. In the prior year peer review report, it was determined that Switzerland's undertakings to identify past rulings and all potential exchange jurisdictions were sufficient to meet the minimum standard. As the implementation in this regard remains unchanged it is determined that Switzerland's implementation continues to meet the minimum standard.

Future rulings (ToR I.4.1.1, I.4.1.2, I.4.2.1)

1286. For Switzerland, future rulings are any tax rulings within scope that are issued on or after 1 January 2017, provided they are still in effect on or after 1 January 2018 (see paragraph 9 f.).

1287. In the prior year peer review report, it was determined that Switzerland's system to identify future rulings and all potential exchange jurisdictions was sufficient to meet the minimum standard. The implementation in this regard remains unchanged and the system to identify future rulings continues to meet the minimum standard.

Review and supervision mechanism (ToR I.4.3)

1288. In the prior year peer review report, it was determined that Switzerland's review and supervision mechanism was sufficient to meet the minimum standard. Switzerland's implementation in this regard remains unchanged, and therefore continues to meet the minimum standard.

Conclusion on section A

1289. Switzerland has met all of the ToR and no recommendations are made.

B. The exchange of information

Legal basis for spontaneous exchange of information (ToR II.5.1, II.5.2)

1290. Switzerland has the necessary domestic legal basis to exchange information spontaneously from 1 January 2018. The domestic legal basis (Revisions of the Tax Assistance Administrative Act and the Tax Administrative Assistance Ordinance) entered into force on 1 January 2017 and allows for exchange of information as of 1 January 2018.

1291. Switzerland's international agreement permitting spontaneous exchange of information is the *Multilateral Convention on Mutual Administrative Assistance in Tax Matters: Amended by the 2010 Protocol* (OECD/Council of Europe, 2011) ("the Convention"). The Convention entered into force on 1 January 2017. According to article 28 paragraph 6 of the Convention, administrative assistance shall have effect for taxable periods beginning on or after 1 January of the year following the one in which the Convention entered into force. Spontaneous exchange of information on rulings issued after 2010 is therefore allowed, provided they were still in effect on 1 January 2018.[4]

Completion and exchange of templates (ToR II.5.3, II.5.4, II.5.5, II.5.6, II.5.7)

1292. The prior year peer review report noted that Switzerland has put in place a process to exchange information on rulings in accordance with the form and timelines required by the transparency framework. As Switzerland has not yet started the exchange of information, this section could not be further assessed for the year in review.

Conclusion on section B

1293. For the year in review, Switzerland did not have the necessary legal framework in place for exchanging information on rulings.[5] The exchange of information on rulings in practice will be assessed in the subsequent report. Switzerland has put in place the administrative practices for the completion and exchange of templates on rulings and applied it to collect relevant rulings in view of an exchange in 2018. Switzerland has met all the ToR that can be met in the absence of a legal basis to conduct the exchange of information on rulings and no recommendations are made.

C. Statistics (ToR IV)

1294. As there was no legal basis for exchange in the year of review, no statistical data can be reported.

D. Matters related to intellectual property regimes (ToR I.4.1.3)

1295. In the prior year peer review report, it was determined that Switzerland's implementation regarding matters related to intellectual property regimes was sufficient to meet the minimum standard. Switzerland's implementation in this regard remains unchanged, and therefore continues to meet the minimum standard.

1296. As Switzerland did not have the legal basis to exchange rulings in 2017, this section could not be further assessed. Switzerland's matters related to IP regimes will be assessed in the subsequent report.

Summary of recommendations on implementation of the transparency framework

Aspect of implementation of the transparency framework that should be improved	Recommendation for improvement
	No recommendations are made.

Notes

[1] The Action 5 Report (OECD, 2015) notes that jurisdictions which do not currently have the necessary legal framework in place for spontaneous exchange of information on rulings will need to put in place such a framework in order to comply with the obligations under Action 5, but that in such cases the timelines are subject to a country's legal framework.

[2] Tax Administrative Assistance Act (TAAA) and the Tax Administrative Assistance Ordinance (TAAO), which are underpinned by an explanatory document to the TAAO published by the Federal Department of Finance.

[3] With respect to the following preferential regimes: 1) auxiliary company regime (previously referred to as domiciliary company regime, 2) mixed company regime, 3) commissionaire ruling regime, 4) holding company regime (cantonal level), 5) licence box (Canton of Nidwalden only).

[4] Parties to the Convention are available here: www.oecd.org/tax/exchange-of-tax-information/convention-on-mutual-administrative-assistance-in-tax-matters.htm.

[5] See note 1.

References

OECD (2017), *BEPS Action 5 on Harmful Tax Practices – Terms of Reference and Methodology for the Conduct of the Peer Reviews of the Action 5 Transparency Framework*, OECD/G20 Base Erosion and Profit Shifting Project, OECD, Paris. www.oecd.org/tax/beps/beps-action-5-harmful-tax-practices-peer-review-transparencyframework.pdf.

OECD (2015), *Countering Harmful Tax Practices More Effectively, Taking into Account Transparency and Substance, Action 5 - 2015 Final Report*, OECD/G20 Base Erosion and Profit Shifting Project, OECD Publishing, Paris. https://doi.org/10.1787/9789264241190-en.

OECD/Council of Europe (2011), *The Multilateral Convention on Mutual Administrative Assistance in Tax Matters: Amended by the 2010 Protocol*, OECD Publishing, Paris. http://dx.doi.org/10.1787/9789264115606-en.

Trinidad and Tobago

Trinidad and Tobago has met all aspects of the terms of reference (ToR) for the calendar year 2017 (year in review) that can be met in the absence of rulings being issued.

Trinidad and Tobago cannot legally issue any type of rulings within the scope of the transparency framework.

As no rulings were issued, no exchange of information was required. No peer input was received in respect of the exchanges of information on rulings received from Trinidad and Tobago.

Introduction

1297. This peer review covers Trinidad and Tobago's implementation of the BEPS Action 5 transparency framework for the year 2017. The report has four parts, each relating to a key part of the ToR. Each part is discussed in turn. A summary of recommendations is included at the end of this report.

A. The information gathering process

1298. As no rulings are issued, this section is not assessed.

B. The exchange of information

1299. As no rulings are issued, this section is not assessed.

C. Statistics (ToR IV)

1300. As no rulings are issued, no statistical data can be reported.

D. Matters related to intellectual property regimes (ToR I.4.1.3)

1301. Trinidad and Tobago does not offer an intellectual property regime for which transparency requirements under the Action 5 Report (OECD, 2015) were imposed.

Summary of recommendations on implementation of the transparency framework

Aspect of implementation of the transparency framework that should be improved	Recommendation for improvement
	No recommendations are made.

References

OECD (2017), *BEPS Action 5 on Harmful Tax Practices – Terms of Reference and Methodology for the Conduct of the Peer Reviews of the Action 5 Transparency Framework*, OECD/G20 Base Erosion and Profit Shifting Project, OECD, Paris. www.oecd.org/tax/beps/beps-action-5-harmful-tax-practices-peer-review-transparencyframework.pdf.

OECD (2015), *Countering Harmful Tax Practices More Effectively, Taking into Account Transparency and Substance, Action 5 - 2015 Final Report*, OECD/G20 Base Erosion and Profit Shifting Project, OECD Publishing, Paris. https://doi.org/10.1787/9789264241190-en.

Turkey

Turkey has met all aspects of the terms of reference (ToR) for the calendar year 2017 (year in review) except for identifying and exchanging information on new entrants to the grandfathered IP regime (ToR I.4.1.3). This recommendation was also included in the prior year peer review report. Turkey is recommended to identify and exchange information on new entrants to the grandfathered IP regimes.

Turkey can legally issue one type of ruling within the scope of the transparency framework.

In practice, Turkey issued three past rulings; for the period 1 April 2016 - 31 December 2016, Turkey issued no future rulings; and for the year in review, Turkey issued eight future rulings within the scope of the transparency framework.

No peer input was received in respect of the exchanges of information on rulings received from Turkey.

Introduction

1302. This peer review covers Turkey's implementation of the BEPS Action 5 transparency framework for the year 2017. The report has four parts, each relating to a key part of the ToR. Each part is discussed in turn. A summary of recommendations is included at the end of this report.

A. The information gathering process

1303. Turkey can legally issue one type of ruling within the scope of the transparency framework: cross-border unilateral APAs and any other cross-border unilateral tax rulings (such as an advance tax ruling) covering transfer pricing or the application of transfer pricing principles. Turkey notes that they are able to issue "written comments" to taxpayers on specific provisions in the tax law, but these are not binding on the tax administration or the taxpayer, and as such they are outside the scope of the transparency framework.[1] In Turkey, unilateral APAs are issued by the transfer pricing unit in the headquarters of the Turkish Revenue Administration.

Past rulings (ToR I.4.1.1, I.4.1.2, I.4.2.1, I.4.2.2)

1304. For Turkey, past rulings are any tax rulings within scope that are issued either: (i) on or after 1 January 2014 but before 1 April 2016; or (ii) on or after 1 January 2010 but before 1 January 2014, provided they were still in effect as at 1 January 2014.

1305. In the prior year peer review report, it was determined that Turkey's undertakings to identify past rulings and all potential exchange jurisdictions were sufficient to meet the minimum standard. Turkey's implementation in this regard remains unchanged, and therefore continues to meet the minimum standard.

Future rulings (ToR I.4.1.1, I.4.1.2, I.4.2.1)

1306. For Turkey, future rulings are future rulings are any tax rulings within scope that are issued on or after 1 April 2016.

1307. In the prior year peer review report, it was determined that Turkey's implementation of a new system to identify future rulings and all potential exchange jurisdictions was sufficient to meet the minimum standard. Turkey's implementation in this regard remains unchanged, and therefore continues to meet the minimum standard.

Review and supervision mechanism (ToR I.4.3)

1308. In the prior year peer review report, it was determined that the Turkish tax administration's review and supervision mechanism was sufficient to meet the minimum standard. The Turkish tax administration's implementation in this regard remains unchanged, and therefore continues to meet the minimum standard.

Conclusion on section A

1309. Turkey has met all the ToR for the information gathering process and no recommendations are made.

B. The exchange of information

Legal basis for spontaneous exchange of information (ToR II.5.1, II.5.2)

1310. Turkey has the necessary domestic legal basis to exchange information spontaneously. Turkey notes that there are no legal or practical impediments that prevent the spontaneous exchange information on rulings as contemplated in the Action 5 minimum standard.

1311. Turkey has double tax agreements in force with 85 jurisdictions which permit spontaneous exchange of information.[2] In addition, Turkey has signed the *Multilateral Convention on Mutual Administrative Assistance in Tax Matters: Amended by the 2010 Protocol* (OECD/Council of Europe, 2011) ("the Convention") and it was ratified by the Turkish Parliament on 20 May 2017. The Convention entered into force on 1 July 2018 and will have effect from 1 January 2019.

Completion and exchange of templates (ToR II.5.3, II.5.4, II.5.5, II.5.6, II.5.7)

1312. In the prior year peer review report, it was determined that Turkey's completion and exchange of templates were sufficient to meet the minimum standard. Turkey's implementation in this regard remains unchanged, and therefore continues to meet the minimum standard.

1313. It takes approximately 90 days from the issuance of the APA for the Turkish Revenue Administration to submit to the Competent Authority the completed template in the form of Annex C of the 2015 Action 5 Report (OECD, 2015). Subsequently, it takes eight days for the Competent Authority to send the template to the relevant exchange jurisdictions. The summary section of the template is completed in line with the internal FHTP suggested guidance.

1314. The timeliness of exchanges is as follows:

Past rulings in the scope of the transparency framework	Number of exchanges transmitted by 31 December 2017	Number of exchanges not transmitted by 31 December 2017	Delayed exchanges Reasons for the delays	Any other comments
	4	0	Procedural problems.	These relate to the delayed exchanges reported in the prior year peer review report and, were exchanged by February 2017.
Future rulings in the scope of the transparency framework	**Number of exchanges transmitted within three months of the information becoming available to the competent authority or immediately after legal impediments have been lifted**	**Number of exchanges transmitted later than three months of the information on rulings becoming available to the competent authority**	**Delayed exchanges Reasons for the delays**	**Any other comments**
	8	0	N/A	N/A
Total	12	0		

Follow up requests received for exchange of the ruling	Number	Average time to provide response	Number of requests not answered
	N/A	N/A	N/A

Conclusion on section B

1315. Turkey has the necessary legal basis for spontaneous exchange of information, a process for completing the templates in a timely way and has completed all exchanges on time. Turkey has met all of the ToR for the exchange of information process and no recommendations are made.

C. Statistics (ToR IV)

1316. The statistics for the year in review are as follows:

Category of ruling	Number of exchanges	Jurisdictions exchanged with
Rulings related to preferential regimes	N/A	N/A
Cross-border unilateral advance pricing agreements (APAs) and any other cross-border unilateral tax rulings (such as an advance tax ruling) covering transfer pricing or the application of transfer pricing principles	12	Germany, Italy, Netherlands, Singapore, Switzerland, United Kingdom, United States
Cross-border rulings providing for a unilateral downward adjustment to the taxpayer's taxable profits that is not directly reflected in the taxpayer's financial / commercial accounts	N/A	N/A
Permanent establishment rulings	N/A	N/A
Related party conduit rulings	N/A	N/A
De minimis rule	N/A	N/A
IP regimes: total exchanges on taxpayers benefitting from the third category of IP assets, new entrants benefitting from grandfathered IP regimes; and taxpayers making use of the option to treat the nexus ratio as a rebuttable presumption	0	N/A
Total	12	

D. Matters related to intellectual property regimes (ToR I.4.1.3)

1317. Turkey has two intellectual property regimes that are subject to transparency requirements under the Action 5 Report (OECD, 2015).[3] It states that the identification of the benefitting taxpayers will occur as follows:

Technology development zone regime

- ***New entrants***: Turkey has not yet been able to identify and exchange information on new entrants to the grandfathered IP regime, and the regime has been found to be actually harmful to the extent of extended grandfathering to taxpayers that entered the regime between 1 July 2016 and 19 October 2017. Therefore the period for enhanced transparency for new entrants on the grandfathered regime is from 6 February 2015 until 19 October 2017. The income from IP benefitting from the regime between 6 February 2015 and 19 October 2017 will be shown in a temporary tax return (specifically designed for the identification of taxpayers with respect to the enhanced transparency requirements). The information will be available to the Turkish Revenue Administration starting from mid-August 2018 including all information on new taxpayers and new IP assets of existing taxpayers dating back to 2015. This will then be exchanged as soon as possible. Turkey is recommended to identify and exchange information on new entrants to the grandfathered IP regime.

- ***Third category of IP assets***: not applicable as the regime does not allow the third category of IP assets to qualify for the benefits.
- ***Rebuttable presumption***: not applicable as the regime does not allow the nexus ratio to be treated as a rebuttable presumption.

5/B regime

- ***New entrants***: as this is a new IP regime rather than a grandfathered IP regime, transparency on new entrants was not required.
- ***Third category of IP assets***: not applicable as the regime does not allow the third category of IP assets to qualify for the benefits.
- ***Rebuttable presumption***: not applicable as the regime does not allow the nexus ratio to be treated as a rebuttable presumption.

Summary of recommendations on implementation of the transparency framework

Aspect of implementation of the transparency framework that should be improved	Recommendation for improvement
Turkey has not been able to identify and exchange information on new entrants to the grandfathered IP regime. This is a continuing recommendation from the prior year peer review.	Turkey is recommended to identify and exchange information on new entrants to the grandfathered IP regime.

Notes

[1] The written comments are made available in anonymised form at www.gib.gov.tr (accessed 20 November 2018).

[2] Albania, Algeria, Australia, Austria, Azerbaijan, Bahrain, Bangladesh, Belarus, Belgium, Bosnia and Herzegovina, Brazil, Bulgaria, Canada, China (People's Republic of), Croatia, Czech Republic, Denmark, Egypt, Estonia, Ethiopia, Finland, Former Yugoslav Republic of Macedonia, France, Georgia, Germany, Greece, Hungary, India, Indonesia, Iran, Ireland, Israel, Italy, Japan, Jordan, Kazakhstan, Korea, Kosovo, Kuwait, Kyrgyzstan, Latvia, Lebanon, Lithuania, Luxembourg, Malaysia, Malta, Mexico, Moldova, Mongolia, Montenegro, Morocco, Netherlands, New Zealand, Norway, Oman, Pakistan, Philippines, Poland, Portugal, Qatar, Romania, Russian Federation, Saudi Arabia, Serbia, Singapore, Slovak Republic, Slovenia, South Africa, Spain, Sudan, Sweden, Switzerland, Syria, Tajikistan, Thailand, Tunisia, Turkish Republic of Northern Cyprus, Turkmenistan, Ukraine, United Arab Emirates, United Kingdom, United States, Uzbekistan, Viet Nam and Yemen.

Note by Turkey: The information in this document with reference to "Cyprus" relates to the southern part of the Island. There is no single authority representing both Turkish and Greek Cypriot people on the Island. Turkey recognises the Turkish Republic of Northern Cyprus (TRNC). Until a lasting and equitable solution is found within the context of the United Nations, Turkey shall preserve its position concerning the "Cyprus issue".

Note by all the European Union Member States of the OECD and the European Union. The Republic of Cyprus is recognised by all members of the United Nations with the exception of Turkey. The information in this document relates to the area under the effective control of the Government of the Republic of Cyprus.

[3] These regimes are: 1) Technology development zone regime and 2) 5/B regime.

References

OECD (2017), *BEPS Action 5 on Harmful Tax Practices – Terms of Reference and Methodology for the Conduct of the Peer Reviews of the Action 5 Transparency Framework*, OECD/G20 Base Erosion and Profit Shifting Project, OECD, Paris. www.oecd.org/tax/beps/beps-action-5-harmful-tax-practices-peer-review-transparencyframework.pdf.

OECD (2015), *Countering Harmful Tax Practices More Effectively, Taking into Account Transparency and Substance, Action 5 - 2015 Final Report*, OECD/G20 Base Erosion and Profit Shifting Project, OECD Publishing, Paris. https://doi.org/10.1787/9789264241190-en.

OECD/Council of Europe (2011), *The Multilateral Convention on Mutual Administrative Assistance in Tax Matters: Amended by the 2010 Protocol*, OECD Publishing, Paris. http://dx.doi.org/10.1787/9789264115606-en.

United Kingdom

The United Kingdom has met all aspects of the terms of reference (ToR) for the calendar year 2017 (year in review) except for collecting and exchanging information on new assets of existing taxpayers benefitting from the grandfathered IP regime (ToR I.4.1.3). This recommendation was also included in the prior year peer review report. As in the previous report the United Kingdom is recommended to identify and exchange relevant information on new assets of existing taxpayers benefitting from the grandfathered IP regime.

The United Kingdom can legally issue three types of rulings within the scope of the transparency framework.

In practice, the United Kingdom has issued 599 past rulings; for the period 1 April 2016 - 31 December 2016, the United Kingdom issued 71 future rulings and for the year in review, the United Kingdom issued 16 future rulings within the scope of the transparency framework.

Peer input was received from four jurisdictions in respect of exchanges of information received from the United Kingdom. The input was in general positive, noting that information was complete, in the correct format and received mostly in a timely manner. One peer noted that it received one past rulings and one future ruling after the respective timeline.

Introduction

1318. This peer review covers the United Kingdom's implementation of the BEPS Action 5 transparency framework for the year 2017. The report has four parts, each relating to a key part of the ToR. Each part is discussed in turn. A summary of recommendations is included at the end of this report.

A. The information gathering process

1319. The United Kingdom can legally issue the three following types of rulings within the scope of the transparency framework: (i) rulings related to preferential regimes[1]; (patent box and shipping); (ii) cross-border unilateral advance pricing agreements (APAs) and any other cross-border unilateral tax rulings (such as an advance tax ruling) covering transfer pricing or the application of transfer pricing principles; and (iii) permanent establishment ("PE") rulings.

1320. Rulings on preferential regimes are issued by specialist team in the tax administration (HMRC). Rulings on APAs are issued by a Delegated Competent Authority in HMRC's Head Office Transfer Pricing Team, and rulings which are Advanced Thin Capitalisation Agreements (a form of unilateral APA for financing issues) are generally signed by a HMRC International Tax Specialist or a Customer Relationship Manager in the field office, normally in the Large Business team. PE Rulings are issued by the Tax Specialist who has reviewed the application, whether on a Customer Team, one of HMRC's Specialist Units or Head Office Functions.

Past rulings (ToR I.4.1.1, I.4.1.2, I.4.2.1, I.4.2.2)

1321. For the United Kingdom, past rulings are any tax rulings within scope that are issued either: (i) on or after 1 January 2014 but before 1 April 2016; or (ii) on or after 1 January 2010 but before 1 January 2014, provided they were still in effect as at 1 January 2016.

1322. In the prior year peer review report, it was determined that the HRMC's undertakings to identify past rulings and all potential exchange jurisdictions were sufficient to meet the minimum standard. In order to identify relevant exchange jurisdictions for past rulings the Delegated Competent Authority now may also use third party data sources and consult with the HMRC caseworker in cases where it seems appropriate to verify the information provided by the taxpayer. As the HRMC further enhanced their system to identify past rulings and all potential exchange their undertakings continue to meet the minimum standard.

Future rulings (ToR I.4.1.1, I.4.1.2, I.4.2.1)

1323. For the United Kingdom, future rulings are any tax rulings within scope that are issued on or after 1 April 2016.

1324. In the prior year peer review report, it was determined that the United Kingdom's implementation of a new system to identify future rulings and all potential exchange jurisdictions was sufficient to meet the minimum standard.[2] The United Kingdom's implementation in this regard remains unchanged, and therefore continues to meet the minimum standard.

Review and supervision mechanism (ToR I.4.3)

1325. In the prior year peer review report, it was determined that the United Kingdom tax administration's review and supervision mechanisms were sufficient to meet the minimum standard. The United Kingdom tax administration's implementation in this regard remains unchanged, and therefore continues to meet the minimum standard. Furthermore the United Kingdom is currently undertaking a full review of all exchanges of past and future rulings to date which could lead to an adjustment of the figures provided for the year of review and the prior year. This procedure is expected to be completed by June 2018.

Conclusion on section A

1326. The United Kingdom has met all of the ToR for the information gathering process and no recommendations are made.

B. The exchange of information

Legal basis for spontaneous exchange of information (ToR II.5.1, II.5.2)

1327. United Kingdom has the necessary domestic legal basis to exchange information spontaneously. United Kingdom notes that there are no legal or practical impediments that prevent the spontaneous exchange of information on rulings as contemplated in the Action 5 minimum standard.

1328. The United Kingdom is a party to international agreements permitting spontaneous exchange of information, including (i) the *Multilateral Convention on Mutual Administrative Assistance in Tax Matters: Amended by the 2010 Protocol* (OECD/Council of Europe, 2011) ("the Convention"), (ii) the Directive 2011/16/EU with all other European Union Member States and (iii) double tax agreements in force with 121 jurisdictions.[3]

Completion and exchange of templates (ToR II.5.3, II.5.4, II.5.5, II.5.6, II.5.7)

1329. In the prior year peer review report, it was determined that the United Kingdom's completion and exchange of templates were sufficient to meet the minimum standard.

1330. Furthermore, the United Kingdom has confirmed that it completes the summary section in section 7 in Annex C of the 2015 Action 5 Report (OECD, 2015) as prescribed in the instruction to the section. The United Kingdom uses the Annex C template and its notes for completion. Caseworkers, who complete the template, receive guidance how to complete the summary section including referring to the internal FHTP suggested guidance.

1331. For the year in review, the timeliness of exchanges is as follows

Past rulings in the scope of the transparency framework	Number of exchanges transmitted by 31 December 2017	Delayed exchanges		
		Number of exchanges not transmitted by 31 December 2017	Reasons for the delays	Any other comments
	23	0	N/A	This relates to the exchanges with new members of the IF that joined in 2017
Future rulings in the scope of the transparency framework	**Number of exchanges transmitted within three months of the information becoming available to the competent authority or immediately after legal impediments have been lifted**	**Delayed exchanges**		
		Number of exchanges transmitted later than three months of the information on rulings becoming available to the competent authority	**Reasons for the delays**	**Any other comments**
	22	16	Resources focused on meeting EU Directive	All future rulings have been exchanged; a new procedure was implemented and additional staff have been recruited, trained and allocated to prevent further delays
Total	45	16		

Follow up requests received for exchange of the ruling	Number	Average time to provide response	Number of requests not answered
	2	40 days	0

1332. The United Kingdom experienced delays exchanging information on future rulings. It states that the delays appeared due to changes in key personnel and pressure on resources due to the implementation of a new system to meet the requirements of the EU Directive. This issue has been addressed by the development of an "end-to-end" process maps, the establishment of a Single Point of Contact (SPOC) Network within the relevant lines of business in HMRC and the recruitment and training of additional staff.

Conclusion on section B

1333. The United Kingdom has the necessary legal basis for spontaneous exchange of information, a process for completing the templates in a timely way and has completed all exchanges on time. The United Kingdom experienced delays in the exchange of future rulings but has addressed the reasons for the delays, which are considered not to be a recurring issue. The United Kingdom was able to complete all outstanding exchanges within the year in review. The United Kingdom has met all of the ToR for the exchange of information process and no recommendations are made.

C. Statistics (ToR IV)

1334. The statistics for the year in review are as follows:

Category of ruling	Number of exchanges	Jurisdictions exchanged with
Rulings related to preferential regimes	18	Australia, France, Japan, Luxembourg, Netherlands, Norway, Spain, United States
Cross-border unilateral advance pricing agreements (APAs) and any other cross-border unilateral tax rulings (such as an advance tax ruling) covering transfer pricing or the application of transfer pricing principles	38	Canada, France, Hong Kong (China), Ireland, Japan, Luxembourg, Netherlands, Sweden, Switzerland, South Africa, United States
Cross-border rulings providing for a unilateral downward adjustment to the taxpayer's taxable profits that is not directly reflected in the taxpayer's financial / commercial accounts	N/A	N/A
Permanent establishment rulings	5	Canada, Germany, Ireland, Malta, United States
Related party conduit rulings	N/A	N/A
De minimis rule	N/A	N/A
IP regimes: total exchanges on taxpayers benefitting from the third category of IP assets, new entrants benefitting from grandfathered IP regimes; and taxpayers making use of the option to treat the nexus ratio as a rebuttable presumption	0	N/A
Total	61	

D. Matters related to intellectual property regimes (ToR I.4.1.3)

1335. The UK offers an intellectual property regime ("IP regime") that is subject to transparency requirements under the Action 5 Report:[4]

- ***New entrants benefitting from the grandfathered regime:*** in the prior year peer review report, it was determined that the United Kingdom's implementation regarding matters related to intellectual property regime was sufficient to meet the minimum standard except for identifying and exchanging information on new IP assets of existing taxpayers benefitting from the grandfathered IP regime. The United Kingdom was recommended to exchange such information.

  The United Kingdom notes that this information has not become available since the prior year peer review report and could therefore not be provided for the year in review. The United Kingdom is currently evaluating ways to collect alternative information for the purpose of exchanging under the transparency framework.

  The United Kingdom stresses that information is not sought when conducting regular field audits, as making use of the IP regime is usually not in the scope of regular subjects of the audits and that it would not be in line with the United Kingdom's legislation to open an enquiry into every company electing into the Patent Box. An enquiry is generally opened because there is a risk that tax has been underpaid, with inquiries limited to that risk. The UK states that it would not be able to use an enquiry procedure to obtain information on new assets without reason to believe that the Patent Box computation had been submitted incorrectly, and that the uses of enquiry powers for this purpose could render the tax administration liable to judicial review. As existing taxpayers in the patent box were not prohibited from bringing new assets into the regime for the period covered by the transparency obligations (i.e. 6 February 2015 - 30 June 2016), there would not be a tax liability at risk. As such, the recommendation to exchange information on new assets brought into the grandfathered regime is unlikely to be able to be addressed. The United Kingdom is therefore proposing to develop a different approach to gather alternative available information which would be exchanged under the transparency framework.[5]

In order to ensure that profits from new qualifying IP assets do not benefit from the grandfathered regimes after 30 June 2016, the United Kingdom introduced provisions. This includes an enhanced risk assessment of existing taxpayers benefitting from the grandfathered regime.

It is noted that in early 2018 the United Kingdom conducted 38 exchanges of information with 13 jurisdictions on new taxpayers who entered the grandfathered regime between 6 February 2015 and 30 June 2016. This information is based on data about elections made in the tax returns up to December 2017, which is identified by the HMRC by using a profiling tool (iXBRL) that detects when a Patent Box election is made in the tax return. As the election can either be made in the tax returns (within a time limit of 12 months from the end of that accounting period) or in amendments to the tax returns (within two years from the end of the accounting period), elections in respect of periods before 30 June 2016 can be made up to 30 June 18. The United Kingdom will update the total number of new entrants in the subsequent peer review report.

- ***Third category of IP assets***: not applicable, as this option has not been incorporated in the United Kingdom IP regime.
- ***Taxpayers making use of the option to treat the nexus ratio as a rebuttable presumption***: the United Kingdom confirms that no taxpayer elected to treat the nexus approach as a rebuttable presumption.

As the United Kingdom's implementation regarding matters related to intellectual property regimes remains unchanged the United Kingdom continues to meet the ToR with respect to intellectual property regimes except for identifying and exchanging relevant information on new assets of existing taxpayers benefitting from the grandfathered IP regime. The United Kingdom should exchange this information to the extent that such information or alternative information does become available in the future.

Summary of recommendations on implementation of the transparency framework

Aspect of implementation of the transparency framework that should be improved	Recommendation for improvement
The United Kingdom experienced some delays exchanging information on future rulings.	No recommendation is made because the United Kingdom completed the exchange of all future rulings in the year of review, implemented new procedures and hired additional staff to prevent further delay, therefore it is considered not a recurring issue.
The United Kingdom has not exchanged information on new assets of existing taxpayers benefitting from the grandfathered IP regime, as this information was still not available. The United Kingdom is currently evaluating ways to collect alternative information on new IP assets for the purpose of exchanging under the transparency framework. This is a continuing recommendation from the prior year peer review.	The United Kingdom is recommended to identify and exchange alternative information on new assets of existing taxpayers benefitting from the grandfathered IP regime.

Jurisdiction's response and recent developments

1336. In relation to the recommendation on the exchange of information for the grandfathered IP regime, the United Kingdom undertook additional efforts during 2018 to collect relevant information on new IP assets of existing taxpayers benefitting from the grandfathered IP regime. The United Kingdom has now collected all relevant information and has exchanged this information with the relevant jurisdictions.

Notes

[1] With respect to the following preferential regimes: 1) Patent box and 2) Shipping regime.

[2] In addition to the system in place, the United Kingdom developed and introduced a new internal database to capture, store and transmit all categories of rulings in scope in line with the ETR XML schema to facilitate the identification and exchange of future rulings. The new database will be in use as of the second quarter of 2018.

[3] Parties to the Convention are available here: www.oecd.org/tax/exchange-of-tax-information/convention-on-mutual-administrative-assistance-in-tax-matters.htm. The United Kingdom also has bilateral agreements with Albania, Algeria, Antigua and Barbuda, Argentina, Armenia, Australia, Azerbaijan, Bahrain, Bangladesh, Barbados, Belarus, Belize, Bolivia, Bosnia and Herzegovina, Botswana, British Virgin Islands, Brunei, Bulgaria, Cayman Islands, Chile, China (People's Republic of), Colombia, Côte d'Ivoire, Croatia, Cyprus, Czech Republic, Denmark, Egypt, Estonia, Ethiopia, Falkland Islands, Faroe Islands, Fiji, Finland, Former Republic of Macedonia, Gambia, Georgia, Ghana, Greece, Grenada, Guernsey, Guyana, Hong Kong (China), Hungary, Iceland, India, Indonesia, Ireland, Isle of Man, Israel, Jamaica, Japan, Jersey, Jordan, Kazakhstan, Kenya, Kiribati, Korea, Kosovo, Kuwait, Latvia, Lesotho, Libya, Lithuania, Malawi, Malaysia, Malta, Mauritius, Mexico, Moldova, Mongolia, Montenegro, Montserrat, Morocco, Myanmar, Namibia, New Zealand, Nigeria, Norway, Oman, Pakistan, Panama, Papua New Guinea, Philippines, Poland, Portugal, Qatar, Romania, Russia, Saudi Arabia, Senegal, Serbia, Sierra Leone, Singapore, Slovak Republic, Slovenia, Solomon Islands, South Africa, Spain, Sri Lanka, Saint Kitts and Nevis, Sudan, Swaziland, Chinese Taipei, Tajikistan, Thailand, Trinidad and Tobago, Tunisia, Turkey, Turkmenistan, Tuvalu, Uganda, Ukraine, United Arab Emirates, United States, Uruguay, Uzbekistan, Venezuela, Viet Nam, Zambia and Zimbabwe.

Note by Turkey: The information in this document with reference to "Cyprus" relates to the southern part of the Island. There is no single authority representing both Turkish and Greek Cypriot people on the Island. Turkey recognises the Turkish Republic of Northern Cyprus (TRNC). Until a lasting and equitable solution is found within the context of the United Nations, Turkey shall preserve its position concerning the "Cyprus issue".

Note by all the European Union Member States of the OECD and the European Union. The Republic of Cyprus is recognised by all members of the United Nations with the exception of Turkey. The information in this document relates to the area under the effective control of the Government of the Republic of Cyprus.

[4] The Patent Box.

[5] Further information on this proposal will be included in the next version of this report.

References

OECD (2017), *BEPS Action 5 on Harmful Tax Practices – Terms of Reference and Methodology for the Conduct of the Peer Reviews of the Action 5 Transparency Framework*, OECD/G20 Base Erosion and Profit Shifting Project, OECD, Paris. www.oecd.org/tax/beps/beps-action-5-harmful-tax-practices-peer-review-transparencyframework.pdf.

OECD (2015), *Countering Harmful Tax Practices More Effectively, Taking into Account Transparency and Substance, Action 5 - 2015 Final Report*, OECD/G20 Base Erosion and Profit Shifting Project, OECD Publishing, Paris. https://doi.org/10.1787/9789264241190-en.

OECD/Council of Europe (2011), *The Multilateral Convention on Mutual Administrative Assistance in Tax Matters: Amended by the 2010 Protocol*, OECD Publishing, Paris. http://dx.doi.org/10.1787/9789264115606-en.

United States

The United States has met all aspects of the terms of reference (ToR) for the calendar year 2017 (year in review) and no recommendations are made.

The United States can legally issue three types of rulings within the scope of the transparency framework.

In practice, the United States issued 114 past rulings; for the period 1 April 2016 - 31 December 2016, the United States issued 21 future rulings; and for the year in review, the United States issued 30 future rulings[1] within the scope of the transparency framework.

Peer input was received from three jurisdictions in respect of the exchanges of information on rulings received from the United States. It was generally positive, noting that information was complete, in the correct format and received in a timely manner.

Introduction

1337. This peer review covers United States' implementation of the BEPS Action 5 transparency framework for the year 2017. The report has four parts, each relating to a key part of the ToR. Each part is discussed in turn. A summary of recommendations is included at the end of this report.

A. The information gathering process

1338. The United States can legally issue the following three types of rulings within the scope of the transparency framework: (i) cross-border unilateral advance pricing arrangements (APAs) and any other cross-border unilateral tax rulings (such as an advance tax ruling) covering transfer pricing or the application of transfer pricing principles; (ii) permanent establishment rulings; and (iii) related party conduit rulings. Certain rulings can be published but this is currently not the case for those which fall within the scope of the transparency framework. In the United States, APAs are issued by a specific office, the Advance Pricing and Mutual Agreement (APMA) programme of the Internal Revenue Service (IRS). The other types of rulings are issued by the IRS's Office of Associate Chief Counsel, with specific offices dedicated to international issues, financial institutions and products, partnerships and special industries, corporate, and tax exempt and governmental entities. The United States notes that PE rulings and related party conduit rulings are not ordinarily issued unless there are unique and compelling circumstances.

Past rulings (ToR I.4.1.1, I.4.1.2, I.4.2.1, I.4.2.2)

1339. For the United States, past rulings are any tax rulings within scope that are issued either: (i) on or after 1 January 2014 but before 1 April 2016; or (ii) on or after 1 January 2010 but before 1 January 2014, provided they were still in effect as at 1 January 2014.

1340. In the prior year peer review report, it was determined that the United States' undertakings to identify past rulings and all potential exchange jurisdictions were sufficient to meet the minimum standard. The United States' implementation in this regard remains unchanged, and therefore continues to meet the minimum standard.

Future rulings (ToR I.4.1.1, I.4.1.2, I.4.2.1)

1341. For the United States, future rulings are any tax rulings within scope that are issued on or after 1 April 2016.

1342. In the prior year peer review report, it was determined that the United States' undertakings to identify future rulings and all potential exchange jurisdictions were sufficient to meet the minimum standard. As the United States implementation in this regard remains unchanged, they continue to meet the minimum standard.

Review and supervision mechanism (ToR I.4.3)

1343. In the prior year peer review report, it was determined that the United States review and supervision mechanisms were sufficient to meet the minimum standard. The United States' implementation in this regard remains unchanged, and therefore continues to meet the minimum standard.

Conclusion on section A

1344. The United States continues to meet all of the ToR for the information gathering process and no recommendations are made.

B. The exchange of information

Legal basis for spontaneous exchange of information (ToR II.5.1, II.5.2)

1345. The United States has the necessary domestic legal basis to exchange information spontaneously. United States note that there are no legal or practical impediments that prevent the spontaneous exchange of information on rulings as contemplated in the Action 5 minimum standard.

1346. The United States is a party to international agreements permitting spontaneous exchange of information, including (i) the *Multilateral Convention on Mutual Administrative Assistance in Tax Matters: Amended by the 2010 Protocol* (OECD/Council of Europe, 2011) ("the Convention"), (ii) Tax Information Exchange Agreements and (iii) double tax agreements in force with 48 jurisdictions.[2]

Completion and exchange of templates (ToR II.5.3, II.5.4, II.5.5, II.5.6, II.5.7)

1347. In the prior year peer review report, it was determined that the United States' completion and exchange of templates were sufficient to meet the minimum standard. The United States' implementation in this regard remains unchanged, and therefore continues to meet the minimum standard.

1348. Furthermore, the United States has confirmed that the summary section of the template is completed as in the internal FHTP suggested guidance. The staff completing the summary section is instructed to insert the description of the covered transaction(s) from the text of the redacted APA and to include a brief description of the transfer pricing method.

1349. For the year in review, the timeliness of exchanges is as follows:

Past rulings in the scope of the transparency framework	Number of exchanges transmitted by 31 December 2017	Delayed exchanges		
		Number of exchanges not transmitted by 31 December 2017	Reasons for the delays	Any other comments
	8	0	N/A	This relates to the exchanges with new members of the IF that joined in 2017.
Future rulings in the scope of the transparency framework	**Number of exchanges transmitted within three months of the information becoming available to the competent authority or immediately after legal impediments have been lifted**	**Delayed exchanges**		
		Number of exchanges transmitted later than three months of the information on rulings becoming available to the competent authority	**Reasons for the delays**	**Any other comments**
	117	0	N/A	The APMA office presented 2 exchanges to the EOI office within the CA slightly over three months after the issuing date, but were exchanged by the EOI office within 3 months after the information was made available.
Total	125	0		

Follow up requests received for exchange of the ruling	Number	Average time to provide response	Number of requests not answered
	23	14 days	0

1350. The two exchanges on a future ruling reported by the United States as being delayed have been exchanged by the Competent Authority within a week after the information was made available to them and therefore are not considered as delays according to the ToR. Instead the reported delays are a result of a slight delay in the transmission of information of one ruling to the Competent Authority and the United States is monitoring its process.

1351. The United States notes that the 23 follow up requests received from different jurisdictions did not provide sufficient explanations to justify foreseeable relevance. The 14 days indicated in the table above therefore refers to the responses sent out by the United States explaining that additional information was needed to allow the requested rulings to be exchanged.

Conclusion on section B

1352. The United States have the necessary legal basis for spontaneous exchange of information, a process for completing the templates in a timely way and have completed all exchanges on time. The United States have met all of the ToR for the exchange of information process and no recommendations are made.

C. Statistics (ToR IV)

1353. The statistics for the year in review are as follows:

Category of ruling	Number of exchanges	Jurisdictions exchanged with
Rulings related to preferential regimes	N/A	N/A
Cross-border unilateral advance pricing arrangements (APAs) and any other cross-border unilateral tax rulings (such as an advance tax ruling) covering transfer pricing or the application of transfer pricing principles	117	Australia, Brazil, Canada, China (People's Republic of), Colombia, Denmark, Egypt, Finland, France, Germany, Hungary, India, Indonesia, Ireland, Italy, Japan, Kazakhstan, Luxembourg, Mexico, Netherlands, New Zealand, Norway, Pakistan, Peru, Poland, Russia, South Africa, Spain, Sweden, Thailand, Turkey, Ukraine, United Kingdom
Cross-border rulings providing for a unilateral downward adjustment to the taxpayer's taxable profits that is not directly reflected in the taxpayer's financial / commercial accounts	N/A	N/A
Permanent establishment rulings	Included in *de minimis*	N/A
Related party conduit rulings	0	N/A
De minimis rule	3	N/A
IP regimes: total exchanges on taxpayers benefitting from the third category of IP assets, new entrants benefitting from grandfathered IP regimes; and taxpayers making use of the option to treat the nexus ratio as a rebuttable presumption	N/A	N/A
Total	117[3]	

D. Matters related to intellectual property regimes (ToR I.4.1.3)

1354. The United States does not offer an intellectual property regime for which transparency requirements under the Action 5 Report (OECD, 2015) were imposed.

Summary of recommendations on implementation of the transparency framework

Aspect of implementation of the transparency framework that should be improved	Recommendation for improvement
	No recommendations are made.

Notes

[1] One of them qualifying both as an APA and as a PE ruling.

[2] Parties to the Convention are available here: www.oecd.org/tax/exchange-of-tax-information/convention-on-mutual-administrative-assistance-in-tax-matters.htm. The United States also has bilateral agreements Australia, Austria, Barbados, Belgium, Bulgaria, Canada, China (People's Republic of), Czech Republic, Denmark, Egypt, Estonia, Finland, France, Germany, Greece, Hungary, Iceland, India, Indonesia, Ireland, Israel, Italy, Jamaica, Japan, Kazakhstan, Latvia, Lithuania, Luxembourg, Malta, Mexico, Netherlands, New Zealand, Norway, Pakistan, Poland, Portugal, Romania, Russia, Slovak Republic, Slovenia, South Africa, Spain, Sri Lanka, Sweden, Thailand, Turkey, Ukraine and United Kingdom.

[3] The three exchanges on PE rulings also qualified as unilateral APAs and were exchanged on templates that identified those two categories of rulings. Because these were included on combined templates, the PE rulings were excluded from the Total to avoid double counting.

References

OECD (2017), *BEPS Action 5 on Harmful Tax Practices – Terms of Reference and Methodology for the Conduct of the Peer Reviews of the Action 5 Transparency Framework*, OECD/G20 Base Erosion and Profit Shifting Project, OECD, Paris. www.oecd.org/tax/beps/beps-action-5-harmful-tax-practices-peer-review-transparencyframework.pdf.

OECD (2015), *Countering Harmful Tax Practices More Effectively, Taking into Account Transparency and Substance, Action 5 - 2015 Final Report*, OECD/G20 Base Erosion and Profit Shifting Project, OECD Publishing, Paris. https://doi.org/10.1787/9789264241190-en.

OECD/Council of Europe (2011), *The Multilateral Convention on Mutual Administrative Assistance in Tax Matters: Amended by the 2010 Protocol*, OECD Publishing, Paris. http://dx.doi.org/10.1787/9789264115606-en.

Viet Nam

Viet Nam has met all aspects of the terms of reference (ToR) for the calendar year 2017 (year in review), except for having in place a process for completion of templates and exchange of information on rulings (ToR II.5). Viet Nam is recommended to continue to put in place a process to complete the templates for all relevant rulings if needed and to ensure the timely exchange of information on rulings in the form required by the transparency framework.

Viet Nam can legally issue one type of ruling within the scope of the transparency framework.

In practice, Viet Nam issued no rulings within the scope of the transparency framework. It has currently received three requests for unilateral APAs which are under review or in a pre-filing stage.

As no exchange of information on rulings was conducted, no peer input was received in respect of the exchanges of information on rulings received from Viet Nam.

Introduction

1355. This peer review covers Viet Nam's implementation of the BEPS Action 5 transparency framework for the year 2017. The report has four parts, each relating to a key part of the ToR. Each part is discussed in turn. A summary of recommendations is included at the end of this report.

A. The information gathering process

1356. Viet Nam can legally issue one type of ruling within the scope of the transparency framework: cross-border unilateral advance pricing agreements (APAs) and any other cross-border unilateral tax rulings (such as an advance tax ruling) covering transfer pricing or the application of transfer pricing principles.

1357. The process for gathering information about past rulings is explained first, followed by the process for gathering information about future rulings.

Past rulings (ToR I.4.1.1, I.4.1.2, I.4.2.1, I.4.2.2)

1358. For Viet Nam, past rulings are any tax rulings within scope that are issued either: (i) on or after 1 January 2015 but before 1 September 2017; or (ii) on or after 1 January 2012 but before 1 January 2015, provided they were still in effect as at 1 January 2015.

1359. Viet Nam only recently introduced the unilateral APA practice. APAs would be issued by the large taxpayers department. When an APA request is received, it is assigned to a specific team of several tax officers within the large taxpayers' division. The team is responsible for issuing the APA and for identifying it is relevant for the purposes of the transparency framework exchange and for identifying potential exchange jurisdictions. In practice, no APAs have been issued within the period defined as "past rulings".

Future rulings (ToR I.4.1.1, I.4.1.2, I.4.2.1)

1360. For Viet Nam, future rulings are any tax rulings within scope that are issued on or after 1 September 2017.

1361. The process for issuing future rulings is similar to the process for issuing past rulings. When a ruling is issued, the hard copy is stored in a cabinet within the large taxpayers' division. A copy of the ruling is also kept at the relevant tax office. Information on the jurisdictions of residence of related parties with which the taxpayer enters into a transaction covered by the ruling is included in the ruling itself.

1362. Taxpayers applying for an APA are obliged to provide information on the jurisdiction of the immediate and the ultimate parent entities. It is noted that in practice, no APAs have been issued within the period defined as "future rulings".

Review and supervision mechanism (ToR I.4.3)

1363. The accuracy of the information-gathering process is ensured by the management of the large taxpayers' division, which supervises the process for all of the issued rulings.

Conclusion on section A

1364. Viet Nam has met all of the ToR for the information gathering process and no recommendations are made.

B. The exchange of information

Legal basis for spontaneous exchange of information (ToR II.5.1, II.5.2)

1365. Viet Nam has the necessary domestic legal basis to exchange information on rulings spontaneously.

1366. Viet Nam is a party to international agreements permitting spontaneous exchange of information, including double tax agreements in force with 72 jurisdictions.[1] Viet Nam is not a party to the *Multilateral Convention on Mutual Administrative Assistance in Tax Matters: Amended by the 2010 Protocol* (OECD/Council of Europe, 2011) ("the Convention").

Completion and exchange of templates (ToR II.5.3, II.5.4, II.5.5, II.5.6, II.5.7)

1367. The team of tax officers responsible for issuing APAs is responsible for completing the template contained in Annex C of the Action 5 report (OECD, 2015). After completing the template, it is sent to the Deputy Commissioner and to the Director of the large taxpayers division, who are both designated as the Competent Authority for exchange of information, and will then exchange it with the relevant exchange jurisdictions. At this stage, timelines for the transmission of the template to the Competent Authority, and for the completion of exchanges, have not been established.

1368. As no rulings within the scope of the transparency framework have been issued in practice, Viet Nam was not required to complete any exchanges of information and there is no data to report on the timeliness of exchanges.

Conclusion on section B

1369. Viet Nam is currently putting in place a process for completion of templates and exchange of information on rulings (ToR II.5). Viet Nam is recommended to continue to put in place a process to complete the templates for all relevant rulings if needed and to ensure the timely exchange of information on rulings in the form required by the transparency framework.

C. Statistics (ToR IV)

1370. As there were no exchanges for the year in review, no statistics data can be reported.

E. Matters related to intellectual property regimes (ToR I.4.1.3)

1371. Viet Nam offers an intellectual property regime ("IP regime").[2] However for the year in review no transparency requirements under the Action 5 report (OECD, 2015) were relevant, as follows:

- ***New entrants benefitting from the grandfathered IP regime***: not applicable for the year in review, because the regime is currently under review by the FHTP.
- ***Third category of IP assets***: not applicable to this regime, which in 2017 was under review by the FHTP.

- ***Taxpayers making use of the option to treat the nexus ratio as a rebuttable presumption***: not applicable to this regime, which in 2017 was under review by the FHTP.

Summary of recommendations on implementation of the transparency framework

Aspect of implementation of the transparency framework that should be improved	Recommendation for improvement
Viet Nam is currently putting in place a process for completion of templates and exchange of information on rulings.	Viet Nam is recommended to continue to put in place a process to complete the templates for all relevant rulings and to ensure the timely exchange of information on rulings in the form required by the transparency framework.

Notes

[1] Viet Nam has bilateral agreements with Australia, Austria, Azerbaijan, Bangladesh, Belarus, Belgium, Brunei Darussalam, Bulgaria, Canada, China (People's Republic of), Cuba, Czech Republic, Democratic People's Republic of Korea, Denmark, Estonia, Finland, France, Germany, Hong Kong (China), Hungary, Iceland, India, Indonesia, Iran, Ireland, Israel, Italy, Japan, Kazakhstan, Korea, Kuwait, Lao People's Democratic Republic, Luxembourg, Malaysia, Malta, Mongolia, Morocco, Mozambique, Myanmar, Netherlands, New Zealand, Norway, Oman, Pakistan, Palestinian Authority, Panama, Philippines, Poland, Portugal, Qatar, Romania, Russia, San Marino, Saudi Arabia, Serbia, Seychelles, Singapore, Slovak Republic, Spain, Sri Lanka, Sweden, Switzerland, Chinese Taipei, Thailand, Tunisia, Turkey, Ukraine, United Arab Emirates, United Kingdom, Uruguay, Uzbekistan and Venezuela.

[2] This is the IP benefits regime.

References

OECD (2017), *BEPS Action 5 on Harmful Tax Practices – Terms of Reference and Methodology for the Conduct of the Peer Reviews of the Action 5 Transparency Framework*, OECD/G20 Base Erosion and Profit Shifting Project, OECD, Paris. www.oecd.org/tax/beps/beps-action-5-harmful-tax-practices-peer-review-transparencyframework.pdf.

OECD (2015), *Countering Harmful Tax Practices More Effectively, Taking into Account Transparency and Substance, Action 5 - 2015 Final Report*, OECD/G20 Base Erosion and Profit Shifting Project, OECD Publishing, Paris. https://doi.org/10.1787/9789264241190-en.

OECD/Council of Europe (2011), *The Multilateral Convention on Mutual Administrative Assistance in Tax Matters: Amended by the 2010 Protocol*, OECD Publishing, Paris. http://dx.doi.org/10.1787/9789264115606-en

Annex A. Glossary

For the purposes of this peer review, these terms have the following meanings:

1. the term "**best efforts approach**" means the efforts undertaken by tax administrations to obtain information on the potential exchange jurisdictions in relation to past rulings, where such information was not included in the ruling itself. The "best efforts approach" does not require the tax administration to contact the taxpayer to obtain this information;
2. the term "**Competent Authority**" means for each respective jurisdiction, the persons and authorities which are responsible for exchanging the information on rulings;
3. the term "**confidentiality**" means a legal right that both the jurisdiction exchanging information and its taxpayers have to expect that information exchanged pursuant to the transparency framework is protected and used only for authorised purposes and disclosed only to authorised persons. All treaties and exchange of information instruments should contain provisions regarding the obligation to keep information exchanged confidential;
4. the term "**Convention**" means the multilateral Convention on Mutual Administrative Assistance in Tax Matters developed by the OECD and Council of Europe;
5. the term "**de minimis rule**" applies for those jurisdictions which conducted fewer than five exchanges of information on rulings in a specific category, whereby they have to list in section D of the report (Statistics) only the number of exchanges in that category and not the jurisdictions with which the information on rulings was exchanged;
6. the term "**future ruling**" means, for jurisdictions which are reviewed in this annual report, a ruling which was issued on or after a date agreed by the Inclusive Framework and which is specified in the report for each jurisdiction; these dates are either 1 April 2016, 1 April 2017 or 1 September 2017 depending on the date at which the jurisdiction joined the Inclusive Framework;[1]
7. the term "**grandfathered IP regime**" means an IP regime which was not consistent with the nexus approach and is treated as abolished, but where certain existing taxpayers in the regime can continue to receive benefits under that regime for a certain period of time
8. the term "**international agreement**" means exchange of information agreements which permit spontaneous exchange of information. This includes, but is not limited to, the Convention (in the circumstances enumerated in Article 7 thereof); double tax conventions based on Article 26 of the OECD Model Tax Convention on Income and on Capital or Article 26 of the United Nations Model Double Taxation Convention, and regional agreements such as the Council Directive

2011/16/EU on administrative cooperation in the field of taxation between European Union member states. A Tax Information Exchange Agreement (TIEA) that is based on the 2002 OECD Model will permit spontaneous exchange of information only if it includes Article 5B contained in the 2015 Protocol, or otherwise explicitly provides for spontaneous exchange of information;

9. the term "**IP regime**" means preferential regimes offering tax benefits in respect of income from intellectual property;

10. the term "**new entrants**" means for the purposes of grandfathered IP regimes, new taxpayers that more recently entered the regime for the first time as well as IP assets which were more recently brought into the regime but were owned by taxpayers already benefitting from the regime. For the purposes of the transparency requirements for jurisdictions reviewed in this annual report, new entrants were generally those taxpayers or assets that entered the regime between 6 February 2015 and 30 June 2016;

11. the term "**nexus approach**" means the requirements set out in Chapter 4 of the 2015 Action 5 Report in respect of IP regimes;

12. the term "**number of exchanges**" means the number of exchanges of information on rulings, counted as the number of jurisdictions that are sent the information on a ruling as opposed to the number of rulings which were the subject of the exchanges. For example, if information on one ruling is sent to three jurisdictions, then this counts as three exchanges;

13. the term "**past ruling**" means, for jurisdictions which are reviewed in this annual report, a ruling which was issued either on or after a date agreed by the Inclusive Framework and which is specified in the report for each jurisdiction. These dates are either 1 January 2010 or 1 January 2012 depending on the date at which the jurisdiction joined the Inclusive Framework and subject to certain of those rulings still being in effect as of a specific date;[2]

14. the term "**peer input**" means feedback provided by other FHTP members on their experience with a jurisdiction. Peers invited to provide input are those which have the legal framework in place for spontaneous exchange of information with the jurisdiction in question and which received information exchanges under the transparency framework from that jurisdiction. The peer input was collected by way of a questionnaire seeking feedback on issues such as the completeness, format and timeliness of exchanges. It is noted that for future rulings, the peer providing input should know the date of issuance of the ruling but would not know when the information on the ruling became available to the Competent Authority, and as such could not opine on whether exchanges on future rulings were late. However, if peers reported consistently long time lags between the issuance of future rulings and the exchanges of information, this would give cause to consider the issue more closely.

15. the term "**potential exchange jurisdictions**" means the jurisdictions with which information on rulings is to be exchanged as set out in Table 5.1 of the 2015 Action 5 Report, which are (i) jurisdictions of residence of related parties with which the taxpayer enters into a transaction covered by the ruling, or which gives rise to income from related parties benefitting from a preferential treatment; (ii) the jurisdiction of residence of the immediate parent of the taxpayer; (iii) the jurisdiction of residence of the ultimate parent of the taxpayer; (iv) for PE rulings,

the jurisdiction of the head office or of the PE, as the case may be; (v) for related party conduit rulings, the jurisdiction of residence of the ultimate beneficial owner of the payment;

16. the term "**preferential regime**" means a regime that applies a preferential tax treatment to certain types of income or activities. Under the transparency framework, there is an obligation to spontaneously exchange information on cross-border taxpayer-specific rulings related to regimes that (i) are within the scope of the work of Forum on Harmful Tax Practices (as described in chapter 3 of the 2015 Action 5 Report); (ii) are preferential; and (iii) meet the low or no effective tax rate factor. Preferential regimes which meet these conditions are thus within the scope of the transparency framework irrespective of whether the regime is determined to have any harmful features;

17. the term "**rebuttable presumption**" means an optional feature of IP regimes, whereby taxpayers have the ability to prove that more income should be permitted to benefit from the IP regime in exceptional circumstances where taxpayers that have undertaken substantial qualifying research and development activity in developing a qualifying IP asset or product can establish that the application of the nexus fraction leads to an outcome where the level of income eligible for a preferential IP regime is not commensurate with the level of their research and development activity, as described in paragraphs 67 – 69 of the 2015 Action 5 Report;

18. the term "**ruling**" means any advice, information or undertaking provided by a tax authority to a specific taxpayer or group of taxpayers concerning their tax situation and on which they are entitled to rely;

19. the term "**rulings within the scope of the transparency framework**" means the five types of taxpayer-specific rulings described in paragraphs 95 – 119 of the 2015 Action 5 Report, which are (1) rulings related to preferential regimes; (2) cross-border unilateral advance pricing agreements (APAs) and any other cross-border unilateral tax ruling (such as an advance tax ruling (ATR)) covering transfer pricing or the application of transfer pricing principles; (3) cross-border rulings giving a unilateral downward adjustment to the taxpayer's taxable profits in the country giving the ruling; (4) permanent establishment rulings; and (5) related party conduit rulings;

20. the term "**third category of IP assets**" means an optional feature of IP regimes, whereby income from certain IP assets may benefit from the IP regime if they share features of patents and are certified as such in a transparent certification process by a competent government agency that is independent from the tax administration, and provided that the taxpayer does not exceed certain revenue thresholds, as described in paragraph 37 of the 2015 Action 5 Report.

Notes

[1] See 2015 Action 5 Report, footnote 11 and 13 of Chapter 5.

[2] See 2015 Action 5 Report, footnote 11 and 13 of Chapter 5.

ORGANISATION FOR ECONOMIC CO-OPERATION AND DEVELOPMENT

The OECD is a unique forum where governments work together to address the economic, social and environmental challenges of globalisation. The OECD is also at the forefront of efforts to understand and to help governments respond to new developments and concerns, such as corporate governance, the information economy and the challenges of an ageing population. The Organisation provides a setting where governments can compare policy experiences, seek answers to common problems, identify good practice and work to co-ordinate domestic and international policies.

The OECD member countries are: Australia, Austria, Belgium, Canada, Chile, the Czech Republic, Denmark, Estonia, Finland, France, Germany, Greece, Hungary, Iceland, Ireland, Israel, Italy, Japan, Korea, Latvia, Lithuania, Luxembourg, Mexico, the Netherlands, New Zealand, Norway, Poland, Portugal, the Slovak Republic, Slovenia, Spain, Sweden, Switzerland, Turkey, the United Kingdom and the United States. The European Union takes part in the work of the OECD.

OECD Publishing disseminates widely the results of the Organisation's statistics gathering and research on economic, social and environmental issues, as well as the conventions, guidelines and standards agreed by its members.

OECD PUBLISHING, 2, rue André-Pascal, 75775 PARIS CEDEX 16
(23 2017 62 1 P) ISBN 978-92-64-30957-9 – 2018

www.ingramcontent.com/pod-product-compliance
Ingram Content Group UK Ltd.
Pitfield, Milton Keynes, MK11 3LW, UK
UKHW051456290926
15471UKWH00008B/1231

9 789264 309579